The
Heartland

ALSO BY KRISTIN L. HOGANSON

American Empire at the Turn of the Twentieth Century
Consumers' Imperium
Fighting for American Manhood

THE
HEARTLAND

AN AMERICAN HISTORY

Kristin L. Hoganson

PENGUIN PRESS
NEW YORK
2019

PENGUIN PRESS
An imprint of Penguin Random House LLC
penguinrandomhouse.com

Portions of this book appeared as "Meat in the Middle: Converging Borderlands
in the U.S. Midwest, 1835-1900" in *Journal of American History* 98 (March 2012):
1025-1051 and "Struggles for Place and Space: Kickapoo Traces from the
Midwest to Mexico," in *Transnational Indians in the North American West*,
Andrae M. Marak, Clarissa Confer, and Laura Tuennerman, eds.,
College Station: Texas A&M Press, 2015.

Library of Congress Cataloging-in-Publication Data

Names: Hoganson, Kristin L., author.
Title: The heartland : an American history / Kristin L. Hoganson.
Description: New York : Penguin Press, 2019. | Includes bibliographical
references and index.
Identifiers: LCCN 2018060308 (print) | LCCN 2019001019 (ebook) |
ISBN 9780525561620 (ebook) | ISBN 9781594203572 (hardcover)
Subjects: LCSH: Middle West--History. | Middle West--Civilization. | Group
identity--Middle West. | Human geography--Middle West.
Classification: LCC F351 (ebook) | LCC F351 .H75 2019 (print) | DDC 977--dc23
LC record available at https://lccn.loc.gov/2018060308

Printed in the United States of America
1   3   5   7   9   10   8   6   4   2

Designed by Amanda Dewey
Map infographic (pages viii and ix) and map painting (pages 4 and 5)
by Meighan Cavanaugh

To the seven generations of my family who have called the heartland home. And in recognition of the first peoples of the tallgrass prairie and their descendants, among them those who struggle for the right to return.

In the middle of everywhere:
Champaign County, Illinois.

Rantoul, the home of the Chanute aviation
field (later Chanute Air Force Base),
established in 1917.

The Illinois Central Railroad: speedway
to the Caribbean and, via Chicago, to the
East Coast and Europe.

West Urbana (later
renamed Champaign)
grew on the outskirts
of Urbana following
the 1854 arrival of the
Illinois Central Railroad.

Upon the organization
of Champaign County,
the town of Urbana
became its seat.

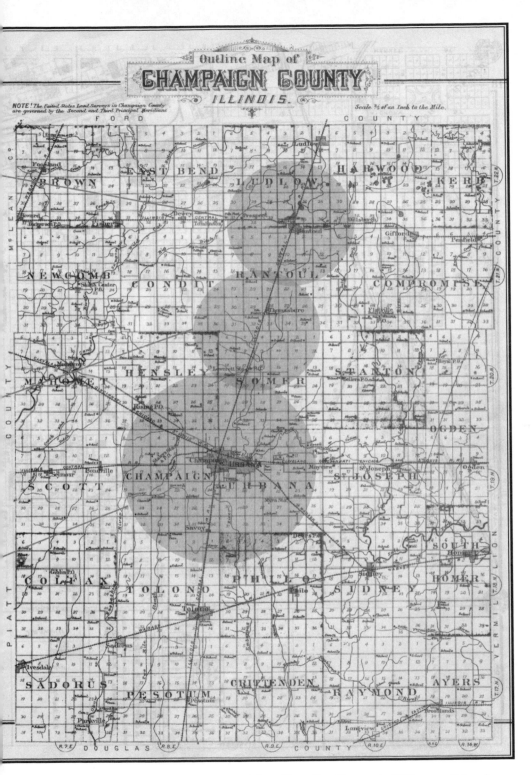

An 1893 map of Champaign County, carved from Vermilion County in 1833 on traditional lands of the Peoria, Kaskaskia, Piankashaw, Weea, Miami, Mascouten, Odawa, Sauk, Mesquakie, Potawatomi, Ojibwe, Chickasaw, and Kickapoo Nations.

CONTENTS

WHAT IS THE NATION, AT HEART?

W hat is the nation, at heart? Who do Americans think they are, as a people? As a nation of many peoples and multiple faiths, assembled from a variety of disparate regions, further divisible into fifty semiautonomous states, over 560 federally recognized Native American polities, a handful of far-flung territories, and the District of Columbia, the United States may seem more a crazy quilt than a body with a heart. Fractured by partisan politics and competing interests, bitter antagonisms and knife-sharp divides, bloody conflicts and histories of soul-wrenching violence, the nation at its starkest seems patched together from a motley mess of parts, held together by straining stitches at their borders.

And yet Americans persist in imagining a heart. Beset by disunity, they imagine their nation as a body with a protected, essential core: the heartland. With the term referring to values as much as to place, its boundaries are a matter of dispute. Though quibbles persist, most mappings of the heartland place it somewhere between the

Appalachian states of the East and Rocky Mountain states of the West, with the long North-South state of Illinois near its core.[1]

Though ostensibly a geographic center, the heartland serves as a symbolic center in national mythologies. Including border states such as Minnesota and Michigan, the heartland could be seen as readily as an edge. But the other moniker for this region—the Midwest—places it between the East and far West, rather than between Canada and Mexico. Instead of being construed as a place of connection, much less a wellspring of global power, the U.S. heartland is more often seen as static and inward-looking, the quintessential home referenced by "homeland security," the steadfast stronghold of the nation in an age of mobility and connectedness, the crucible of resistance to the global, the America of America First.[2] Walls might be built on the margins, but the impetus for them putatively comes from here.

References to the heartland tend to depict it as buffered and all-American: white, rural, and rooted, full of aging churchgoers, conservative voters, corn, and pigs. Those who have denounced this stereotype as a gross distortion, invoking cities like Chicago as proof, have not refuted the myth, they have only tied it to rural areas dotted with small towns. This pastoral heartland is a place of nostalgic yearnings. It is the garden of prelapsarian innocence before the fall into global entanglements. Critics view the rural heartland in grimmer terms, seeing it as a holdout of compulsory normativity, exclusionary politics, and national exceptionalism. Flyover jokes deride it as a provincial wasteland. Out of touch, out of date, out of style—the heartland is the place that makes isolationism seem possible, the place where people think it desirable.[3] It is the mythic past that white ethnonationalists wish to return to, the place that animates their calls to the barricades.[4]

Americans may not agree on who they are as a whole, but they think they know the nature of their heart. Local. Insulated. Exceptionalist. Isolationist. Provincial. The ultimate safe space. Love it or hate it, the heartland lies at the center of national mythology. This mythology seems so natural and inevitable, the inexorable outcome of history and geography, that it is easy to forget that the heartland myth emerged only in the mid-twentieth century, from the crucible of total war.

THE ORIGINS OF THE HEARTLAND MYTH

Coined by British geographer Sir Halford Mackinder in 1904, the term *heartland* initially encapsulated the idea of central Europe as a geostrategic pivot point. In opposition to prevailing theories that saw naval power as the key to global power, Mackinder argued that whoever controlled the Eurasian heartland would control the world. The efforts of Adolf Hitler and his Nazi war machine to prove Mackinder's theory right brought the word *heartland* into circulation in the United States.[5] During World War II, dispatches from Europe referred to fighting in—and for—the European heartland.[6] In the aftermath of the war, as Cold Warriors began to identify Soviets as a greater menace than Nazis, U.S. references to the heartland continued to locate the most critical geographic area where Mackinder had placed it: Eurasia.[7]

Yet the midcentury fixation on geostrategy also prompted Americans to take a new look at their own landmass and the power base it could provide. Commentators began to affix the word *heartland* to the U.S. Midwest, using it alongside terms such as *the middlewest* and *midlands*.[8] From the start, references to the U.S. heartland implied more than just geographic centrality. In keeping with the word's original usages, the term brought to mind national might, especially in references to the "industrial heartland."[9] While seeming to deny American empire, the word *heartland* evoked the tremendous strength

xv

emanating from the United States. The cockiest of Cold Warriors heralded the U.S. heartland as the center of the greatest power ever known.

The idea of the American heartland as an imperial center (in essence, though not name) may have bolstered confidence, but it did not put existential anxieties to rest. The lurking fears of superpower showdown, of airborne bombs obliterating the fields of corn, launched a very different conception of the term. This was not the heartland of ethnically and racially mixed industrial assembly lines. It was instead figured as a land of farmers of northern European descent, less the core of an expansive empire than a psychic fallout shelter in which to seek refuge from a changing and dangerous world. From the start, the vision of security offered up by this heartland came wrapped in nostalgia, for it seemed just as imperiled by the urbanizing, multi-hued, industrial heartland as by distant threats.[10]

This soft-focus version of the heartland could trace its ancestry back to ideas about the Midwest that took hold between the Civil War and World War I. As the region once known as the Old Northwest and Great West moved from the edge of national maps to the center, it came to appear as a middling place. "The most American part of America," noted a British traveler in 1891. When its hyphenated inhabitants foreswore their German ancestry in the great Hun hunt of 1917, they cast their lot with the 100 percent Americanism that was coming to signify the region.[11]

As the word *heartland* began to gain currency as a synonym for the Midwest, Americans in search of a national essence faced a choice: Which heartland would come to represent the mythical core of the nation? The one that drew attention to power and imperial reach? Or the more defensive one, of picket fences and clapboard houses symbolizing the dream of security?

In the struggle over nation-defining mythologies, the picket fences won. Americans bound the center of their country up in myth as they struggled to keep the nation as a whole from unraveling into the world. The more they bound, the more they obscured the full spread of American power. The more entrenched the myth became, the more natural it seemed. The more distant its origins, the easier it became to forget that it did not arise from solid historical and geographical analysis but from the stuff of political need.

This is not to say that there was no historical basis for the heartland myth. To the contrary, its lineage can be traced back beyond the first tendencies to regard the Midwest as the all-American region, to an older set of stories about place. The originators of the heartland myth were able to weave their stories so deftly—and convincingly—because they had inherited a big basket of yarns.

THE LOCAL HISTORY PLOT

The nineteenth century was a golden age of local history. Not the kind of local history that used locality as a method to explore wider themes such as witchcraft or family life, but the hoarier form of local history, of a more calcified, antiquarian vein.[12] Starting with stories of the European explorers, these histories move on to the first white inhabitants and last Native Americans.[13] The establishment of churches, courthouses, schools, and parks all merit mention, as do gleaming hospitals, depots, and streetcar lines. These histories make nearly everyone within their ambit look good, by slighting everyone who didn't fit the proper mold, whether transients, radicals, people of color, audacious women, unruly children, the disabled, the queer, or the poor. Even as they speak in nostalgic tones, these antiquarian accounts serve norm-making, particularist, and boosterish ends.

Nineteenth-century local histories and the generations of descendants that followed in similar veins have helped individuals situate themselves in history by placing the known into a *longue durée*. They have fostered community and advanced historic preservation. They have served as fabulous teaching tools by helping students to draw connections between the familiar and the far-reaching, the tangible and the foundations obscured by time.[14] Antiquarian local histories have held enduring appeal because they speak in an intimate voice. Even the commercialized versions slapped together by out-of-town corporate agents tell stories of neighbors who, whatever their differences, are bound to us through ties of place. They make us feel that our lives, our surroundings, our very localness is historically meaningful. As the global has seemed to swamp the world in a homogenizing tide, local history has won new adherents. Local histories provide glimpses into repositories of distinctiveness. They present the refuge of small-scale relationships in which individuals matter, the possibility of more consensual politics, the importance of place.

Yet in teaching us that we matter in both time and place, antiquarian local histories also run the danger of teaching xenophobia and parochialism.[15] Though long associated with boosterism and elite biases, these histories have anchored another, less recognized, kind of politics. They have advanced a particular plot, the locality plot as it were. This plot starts and ends in the same place, for it is tidily fenced. There may be a nod here or there to distant ancestors, the backgrounds of new arrivals, the departures of native daughters and sons, but in general, the story unfolds within set boundaries, rarely venturing outward.[16] And it looks inward in a particular way, addressing the questions: Who are we as a people? What sets us apart? Antiquarian local histories may help us see beyond our own time, but they reinforce the most myopic perceptions of place.

Antiquarian local histories appear, in sum, to be the heartland myth writ small—or, to get the sequence right, the archetype that makes the heartland myth seem plausible. They have served as the gateway histories to much stronger stuff, in the process dulling more critical perspectives. For all their seeming innocence, they have sustained the heartland myth, preventing us from seeing it as bunk.

THE LAST LOCAL PLACE

The end of the Cold War ushered in a seismic shift in our understanding of the nation. As superpower rivalries faded in importance, globalization became the word of the day. Geographers began to question the local history plot as soon as the Berlin Wall came down. "Can't we rethink our sense of place?" asked geographer Doreen Massey in 1992. "Is it not possible for a sense of place to be progressive; not self-enclosing and defensive, but outward-looking?"[17]

Such questions formed the backdrop against which historians began to question their tendency to carve history into national units, each served on a separate plate. Thomas Bender became a leading advocate for histories that followed their subjects wherever they went, making his case in *Rethinking American History in a Global Age*. His rallying cry shook national history like an earthquake, rattling the foundations and changing the lay of the land. Increasing attention to border-crossing people, politics, goods, culture, and capital began to transform understandings of the national past, as did histories of environmental issues that transcended jurisdictional lines. Metaphors of webs began to outpace references to blocs. The emerging narratives showed the nation to be far less local, insular, and provincial than previously thought, and many of them helped flesh out narratives that were far less white.[18]

And yet in the frenzied rush to rewrite histories, some places got left behind.

This dawned on me in July 1999, the month I moved from the

East Coast to a college town in the Midwest. The first morning in central Illinois, assessing the bare kitchen, the dirty grout, the sticky walls, on a day so hot it was melting, no water to be had for cleaning because of a break in the main, wondering where in the world to begin, I turned on the radio. Static . . . more static . . . a buzz . . . then out poured weather forecasts for China, Argentina, Brazil.

Listening to the news from China, I registered something that I had missed in my readings on global connection. All those histories were not really global at all. They had advanced the conceit that there were particular geographies of global connectedness, involving places such as coastal areas, borderlands, major cities, and tourist destinations. Through omission, they implied that there were geographies of disconnection, of left-behind places. Where to find the U.S. heartland in these geographies of globalization? Somewhere close to Appalachia on the list of the last local places, never mind the weather report.

The utter surprise of that broadcast sharpened my antennae for other signs of dissonance. The more I settled in, the less my environs seemed to fit my preconceptions. It wasn't just the news reports of global commodity markets or my dawning recognition of the ways that NAFTA benefited nearby industrial farms. It was the realization that the rural and small-town Midwest also held stories of immigrants and refugees, of military service and mission trips, of exchange students and Caribbean cruise passengers, of invasive species and farm families investing in land in Brazil.[19] People in the Corn Belt buy pretty much the same imported products in pretty much the same box stores as people on the coasts. They eat Chilean grapes in the winter and Mexican strawberries in the spring. They stay in touch with family members who have left for cities such as New York and L.A. They adhere to faiths with cobelievers around the globe.

Which is not to say that they are all passport-holding, sophisticated one-worlders. To the contrary. There *is* something to the assumption that we can find evidence of locality, insularity, national exceptionalism, isolationism, provincialism, and white tribalism in the rural heartland. Like other rural people, those in the Midwest have had fewer proximate neighbors than apartment dwellers have. They have likewise lived in comparatively homogenous communities, many of them formed by chain migration and buttressed by antiblack legislation, such as the 1853 Illinois statute forbidding people with one or more black great-grandparents from settling in the state.[20] Despite the crop subsidies, insurance programs, and other federal payouts that have propped up rural economies, farm dwellers have prided themselves on being more self-sufficient than city folk. There are stories of homesteaders so eager for companionship that they danced after barn raisings until their toenails fell off.[21] There is some substance to claims that those wanting glitter and excitement (and perhaps smoother dance floors) took off for other places, leaving behind those more inclined to safety, familiarity, and belonging. The *Illinois Agriculturalist* essay that admonished the farm boys who were eager to see the world that "there is much of the world that is best not seen" seems to exemplify the region's parochialism.[22]

Historians have countered such perceptions by alluding to various forms of connection, ranging from Asiatic cholera epidemics to itinerant harvest crews, ambitions of global markets, and the ability to buy the fashionable Staffordshire tea sets of the 1820s within a year of their appearance in London.[23] But historians have also reinforced perceptions of rural midwesterners as living on remote islands in the midst of the vast American landmass. They have painted vivid pictures of incessant, exhausting efforts to coax a living from the soil, small-scale communities, church-centered social lives, family economies, and ties to place extending over generations. They have told stories of hellish conditions inhibiting travel: mud, dust, mosquitoes, assailants, unbridged rivers, dangerous fords, verminous lodgings, potholes, ice, snags, and paths that faded into morasses of tallgrass.

Histories of the rural Midwest have emphasized the particular isolation of women, bound to home by male privilege, tied tighter by the unremitting burdens of childbearing, child care, and tasks such as cooking, cleaning, vegetable raising, poultry tending, dairying, sewing, and food preservation.[24] The heartland myth has sprung from a kernel of truth.

And yet to stereotype the entire rural Midwest—and all the people in it—as narrow-minded locals is akin to imagining everyone in Appalachia as drug addicted, junk-food eating, violence prone, and white. Such simplistic caricatures not only belittle an entire region, they also explain behavioral patterns in terms of site-specific ethnic depravity, thereby hiding their true origins and extent.[25] To write such stereotypes into the past creates further distortions, because rural communities have never been static. Indeed, they have declined over the past century as farming has become more mechanized. They have become comparatively smaller as the world has urbanized, comparatively poorer as capital has become more concentrated, comparatively off the beaten track as long-haul flights have joined major hubs.[26] The contemporary tendency to associate the U.S. Midwest with spatial fixity would have made little sense to peripatetic pioneers. The rural Midwest may appear to be a cultural backwater now, but in 1800 it had a different kind of reputation: the cutting edge of Western civilization; a place free from the ruts of tradition and open to the possibilities of change: a true city on a hill, however rural and flat.[27]

Although we can find evidence of all the things the heartland supposedly represents in plenty of other places as well, national mythologies have dumped an overwhelming load of baggage on the heartland's shoulders. This burden is far too heavy for one region to carry by itself. It bogs the heartland down in place and traps its history in expired approaches to the past, dating back to before scholarship began opening out to the global. By rendering the heartland as one of the last local places, it associates insularity more with geography than with politics, thereby distorting both.

THE HEARTLAND, UNBOUND

The discordance between the heartland of myth and the one that stared me in the face led to the question: What *really* lies at the heart of the nation? The realization that the heartland of myth was at odds with what was so apparent on the ground made me suspect that we find in the heartland what we're looking for. Our assumptions about the heartland are so deeply rooted that they can withstand counterevidence howling as loud as prairie winds.

But what if we look out as well as in, going back before the heartland myth took hold, to the time when the meaning of the Midwest was wide open? What if we went back to the point of origin, the local history plot, but instead of stringing more wire on the fences, we let the stories we found there unspool? Might we better comprehend the full complexity at the heart of the nation? Might we uncover a different past upon which to build?

Local. Insulated. Exceptionalist. Isolationist. Provincial. The ultimate safe space. What if, instead of treating these components of the heartland myth as foregone conclusions, we approached them as questions, as invitations to explore?

I nearly started with my backyard, a classroom-sized mess of prior plantings jostling against the shaggy patch of prairie I had seeded and the tomato vines entwined in the forsythia. Tomatoes: Central and South American in origin. Forsythia: a Eurasian shrub that traveled to the United States from Britain. The nitlike starlings on the telephone wires? Invasives. The lady beetles climbing on the screen? Natives of Japan. The mosquitoes lurking somewhere in the shade? For all I knew, bearers of West Nile virus, which was hitting Illinois harder than any other state at the time.[28] Internet searching traced the hostas and the peonies to Asia; the creeping Charlie to Europe (brought to the Americas as an herb). The ornamental grass spilling over the fence was not the native switchgrass, but pampas grass from South America. And the compost pile? A heap of tropical and out-of-season peels from someplace else. The very soil of my yard was laced with equatorial residues, all run through the guts of nonnative worms. And at least some of the runoff would flow to the Gulf, where midwestern lawn and farm chemicals have spiked an algae-choked zone of death.

Doubtful that my backyard could really help me go back to the very grounding of the heartland myth and mortified by the prospect of it appearing on a book cover, I decided to make the backyard a bit more figurative by widening my scope to my new home county, Champaign.

Located about 130 miles south of Chicago, 160 miles northeast of St. Louis, and 110 miles to the west of Indianapolis, Champaign is a rural county in east-central Illinois. An 1858 newspaper positioned one of its northernmost towns, Rantoul, "four miles nearer the centre of the world than any other place," bounded on the north by Chicago, on the east by Sebastopol, on the south by New Orleans, and on the west by Kansas and Sodom.[29] The county seat, Urbana, also lies to the south, along with its twin city, Champaign. These cities now house a University of Illinois campus, which grew from the Illinois Industrial University, founded in 1867. Boosters describe the campus area as microurban, but despite the international flavor of the university, its host cities (with a combined population of about 126,000) are not the kinds of places that references to global cities bring to mind. The smaller towns that speckle the surrounding countryside are even less so. A Corn Belt county, Champaign is a landlocked stretch of what was once tallgrass prairie. For as long as I have lived there, the county has skewed red in congressional matches. The highways that bisect it have pro-gun signs along their shoulders, like labels for the rows of corn and soy. The population is predominantly white (over 75 percent), Christian, and native-born; the poverty rate hovers around 20 percent.[30]

Champaign is by no means typical in its particularities, but no single place in the heartland could serve as a microcosm for such a vast and variegated whole. So Champaign seems as good a starting point as any to figure out if the rural and small-town communities that came to figure at the center of the heartland myth have always been as insular as that myth suggests, and if so, how. Having settled on a starting point, I set out, sans map, guided by the question: What is the nation at heart, when we unbind it from myth? Intending initially to go back to the moment of origin—the golden age of locality between the region's incorporation into the newly formed United States and its enshrinement at the heart of the world's leading power—I discovered that the story was as hard to contain in time as in place.[31] To understand the making of the modern heartland, I had to stray from the most heartlandish of times, following strands that stretched further into the past even as others tugged me inexorably toward the present.

The journey took me down all kinds of paths I did not know existed. It led to Anglo-Saxonist pigs, Chinese miracle plants, celebrity bulls, polar explorers, African winds, World War I aces, racialized bees, Cuban radio chatter, and UFOs. One thread led to an 1873 cavalry invasion of Mexico; another to diarrhea-induced scandals on British ships. Still other threads connected Champaign to consular outposts in Germany, bioprospectors in Manchuria, congresses of the Inter-Parliamentary Union, and a fledgling agricultural college in Piracicaba, Brazil. I learned of reservations for westward-moving native tribes of birds, the politics of tornado mapping, an Algonquian people living under an international bridge, Malthusian fears of a global race war, a Hindu student's arrival in a place he hadn't known existed, and people on the ground wondering when the next bomb would fall.

I found so many leads that I could not possibly follow them all. Abandoning all pretense to comprehensive coverage, I pursued the larger goal of comprehension as a process and intent. After letting go of some of the most tempting leads by registering them in the "archival traces" that launch each chapter, I scrapped plenty more because they seemed too generalized to tell me much about the heartland per se. The rest became the themes that structure this book: human mobility, border brokering, economic ties, alliance politics, geographic awareness, and homeland insecurities.

Having set off in search of a heart, I had found settler colonialism, borderlands, empire building, agrarian solidarity, global consciousness, and a displaced people's struggle for the right to return. I had found histories that did not advance ring by ring from the local to the global but that unfolded on multiple scales simultaneously. I had found, in sum, histories of foreign relations. Having dug down to the core of the nation, I had unearthed a mesh of global entanglements, stemming from searches for security and power.

Who are the American people at heart?

Judging from their mythologies, a people who have yet to fully reckon with the long, tangled roots of their past.

The
Heartland

ARCHIVAL TRACES

An exile's home

Records Relating to Indian Removal, Bureau of Indian Affairs, 1832: First five entries from a Muster Roll of Kickapoo Indians "who have emigrated West." The document names only those assumed to be heads of families. Given that it is hard to decipher the handwriting, some of my transcriptions may be off.

Posh. e. che. hoy. (with three male and four female family members)
Ke. an. a. Kuck (with one male and one female family members)
Ah. que. pah (with two male and four female family members)
An. ah. be (with two female family members)
Ah. mah. mo (with two female family members) . . .[1]

Urbana Union, **1853:** Spanish slave dealers captured 180 Yucatan Indians with the intention of transferring them to Cuba for plantation labor. British authorities at Honduras intervened and they were released. "What will not a Spaniard do when he has prospect of gold?"[2]

Urbana Union, **1854:** "How few in this land of plenty can realize the sufferings and privations which fall to the lot of those, who, oppressed on their own native shores are forced to find an exile's home within the borders of the United States." (Preface to a story of a Prussian family that succumbed to cholera, one by one, in the lonely prairie on the outskirts of town.)[3]

Urbana Union, **1855:** "Farmers! Champaign County Illinois offers inducements that will attract you all! No better soil exists in the world . . . Come

1

and settle our towns. For all we have room, and all we will heartily welcome with true American hospitality."[4]

Appeal signed by Na she nan and others, 1855: "We, the undersigned old men of the Kickapoo Nation, in the absence of our Agent (We believe he is at Iowa) get our old acquaintance, Mr. Talbott, to write for us to you. We think we have been treated badly by some means. The present Agent we do not know, having never seen him, and we fear our Interpreter has not been careful to make us understand every thing. . . . We are broken up and scattered . . . but few are on our Reserve (to which we have objected). . . . We, some old and poor, some widows and orphans, broken up as we are. We have raised but little and what must we do?"[5]

Champaign Gazette, **1899:** ". . . we have been expanding ever since the formation of the government, and have done good and not evil to the people we have absorbed. Our whole acquisition by the process of expansion has exceeded a billion acres and not a single human being has thereby been enslaved or made a vassal, or a serf, or was crushed, or trodden down, or chained to a chariot wheel, or passed under a yoke, or was deprived of any natural right, or of any imaginable liberty. The long process of expansion, now entering upon its second century, has redounded to the glory of the United States and the advantages of all its people."[6]

BETWEEN PLACE AND SPACE

The Pioneering Politics of Locality

INVENTING THE LOCAL

Cosmopolitanism has signified elite status since well before Gilded Age robber barons began cramming their palaces with imported stuff. Overlooking the passengers belowdecks in steerage, first-class ticket holders have claimed that status for themselves, believing that to be traveled, open-minded, connected, and geographically aware has meant to be modern, cultured, progressive, urbane, and rich.[7] To be local, in contrast, has meant to be left behind: close-minded, isolated, ignorant, backward looking, peasantlike, and probably rural. The more recent sense of "the local" as a site of resistance to global capital—as the rock that can speak truth to power—has challenged these perceptions, but it also draws on them. The academics who theorize about "the local" tend to position themselves as cosmopolitan outsiders, peering in and down. In reifying locality, they have perpetuated its reputation as a stubborn holdout from a less dynamic age. Even those

In the long nineteenth century, stretching from the American independence era through World War I, various groups of Kickapoos traveled from their villages in what is now the U.S. Midwest south to Mexico City, north to the trading posts in the Straits of Mackinac, west to the Douglas, Arizona, area, and east to Washington, D.C., and Florida. In these travels, they not only passed through the domains of other indigenous peoples—including those of the Delawares, Shawnees, Potawatomis, Piankashaws, Miamis, Eel River people, Osages, Comanches, Kiowas, Apaches, and Yaquis—they also engaged with a staggering number of Euro-American polities: the Spanish empire, British empire, United States, Mexico, Lone Star Republic, Confederate States, Canada, and a number of U.S. territories and states. This map depicts their pre-removal villages in Illinois and Indiana and their subsequent reservations and communal land, or *ejido*, in Coahuila, Mexico.

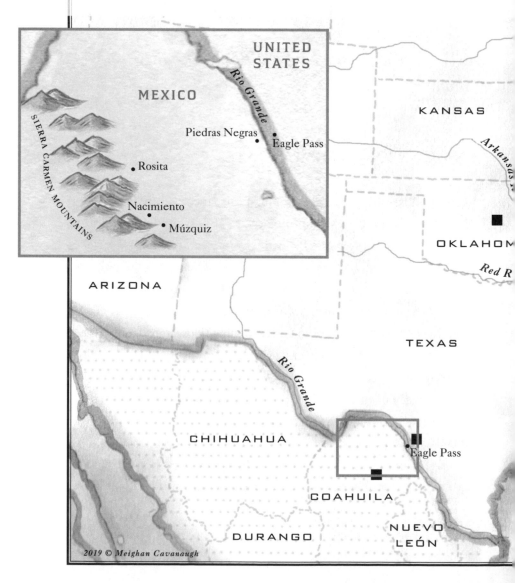

2019 © Meighan Cavanaugh

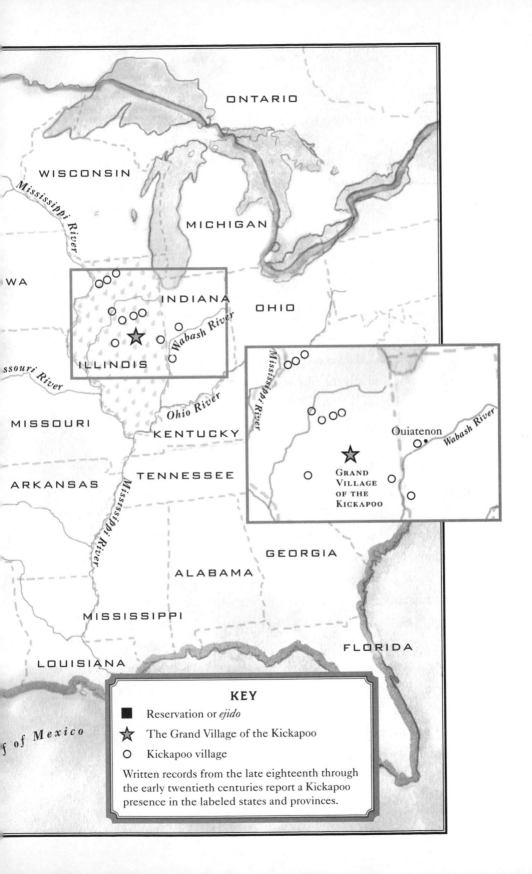

KEY

■   Reservation or *ejido*

★   The Grand Village of the Kickapoo

○   Kickapoo village

Written records from the late eighteenth through
the early twentieth centuries report a Kickapoo
presence in the labeled states and provinces.

who insist that "the local" can no longer be separated from "the global" assume that the former preceded the latter in time.[8]

That chronology may be true for some parts of the world but not for the U.S. heartland. Locality did not exist in what became the U.S. Midwest until the so-called pioneers invented it, in large part through their self-serving local histories. The politics of these histories can be hard to spot amid their biographical notes and anecdotes. But they can be detected at the margins, in the stories of the people squeezed aside. These people were, for the most part, Native Americans. Their presence is why the pioneers are so-called.

If the heartland seems local today, it is not because of geography but in spite of it. The tallgrass prairies that the pioneers plowed lay in the middle of everywhere. The pioneers strove to make these prairies local to advance their own status and power.

AN AMERICAN WAY OF BEING IN THE WORLD

Much of the prepioneer Midwest was inhabited and traversed by the Kickapoos, an Algonquian people with affinities to Potawatomis, Mascoutens, Delawares, Miamis, Shawnees, Sacs, and Mesquakie (Fox).[9] The Kickapoos considered the ability to move freely through space to be a fundamental aspect of their identity, their very name translating roughly as "he moves about, standing now here, now there."[10]

Much as the Kickapoos cherished their homes, they did not have a single homeland, for the Kickapoos were mobile across generations. In the seventeenth century, most Kickapoos lived in what is now the area around Detroit, Michigan, and Windsor, Ontario. As the Iroquois strove to increase their power in the fur trade with the French, they pushed the Kickapoos westward. They also decimated the Illiniwek Confederacy in the Illinois country, thereby opening up new possibilities for the Kickapoos, who sought a respite from fur-trade-induced violence by relocating to southwestern Michigan, southern Wisconsin, and northern Indiana and Illinois. By 1712 some Kickapoos had moved south to central Illinois.[11] Among the places they claimed as their own were sites along the Salt Fork River, which meandered into what later became Champaign County.[12] The Kickapoos also established a village, later known as the Grand Village, on a trail between the Illinois River (to the west) and the Wabash (to the east).[13]

In addition to moving vast distances over the years, the Kickapoos were seasonally mobile: they congregated in villages during the planting season and dispersed to hunt in winter. When the soil was exhausted, they established new villages elsewhere.

It was not unusual for Kickapoos to intermarry with related groups, especially the Mascoutens and Potawatomis.[14] They also absorbed captives—not all of them Native American—and mingled with neighboring peoples who were culturally and linguistically distant.[15] Given the Kickapoos' incorporation of non-Kickapoos, any effort to identify one particular place of origin would have to value some ancestral histories over others.

The more than two thousand Kickapoos of the nineteenth century lived in bands of about fifty to four hundred people.[16] Although the Kickapoos visited across bands and sometimes shifted their membership from one band to another, they did not all live in close proximity. In time of war, bands broke into smaller groups to avoid crushing defeats.[17] Bands also broke up for hunting. By the early nineteenth century, the Kickapoos of central Illinois and western Indiana had divided into two major bands. A man named Kenekuk led the band with a notable admixture of Potawatomis, and a man named Mecina played a leadership role in the other group.[18]

What mattered most to Kickapoo identity was not a specific, bounded, common location, but social relations and linguistic, cultural, and spiritual ties.

Ke-chím-qua, also known as the Big Bear, likely posed for this portrait at Fort Leavenworth (in today's Kansas) in 1830. Around his neck he wears wampum beads: a trade good from the Atlantic coast. His woven white shirt also hints at the trade relations in which he and other Kickapoos were enmeshed. The artist, George Catlin, would have been one of many strangers that Ke-chím-qua encountered at the polyglot fort.

George Catlin, Ke-chím-qua, Big Bear, *Gilcrease Museum, Tulsa, Oklahoma.*

A'h-tee-wát-o-mee apparently sat for this portrait around the same time that Ke-chím-qua, Big Bear, sat for his. She, too, wears a mix of trade goods, including silver brooches that resemble ones manufactured in Germany. Though posed in a sitting position, A'h-tee-wát-o-mee was by no means sedentary; she would have traveled long distances from the Kickapoo villages near the Illinois-Indiana state line to reach Fort Leavenworth.

George Catlin, A'h-tee-wát-o-mee, a Woman, *Smithsonian American Art Museum, Washington, D.C./Art Resource, New York.*

KICKAPOO GEOGRAPHIES

Although it is impossible to fully trace all the nineteenth-century Kickapoo geographies, even a partial mapping reveals that they were remarkably extensive, given the routes and means of transport at the time. Following their arrival in the Illinois country, Kickapoos hunted west of the Mississippi, in the present-day states of Iowa and Missouri.[19] They traveled hundreds of miles to trade as well as to hunt, often to the post at St. Louis.[20] They also journeyed many miles to find salt.[21]

In addition to covering vast distances to provision themselves, the Kickapoos did so for diplomacy and in the course of warfare.[22] Early in the century, a group of Kickapoos took prisoners about 135 miles "west of the Natchez," putting them in western Tennessee and Mississippi.[23] In 1814, "wandering hordes" of the Kickapoo nation committed "many depredations on the white inhabitants residing near the Floridas."[24] The year after that, some British-allied Kickapoos attended a peace conference at Fort Michilimackinac, at the confluence of Lakes Huron and Michigan. In the 1820s, "disaffected" Kickapoos surfaced in reports of trouble north of Fort Towson (in present-day Oklahoma), in Texas, and in Arkansas.[25]

The Kickapoos followed their own footpaths and (especially when farther afield) those under the purview of other groups.[26] They traveled by water, relying on pirogues (shallow draft boats, sometimes made from hollowed logs) and canoes.[27] They also waded and swam across ponds, creeks, and rivers.[28] By the 1760s, some Kickapoos had obtained horses, which they came to rely on for hunting and long-distance travel. Their vocabulary hints at some of the challenges they encountered while en route: *aahkatahoko* means to be stranded by water or snow and *pietapenee*, to arrive hungry.[29]

Their captives told tales of exhausting journeys. A British Indian agent taken by some Kickapoos in 1765 reported traveling about forty-two miles the first day and about thirty miles a day thereafter, "crossing a great many swamps, morasses, and beaver ponds" on the way.[30] Another captive, taken as a youth in 1793 near the Ohio River, reported running all day and pressing on all night, so that he was "much fatigued, and well nigh worn out by means of constant and hard traveling." Stopping did not necessarily mean resting, because the Kickapoo captors "danced the war-dance, and made their young prisoners walk round with them, and would have had them dance, had they not been too much exhausted."[31] Mary Smith, taken captive in the War of 1812, claimed to have traveled "nearly six miles an hour," at the cost of beatings and death threats for a slackened pace. By her account, the group went nearly forty miles in one day, sustained by roasted bear meat.[32]

The challenges faced by the Kickapoos in covering so much ground can be deduced by their enemies' struggles to negotiate Kickapoo landscapes, or, to be more precise: Kickapoo land and waterscapes. When General Charles Scott launched an expedition against the Kickapoos in May 1791, he had to travel about 135 miles from the Ohio River.[33] This "long laborious march" through sodden wetlands so exhausted his horses and men that Scott turned back before reaching the Kickapoo villages of central Illinois.[34]

Lieutenant Colonel James Wilkinson had a similar experience, only worse. In his 1791 effort to locate a Kickapoo town, he had to cross a deep bog, "which injured several of my horses exceedingly." Conditions did not improve. He found, as he pressed forward, that the country was "pondy, in every direction." He pushed on, "through bog after bog, to the saddle skirts in mud and water" until he found himself surrounded on all sides "with morasses which forbade my advancing." The horses had softened the route so much that the men had to dismount and slog through armpit-deep mud. "Under these circumstances," wrote Wilkinson, "I was compelled to abandon my designs upon the Kickapoos of the prairie."[35] The Kickapoos' ability to navigate terrain that invaders found impassable offered them protection from attack as well as advantages in eluding pursuit.

Their pursuers gained the edge over time, however. They drained the wet prairies. They constructed roads. They dug canals, launched steamships, and laid railroad tracks. They saw these engineering accomplishments as more than a means of establishing control, they saw them as proof of their alliance with progress. To the pioneers, enhanced mobility was a sign of civilizational attainment, though only for themselves, not for Kickapoos, whose mobility struck the pioneers as evidence of their savagery.

Just as eighteenth-century Kickapoos embraced horses, nineteenth-century Kickapoos took advantage of new routes and forms of transportation to expand their range and quicken their pace. They traveled on the roads constructed by settler colonists.[36] They used ferries to cross the Mississippi and they traveled by steamer to St. Louis to testify in court.[37] They also took advantage of railroads, though not always as fare-paying passengers.[38] Keyword searching "Kickapoo" in nineteenth-century newspapers turns up multiple accounts of terrible accidents involving trains. The Kickapoos who were struck while walking on the tracks may have been using the railbed as a trail but were most likely killed while trying to jump on.[39]

Their ability to move through space enabled the Kickapoos to make use of more resources than those in the immediate vicinity of their villages. It enabled them to develop alliances, seek redress, and socialize; to inhabit challenging terrain and to evade pursuit. To a people who invested much meaning in the landscape—in trees, rocks, rivers, and streams—mobility enabled a kind of spiritual expansiveness. As their dancing and mastery of dangerous feats of horsemanship suggest, the Kickapoos opened up to the world through different types of movement.[40] Through mixing village life and life on the trace, the Kickapoos blurred the distinctions between home and the world even in the face of empire.

THE LOCAL HISTORY STAKES

Having navigated place and space among similarly wayfaring peoples for generations, the Kickapoos ultimately found their foil in the pioneers. Their ideological foil, that is, for the pioneers were far more like the Kickapoos in reality than they cared to admit. Well before the creation of the heartland myth, the pioneers projected locality onto places where it had never existed. They did so, in large part, through published reminiscences, county histories, and the formation of nostalgic old-settler societies.[41]

Having started out in many cases as squatters, as devoid of legal titles as the people they displaced, the pioneers and their descendants approached local histories as a way to register and publicize their claims.[42] These original local histories advanced two propositions, both pertaining to community and place. The first was that place could determine community. This assumption made sense for pioneers who relocated as individuals or in family units. Their experience was not one of fully fledged groups drawing well-defined boundaries, but of geographic proximity creating collective identity over time. In distinguishing between insiders and outsiders, local historians relied on residence.

Yet even as these local histories defined belonging in geographic terms, they also made it clear that some residents belonged more than others. Leading citizens, mostly male, had particular claims to prominence—and to the political authority that followed—because of their property holdings. Local histories also heralded smaller stakeholders who had put down sufficient roots. But marginal people and newcomers merited scant attention, and transients, travelers, and sojourners even less. The people at the center of local histories were the ones who literally owned the place.

These propositions may seem to be self-evident. And even if not, they may seem an unimportant aspect of fusty old accounts—the kinds of books that make you sneeze from so many years on the shelf. Yet these underlying assumptions are fundamental to understanding the politics of the heartland myth. To understand the nature of these politics and their significance, we need only ask: Where did these assumptions leave the Kickapoos?

There is a narrative trajectory to local histories that starts with colonial contacts and ends with snug farms and fenced fields. In between, there are stories of danger, savage beasts, and Indians. The point of these in-between stories is that the pioneers earned their central position in the community through their struggles to secure their homes. As the authors of a history of Champaign County put it, "We are prone, in the midst of the activities of the present, to forget our obligations to the bold, self-sacrificing pioneers and early settlers who, amid privations and dangers, founded an empire in the wilderness and thus made passable the comforts and blessings of civilization that we, today, enjoy."[43] Those pioneers and settlers were, in other words, colonists. They had forged an empire by overcoming dangers, chief among them the people they supplanted.

For all the self-congratulation, there is also a note of anxiety in these celebrations of pioneer deeds. In calling for gratitude and veneration, such histories address the possibility that newer arrivals might not defer to old-timers. To the contrary, newcomers might interpret the pioneer story to mean that anybody could dislodge older occupants, thereby claiming place for themselves. They might see the pioneers and their offspring less as founders than as natives, who could in turn be pushed aside.

These local histories foreclose the possibility of such a subversive reading by casting the pioneer experience as fundamentally different from that of later immigration streams. What made it different (according to these histories) was that the people who preceded the pioneers had not put down roots. Unlike the pioneers and their offspring,

Indians had never fully laid claim to place because they were too mobile. The pioneers had not really displaced anybody, because Indians had never made the place their own. The whole pioneering enterprise rested on that deceit. Without it, the pioneers would have been recognized as colonists from the start.

Pioneering local histories present Indians as people who came and went, wandering at will. As Milton W. Mathews and Lewis A. McLean put it in *Early History and Pioneers of Champaign County*: "Wild Indians roamed and hunted at pleasure over these prairies and through these groves." In addition to roaming, the Kickapoos ranged—"with all the freedom of wild turkeys." They also roved, so much so that one observer described them as addicted to it.[44] They did not truly live in the area, they merely camped. Insofar as they left a mark on the landscape, it was in the form of trails and paths. When told to clear out, they "gathered up ponies, dogs, squaws, tents, and papooses, and never returned."[45]

Purported Indian experts shared the pioneers' views of the Kickapoos as ever on the move. An English traveler who saw Kickapoos at Fort Leavenworth, Kansas, in the 1830s described them as "constantly coming and going."[46] In his 1851 tome on American Indians, Henry Rowe Schoolcraft characterized the Kickapoos as an "erratic race." They have "skipped over half the continent," he wrote, "to the manifest discomfort of both German and American philologists and ethnographers."[47] Other Indian agents took advantage of their vast geographic knowledge by hiring them as messengers and guides.[48]

Depicting Native Americans as comparatively mobile—frustratingly so to those who would categorize them according to geography— served expropriative purposes well beyond the Kickapoos. European colonists came to North America with disparaging views of pastoralists, gypsies, and vagabonds. From their first contacts with native peoples, they regarded mobility as evidence of savagery and attenuated ties to place.[49] They claimed that Native Americans merely used land without fully possessing it to justify their seizure of that land.[50] An 1827 tract championing Indian removal cited the example of the Kickapoos (among other groups) to demonstrate that Indians were mobile even without being forced and hence that they "may be removed by fair and honorable measures."[51]

THE GREAT ERASURE

Just as the propertied inhabitants of the nineteenth-century United States regarded tramps as social outsiders deserving of punishment, rehabilitation, and incarceration, they regarded Native Americans as shiftless vagrants.[52] The local histories that sprang up in Champaign typically ceased to mention native peoples after the first few pages. Out of sight, out of mind. Or, as one history of central Illinois put it, "The Indian is gone . . . doomed to extinction." That the Illinois pioneers were not alone in this conviction can be seen in an article on the sale of Kickapoo Indian land in Oklahoma, where some of the Kickapoos had gone after the pioneers had pushed them out of Illinois. This article observed that the Kickapoo reservation would soon be "owned and occupied entirely by white people and their heirs, inheritors and assigns forever. Thus another step will be taken in the wiping out of the name Kickapoo from the map of the United States, as it will be eventually dropped from history and from the memory of men."[53]

The Kickapoos were not wiped off the map. To the contrary, the more they were displaced, the more they appeared upon it. From Kickapoo Creek to Kickapoo River, Kickapoo Hills, Kickapoo coal mines, Kickapoo Falls, Kickapoo Prairie, Kickapoo City, Kickapoo Cave, and the Kickapoo road, place names in at least fourteen states have borne witness to the Kickapoos' onetime presence.[54] In large part, however, Kickapoo places are now without visible Kickapoos. The practice of naming places after Native American groups paradoxically underscored the pioneers' claims to place, for it was, after all, the pioneers who affixed words like *Kickapoo* to their maps. If there is any doubt that settler colonists asserted their own power through naming things after Native Americans, consider the Kickapoo bomb. The U.S. government detonated this over the South Pacific in 1956, as part of the Redwing tests. The seventeen atomic bombs in this series may have seemed to honor indigenous people, each being named after a Native American nation. But these seventeen bombs spewed their fallout on the indigenous people of the Marshall Islands.[55] Kickapoo traces, without Kickapoos.

Removal so fully effaced the Kickapoos from the consciousness of settlers that when some local historians in the early twentieth century became interested in Native American precursors, they did not know where the Kickapoos of Illinois had gone. This was true for Milo Custer, who lived near the Kickapoo Grand Village site about fifteen miles west of the Champaign County line. After doing some basic research on removal, Custer started to correspond with John Masquequa, a Kickapoo man living in Kansas. Custer described his fervent hopes of learning more about Masquequa's people: "I have always wanted to know about the Kickapoo Indians for they once lived here in the country where I was born, and I have heard some of the old people who live here tell about them and I wanted to know more."[56]

When the youthful Custer finally saved enough money to travel to Kansas, he sought out Kickapoo elders, hoping for stories of Illinois. The oldest woman he met, Omubyah, was not forthcoming. Custer sadly reported that, having left Illinois when she was eight, she did not "remember anything in particular about our locality." The oldest man, Old Jesse, had been born in Missouri. He told Custer of "a tradition of the 'Salt Lands' in Illinois." Despite Old Jesse's knowledge of a place he had never seen, Custer did not think to ask younger Kickapoos what Illinois meant to them. It did not occur to Custer that Illinois may have had meanings that passed on through the generations. This became especially apparent in Custer's farewell address. Before going home, Custer spoke at the Kickapoo School. "I was able to tell them more about the past history of the Kickapoos than they had ever heard before," he noted, oblivious to the possibility that the Kickapoos had their own histories, ones that certainly included stories of Illinois from as recently as their parents' and grandparents' times.[57]

Although local historians such as Custer professed greater interest in the Kickapoos by the early twentieth century, their intentions were strictly historical—to understand the past, not the possibility that the Kickapoos' attachments to Illinois continued into the present. As one late-nineteenth-century account put it: "The Kickapoos are, or were, a red Indian tribe."[58] *Were.* Out of sight, out of the ongoing stream of time—except as symbols of mobility.

Even as pioneering accounts declared the Kickapoos gone, newspapers across the country ran testimonials from a Champaign resident (among others) who attributed his restored health to a Kickapoo tonic.[59] This was due to the advertising campaign of the Kickapoo Indian Medicine Company, based in New Haven, Connecticut. The company sold a variety of products that cured diseases of the kidney and other vitality-sapping ailments. All its tonics and exotic-sounding "sagwas" purportedly came from the secret herbal formulas of the Kickapoos. To hawk its products, the company sent agents—many of them real Indians, though fake Kickapoos—to travel the country, as far as the new territory of Hawaii,* performing Wild West show feats of daring. Its printed materials—which circulated even more widely— trumpeted the Canadian, Egyptian, Mexican, and European markets for the company's various rheumatism, neuralgia, cough, and worm medicines. These materials depicted scenes of buffalo hunts on the

---

* I use *Hawaii* to refer to the state and Hawai'i to refer to the kingdom and the territory.

WOMAN'S HOPE.

A Story of Rescue Due to the Indians.

An Example That Goes to Prove the Tremendous Benefit that the Indian Has Been to Mankind.

The following letter is of interest to women, and especially to that class of women who drag themselves through life, suffering innumerable tortures, living without hope of release from pain, and looking forward only to death as the great doctor who will make them well.

"Parham, Minn., Kickapoo Indian Medicine Co.; Gentlemen:—I heartily recommend Kickapoo Indian Remedies. I suffered with poor health for years and tried everything without relief, until at last I was made well by your won-  derful medicine. It worked like magic. I now enjoy perfect health and I am over 30 pounds heavier than before taking your remedy I have also used your Worm Killer for my children. It has done wonders for them and never will we be without the Kickapoo Indian Remedies in the house. Yours respectfully, ELIZABETH LATTERER."

These words, coming from a woman, should appeal strongly to other women. Her sufferings gave way to one of the wonderful Kickapoo Indian Remedies. Other sufferers have the same chance of regaining lost health. Kickapoo Indian Prairie Plant for all female diseases is the most wonderful remedy known, to man. It is for sale by all druggists, for $1. per box. Kickapoo Indian Sagwa for a general breaking down of the system and for the cure of diseases resulting from a disordered condition of the kidneys, liver, stomach and blood is positively invaluable. These, as well as other Kickapoo Indian Remedies, are harmless, although powerful and quick in their action and should be resorted to for a cure which they will effect where doctors and other remedies have failed.

An excerpt from an advertisement for Kickapoo Indian Remedies, from 1897. It hawks Kickapoo Indian Sagwa as the cure for "a general breaking down of the system" and for disordered kidneys, liver, stomach, and blood.

"Woman's Hope," Milwaukee Journal, *April 15, 1897, 19th-Century U.S. Newspapers.*

Along with turning the Kickapoo people into commodified symbols of vigor, patent medicine ads spread bogus representations of Kickapoo culture.

Everett W. Doane, Life and Scenes Among the Kickapoo Indians, *New Haven: Healy & Bigelow [nd].*

open plains and white women astride fast-moving horses, clasped firmly in the arms of bare-chested Indian men.[60]

That at least some readers took this message to heart can be seen in the newspaper stories reporting on white girls eloping with the Indian sales agents. It can also be seen in the decision of a Traveling Men's Union chapter to call itself the "order of the Kickapoos."[61] Thanks to the Kickapoo Indian Medicine Company, the Kickapoos became placeless symbols of vigorous movement, whose name continues to circulate in connection with Kickapoo Joy Juice, a gingery soft drink popular in Malaysia and Singapore and now on offer in my grocery store in Champaign.[62]

HOME ON THE RANGE

The pioneer vein of local history is deeply ironic, though not intentionally so. Those who dismissed the Kickapoos as ramblers did not seem to realize that the Kickapoo people could have written their own accounts of roving outsiders, with the roles reversed. Most of the white Americans the Kickapoos met were people on the move. The Kickapoos encountered British travelers; Belgian missionaries who moved from post to post, as their Jesuit superiors determined; German émigrés newly arrived in America; a Prussian explorer heading up and down the Missouri.[63] The Great Overland Trail to the far West cut through the land allotted the Kickapoos in the removal era. The emigrants who trudged along that trail stole the Kickapoos' oxen, hitching them to their wagons heading west across the plains.[64] The Kickapoos knew, as well as anyone, that it was the short-lived military man who did not travel from post to post, the unambitious Indian agent who was content to stay put, the pointless trader who obtained his goods in the neighborhood, the misnamed pioneer who hadn't come from someplace else.

Despite their insistent claims to locality, the pioneers who penned the first local histories of the Midwest were not really locals. What made them pioneers was their mobility. Many of them moved several times before putting down roots, others just passed through the area, and some took off and came back. The settlers who figured so largely in histories of Champaign are no exception. They came from New Hampshire, Massachusetts, Maryland, New Jersey, New York, Pennsylvania, Indiana, Ohio, and Michigan; from North Carolina, Virginia, Tennessee, and Kentucky; from Ontario, England, Scotland, and Ireland; from Switzerland, Hannover, Bavaria, and the Kingdom of Württemberg. Some came from families with longer histories of mobility, as in the case of Thomas Jonathan Burrill, whose mother hailed from the vicinity of Belfast, Ireland, though "Scotch by ancestry," and George Besore, whose Huguenot forebear had traveled from France to Pennsylvania via a German province.[65] The ancestral homes of such pioneers were many removes away: as the wandering children of wandering parents, these pioneers felt no particular compulsion to stay.

Some of the founders of Champaign County had spent years on the move, working as slave traders, soldiers, drovers, salesmen, and sailors. Pennsylvania-born Henry Sadorus applied to accompany Lewis and Clark. Unsuccessful in that pursuit, he journeyed to Cuba instead. Another pioneer traveled the country with a menagerie, in charge of an elephant, two monkeys, and a tiger. The Ontario-born John Rogerson circled Lake Superior on snowshoes, in the company of two Indians. Elisha Stevenson, originally of Ohio, had "drifted about to different places," practicing his trade as a hatter. One of the county's Lutheran pastors had been born in Rio de Janeiro in 1847. The son of a minister, he studied at a mission institute in Hannover before coming to the United States. The Irish-born Father Shanly had studied for the priesthood for six years in Rome.[66]

Not only did the pioneers arrive after long and circuitous journeys, they refused to stay put. Malinda Busey Bryan, born in Kentucky in 1812, rode the same horse from Champaign back to Kentucky five times.[67] Other pioneers hitched their ox teams to their wagons to trade in Chicago. They did business downriver in New Orleans. They drove hogs to the Wabash River in Indiana and got short-term jobs there in the pork-packing plants. They took off to California for the gold rush, some across the continent, some via Panama and Nicaragua. When the railroad came, they sought jobs as conductors. They departed for Arkansas to lay track, to Pike's Peak, again in search of gold. They left for education, to serve in the legislature, to buy livestock, to exhibit stock in fairs, and just to "look around a little." Sometimes settlers left for reasons unknown, as in the case of Myron Stoddard Brown, who "went away for a while but came back in 1858 with his wife."[68]

As the desire to "look around" suggests, Champaign residents left for more than just economic reasons. Some left to fight—in the Blackhawk War, the Mormon War, and the Mexican War—motivated perhaps in part by the knowledge that since the Revolution, bounty-warrant acts had offered land to veterans of Indian and other campaigns.[69] They served the Union in places such as Vicksburg, Chickamauga, Atlanta, Mobile, Pensacola, Galveston, and Chickasaw Bayou. One scouted for the Union Army in Kansas; another escaped from Andersonville Prison, fleeing to freedom with a black man, hiding in swamps by day. Others left to visit family, including across the Atlantic. Men traveled east to secure a bride. One of the early pioneers, William Sadorus, took off on three-week hunting trips, living by the chase. The more that game dwindled in the area, the farther afield he went, traveling to Arkansas and other hunting grounds to the west. As the nineteenth century wore on, wealthy Champaign residents went to Florida for their health and to Europe and elsewhere for pleasure.[70]

Some of the moves were for good. The *Early History* of Champaign speaks of men who became restless over time and "sought broader fields in the far west." As the population of the county grew, families packed up and went to Iowa, Wisconsin, and Oregon.[71] Following in the footsteps of their forebears, many of the pioneers' children displaced Native Americans down the road.[72] The *Early History* mentions daughters settled from Michigan to Montana and sons from Texas to British Columbia. One son became a miner in "old Mexico," one a baggage master in Las Vegas, one a vintner in San Diego; one a rancher near Leadville, Colorado. Anticipating a time when immigration and natural increase would lead to crowding and ever-smaller patches of inherited land, the *Prairie Farmer* newspaper drew attention to real estate opportunities in Canada, Mexico, and the West Indies in the early 1870s.[73] The *Urbana Courier* also tempted readers with advertisements for land. Read one for eight hundred acres in Alberta: "Choicest soil. Deep black loam, comes with a hog pen."[74] In 1890, sixteen men in Monticello, Illinois (one county to the west of Champaign), pooled their funds to purchase fruit farms in Honduras.[75]

In addition to moving themselves, the pioneers moved borders. They lived in a time of outward-pressing U.S. boundaries, with the mappings of their new homes likewise in flux. Those who colonized Illinois saw it change over time from Indian territory with European footholds, to a western edge of the United States, to a border state abutting the breakaway Confederacy, to a state smack in the center of the country. Such flux seemed unexceptional given simultaneous changes in the middle of Europe. The pioneers who spoke various German dialects came from several German kingdoms, only unified in 1871.[76] They arrived with firsthand knowledge of Schleswig-Holstein falling to the Danes and Alsace-Lorraine to Germany; of growing up in jurisdictions, such as Austrian Poland, that could no longer be found on maps.[77] Like their relatives who had advanced European imperialism in places such as the Transvaal and Ceylon, they treaded expansive new paths.[78]

If foreign relations is considered in a broad sense, so as to encompass relations with foreigners, then the presumption that Illinois was thoroughly domestic would have seemed nonsensical to the polyglot settlers who wrested it from Indians. Foreign relations could be found in money sent to sisters in Ireland and in everyday encounters with neighbors. It unfolded at home, between immigrant parents and Americanized children; naturalized citizens and European relatives. Marriages were often transnational alliances, joining Swiss to German, Danish to Canadian, Rhinelander to Irish.[79] For the restless people who made the Midwest a tapestry of northern European diasporas, foreign relations was the stuff of daily life.

DISLODGMENT

It is not only the pioneers' position in the midst of such a turbulent brew that makes their claims to locality so deeply ironic. Contrary to pioneer depictions of Kickapoo homelessness, the Kickapoos did indeed build homes, modeled after those of Kitzihiat, the Great Spirit.[80] Built largely by women, Kickapoo *wickiups* had mat walls over a bentwood frame. Whether for winter or warmer-month use, they had a fire circle in the center and a smoke hole in the roof.[81] The Kickapoos cherished their dwellings as spiritually significant places associated with warmth, cooking, and nighttime light. They also valued the land on which their dwellings were located.[82] This can be seen in their resistance to land seizures and forced removal and in their spiritual beliefs that have carried forward through time, to today.

The Kickapoo poet Ekoneskaka (also known as Aurelio Valdez Garcia) revealed some meanings he attached to place in a 1992 oral history. Having arrived with a friend at his village, he gestured toward a rock. "Hey, hombre, come here, take a look at this," he said. "Put your hands on it. See? This is the heart of Nacimiento [the name of his village, meaning *birth* or *source* in Spanish]. Everything goes out from here to there, and from there to here, and at the same moment it all goes back out again and on and further on around all these places we call Nacimiento. This is the living place of the rock. It's the heart of the village too. See how the stone moves around inside the rock, as if all those grains of rock were moving like a pure river at dawn, and you can drink it. . . . This is the heart of Nacimiento and that is what our heart must do, even when we sleep, it's breathing this place for us, beating and breathing out and breathing back in this place for us, our heart of Nacimiento."[83]

Pioneer claims notwithstanding, place profoundly mattered for Kickapoos such as Ekoneskaka. Generations after his ancestors had been driven from Illinois, Ekoneskaka still felt a deep attachment to Nacimiento, the place where they had gone. There, in the northern Mexican state of Coahuila, they had started over. And yet they and their descendants had continued to go out into the world, including to places that had sustained the Kickapoos in the past. This sense of the connection between the solidity of place and fluidity of space helps explain his sense of the heart of his village as a living thing.

Recognizing the importance of place claims to the Kickapoos is not to say that the Kickapoos understood land in the same legal ownership terms as the pioneers. Their lands overlapped with the lands used by other groups such as the Delaware, Shawnee, Potawatomi, Eel River, Weea, Piankashaw, and Miami. Even as they negotiated their first treaties, the Kickapoos regarded land as something held in common, rather than by individuals. The idea of buying and selling land was alien to them, for they regarded land rights more in terms of use than in terms of permanent ownership. This conception of land rights helps explain why the Kickapoo men who signed the 1795 Treaty of Greenville, ceding lands in Illinois and Indiana to the federal government, insisted on a provision stipulating that they could continue to hunt on them, "without hinderance or molestation."[84] Whatever they had transferred, it was not the ability to replenish themselves on the land.

If anyone had asked what the Kickapoos thought about the pioneer accounts that disparaged them as rootless, they could have pointed out that in many cases, it was the pioneers' fault. The homes the Kickapoo built south of the Great Lakes were no more secure than those they had left during earlier waves of colonial warfare. After the American Revolution (supported by most Illinois Kickapoos, at least by the end), pioneers flowed into the Old Northwest, precipitating retaliatory raids.[85] In 1791, General Charles Scott and seven hundred Kentucky volunteers responded by destroying the Kickapoo village near the convergence of the Tippecanoe and Wabash Rivers (near present-day Lafayette, Indiana).[86] The following month, General James Wilkinson and five hundred mounted Kentuckians destroyed another Kickapoo village, at the confluence of the Eel and Wabash Rivers, about twenty-eight miles upstream.[87] "I have burnt a respectable Kickapoo village, and cut down at least 430 acres of corn, chiefly in the milk," reported Wilkinson, fully aware that destroying the Kickapoos' corn threatened their existence, that without their stores of provisions, they would suffer keenly in the impending winter and have no seeds to plant in the spring.[88]

The War of 1812 led to further displacement. In anticipation of war, the Kickapoos abandoned their villages.[89] They had good reason to fear attack: as allies of Tecumseh, they had been resisting U.S. incursions.[90] Illinois forces under Governor Ninian Edwards burned their deserted villages and then struck the encampment where the Kickapoos had concentrated. According to Edwards, he and his men destroyed "upwards of 1000 bushels of corn" at the principal Kickapoo village, along with "a prodigious quantity of Beans and dried Meat, Pumpions, Tallow, Furs, and Peltry."[91] This caused the Illinois Kickapoos to disperse and seek protection among the Sauk in northern Illinois. About a month later, a detachment of U.S. forces under Colonel

Philip Barbour destroyed a "large Kickapoo village" on the Wabash River.[92]

In addition to fleeing villages in time of war, the Kickapoos deserted them during epidemics. Lacking inherited immunities to the diseases carried across the Atlantic, the Kickapoos suffered tremendously from colonial contagions. When smallpox ravaged the Kickapoos who lived along the Wabash in the late 1700s, the survivors abandoned the pestilential site and headed west, to Illinois.[93]

FORCED RELOCATION

Pioneer histories do not confess that U.S. forces burned down Kickapoo villages and fields. They do not acknowledge that colonial diseases had made them into places of death. They do not admit that hunger may have driven entire communities—gaunt women and men and their suffering children—to look elsewhere for the nourishment once provided by corn and more abundant game. They depict the Kickapoos as rovers by choice.

Things got worse when the pioneers embarked on a purposeful program of ethnic cleansing, known at the time and onward by an even more euphemistic term: *removal*. In their treatments of Indian removal, most textbooks emphasize the story of the "Five Civilized Tribes" from the Southeast—the Cherokee prominent among them—and the tragedy of the Trail of Tears. But Indian removal did not begin in Georgia, nor did it end there. The Midwest has its own terrible stories of Indian expulsions, including of the Kickapoos.[94]

The process of expelling the Kickapoos from their villages east of the Mississippi began in 1809, when the group living between the Wabash and Vermilion Rivers lost land in the Indiana Territory.[95] The Edwardsville and Fort Harrison treaties that ceded land in Illinois followed within a decade. In exchange, the Kickapoos got a tract of land on the Osage River, "west of the contemplated boundary of the proposed state of Missouri." The treaty writers cast this as a good deal for the Kickapoos, noting that their new tract was large and their title to it "indisputable."[96] This view of the transaction overlooked the Osages living along the river that bore their name, less than thirty miles from the Kickapoos' new homes.[97] Disregarding the Kickapoos' connections to place, it assumed that moving from the wet prairies of central Illinois to the drier grasslands of Kansas would make no difference to a people thought to be inherent rovers.

According to War Department registers, more than two thousand Kickapoos had resettled along the Osage by 1820.[98] Whatever their initial expectations, they found their new home to be a land of disappointment. As they told the Indian superintendent in St. Louis, instead of getting the expansive lands they anticipated, they had been placed "in a small hole."[99] The nature of the land selected for them compounded their frustrations. Defying instructions, they settled in Missouri instead of to the west of it. Yet even so, a nearby Indian agent reported them as being "destitute of every comfort."[100]

The Kickapoos' dissatisfactions contributed to the 1832 Treaty of Castor Hill, in which the Kickapoos who had recently settled in western Missouri exchanged their unsatisfactory new holdings for land "southwest of the Missouri river, as their permanent place of residence as long as they remain a tribe." The treaty identified the boundaries of this new reservation as "lying generally north and west of Fort Leavenworth," a vague designation for land in northeastern Kansas. Members of the Kickapoo band that had stayed in Illinois also signed the treaty, thereby leading U.S. officials to believe that the Kickapoos had relinquished all land claims in the state.[101]

Even before the Kickapoos reached their new lands, white critics complained that they should have been moved farther still, beyond the Rocky Mountains, "to the remotest space that can be found for them on this side of the Pacific."[102] In response to such demands, the

U.S. government seized some of the Kickapoos' Kansas lands in the 1860s. It relocated those who objected to Indian Territory, in what later became Oklahoma.[103] By the time of this removal, the Kickapoos had good reason to worry that no matter where they went, land-hungry white settlers would soon follow. Despite their claims to locality, the pioneers and their children had a tendency to see opportunity wherever they saw Indians, and this opportunity typically meant forcing Indians to go elsewhere.

KICKAPOO PRESENCES

So many Kickapoos left Illinois for Missouri in 1820 that it took the ferries of St. Louis fifteen days to carry them and their wagons of household goods across. Nonetheless, several bands remained in central Illinois into the 1830s. As Indian Agent William Clark reported more than a decade after the Edwardsville treaty, those who opposed it "have continued their resistance to the wishes of the Government, and have withstood every inducement to move to their own lands west of the Mississippi."[104]

When some Kickapoos joined Black Hawk's supporters in 1832, Champaign settlers fearful of attack appointed a committee to tell the "red men" in the vicinity to go. According to a later pioneer history, the Indians subsequently left.[105] Yet Kickapoos were still in the area the following year, when an Indian agent reported that "their situation is now very deploring, being in a country thickly inhabited and affording little or no game."[106] The last of the Kickapoos reportedly crossed the Mississippi in the spring of 1834, leaving only their dead behind.[107]

Rather than interring their dead in the ground, the Kickapoos who had not adopted Christian burial practices preferred to hang them in slings from the lower limbs of trees. Although the Kickapoos believed that the dead traveled to the spirit world, they treated the bodies of the dead with respect because of the possibility that they still harbored spirits.[108] This respect for the deceased had contributed to the Kickapoos' unwillingness to sell their land, for to sell it meant to sell the bodies of family members, an act akin to selling their own flesh.[109] As the pioneers saw the last of the Kickapoo wagons roll past, they may have thought the Kickapoos gone, but from a Kickapoo perspective, their people remained, many of them still swaying in the breeze.

Their ongoing ties to the land of their ancestors help explain another development glossed over by the pioneer histories: why some Kickapoos returned. One pioneer who arrived near the southwest corner of Champaign County in 1837—four years after the last of the Kickapoos had supposedly crossed the Mississippi—found that "the smoke of the camp-fire of the Indians still ascended from the Big Grove."[110] In the 1840s, a stricken Kickapoo man died in Urbana after being bled by an ineffective doctor summoned to his side.[111] In 1854, twenty years after the Kickapoos had ostensibly left, a Kickapoo man from Kansas returned to the scenes of his boyhood, where he told curious residents about his life prior to removal and about his parents, whose bodies had been laid to rest nearby.[112] An English immigrant who arrived in Champaign in 1867 claimed that there were still "many Indians" there and that he saw them performing their dances.[113]

An 1887 dispatch from Tuscola, Illinois (about five miles south of the Champaign County line), also hints at ongoing Kickapoo attachments to east-central Illinois. "For many years past a small band of Indians has been accustomed to encamp on the banks of the Okau, about nine miles southeast of this city, near Uncle Eph Gardner's farm, and there spend several days." One of the men in the encampment explained that "sixty years ago, when that tribe of red men made this section of country their hunting grounds, a great chief was buried on a prominence overlooking the Okau, near that point, and that they came to do honor to his memory." The article went on to confirm that there had been a "great camping grounds and head-quarters of the Kickapoos" in the vicinity.[114]

Over fifty years after removal, some Kickapoos either had never left or had come back. Sometime in the spring or early summer they went from Tuscola north to Paxton (about fifty miles away), where they set up camp. This would have gone unnoticed in the historical record, except they gave bow and arrow shooting demonstrations as part of the Fourth of July festivities, and this spectacle got a passing mention in the papers.[115]

That the Kickapoos continued to see east-central Illinois as meaningful can be seen in another, still later, return. In the 1990s, farm owners Bill and Doris Emmett came to realize not only that their land in McLean County encompassed part of the onetime Grand Village of the Kickapoos, but also that a mega–hog farm proposed for an adjacent parcel would desecrate the Kickapoos' grove for the dead. Using their life savings and pension funds, they purchased 250 more acres of land.[116] Then, with the help of friends and volunteers, they established a private park and organized a homecoming. The three hundred or so Kickapoos who attended the 1998 gathering came from Kansas, Oklahoma, Texas, and Mexico.[117] Among them was Texas resident Marguerita Salazar, age 104. She had grown up hearing her grandparents' stories about the Illinois territory, for both her grandmother Kelkowah and her grandfather Neepaha had lived at the Grand Village.[118] For Salazar and the other Kickapoos who danced in sight of the trees that had held their ancestors' remains, Illinois had never lost meaning.

THE CONCEIT OF THE LOCAL

Although the pioneers admitted the ties between place and space when they filled their local histories with discussions of wide-branching family trees and jottings on who went where when, these histories advanced the fundamental premise that they had carved locality from the vast expanses of the West. They grounded the supposition that place could be severed from space, that the local could stand on its own.

This premise has long survived them. Even as other places have come to seem connected to the global, the heartland's position in the middle has seemed to buffer it from the world. Its rural areas and small towns have seemed especially impervious to connection, seen more as outcroppings in the middle of nowhere than as junctions in the very thick of things.

To construe this seeming locality as inherent to place misconstrues both its fabrication and its nature. Locality began, in the heartland as elsewhere in the United States, as an ideology of conquest. By suggesting that Euro-American settlers were rooted in place, local histories turned groups such as the Kickapoos into outsiders, existing only in space. In addition to mischaracterizing people like the Kickapoos, who valued their homes as much as any pioneer and who maintained attachments to place long after becoming displaced, such distinctions exaggerated the pioneers' ties to place, for they, too, valued mobility and they, too, cherished ties based more on affinity than on geography.

Those who disdain the rural Midwest as a last holdout of locality misread its history. Since the beginning, the seeming locality of the Midwest has served colonialist politics, having originated in colonial denial.

ARCHIVAL TRACES

Not enough of the war to 'go round'

Urbana Clarion, 1860: "The colored residents of Urbana and Champaign celebrated the anniversary of emancipation in the British West Indies, on Wednesday, by a pic-nic."[1]

The Illinois Farmer, 1864: The Canada thistle "is sometimes called the 'cursed thistle'—and very properly too. It is certainly a curse and ac-cursed! But we do not suppose it is so called because 'cursed' is synonymous with Canada! We would not be so understood. But there is no sort of doubt but Canada is cursed with it, as well as some of the United States . . . The seed has wings. It is migratory. It travels in the air, in crockery crates, on railway trains, in emigrant wagons, in dry goods boxes, in tree packages, with grass seed, grain, and it is not altogether impossible that the government may distribute it through its Agricultural Department . . ."[2]

From *The History of Champaign County*, 1878: Charles Miner came to Champaign in 1849, obtaining his land with Mexican land warrants, that is, with bounty payments from his service in Mexico.[3]

From *The History of Champaign County*, 1905: "The late war with Spain, entered into on account of the cruel oppressions and misgovernment of the Island of Cuba, near the American coast, while not in defense of the integrity of American territory, was truly in defense of American honor. . . . The only trouble that most of our patriotic young men encountered during the progress of this war, was that there was not enough of the war to 'go round' and give all a chance."[4]

Urbana Daily Courier, 1909: "Señor Zeferino Dominguez, a prominent farmer and land owner of Mexico, is organizing a party of wealthy Mexican farmers for a trip through the corn belt of the United States during the coming year. The Señor has written that this party will consist of about 100 people who will travel by special train. The purpose of the organizer is to convince his countrymen what is being done along scientific lines in the United States particularly in corn raising." The group will visit the University of Illinois and the Funk Brothers Seed Company.[5]

Urbana Courier, 1909: The story of the dash to the North Pole "will be told in graphic pictures at the Walker Opera House on Christmas day." The pictures show the frozen regions of the Arctic and "why the polar prize fell to America." The program also includes Big Guns in Action, Algeria, Canada, and twenty other features.[6]

Urbana Courier, 1912: "Mrs. R. A. Wells of this city, who for some time has been visiting her daughter at Mexico City, Mexico, has fled with the latter and family across the Rio Grande into Texas, following the ultimatum that Americans in Mexico would be slaughtered at the first appearance of United States troops across the border."[7]

MEAT IN THE MIDDLE

Converging Borderlands in the U.S. Midwest

FROM MIDDLE GROUND TO BORDERLANDS, BY WAY OF THE OLD NORTHWEST

Even before the coming of the pioneers, the place that became the heartland already lay in the thick of things. In the years leading up to the American Revolution, indigenous polities and European empires struggled mightily for power there, with the outcome up for grabs. Though later historians have characterized this contested area as a *middle ground*, eastern mapmakers saw it at the time as an edge.[8] From U.S. independence to the Louisiana Purchase of 1803, the nation officially ended at the Mississippi. When the nation leapt beyond that squiggly line, Illinois moved from the dynamic far horizon of the nation—from a place in what was variously called the *Old Northwest*, *Great West*, or *West*—toward the stodgy center. As pioneers wrote themselves into local history, nation builders wrote Illinois out of the wild landscape of diplomatic maneuvering, exploration, and warfare, and into the thoroughly domestic landscape of the *Midwest.*[9]

The idea of the heartland as an insulated core is so entrenched that it is easy to forget the history of the middle ground, stretching across what is now the U.S.-Canadian border and south along the Mississippi as it flowed toward the Gulf. But the history of the middle ground is worth recalling if we are to understand what followed its demise, for this history reminds us that the middle has existed in the round. Before the nation closed in, the Midwest lay between all the compass points, not just east and west. By pinning it between the two coasts, nation builders fixed it solidly in the middle of the country.

But *country* has a second meaning: an expanse of land. Maps that end at the nation's borders hide this larger sense. The seeming insularity of the heartland may tell us more about our angle of vision than the scope of the field. If we tilt the axis, the Midwest suddenly emerges as a place between two borderlands.

The term *borderlands* refers to an intermediate area between two separate states. Upon originating in studies of the U.S. Southwest, borderlands scholarship focused on the communities that have abutted—and transcended—the U.S.-Mexican border. More recent scholarship has taken a borderlands approach to peoples and places along the U.S.-Canadian line, finding spillage and mixing there, too. Yet although such studies have begun to open up our understanding of national dividing lines, they have done little to shake up the myth of heartland insularity. Borderlands just seem to move the real borders inward a bit, not to suggest the permeability of the nation as a whole.[10] They peter out on the fringes of the heartland, daring to reach only so far. The possibility that a state such as Illinois may have had its own borderlands histories seems too much of a stretch, unless the subject were its relations with Indiana, Kentucky, Missouri, Iowa, or Wisconsin.

But where do borderlands end? What if they just keep receding until they finally converge, in places such as the flat fields of central Illinois? How insular would the Midwest seem then? Given the heartland metaphor, it seems fitting to approach these questions with blood in mind. Animal blood, that is, in keeping with nineteenth-century farmers' tendency to use *blood* as shorthand for all the attributes of *breed*. If their attention to blood reveals quite a bit about race-making and boundary drawing in an agrarian society, their animals and the paths they traveled tell us just as much about the cross-border history of a region.

THE RISE AND FALL OF THE MIDWESTERN RANGE

Texas and other states west of the Mississippi did not become the center of the U.S. beef-raising industry until after the Civil War. Starting in the mid-1830s, the cattle frontier could be found on the prairies of what is now the Midwest.[11] Among the counties that offered rich pasturage was Champaign: In 1850, four years before the Illinois Central Railroad connected Champaign to Chicago, fewer than three thousand people lived in its 1,004 square miles.[12] It was no accident that this was one of the last parts of the state to be intensively settled by the pioneers. Besides lacking natural transportation routes, the county consisted largely of wetlands (hence the term *wet prairie* to characterize this ecological region) that were ill suited for cultivation. But the vast expanses of inexpensive land did lend themselves to grazing.[13]

Cattle pioneers benefited from the unsettled nature of the prairie insofar as they could pasture their stock free of charge on the "unclaimed" land recently taken from Native Americans. Federal land distribution policies also proved favorable to white cattle raisers. Those who had accumulated some capital as small-scale herders or drovers took advantage of the U.S. government's cheap prices for marshy land and the Illinois Central's willingness to dispose of its land grant in big parcels, more suitable for grazing than plowing. In the mid-nineteenth century, Champaign contained some of the largest farms in the state. By 1870, ten of its farms contained one thousand or more acres, too large for family cultivation but well suited for commercial stock raising.[14] Many of the men who populate the late-nineteenth-century directories of Champaign's leading citizens made their fortunes in the livestock business.[15]

One of Champaign's most prominent stockmen, Benjamin Franklin Harris, started purchasing cattle in Illinois in 1835 to drive them to Pennsylvania markets. This demanding three-month trip required Harris and his herds to swim the Wabash, the Ohio, and several other formidable rivers and then climb the Allegheny Mountains en route to Lancaster. After seven such drives, Harris understandably tired of the work. In 1841, he purchased a farm in Champaign. Harris sold his cattle to drovers, who herded them to farms in Ohio to be fattened before slaughter.[16] With the arrival of the railroad in the early 1850s, there was no need to fatten his animals close to market, so Harris did it himself, with tremendous success. He specialized in the heavy cattle popular at the time, mostly in the four-thousand-pound range but some over five thousand pounds. Following his death in 1905, an obituary noted that Harris had once sold the heaviest one-hundred-head lot of cattle ever marketed in the United States "and, so far as the records show, in the world." Harris sold his herds to railroad shippers, including the Boston Exporting Company, which delivered them to the slaughterhouse and then marketed the meat in the northeastern United States and Britain.[17]

Although the large farms of Illinois started to break up after 1870,

"CORN-FEEDING" ON JOHN T. ALEXANDER'S FARM, MORGAN COUNTY, ILLINOIS.

Corn-feeding in central Illinois in the 1870s. Note the pigs gleaning in the lot.

Joseph G. McCoy, Historic Sketches of the Cattle Trade of the West and Southwest *(Kansas City, Mo., Ramsey, Millett & Hudson, 1874), 170. The Newberry Library.*

giving way to mixed farming on smaller holdings, the state's cattle industry did not peak until around 1890.[18] In 1850, Champaign had fewer than 1.5 beef cattle per one hundred acres; by 1890, it had over 4.6. Champaign cattle producers remained competitive for so long by adjusting their operations, taking advantage of their increasing capacity to grow corn to shift their emphasis from grazing to the feedlot-style fattening of range cattle.

They also used their capital and livestock expertise to breed and raise animals that matured faster (meaning they could be sold at two years, instead of four), fattened more readily (thereby reducing feed costs), and marbled so finely as to appeal to the most discriminating consumers.[19]

These competitive strategies can be seen in the case of Broadlands, the largest farm in the county, indeed, the largest in the Old Northwest. The Ohio livestock grazier Michael L. Sullivant established the farm in 1853 on 20,000 acres, which grew to 26,500 after he sold the farm to John T. Alexander, a former drover, in 1866.[20] For a number of years, Alexander fattened Texan stock on his land. He also bought cattle from fellow feeders to ship to eastern markets. In 1870, he shipped 70,000 head, an achievement that earned him the sobriquet "the cattle king of the world." In 1873, he was elected president of the Live Stock Men's National Association.[21] But soon after, losses from disease bankrupted Alexander, and by the end of the century, the center of the Illinois cattle production had shifted to the northwest corner of the state.[22]

THE PURSUIT OF BRITISH BLOOD

British export markets were not the only way the wider world helped shape the region, in the process turning the United States from a nation of pork eaters into a land of beef eaters in the early twentieth century. Imported genetic material mattered profoundly as well. Many of the animals unloaded at the Liverpool docks—whether dead and dressed or staggering wildly after horrific North Atlantic crossings—were making a homecoming of sorts, as the herds traced increasing percentages of their ancestry to the "blooded" bulls bred in Britain in the nineteenth century.[23]

The cattle driven east to market by men such as Harris were largely descended from the herds brought to North America from England, Holland, Denmark, and Sweden during the colonial era. In the 1820s, however, eastern breeders began to import pure breeds to improve their common stock.[24] They turned primarily to Britain, the world's premier supplier of pedigreed cattle. Nineteenth-century British breeders narrowed the genetic diversity that had previously characterized livestock production by creating select lines (often by crossing prize bulls with their female offspring), which they then sold to buyers in the United States, Argentina, Australia, Canada, New Zealand, Russia, and other nations with beef industries geared toward export markets.[25]

Among the purchasers who sought better animals were the Illinois farmers looking to compete against Texan scrub cattle. Their first direct links to British breeders (rather than those mediated by importers in other states) came in 1857 with the formation of the Illinois Stock Importing Association. The investors pooled their resources to send three agents to the United Kingdom. Visiting well-known herds and livestock shows, the agents purchased thirty head of Shorthorn cattle and some sheep, pigs, and horses.[26] Upon their return to the United States, they auctioned the animals they had acquired, which, along with ones obtained from U.S. farmers who bred imported stock, helped found a pedigreed livestock industry in the state. By 1861, nearly all the common cattle in Illinois had some Shorthorn ancestry.[27]

Harris's prizewinning animals were not the only well-bred cattle in Champaign. An 1878 history of the county dated the introduction of "short-horn" cattle to 1836. Claiming that the county's herds had since won some note, this history also observed that "the farmer who now feeds cattle, and who does not breed short-horns, is behind the times; in fact few such exist."[28] According to another boosterish local history, a farmer named William Owens had some of the "finest specimens" of Shorthorn cattle to be found in the county. Another prominent resident, Albert Carle, was "well known to the stockmen of the entire state and in fact of the west."[29] A 1917 directory of the farmers and breeders of Champaign listed 105 Shorthorn breeders and smaller numbers specializing in other types of cattle (including 20 Aberdeen Angus breeders, 21 Polled Durham breeders, and 1 Hereford breeder).[30] Although Champaign never won extraordinary fame as a cattle-breeding area, its livestock breeders did compete at the highest levels. In 1900, a prize bull owned by the Champaign breeder

O. H. Swigart won the "second premium" award at the Paris World's Fair. Swigart boasted of seventeen cows from imported bulls "and as many more from imported dams."[31]

To improve their herds, leading Illinois breeders continued to purchase stock in Britain through the nineteenth century. The trip was expensive, however, as was the transatlantic shipment of the animals. European disease outbreaks and quarantine regimes added to the difficulties. Hence top breeders also sought to acquire stock from their associates in states such as Kentucky, Ohio, and New York, and from across the border, in Ontario.

THE CANADIAN CONNECTION

There was a long history of livestock mobility from what is now the United States to what is now Canada, and vice versa. The pioneers who drove their own cattle to Illinois in the early nineteenth century found that the state already contained abundant herds, of Normandy ancestry, that had been brought via Canada by French colonists.[32] By the early nineteenth century, Illinois stock raisers had begun exporting some of their animals to Canada for consumption. In the 1830s, U.S. competition from Ohio, Indiana, and Illinois had put a damper on Canadian stock raising. Despite duties as high as 20 percent, American drovers brought large herds into Ontario during winter and summer.[33]

This trade pattern shifted over time as the Ontario livestock industry grew. The 1854 Reciprocity Treaty that permitted duty-free movement of farm products between the United States and Canada aided the animal trade. Until the treaty's expiration in 1866, Canadians exported large numbers of cattle, especially during the Civil War, when there were reports of "Yankee speculators . . . scouring the country for cattle and horses, and buying up all they can get."[34] After the abrogation of the Reciprocity Treaty in 1866, Canadian beef exports declined. Nevertheless, Canadian statisticians reported that Ontario farmers exported approximately a hundred thousand head of cattle to the United States in 1870.[35] Just as important as the numbers was the nature of the trade: in the post–Civil War period, an increasing number of these animals were pedigreed cattle, sold for breeding purposes, not meat.

The Canadian breeding industry took off in the 1860s when well-to-do Canadians started investing in high-end livestock.[36] Ontario cattle breeders formed notable herds of Shorthorns (sometimes conflated with Durhams), Herefords, Aberdeen-Angus, Galloways, Devons, Sussexes, and West Highland breeds. Not coincidentally, each of these lines originated in the United Kingdom.[37] This is not to say that Canadian breeders purchased all their blooded animals directly from Britain—some of their quality stock came from the United States.[38] But just as U.S. breeders turned to Britain for top-notch stock, so, too, did Canadians.

The rise of the Canadian breeding industry coincided with Canada's emergence as a federated nation. In 1867, Upper and Lower Canada (Ontario and Quebec, respectively) entered a union with Nova Scotia and New Brunswick. The union soon expanded with the additions of Manitoba and the North-West Territories (1870), British Columbia (1871), and Prince Edward Island (1873).[39] Yet even after uniting as a dominion, Canada retained close ties to Britain through investments, labor migrations, and official imperial affiliation. Many Anglophone Canadians felt a special affinity to Britain because of language, ethnicity, and family bonds. Since Britain's cattle breeders were industry leaders, these relations proved to be an enormously valuable asset to the Canadian farmers. Some of the earliest Canadian breeders were wealthy hobbyists who relied on British-born immigrants to manage their farms. Other breeders relied on family connections, friendships, and comfort navigating the British live-stock markets to establish transatlantic businesses.[40]

From their origins as second-tier sellers, Canadian Shorthorn breeders soon became globally competitive. As early as the 1870s, agricultural papers reported on Canadian breeders who reversed ear-lier relationships by exporting stock *to* Scotland.[41] By the 1880s, the U.S. consul in Port Sarnia reported that "the transition from Scotland to Canada" had been successful, for "the animals bred in Canada from imported Polled Angus stock are superior in size and general appearance to the cattle from which they were bred."[42] Robert Miller, a leading Ontario livestock dealer who crossed the Atlantic twenty-five times to build his business, had dealings with cattlemen in places as distant as Mexico and South America by the 1890s. Regard-less of such successes, the most important export market for Cana-dian breeders remained the United States. Ambitions for midwestern markets helped drive the Canadian livestock-breeding industry from its inception.[43]

Putting a precise number on the U.S-Canadian cattle trade in this period is a tricky business. The U.S. Revenue Cutter Service lacked the resources to adequately patrol the Great Lakes. Land borders were still more permeable.[44] But even the traffic that passed through customs stations is hard to tabulate. Given that livestock could be imported duty-free under the terms of the 1854 Reciprocity Treaty and duty-free for breeding purposes after its expiration in 1866, cus-toms agents lacked a major motivation for keeping close count. Through 1883 U.S. commerce reports use the category "animals, liv-ing" to keep track of livestock that entered the United States from Canada, failing to distinguish between cattle, horses, sheep, and swine. Rather than providing head counts, some reports list only the general monetary values of living animals. Canadian officials did track cattle exports to the United States prior to 1883, but when the data is comparable there are frequently discrepancies between U.S. and Canadian statistics.[45] Finally, when the western Canadian ranching industry took off in the late nineteenth century, stocked in large part by U.S. animals, border crossings became harder to scrutinize. As *Bradstreet's* reported in an 1890 piece on trade with Canada: "Congress blindly neglects to make provision for correct returns of the overland movement."[46]

Despite these obstacles to an exact count, it is possible to get a general sense of U.S. cattle importations from Canada. Unlike goods such as whiskey, cattle did not lend themselves to Great Lakes smuggling. By 1884, U.S. customs officials did regularly distinguish between livestock species. And there are patterns to U.S.-Canadian trade discrepancies: as one Canadian report put it, they could be attributed "to carelessness in valuation of exports on both sides of the line."[47] Hence we can assume that import statistics are more accurate than undercounted export statistics. Canada's report of 249,361 cattle exports to the United States from 1872 to 1883 (which averages out to 20,780 head per year) probably undercounts the trade. The U.S. Treasury report that noted 469,771 Canadian cattle imports from 1884 to 1898 (which averages out to about 31,318 a year) is probably closer to the mark for the covered years. Of these, 13,746 (about 916 a year) entered duty-free, meaning for breeding purposes, mainly through Great Lakes customs houses. This may not seem like a particularly large number, but prize bulls had celebrity status in livestock circles and the potential, through their progeny, to make a prodigious mark on herds.[48]

Farm publications can help contextualize these government statistics, in the process making it clear that Canadian breeders had a notable presence in the pedigreed livestock circuits of the Midwest, sometimes to buy and, more often, to sell.[49] Some of the most important sites of contact were agricultural fairs. The records of the

We may now safely challenge any part of the world for fine stock, and it would not surprise us to see announcements of the purchase here of choice stock for the English farms. The genial climate and rich feed of the prairie tends to the full development of the bovine race, and breeders must sooner or later look here for the best animals. Col. Wentworth can accommodate them. Now that the cattle disease has put an embargo on importations, we hope to see a little justice done to our home breeders who have invested so largely in choice stock.

SHORT HORN DURHAM COW ADELAIDE.

The English Herd Book, volume XI, describes her as bred by Hon. Adam Ferguson, Woodhill, Canada West, red roan and calved 20th April, 1850.
She was got by the celebrated prize bull Halton (11,552,) out of Lady Elgin by Symmetry (12,170,) Flora by Wellington (13,987,) Victoria by Agricola (1,614,) Beanty by Snowball (2,647,)—by Lansleeves (865,)—by Charles (127.)
She was bought by Hon. John Wentworth for the Illinois Breeding Association at Summit, Cook county, Illinois.

The Illinois Farmer joined other agricultural publications in trumpeting
the aristocratic English ancestry and Canadian connections
of prize bulls and cows, such as Adelaide.

"Short Horn Durham Cow Adelaide," The Illinois Farmer, *June 1860, 88.*

Illinois State Fair reveal that Canadian breeders competed regularly in the livestock competitions and often took home a handful of prizes.[50] Beyond the state fair circuit, Canadian breeders entered their herds in exhibitions with grander titles, such as the United States Fair in Chicago.[51] The participation of Canadians in such events was so common that it did not attract special notice. Their absence did, however. In 1914, foot-and-mouth disease struck the Chicago Union Stock Yards, and the agricultural press reported that the outbreak was keeping Canadian exhibitors away from the International Live Stock Exposition.[52] The more that Illinois breeders set forth on Canadian herd tours, bid at Canadian auctions, and welcomed Canadian breeders at their own livestock events, the more that reports on their prize herds trumpeted Canadian ancestry.[53]

A TRANSBORDER AGRICULTURAL REGION

As the agricultural papers reveal, Illinois and Ontario cattle producers participated in a transborder agricultural system. Despite trade barriers that waxed and waned, a variety of farm products crossed the eastern Great Lakes, heading in multiple directions. Yet it was not just commodity exchanges that gave Illinois farmers grounds to consider Canada as an important part of their agricultural region: human mobility also tied the U.S. Midwest closely to Canada. Descendants of Loyalists who had fled to Canada at the time of the American Revolution joined the flow of Canadians who resettled the upper Midwest (especially in Michigan, but also in Ohio, Illinois, Wisconsin, and Minnesota) in the nineteenth century. Would-be emigrants from Britain read accounts presenting Ontario and Illinois as fairly comparable destinations.[54] This low-key competition for settlers received a jolt in 1859, when James Caird, a member of Parliament and an investor in the Illinois Central Railroad, published an emigrant's guide that strongly favored the lands along the Illinois Central's tracks. A Canadian reviewer responded to this piece of self-serving propaganda by harshly critiquing conditions in Illinois. After professing "no feelings but those of amity towards our American brethren," the booklet went on to characterize Illinois as a land of "disappointment and ruin."[55]

To counter these charges and restore cordiality, the railroad invited prominent Canadians to tour the state. The *Prairie Farmer* applauded this effort to foster friendship: "We are so nearly cosmopolitan in our commercial relations, that it is important we should become so socially."[56] The group (numbering about sixty) rode the rails from Chicago to the small town of Loda, about fourteen miles north of Champaign County, where everyone disembarked for dinner. The men who rose to speak emphasized goodwill, trade reciprocity, and the annexation of Canada to the United States. From Loda, the excursionists proceeded on to Champaign, to meet Sullivant and learn about his steam plow. (Readers of the *Canadian Agriculturalist* would have been familiar with Sullivant's farm, from a piece in an 1857 issue.) Then they departed for points farther south. The Illinois hosts relished the visitors' praise, including one man's confession that he had been wary of making the trip, "because I was afraid I should want to come here for a home!"[57] In keeping with the boosterish spirit of the day, the editor of the *Illinois Farmer* predicted that the tour would have the beneficial effect of an "influx of well-to-do Canadian farmers, just such men as we shall be most happy to welcome to the great corn zone of the west."[58]

Despite the speechifying and polite compliments, Champaign was not swamped by a sudden flood of Canadians. Nevertheless, there was a noteworthy Canadian presence in Illinois, estimated at seven thousand to the south of Chicago in 1870.[59] Nineteenth-century naturalization records from Champaign list only the foreign potentate repudiated by the new citizens (thus making it impossible to distinguish between settlers from Canada, Ireland, and Britain, all of whom renounced Queen Victoria), but the records kept for those who came to the United States as minors and were naturalized between 1866 and 1896 do list place of birth. These reveal that 24 out of 320 naturalization cases involved Canadian-born men.[60] Census data also reveals a Canadian presence: in 1850, 9 of 2,649 enumerated Champaign residents were reported as being born in "Canada," "Nova Scotia," or "New Brunswick." By 1860, the number was 126 of 14,629; and by 1870, it had risen to 281 of 32,743.[61] Entries for families such as that of Henry and Ann Tucker, born in England and Ireland, but with four Canadian-born children, suggest the likelihood that these numbers should be higher still because some of the many residents born in the British Isles came to Champaign after a stint in the British dominion.[62]

Although census records identify many Canadian-born men as farm laborers, others owned considerable property and occupied high-status positions in the community. Canadian transplants who made it into the ranks of the Champaign County elite included David Gay, a minister from Prince Edward Island; Willard Samson and Margaret Crandel Samson, farmers from Ontario; John Rogerson, a lumber, grain, and merchandise dealer from Perth, Ontario; Patrick Richards, a banker from Quebec; Joseph O'Brien, an Irishman by birth who had studied engineering in Hamilton, Ontario; Daniel P. McIntyre, a farmer and banker from Ontario; William H. Lock, an importer and breeder of sheep from London County, Ontario; Harman Stevens, a Canadian-born doctor; and Lucretia Crawford Larkin, a mother of five.[63] The University of Illinois, begun as the Illinois Industrial University in 1867, brought additional Canadians to Champaign to participate in Farmers' Institute programs. Tellingly, for the history of cross-border cattle connections, animal husbandry instructor W. J. Kennedy had been born and reared on a Canadian stock farm.[64]

Border crossing went the other way as well. Censuses do not track temporary sojourns outside the United States, but they do reveal that some U.S.-born residents had children born in Canada.[65] Further evidence of temporary Canadian residence can be found in community histories. One of the first pioneers who settled in the county was Henry Sadorus, a Pennsylvania native who had spent some time in Canada before putting down roots in Illinois.[66] Another pioneer, the New York native Mark Carley, had lived in New Brunswick before heading west.[67] Residents had grown children in places such as Vancouver and Toronto, and at least one Champaign household served as a way station on the Underground Railroad.[68]

If, from the 1850s through the 1870s, Canada lost population to the U.S. Midwest, by the 1890s, the flow had reversed course. Thanks in part to the active recruiting efforts of Canadian immigration agencies, as many as a million U.S. residents settled in Canada between 1898 and 1914. Railroad companies also propagandized for Canada. In the 1890s, the *Champaign Daily Gazette* ran advertisements for "Home-seekers' Excursions" to various destinations, including British Columbia and Manitoba.[69] An American settler reportedly found it "just as easy to visit Saskatchewan as to go from his own State to the next. He runs up here in the fall to select a Government free grant, or to buy a farm from a railway or land company, and build a 'shack.' He returns in the spring with his outfit, and starts breaking the soil for his first crop the next morning. If he has bad luck or poor health overtakes him, he can always sell his land to advantage, and go back to his old home without much trouble."[70]

Not all emigrants were good ambassadors for Illinois, as seen in the case of a onetime Champaign resident who was extradited from Chicago for cracking bank safes in the dominion.[71] Some Canadians began to fear that the flood of U.S. settlers would carry Canada into their Union, just as they carried Texas from Mexico." Nevertheless, the two-way mobility between the Midwest and Canada contributed to a sense of affinity that cut across the border. As a commercial journal put it, there was "scarcely a family in the Dominion but what has members or kins-people living in the United States, and this operates as a mighty force in the interest of peace and closer communion."[72]

NORTHERN TRAFFIC

In the early nineteenth century, a significant amount of midwestern agricultural production traveled to eastern markets via the Great Lakes and St. Lawrence River. Although U.S. canal and railroad construction diverted traffic from Canadian routes, reducing their relative significance, Canadian investments in canal construction and expanded commerce after the Civil War led to an increase in U.S. tonnage on the St. Lawrence. In 1885, 3,795 U.S. vessels passed through the Canadian canal system; by 1899, the number had risen to 6,101.[73]

Ongoing improvements and expansions in U.S. railroad lines did not cut Canada out of U.S. shipping maps, because some of the freight cars that headed east from Chicago ventured north of Lake Erie. In 1876, with the completion of the eastern Intercolonial Railway, it was possible to ship goods by rail from Chicago to Halifax via Canadian lines, some of which added third rails to their wide-gauge tracks to accommodate traffic from the United States. Halifax was not much of a market, but it was one day closer to Europe than any U.S. port. (This helps explain why most of the cattle imported to the United States from Britain landed there.) Alternatively, freight could reenter the United States near Niagara and travel through Upstate New York to eastern U.S. markets.[74]

By 1880, Sir Henry Tyler, president of Canada's Grand Trunk Railway Company, claimed that his line was carrying 10 percent of the traffic east from Chicago, including 6 percent of the livestock traffic. This may not seem particularly noteworthy, but considering that the Grand Trunk had just completed its own line to Chicago, those numbers show a remarkable ability to attract business.[75] The rise of refrigeration, beginning with an 1878 shipment from Chicago to the Eastern Seaboard, added to the Grand Trunk's competitiveness.[76]

Prior to refrigeration, beef had to be shipped east in tins or on the hoof. The former was unsavory, the latter expensive. Live cattle needed food, water, and rest en route, and that necessitated an expensive infrastructure of feed bins and stockyards. Shipping cattle also posed public relations challenges: by the 1870s, investigators were accusing live-animal transporters of cruelty. They published gruesome reports of animals goring each other in their close-packed

Though aiming primarily to improve the lot of mariners,
British reformer Samuel Plimsoll also drew attention to the slave-ship-like
conditions for cattle in the transatlantic crossing.

Samuel Plimsoll, Cattle Ships *(London: Kegan Paul, French, Trübner and Co., 1890), 3.*

quarters during transport. Investigators claimed that boxcar cattle lost their appetites and became too alarmed to drink, losing one hundred to five hundred pounds in a thousand-mile trip. In 1870, the U.S. commissioner of agriculture called for a "well-regulated beef express" with padded and partitioned cars, but shippers balked at the added expense.[77]

Animals continuing their journey across the Atlantic faced even more horrific conditions. In 1890, the British seaman's advocate Samuel Plimsoll published an exposé on cattle ships. His account brought to light the animal equivalent of slave ships, with cattle packed like sardines, heads alternating with rumps, in spaces as small as two feet three inches across per bullock. Plimsoll wrote of oxen "mad with terror and unrest" forced to stand for sixteen days at a stretch. That alone would have been "prolonged torture," but crippling seasickness made things worse for the "dumb brutes." Animals that might have been put down under other circumstances, due to maiming and other excruciating injuries, had to die a so-called natural death on ship for insurance to be claimed. Upon arrival, surviving animals staggered off the ships, barely able to stand, with broken legs, torn-off horns, and frightful wounds from which "trail through urine and ordure the animals' intestines."[78]

And if the ordinary crossings were not bad enough, the stories of journeys gone awry were much worse. On the steamer *Santiago*, the "poor brutes" were "slowly roasted in their stalls" by a fire. When the passengers abandoned ship, they had to beat the bullocks that had jumped from the flaming vessel away from their lifeboats with hatchets and oars. Another ship, caught in a cyclone three days out, arrived with only 14 live cattle, from a cargo of 360. And here even Plimsoll drew the veil, saying that the captain's report of the suffering was too horrible to publish.[79] It was in this context that refrigerated meat took off.

The administrators of the Vanderbilt and Pennsylvania railroad companies had such large investments in cattle cars and stockyards that they regarded the advent of refrigerated cars as more of a threat than an opportunity. But the Grand Trunk Railway was not committed to the live-cattle trade. Indeed, the special measures mandated during pleuropneumonia outbreaks to prevent the spread of the disease across national borders provided extra incentives for Canadian shippers to cast their lot with dead meat.[80] Carcasses did not require posted bonds guaranteeing quarantined cars, "double isolated" enclosures, clean bills of health from veterinarians, keepers to collect and disinfect droppings, or government-supervised teams to bury animals that perished en route.[81] All dead meat required was ice, and Canada had plenty of that. By 1885, the Grand Trunk was carrying 138,000 tons of dressed meats (59 percent of the trade) on its eastbound tracks.[82]

Chicago meat-packers turned to the Grand Trunk not only because of its investments in refrigeration but also because of its competitive prices. By undercutting the rate agreements of the major U.S. lines, the Grand Trunk railroad sparked several rate wars in the 1880s.[83] In an age when nationalists were calling for a larger merchant marine to end U.S. dependence on foreign vessels, Illinois farmers heralded the Grand Trunk as the vehicle for obtaining more favorable shipping contracts.[84] Rather than regard Canadian lines as a threat to U.S. interests, the commodity producers of the Upper Midwest hailed them as a means to advance the interests of a different polity: *farmers*, on both sides of the line.

FAMILY TIES

The railroad lines that linked the U.S. Midwest to Canada carried awareness along with animals and people. A sense of cultural affinity may be less tangible than commodity exchanges, migration flows, and railroad ties, but this was just as important in making a Great Lakes agricultural region. For midwestern farmers, the agricultural press played a significant role in building feelings of cross-border attachment. The *Prairie Farmer* serves as an example. On first glance, it may seem to testify to the expansive influence of midwestern farm culture, for it boasted that its readership stretched from Texas to Canada.[85] Yet information also flowed *into* Chicago: the *Prairie Farmer* attributed some of its world news to Canadian outlets, and it republished material from serials such as the *Canada Farmer*.[86] Readers of the *Prairie Farmer* found articles praising Canadian (or at least Anglophone Canadian) agricultural attainment, including one which claimed that "we 'Americans' have a great deal to learn from our British American cousins . . . we are, even in our best cultivated regions, very much behind the Canadian standard of farming."[87]

As they stressed the cultural affinities between the farmers of the

Great Lakes borderlands, agricultural publications downplayed the significance of the U.S.-Canada border. The *Cyclopedia of American Agriculture*, for example, identified its scope as "North America north of Mexico," with some incidental treatment of "the tropical islands with which the United States holds governmental relations." It went on to say: "There is no geographical or agricultural distinction between the United States and Canada except such as arises from difference in latitude."[88] Similarly, the *Breeder's Gazette* pledged in its inaugural issue to "always keep a vigilant eye upon the business in the States, Canada and England"—thus suggesting that these three places together constituted a breeding community.[89]

Agricultural associations joined the agricultural press in linking U.S. and Canadian farmers together in common pursuits. Although Canadian and U.S. farmers organized independently, the U.S. National Grange and the Dominion Grange established formal contacts.[90] Despite some disagreements over the desired relations between the two national organizations, the 1876 Grange encampment in Philadelphia attracted representatives from twenty-six states, England, and Canada.[91] In 1877, the secretary of the Dominion Grange credited the U.S. National Grange with helping to spark the Canadian movement, and he professed respect for the National Grange's ongoing dedication to elevating "our class." He continued in this brotherly vein: "I trust those fraternal feelings, which should exist between our members everywhere, may grow stronger as time rolls on, and that we may ever be found working hand in hand for the common good."[92]

This sense of fraternalism guided the activities of more specialized agricultural groups such as the American Shorthorn Association, also called the Short-Horn Breeders of the United States and Canada.[93] Founded in 1871, the association drew its membership and leadership from both the United States and Canada, addressed its announcements and publications to audiences in both nations, and chose cities in both countries for its annual meetings.[94] Among those who traveled to Toronto for the association's 1875 meeting was Manly Miles, a professor at the Illinois Industrial University in Champaign.[95]

The fellowship fostered by the association did not render national differences moot. In the 1880s, U.S. members pressed the Department of Agriculture to make the duty-free entry of breeding animals contingent on registry in U.S. herd books. The prospect of paying $100 to register animals already listed in British and Canadian books led Canadian breeders to ask their government to impose comparable restrictions.[96] But not all Shorthorn breeders took the nationalist route—some called for a single American herd book, arguing that "the States are constant customers of the Canadian breeders."[97] Furthermore, the fractures along national lines crossed others that cut different ways. In 1872, the *Prairie Farmer* observed that differences of opinion about pedigree standards were "not confined to the breeders of Canada on the one side, and those of this country on the other, but are common to individuals of both countries."[98] Personal—rather than national—economic interests determined members' stances on inbreeding.[99] Association members felt the nationalistic strains in their relationship keenly because their cross-border relationships were so close.

Indeed, contemporaries often described these relations in familial terms. Histories of Illinois typically cast French Canadians as forebears because of their early presence in the area.[100] Contemporary Canadians (or at least the Anglophones among them) conjured visions of brotherhood. The editor of the *Prairie Farmer* praised the Canadians he met on the 1860 Illinois Central excursion for their "family traits" of frankness, pertinacity of opinion, adherence to naked facts, and reasoning.[101] To welcome a speaker from Nova Scotia, a spokesman for the Illinois Farmers' Institute rhapsodized about "unity and fellowship throughout the entire farming brotherhood."[102] As these familial references suggest, Illinois farmers did not really regard English-speaking Canada as foreign. It was not careless record keeping but a process of domestication that explains why U.S. stud-books failed to identify cattle from Canada as "imported."[103]

Despite the feeling that the border did not or should not matter, tariff policies reminded farmers that it did. From the end of the Civil War into the 1890s, protectionist policies that were aimed at national consolidation (understood in Canada as particularly beneficial to urban economic interests) led to demands for more transborder integration, including trade reciprocity, commercial union, political union, and annexation.[104] Advocates of closer relations emphasized not only the existing ties between Ontario and midwestern states but also their proximity and similar "physical conditions."[105] As one unionist put it: "the United States and Dominion of Canada belong as it were to each other . . . they are the geographical and commercial complement of each other."[106] Those who called for greater unity between the United States and Canada insisted that the nations' common fundamental interests and geographic logic should outweigh their political differences. In the words of a reciprocity advocate: "The interests of these two peoples are as similar as the territories which they occupy . . . Nature knows no artificial boundaries."[107] According to this reasoning, the U.S.-Canada border was an arbitrary and permeable political line that bisected a biologically, culturally, and economically coherent community. Even episodes of state-to-state conflict (such as the tensions created by Canada's havening of Union draft evaders and Confederate raiders) did not fundamentally shake the conviction that when it came to the Great Lakes region, the border figured more prominently in treaties and maps than in on-the-ground relationships.[108]

THE HIDDEN HISTORIES OF "TEXAN" CATTLE

Given the absence of comparable social and cultural ties with Mexico, it may seem that the influence of southwestern borderlands petered out well before reaching central Illinois. Indeed, when mapping their southernmost connections, nineteenth-century Illinois farmers often stopped, misleadingly, in Texas. Nevertheless, focusing on commodified cattle reveals that Great Lakes borderlands were not the only ones to stretch deep into the Illinois countryside. Midwestern farmers were bound as well to Mexico, in ways that resembled their ties to yet another place at the edge of the nation: Indian Territory. These southern relationships differed qualitatively from those that connected them to Canada, but they, too, played a significant role in shaping the region.

There were, of course, good reasons for Illinois fatteners to dwell on the importance of Texas cattle. As Illinois shifted from grazing to fattening in the 1860s, its beef industry became increasingly reliant on Texas ranches for supply. Illinois beef producers had started to fatten Texas cattle in the 1840s, but epidemics and the Civil War disrupted these shipments.[109] After the war, midwesterners reestablished connections with Texan suppliers. Early drives were beset by problems, including unfamiliarity with territory, swollen rivers, and resistance by Native American peoples who objected to damaging incursions on their land.[110] In the following years, however, Mississippi River steamers and newly built railway lines facilitated the movement of increasing numbers of Texas animals to Illinois feedlots. As an 1871 agricultural report noted, Texan cattle were driven six hundred to nine hundred miles to the coast, by "energetic frontiersmen in small bands, armed to the teeth."[111] At the Gulf of

Mexico, the animals were loaded on steamships for New Orleans. From there some traveled up the Mississippi. After arriving at Illinois feedlots, they met animals that had left Texas on foot for the arduous drive to the depots in Kansas.[112]

In contrast to the expensive Ontario animals imported for breeding purposes, Texas animals were cheap. Whereas purebred Canadian animals had aristocratic names, such as Lady Highthorn and the Seventh Duke of Airdrie, it would have been ridiculous to give a Texan steer any name at all, because of the castrated animal's inability to produce his own line of descendants and because of his interchangeability with other low-cost animals.[113] Whereas a celebrity bull might sell for thousands of dollars, and a "ripe graded steer" for as high as $6.85 per hundredweight in Chicago markets, Texas cattle sold for as little as $3.00 a hundredweight (or $36 for a steer in the common twelve-hundred-pound range). Prices in Texas were far lower than in northern packinghouses: $3.50 to $4.50 a head.[114] As an 1875 agriculture report pointed out, Texas cattle were "comparatively valueless," worth rearing only because of the abundance of forage and their ability to fend for themselves.[115]

According to livestock writings of the time, different assessments of worth boiled down to the matter of blood. Whereas Illinois farmers associated Ontario animals with highly cultivated British blood, they characterized Texas Longhorns as the degenerate descendants of Spanish stock, introduced into Mexico by the conquistadors in the time of Cortés.[116] Citing their wide variations in color as evidence of their motley ancestry, U.S. livestock experts traced the origins of Texan cattle back from Spain to North Africa. Rather than improving over time, as had inbred British animals, Texas cattle had "relapsed from a state of domestication."[117] Left to fend for themselves, they had only degenerated, returning to their African nature.[118] The fact that not all "Texan" cattle came from Texas and that they were indistinguishable from Mexican and Native American

COMPARISON OF LONGHORN STEER
OF THE TYPE COMMON FIFTY YEARS AGO, WITH AN IMPROVED BEEF ANIMAL OF TO-DAY.

U.S. livestock experts regarded longhorn cattle descended from Mexican stock as inferior to pedigreed Shorthorns but capable of uplift if crossed with purebred bulls that were traceable back to northern European lines.

J. R. Mohler, "Science in the Live-Stock Industry," The Scientific Monthly *32 (June 1931), 507–12.*

animals did nothing to raise them in the estimation of Illinois farmers.

CATTLE CROSSINGS ON THE RIO GRANDE

The border between the United States and Mexico was highly permeable in the late nineteenth century, and this applied to cattle no less than to people and inanimate goods. Although the combination of Mexican export taxes and U.S. import taxes inhibited licit trade, cattle production straddled the border.[119] Would-be U.S. ranchers gained a foothold in the business by rounding up feral cattle from

Mexican herds in Texas and by purchasing comparatively cheap animals in Mexico. Among them was Ohioan John T. McElroy, who purchased a herd in Sonora and then set off on a two-thousand-mile cattle drive to Kansas. The journey took three years, but the profits enabled McElroy (who had grazed the animals without cost on Indian lands) to buy ranch property in Texas.[120]

Established ranchers attempting to increase their herds continued to look to Mexico, though not for bulls. As the U.S. consul in Chihuahua put it, "There are no cattle in this State that would be worthy of importation to the United States for male breeding." Mexican cows were more attractive, however: the consul described them as "much superior to the bulls" and noted that the first crossbreed with a Shorthorn or Hereford bull resulted in "marked improvement."[121]

The comparatively positive appraisals of Mexican cows resulted not only from their utility in maximizing the genetic material carried by one high-value bull, but also from cultural assumptions about interbreeding. Nineteenth-century farmers believed that sires had more influence over their offspring than their female partners. Moreover, the farmers of Champaign (over 99 percent of whom were identified as white in the 1870 census) approached the issue of animal crossings from a cultural system that saw white men's excursions across the sexual color line as potentially blanching but saw other men's forays as inevitably corrupting. Cultural considerations influenced livestock breeding to such an extent that illustrious ancestry sometimes trumped meat-producing potential. Some prize bulls were too fat or sluggish to serve; others were too inbred to produce sound offspring. Yet midwestern farmers were far more critical of hardy Mexican bulls than of their own sometimes faulty stock.[122]

Besides acquiring cows from Mexico, some U.S. ranchers invested in Mexican land for grazing purposes. These ranchers joined Mexican *hacendados* in dispossessing peasants and outcompeting small-scale *rancheros*. Like northern Mexico cattle barons, late-nineteenth-century U.S. ranchers exported cattle from their Mexican holdings to the United States for consumption.[123] One rancher crossed about two thousand head of cattle into the United States near Eagle Pass on a single drive in 1895. Although ranchers at that time were supposed to cross their cattle at designated spots for health inspections, they preferred to wade their cattle across the border at the most proximate place.[124] Displaced Mexicans also headed north, in many cases to work on U.S. ranches alongside Texas-born Mexicans who were likewise losing ground to Anglo landowners.[125]

The number of Mexican cattle exported to the United States defies precise calculation. If U.S.-Canadian trade statistics are sketchy for the years leading up to World War I, U.S.-Mexican statistics are worse because the Rio Grande afforded easier crossing than the Great Lakes. In the 1880s, the U.S. customs service attempted to monitor imports into Texas through five customs districts (Brazos de Santiago, Corpus Christi, Galveston, Saluria, and Paseo del Norte— all but the last located on the Gulf of Mexico) with a total of about 110 employees (including storekeepers, messengers, and porters).[126] Such a minor inland presence meant that customs inspections were easily avoided, as Treasury reports on the prevalence of smuggling acknowledged.[127] The Mexican monitoring system—consisting of seven *aduanas* (customs houses) and four substations along the entire Texan border—was no more effective.[128]

The establishment of free trading zones in northern Mexico— starting with the state of Tamaulipas in 1858 and extending to the entire frontier in 1885—did not reduce the prevalence of smuggling in the surrounding borderlands. Prior to the establishment of these zones, Mexicans had crossed the border to do much of their trading. By smuggling their purchases across the Rio Grande, they had avoided steep Mexican duties. Rather than putting a stop to smuggling, the establishment of duty-free zones pushed lawbreaking activity six to twelve miles into the Mexican interior. The new trade zones also drew Texans into Mexico to shop. Texas merchants began to complain that the earlier dynamics of the border had flip-flopped—that their onetime Texan customers were now smuggling goods into the United States.[129]

Although the border was too permeable to permit a close count, significant numbers of cattle crossed from Mexico into Texas. A minimum estimate of the traffic can be gleaned from U.S. trade reports, which put the number at about 180,963 a year from 1884 to 1898.[130] U.S. consular reports hint at higher numbers. In 1888, the U.S. consul general in Matamoros estimated that about a third of the roughly 1.5 million cattle produced in Tamaulipas, Nuevo León, Coahuila, and Chihuahua went to the United States. The consul in Monterrey concurred with these findings.[131] An 1895 article in *The National Provisioner* put the import figure at 63,716 for the last six months; an 1898 article in the same publication counted 10,830 for the previous month.[132] A 1902 Bureau of Animal Industry report claiming that "Mexico raises great numbers of cattle for the United States" provides an additional glimpse into the trade. This report estimated that prior to an 1897 increase in tariffs, as many as four hundred thousand Mexican cattle crossed the border annually. The report estimated that increased tariffs had caused the number of imported cattle to fall to approximately a hundred thousand per year.[133]

Official efforts to calculate the cross-border trade do not track Mexican animals to their final destinations, but commercial accounts reveal that many were shipped north for fattening and then slaughter. In 1875, a *Railroad Gazette* article noted that Mexican cattle were among the animals that suffered on northbound U.S. freight cars.[134] In 1898, the Illinois Farmers' Institute found that Mexico was sending "thousands of cattle to the great Chicago and other markets."[135] Following the outbreak of the Mexican Revolution, a reporter for the *Chicago Live Stock World* registered his hope that the "rumpus" might benefit U.S. cattle feeders by leading to the U.S. acquisition of the northern Mexican "stocker" supply states.[136] If the cattle-raising borderlands finally ended on the packinghouse floor, their ambit encompassed the feedlots of Champaign. For hundreds of thousands of Mexican-born cattle, the heartland meant the final supper and bloody terminus to their far-reaching life journeys.

MAGNIFYING DISTANCE

Trying to track imports of Mexican cattle to Illinois begs a question: What counted as Mexican and what as Texan, given that cattle production was a border-straddling endeavor? In addition to operating ranches in Mexico, Texan ranchers did not think twice about crossing into Mexico to recover wandering stock—at least before a quarantine regime was put in place in 1890. (Subsequently, they complained that in contrast to Mexican ranchers, who could cross the Rio Grande to bring their errant cattle home, they could not legally do so.)[137] Texan ranchers also crossed the border in search of animals that had been rustled. The *Prairie Farmer* depicted the Texas-Mexico boundary as a lawless area, in which hundreds of thousands of animals were stolen from Texas ranches and armed vigilante groups were justified in their efforts to demand restitution from "cowardly, murderous greasers."[138] When a U.S. commission investigated cattle stealing across the Rio Grande in 1872, the *Prairie Farmer* reported on its findings: Texan ranchers had lost $100 million in stock to cross-border Mexican and Indian raids between El Paso and Brownsville.[139]

At times, the U.S. Army backed up ranchers' efforts to curtail rustlers from Mexico. It did so in spite of objections that nations at peace should not permit their armies to "invade" each other's territory to "capture and carry away property upon the claim that it has been stolen," that such action would have been unthinkable "had the stolen stock been transported to Canada."[140] Among the suspected cattle thieves pursued by the U.S. military were the Kickapoo Indians of Coahuila, formerly of the Champaign area. An 1873 U.S. cavalry raid on the Kickapoo village near Nacimiento, Mexico, gained press attention as far as London, but it did not stop cross-border cattle thievery or the cross-border pursuit of "cattle stealers." Although the U.S. press emphasized Mexican depredations, the raiding went both ways. Indeed, Mexican investigators found that their nation was the greater victim of cross-border plundering. Besides fostering bad feelings on both sides, the raids added to the difficulty in distinguishing between Mexican and Texan cattle.[141]

Canadians, some of them native peoples, raided across the border, too, but depredations in Montana did not figure as largely in the midwestern agricultural press as did those in Texas. The strenuous efforts of the Mounties to track down offenders bolstered assertions that cattle stealing on the northern ranges had become "almost entirely a thing of the past" by the 1880s. Even so, the tendency to stress the civilizing role that cowboys of northern European ancestry were playing in the region also explains the popular conception that people of the northwestern rangelands were relatively law-abiding.[142] The *Prairie Farmer* presented thievery along the Mexican border as part of a pattern that extended to rampant smuggling and a complete absence of "responsible government."[143] In circular fashion, the comparatively greater attention paid to Mexican raids contributed to negative views of Mexicans, described in the *Prairie Farmer* as "plunderers," "marauders," and "the savage Indian and the scarcely less savage border Mexican."[144] By paying more attention to Mexican than Canadian or U.S. lawlessness, the midwestern agricultural press advanced stereotypes of Mexicans as predatory bandits a world apart from the law-abiding Ontario breeders who could precisely document not only the aristocratic genealogies of their prize animals but also their legal ownership of these animals.

The disparaging assessments of Mexican criminality contributed to a larger pattern of disassociation. Even though British-style agricultural exhibitions and breeding practices took off in Mexico in the 1890s, Mexicans do not appear in nineteenth-century reports of midwestern agricultural fairs, livestock sales, university institutes, farmers' alliance meetings, or breeding associations. Champaign histories did mention Mexico in passing, alluding to former residents in the mining business in "Old Mexico" and "in old Mexico when last heard from," and to a current resident who had been "delayed some time at Acapulco" on his return from California. Nevertheless, most of the firsthand knowledge of Mexico that circulated in central Illinois was imparted by the veterans of the 1846–1848 Mexican-American War— that is, by people who knew Mexicans as vanquished adversaries.[145]

Significantly, most Champaign residents did not know people of Mexican origin as neighbors. The Champaign County naturalization records are dotted with Canadian cases but contain no references to Mexican birth, nor do census records reveal any Champaign residents of Mexican birth prior to 1910.[146] If any residents had obviously Hispanic surnames, the sometimes semiliterate census takers altered them beyond recognition. The one nineteenth-century resident of the county who seems likely to have been Mexican—a woman named Donena Sweet—is not identified as such. The only census in which she appears—for 1860—identifies her as having been born in Spain around 1800. It is possible that she was, indeed, born in the Iberian Peninsula, but geographic proximity makes onetime Spanish holdings west of the Mississippi seem her more likely place of origin. Sweet lived on a modest farm owned by a son; neither she nor her family members made it into published histories of the county's illustrious residents.[147]

Due to their comparative docility, farm-raised Shorthorn cattle could
be tended very differently from the ornery Longhorns rounded up on the
range. In this detail from a depiction of a Champaign County stock farm,
the farmer walks his well-behaved cattle down the road.

Detail of "Residence and Stock Farm of J. C. Kirkpatrick," History of Champaign County, Illinois
(Philadelphia, 1878), plate after 116. The University Library, University of Illinois at Urbana-Champaign.

It is possible, of course, that census takers missed Mexican-origin
workers, especially if they were transient. Because railroad companies assumed no responsibility for cattle deaths caused by heat, cold,
trampling, or smothering, shippers had good reason to take them up
on their offers to allow the owner of a carload of stock to ride free as
a caretaker. Yet railroads also paid the return fare for those who accompanied two or more cars of cattle to Illinois, thereby reducing the
likelihood of a long-term stay.[148] Men who passed too quickly through
boardinghouses to attract a census taker's notice would have had
limited opportunities to make favorable impressions on Champaign
farmers, who had no compelling economic reasons to seek their company. By the 1870s, midwestern farmers, like farmers in Ontario, had
fenced their fields and were carefully tending their comparatively
docile stock.[149]

In such a system, the specialized riding and roping skills that
Mexican vaqueros relied on to manage ornery range cattle had no
particular value. Whereas Champaign farmers were likely to know

Canadian people, their main encounters with anything Mexican involved low-value animals destined soon for the shambles. Countless Mexican cowhands (both native-born and immigrant) worked on Texas ranches, but, in keeping with Anglos' disparagement of Mexican cowboys (on class, ethnic, and racial grounds), the midwestern farm press took little note of their labor or its significance for their own economic well-being.[150]

This sense of distance from the people of Mexico carried over to assessments of Mexico's economic position. Canadian farmers had valued connections to British breeders, but Mexico's former colonial ruler, Spain, did not have a noteworthy beef industry. When Argentinian ranchers became major players in the global beef market, they purchased their high-end bulls from Britain, not from their former colonial ruler.[151] Canadian breeders had higher profit margins than Mexican ranchers, who were shut out of the more lucrative fattening and packing sectors of the export business.[152] Whereas Canadian railroad lines competed for U.S. traffic, Mexican lines did not lead to harbors teeming with ships bound for the U.S. Northeast or Liverpool. Canada served as an outlet to lucrative beef markets, but Mexico was, in comparison, a dead end.[153]

The *Prairie Farmer* did provide some notice of Mexican efforts to entice immigrants and of public land offerings in Baja California, Sonora, Chihuahua, Sinaloa, and Durango. But in contrast to its coverage of Canadian opportunities, it did little to drum up enthusiasm for Mexican grants, noting that, "even at those rates, the sale will probably be dull. It is not the price that attracts buyers so much as the productiveness, the security, the opportunity for selling again, the accessibility and the society. If Northwestern Mexico were annexed and Americanized, provided with railroads and schools, the land would soon rise a hundred-fold in value." Illinois farmers called for Canadian annexation as well, but for reasons of affinity rather than colonial uplift (or, in other calls for Mexican annexation, to put an end to plundering).[154] Mexico, it appeared, was a country apart, and its cattle marked difference as much as anything else.

From the perspective of Illinois cattle producers, Mexico was a land crying out for improved blood. And who better to supply it than cattlemen such as themselves? A 1902 report titled *Mexico as a Market for Purebred Cattle from the United States* made precisely that point. Drawing heavily on the testimony of U.S. consular officers, it found a significant Mexican demand for the services of U.S. bulls.[155] Claims that U.S. bulls could improve the size and quality of stunted Mexican scrub cattle resonated with claims that the "half-breed" Mexican nation would benefit from an infusion of better blood. As one pioneer history put it, without the industry and vigor of Champaign's leading men (all assumed to be white and many identified in terms of European lineages and revolutionary stock), the community "would soon sink into the lethargic condition that characterizes the Mexican and Spaniard, and ultimately destroys their manhood, their nation."[156] A Champaign stock raiser put the matter more bluntly: "a well bred man is better than a 'scrub.'"[157] Farmers familiar with the principles of breeding would have gotten the point: Mexico desperately needed U.S. studs.

THE INDIAN TERRITORY TRADE

The tendency to characterize the southwestern cattle sent to Illinois for fattening as "Texan" hid not only Mexican ancestry and more recent origins but also links to Indian Territory. Although some Native Americans relied on government beef, especially as supplies of buffalo dwindled, other groups raised cattle for their own consumption and for market.[158] Before the Civil War, cattle production was the leading enterprise of Oklahoma's "Five Civilized Tribes" (Cherokee, Choctaw, Chickasaw, Creek, and Seminole). Despite raids by the

Kickapoos and other Native American groups, the Cherokee Nation had about 20,000 head of cattle in 1839. Prospering on the extensive grasslands held communally by the tribe, the Cherokee herds grew to about 240,000 in 1859. They declined during the Civil War, when Union and Confederate troops joined civilian thieves and roving Native American bands in plundering Indian Territory herds. This widespread lawlessness continued through the war, resulting in the loss of about 300,000 animals before federal troops finally reduced the rustling. Thereafter, herd sizes increased, to an estimated 700,000 cattle in Indian Territory in 1884. The Cherokees had the largest holdings—about 250,000—followed by the Choctaws and Creeks.[159] Other groups—including for a while the Kickapoos who had been relocated to Kansas—allowed non-Indian cattlemen to graze their herds on their lands in exchange for fees.[160]

Like Mexican cattle, Indian Territory cattle crossed boundaries and mingled with other herds. It was not uncommon for Anglo drovers to drive across Native Americans' land, adding and sometimes losing animals on the way. Although an 1834 Indian Act penalized drovers a dollar per head for cattle driven across land belonging to an Indian or Indian tribe, enforcement was another matter. The great long drives from Texas north to Kansas often crisscrossed Indian lands in Oklahoma, sometimes at a purposefully slowed pace so that the animals could fatten en route, arriving at their destination after the cold had set in.[161]

Recognizing their inability to keep the Texan animals off their territory, the Cherokees settled instead for a ten-cent tax. Though poor compensation for the grasses consumed, it was better than nothing. And nothing was what the Five Tribes got after an Arkansas judge ruled that the transit tax represented undue regulation of interstate commerce. It was in this context that some members of the Five Tribes and the neighboring Osages leased land to Texas ranchers, thereby contributing to further mingling of wayward animals.

The greatest blow to the Five Tribes' ranching endeavors came in 1893, when the Dawes Commission, tasked with privatizing collectively held Indian land, began the allotment process that greatly reduced the Five Tribes' holdings. Regarding Indian grazing lands as excessive, the commission members put over three million acres of unallotted land on the market. White settlers snatched up the newly available prairies, bringing the great age of Indian livestock production in Oklahoma to an end.[162]

As the story of Oklahoma allotment reveals, many of the lands placed on the market after the Civil War for grazing use and purchase were Indian lands. This expropriation of Native American land had major implications for Illinois fatteners. To begin with, they numbered among those who took advantage of land offerings. When nine million acres of the Sioux reservation in South Dakota were thrown open to settlement in 1890, the *Champaign Daily Gazette* reported enthusiastically on the "Preparations for a grand rush."[163] Local directories mention residents who owned "western lands" and grown children who decamped for South Dakota, Kansas, Arizona, Oklahoma, Oregon, and elsewhere. Even those who stayed on the wet prairie benefited from the ongoing colonization of Indian lands, for the grass-fed animals of the Northwest joined those of the Southwest on their feedlots.[164]

Like Mexican stock raisers, Native American stock raisers were not as integrated into midwestern farming webs as Ontario breeders. In contrast to their fraternal ties with the men who dominated the Canadian breeding industry, Illinois cattlemen had little common ground with the Native American groups that regarded cattle tending as women's work, comparable to the cultivation of fruit trees.[165] This sense of difference held fast even as the Five Tribes became more fully incorporated into the commercial cattle industry. After the Civil War, the Five Tribes joined Illinois farmers in investing in improved breeds such as Durhams and Devons.[166] As a result, the

Cherokees won occasional recognition for their herds. The *Prairie Farmer*, for example, reported on a thousand-head Cherokee herd brought to Indiana for fattening that resembled "our native stock," due to evident Durham blood.[167] However, such herds appeared to be exceptions that proved the general rule. When a team of livestock investigators in Abilene noted "one drove of especial merit" that had been "raised among the Cherokee Indians by Col. Gains, an Indian notable of much intelligence," they cast merit and intelligence as atypical qualities in Indian country.[168] The reason the team had taken the trouble to inspect Gains's operation was their conviction that most Cherokee cattle were a deadly menace to the herds of the Midwest.

BAD BLOOD AND BOUNDARY DRAWING

Although boosterish articles on the cattle-fattening business did not stress the Mexican or Indian Territory origins of some ostensibly "Texan" cattle, Illinois farmers were not oblivious to these connections. Reportage on "Spanish fever," also known as "Texas fever," "Cherokee cattle disease," and "the cattle disease," made these connections difficult to miss.[169] Spanish fever was a mysterious ailment that had little outward effect on animals driven north from Texas, but that devastated the northern cattle exposed to southern stock. Signs of infection included restlessness, a wild gaze, swollen eyeballs, elevated temperatures, and blindness. As the disease worsened, the animals retained their urine and their bodies stiffened, even as their neck muscles twitched uncontrollably. Prostration and death followed within days. Autopsies revealed kidneys "turgid with blood," bladders "much distended by bloody urine," and windpipes full of "frothy blood."[170]

Spanish fever hit Champaign fatteners hard in the summer of 1868. From June to July of that year, the Illinois Central Railroad shipped about fifty carloads of cattle a day from Cairo, Illinois, to its Tolono stockyard in southern Champaign County. The animals—about fifteen thousand total—had traveled from the Red River area near Shreveport, Louisiana, up the Mississippi. As one shipper described it, the animals had stood on the hard, hot deck for about a week, without room to lie down. Having been denied food and drink as well as rest, they landed in Cairo "in great poverty of flesh and famishing with hunger, and so near dead from exhaustion that in many instances they had to be helped up the levee to the shipping yards of the I.C.R.R." From Tolono, the cattle were distributed to nearby feedlots in and around Champaign. Wherever they went, they came into contact with native animals, and an epidemic ensued.[171]

Desperate fatteners rushed their diseased cattle to market, but many died on the way east, causing considerable financial losses. Among those who suffered grievously was John T. Alexander. In that terrible summer, he took in one hundred to six hundred cattle a week, mostly from Cairo via Tolono, but some from Abilene via Chicago. Even as these southwestern cattle fattened on his farms, his own cattle, and those of his neighbors, sickened and died. When a veterinarian came to investigate, he found men skinning and burying the carcasses from sunrise to sunset.[172]

Counting the payments he made to his neighbors to cover their losses, Alexander suffered a $75,000 blow. No longer able to maintain his large holdings, he frantically sought a buyer, turning at first to a Canadian company that he thought would be able to take everything and then finally breaking Broadlands into parcels for sale.[173] As his payments to his neighbors suggest, Alexander was not alone in misfortune. Across the county, the toll exacted from the "dreadful scourge" amounted to about five thousand deaths. Though not the only stricken part of the state, Champaign was the hardest hit.[174]

Though the worst epidemic, it was not the last: Spanish fever became a matter of ongoing concern.[175]

As the moniker "Spanish fever" suggests, this disease struck contemporaries as foreign in its origin. Since no cases were reported in Spain, the word *Spanish* implied Mexican origins.[176] Indeed, reportage on the fever made it clear that Texan animals were not the only ones to spread it to vulnerable midwestern herds; Mexican and Cherokee cattle did as well. It was the threat of disease that drew the greatest attention to the presence of these animals in Illinois.[177]

Northern farmers responded to the danger by urging health inspections and quarantine for "all foreign cattle."[178] Heeding their outcry, the governor of Illinois appointed two cattle commissioners and called a convention, which was attended by delegates from several northern states (including at least one from Champaign) and Canada. This gathering failed to solve the problem. Delegates did bring up the issue of ticks (later discovered to be the transmitters), but they focused on the problem of cattle ingesting ticks that had dropped into their feed rather than the problem of ticks biting cattle.[179] In 1869, the Illinois legislature decided that the most effective strategy would be to limit mobility. It passed a bill excluding the entry of southern cattle from March through October, with the exception of animals that had wintered in northern states.[180] Illinois was not the only state to pass such legislation, nor even the first: Kansas had restricted the importation of southern cattle in 1861 and Missouri had done so thereafter. (Indeed, the restrictions those states placed on overland routes had benefited the Mississippi River route that funneled cattle to central Illinois.) After Bureau of Animal Industry studies had conclusively proved in 1889 that ticks were the culprits, the federal government passed a national quarantine law.[181] When it came to the movement of livestock, the role of tariff barriers paled beside health-based barriers to mobility. The disease threat posed

by Mexican and Indian animals did little to foster feelings of attachment to Mexico or Indian Territory, much less their people.

Canadian cattle also suffered from disease, most notably the deadly
pleuropneumonia.[182] Yet rather than providing evidence of Canadian
depravity, pleuropneumonia provided further evidence of Canada's
tight connections to northern European breeders, because the disease
had come to North America from Europe. Instead of causing midwestern farmers to look upon Canada as a pestilential and menacing
neighbor, pleuropneumonia reminded them of the essential commen-
surability of the two countries, as Canadian officials were as likely to
slap restrictions on U.S. animals as the reverse when outbreaks occurred.[183] Recognizing the common interests of U.S. and Canadian
breeders, the American Association of Breeders of Short-horns pressed
both U.S. and Canadian officials for tougher quarantine regulations.[184]
By the 1880s, Canada had instituted such strict quarantine provisions
for imported cattle that the United States required no additional surveillance of transshipped animals. When the United States quarantined Canadian cattle in the Northwest in 1895, it did so because the
British government had warned of contagious disease in the area.[185]

Illinois farmers recognized Canadians as fellow victims and worthy allies, but they saw Mexicans and Native Americans more as
threats, aptly represented by disease-ridden animals. Seeing them as
such helped lay the groundwork for further border-drawing efforts,
among them the extension of health inspections and quarantine
practices from animals to people.[186]

CONTINENTAL CROSSROADS

Given that most people in Champaign never went to Canada or
Mexico, it may seem a stretch to claim that borderlands, north and
south, extended to their mucky roads and flat expanses of puddled

farms. Yet it has long seemed commonsensical to place the same people at the very heart of a continent-spanning nation because of the larger forces at work. Midwestern farmers did not need to personally tour the surrounding country to be woven into its fabric. As tariff policies, quarantine restrictions, railroad grants, and Department of Agriculture veterinary inspections demonstrate, the reach of the federal government extended far beyond mustering troops and distributing land. Even in the government's sproutlike nineteenth-century form, its tendrils enlaced the country. Economic, social, and cultural relationships further stitched the Midwest into the very heart of the land.

Nationalist maps that come to a screeching stop at borders notwithstanding, this land sprawled to the north and south, extending beyond the Great Lakes and Rio Grande. The Illinois farmers who looked northward for breeding stock and southward for animals to fatten made the most of their position in the middle. In the process of advancing their own particular fortunes, they brought seemingly disparate borderlands together. By framing the Midwest as thoroughly domestic and quintessentially American, the heartland myth has prevented us from seeing the Midwest as a place where borderlands converged.

Which is not to say that the people in the middle regarded both borders as commensurate. When midwestern stock producers looked to the north, they did not see many threats. Although Canadians could be economic rivals, their complementary productive systems, familiarity, and ties to the British Empire enhanced the appeal of an integrated borderlands region. If it had been up to the rural residents of the Old Northwest to draw the lines and fix the boundaries, the region we know as the Midwest might very well have become the *Lower North*.

To the south, in contrast, the farmers in the middle saw a gulf—in economic competitiveness, in human relationships, and in the quality of stock. The midwestern livestock producers who knew Mexico through animals worked hard to erase the marks of difference and danger from these animals, to homogenize meat through diet and breeding. Yet despite the profits they derived from fattening range cattle, in the process hiding their points of origin, they did not embrace Mexico or Mexicans as economic equals. To the contrary, when they looked to the south, they saw the need for a well-patrolled border, with crossings of more an imperialist than a familial kind.

Insofar as they pressed for more border enforcement, midwestern farmers may seem to provide evidence for the myth of heartland insularity. But their support for new border-policing practices did not result from distance. To the contrary, it resulted from their intimate relations with, and, indeed, economic dependence on, border-crossing animals, and from the comparative perspectives derived from a place in the middle.

ARCHIVAL TRACES

The ordinary meat-eating races

Urbana Union, **1855**: "We have ourself seen a hundred bushels to the acre raised on old 'Indian corn patches' which had been cultivated probably for hundreds of years."[1]

Champaign Daily Gazette, **1899**: A First National Bank advertisement: steamship passage, "via all the principal lines, sold to any part of the world . . . foreign exchange bought and sold, and letters of credit issued available the world over."[2]

The Illinois Agriculturist, **1902**: A. D. Shamel, an Instructor of Farm Crops at the University of Illinois, has ambitions of spreading corn into "great territories now undeveloped," and Africa in particular. "Some prominent agriculturalists confidently predict that upon the development and settling up of our corn belt, when the farms become small and intensive cultivation is the rule that then this great African corn belt may be taken advantage of."[3]

Urbana Courier, **1905**: Advertisement for International Stock Food-coupon holders can obtain free samples of International Poultry Food, International Worm Powder, International Heave Cure, International Gall Cure, International Colic Cure, International Distemper Cure, and International Louse Killer, provided they purchase a pail of International Stock Food at the regular price.[4]

Chicago Daily Tribune, 1909: "Champaign, Ill. has three track buyers, who buy for export, they have already taken over 10,000,000 bu [bushels] for export via New Orleans, to be shipped by Jan. 1."[5]

The Breeder's Gazette, 1911: "The porcine species is purely the associate of home-making humanity. The American Indian never produced a hog, nor have the Asiatic tribes of wandering proclivities. His very nature renders him a product of civilization and the associate of progressive mankind."[6]

Urbana Courier, 1918: "With food the United States made it possible for the forces of democracy to hold out to victory. To insure democracy in the world, we must continue to live simply in order that we may supply these liberated nations of Europe with food. Hunger among a people inevitably breeds anarchy. American food must complete the work of making the world safe for democracy."[7]

The World's Meat, 1927: "Those nations which have been the most vigorous colonizers of modern times and which are the most advanced in the achievements of this industrialized age are the heaviest meat eaters." Meat eating "may not be the cause of greater virility," but "all the racial evidence available indicates that the ordinary meat-eating races are the most virile races of the world."[8]

HOG-TIED

The Roots of the Modern American Empire

WISCONSIN SCHOOLS

Since its inception the heartland myth has insisted on American exceptionality. The heartland of myth is God's country. Its wholesome farms, with their tall tasseled stalks standing golden in the sun, provide the rural counterpart to the Puritans' city on a hill. More seat of virtue than throne of power, the heartland of myth seems innocent of imperial designs.

The founders of the republic, however, imagined their creation as a new Rome, destined to expand over time. The term *empire* later fell into disfavor as it came to be associated with European colonial injustices, but for the first century following independence, Americans did not hesitate to speak of their expanding republic as an empire, mostly "of liberty" but sometimes just plain. The Northwest Ordinance of 1787 provided the legislative mechanism for their expansive vision. By enabling the incorporation of new states, on an equal basis, it headed off the possibility of subordinate western colonies. Yet by promoting the conquest, dispossession, and displacement of indigenous nations, it also advanced the imperial project. It was under the auspices of the Northwest Ordinance that the ostensibly anticolonial settler colony of Illinois became another stately jewel in the imperial orb.[9]

Frederick Jackson Turner, of the University of Wisconsin, moved the Old Northwest out of the realm of empire and into the domain of democracy in his frontier thesis of 1893. Rather than compare U.S. expansion to European colonialism, he compared the American frontier to the boundaries that European states drew with each other. This sleight of hand enabled him to keep the American empire out of the imperial world system of the time, placing it in a special world of its own, a world of nonimperial democracy building on the part of white men gifted with vast expanses of free land. Turner provided such a powerful national narrative that it took generations of historians (notably including one of Turner's successors at Wisconsin, William Cronon) to retire it from active duty history, relegating it to an office in the echoing halls of myth.

Along with historians of the American West such as Cronon, the foreign relations historian William Appleman Williams (yet another Wisconsin luminary) played a major role in debunking Turner's thesis. In *Empire as a Way of Life* (published in 1980), Williams drew attention to colonial violence, as it played out in land grabs and removal policies. But it was Williams's earlier work that had put the word *empire* back into play. In *The Roots of the Modern American Empire* (published in 1969), Williams construed the Midwest very differently from both the founders and the Turner school. Focused more on overseas expansion than the continental variety, this book treated the Midwest as fully incorporated into the nation, its history as thoroughly domestic, until the flood of its abundance broke the dam. Writing in the midst of the Vietnam War, a conflict that he vigorously opposed, Williams had set forth to discover the wellspring of

American empire. He found it on the farm, and, more specifically, in farmers' desire for export markets in Asia and Latin America.

The Roots soon became a classic, and deservedly so, not just because of its efforts to trace American empire to its literal roots, but also because of its insistence that there was something that could be called an American empire outside of 1898. Yet even as Williams braved the patriotic gales of the Cold War to speak of the United States in such terms, he joined Turner in fencing the United States off from the larger global history of empire. Williams's study of agrarian politics made American empire seem exceptionally American, sprung from the soil, as it were. The "farmer businessmen" who people the pages of *The Roots* are far more colonizing than postcolonial. They are the originators of American empire, not the inheritors. Useful though *The Roots* continues to be in explaining midwestern farmers' interests in overseas empire building, it does not fully account for their entanglements with the global imperial system of their day. That would take a different species of imperial story, one more along the lines of the rise and fall of the Berkshire hog.

IMPERIAL STOCK

The Berkshire hog was a creature of empire. As the name suggests, some of its ancestry was English, traceable back to animals "strong in tusks . . . high backed, long-legged, and villainously carnivorous."[10] Over the centuries, the breeders of Berkshire, England, worked to eradicate these uncouth characteristics, in the process creating a fixed line of buff, sandy, or whitish-brown animals spotted with brown and black.[11] Improved though they were over their ancient forebears, these pigs were known for being "unthrifty," for "consuming more food than was repaid in the flesh."[12] This problem extended far beyond Berkshire hogs to European pigs in general, which ate scraps for most of the year but fattened each fall on mast (the acorns and beechnuts that had fallen to the forest floor). Mast-fed pigs had to be hardy enough to range widely through the forest in search of food and agile enough to avoid whatever predators they encountered there. As a result, they resembled the wild boars with which they often interbred—big framed, long legged, and lean bellied. Although deforestation and human population pressures had led to continual confinement in stys and more purposeful breeding efforts by the seventeenth century, European pigs of the era were not that far removed from the forest. Berkshire breeders, like other farmers, eagerly sought crosses that would make pigs worth raising in the absence of mast. They eventually got these crosses from the ships of the British Empire, particularly those that sailed to China.[13]

In contrast to European pigs, Chinese pigs had been trough-fed and selectively bred for thousands of years. The resulting short-legged, potbellied animals fattened more readily than European pigs. Even better, they seemed to fatten on just about anything. Nineteenth-century writings tended not to dwell on the remarkable length of their intestines, which enhanced nutrient absorption. Instead of highlighting biology, these writings advanced social theories maintaining that Chinese pigs, like Chinese people, lived in an economy of scarcity. To survive in such a setting, pigs and people alike had to prosper on foods that more fastidious eaters would have spurned. To survive, the Chinese had to "devour almost everything that grows on the earth, or in it, or in the sea. Their main characteristic is that of a foul-feeding race; consequently the food of the pig in such a country, must be confined to the very few things the human natives do not eat."[14]

In later debates over Chinese exclusion, the supposed omnivoraciousness of Chinese people helped make them seem alien and threatening to the white working class. Exclusionists roused their audiences with the specter of having to compete against rat eaters.

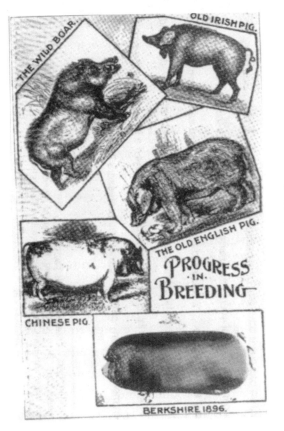

This depiction of the history and evolution of the Berkshire pig shows how crossing the old English pig with a Chinese line resulted in a veritable sausage of a pig that far surpassed its ancestors.

C. Fred Boshart, "History and Evolution of Our Common Pig," Berkshire Yearbook, 1896 (Springfield, Ill.: Illinois State Register Book Publishing House, 1896), plate after 20.

But a century earlier, claims of omnivoraciousness had added to the appeal of Chinese pigs. Though stigmatized for their color—so dark that they came to be known as the "black breed"—and for their soft and oily flesh, their meat-making ability redeemed them.[15] Seeing the ability to fatten on whatever they were fed as a saving strength, English breeders welcomed Chinese animals into their pens.[16] By crossing the small but meaty Chinese pigs with large but lean domestic lines, Berkshire breeders created one of the heaviest breeds of England, weighing from seven hundred to one thousand pounds when grown.

Enthusiasts described Berkshires as unsurpassed meat makers. They matured so early that they could be made to weigh three hundred pounds in ten months. No breed could compete with them when it came to the amount of food required for each pound of growth, but their attractions went beyond sheer poundage. Packers reportedly favored them because their meat was not oily but marbled, their hams choice and heavy, and their bacon of "unexcelled quality."[17] Long-distance shippers praised their meat as less prone to shrinkage than that of fattier breeds.[18] Were this not enough, their offal was light in comparison to carcass weight, meaning ounce for ounce, they outcompeted—or outmeated—other pigs.[19]

The improved Berkshire hog may have had some common ancestry with the swine that sustained the pioneers, but Chinese genetic material had altered British lines to such an extent that an Englishman who traveled through Illinois in the 1840s expressed horror at the hogs he saw there. "The breed of hogs in this part of the country is very bad," he wrote. "They are long-nosed, thin creatures, with legs like greyhounds, and, like the greyhound among dogs, seem to be the kind formed for speed and agility among swine, as they think nothing of galloping a mile at a heat, or of clearing fences which a more civilized hog would never attempt." The traveler admitted that such animals might be "the best fitted for the backwoods," given their ability to fend for themselves, but he had only contempt for their savage nature.[20]

As frontier conditions gave way to more commercialized farming, Illinois farmers came to agree. Hardy though they were, woods hogs rarely weighed more than two hundred pounds at three years of age, one hundred pounds less than a prize Berkshire at ten months.[21] Comparing the numbers, farmers ambitious of profit had to admit that domestication and controlled breeding offered advantages over the "reckless matings" of "mongrel" animals.[22]

As in the case of the cattle industry, the quest for herd improvement led Illinois pig farmers to purchase purebred strains. Some of these strains had been developed by U.S. breeders. Like British farmers, they benefited from far-flung trading networks. Merchants and naval officers carried animals to the United States on their vessels.[23] The Mackay breed, for example, can be traced back to the Boston-based Captain John Mackay, who procured hogs from "various parts of the world, whither he was led in his commercial intercourse." His subsequent breeding efforts led to "the production of a stock to which his name was applied."[24]

Yet even as U.S. breeders refined various lines, U.S. farmers looked to Britain as a leading source of quality pigs. As in the case of cattle importations, it was not only the reputation of the British breeding industry that made it the top place to look for pedigreed animals, it was also the long-standing connections between Britain and its onetime colony. Not coincidentally, Berkshire historians traced the start of the line in the United States back to an English emigrant who had a farm in English Neighborhood, New Jersey. That importation was in 1823. The next came in 1832, also by an English emigrant, this one settled in the vicinity of Albany, New York. "I have heard," wrote a Berkshire historian, "that by the year 1838 a few followed into Canada, and some of the Western States, from England."[25] Their popularity grew so quickly that by the 1840s the demand for them "amounted almost to a craze."[26] Even as the U.S. Berkshire breeding industry took off, U.S. breeders continued to import English Berkshires, such as Lord Liverpool 221, who sold for $700 in 1874 (meaning about $14,400 in inflation-adjusted 2018 dollars), and Lord Bromley-Manley, imported in 1914.[27]

The Berkshire rose to glory from a wider field of globe-trotting contestants, all polished in the British Isles. The Neapolitan breed, "descended from the Roman pigs of antiquity," might seem Italian, but it came to the United States from Britain. So did the Essex, a Neapolitan cross. The Middlesex had a larger infusion of "the

Chinese." The Suffolk mixed old Suffolk lines with Berkshire and Chinese breeds.[28]

Though each of the imported British breeds had its advocates and investors, the Berkshire won particular favor among Illinois farmers. In the late 1870s, Berkshires were the most popular hog at the Illinois State Fair.[29] And the Illinois State Fair was a good place to look at hogs, for in 1870, Illinois had more swine than any other state.[30] The pioneers had depended on hogs from the start, but the pig population of Illinois took off in the second half of the century, plateauing in the 1880s at nearly six million snouts.[31]

THE BERKSHIRE CRAZE
IN ILLINOIS

The farmers of Champaign County contributed to the count. According to the 1850 census, the average farm in the county held between thirty-five and thirty-six swine.[32] That was enough to give the county seat the moniker "Hog Town," due to the animals that thronged the streets and blocked the sidewalks, irritating the fastidious with their abundance of fleas.[33] If the county seat was a hog town, the surrounding area was increasingly a hog district. As they shifted from cattle grazing to fencing fields and feedlot fattening, the farmers of central Illinois rounded up the last semiferal pioneer hogs and set to work constructing pigpens.

A more hands-on style of pork production meshed well with more managed approaches to beef. After the harvest, farmers gave their cattle first crack at the stubbled fields and then let loose their pigs to scour what was left (thereby providing some grounds for claims that they fattened on manure).[34] In the 1860s, Champaign farmer Isaac Funk kept four to five hundred hogs for this purpose.[35] A generation later, cattle raiser H. H. Harris fattened about six hundred to seven hundred hogs on the side.[36] If, for some farmers, pigs provided a means to make money from leftovers, for others, pigs became the main means to condense grain into meat. Pig production took off in Illinois, as in other parts of the emerging Corn Belt, because pigs waxed well on corn.

Looking from the windows of his office in the mid-1850s, the editor of a Champaign newspaper saw "hundreds of acres of corn, luxuriant in its growth . . . promising food to the hungry and wealth to the growers," towering so tall that it took "two looks to see the top."[37] In 1869, the county had 120,428 acres planted in corn, yielding nearly four million bushels of grain.[38] The more that farmers drained their swampy fields, the more they planted, with corn gaining ground against wheat.[39] By 1898, Champaign resident H. J. Dunlap boastfully referred to Champaign as a leading county of the corn zone.[40] Although Illinois fell in the hog-producing rankings to the fifth-place state by the turn of the century, pig counters continued to place Illinois at the "center of the world's swine producing industry," thanks to its fields of corn.[41]

The history of Berkshires in Illinois can be traced back at least as far as 1857, when the Illinois Stock Importing Association purchased several Berkshire hogs to breed with native sows. Three years later, Champaign County resident Benjamin F. Johnson claimed that "the Berkshire hog is surely, and in some places swiftly, winning its way to general favor, and promises in a few years to take the eminent rank among swine, that the noble Short Horns do among our cattle."[42]

The farmers of Champaign joined in the larger enthusiasm for Berkshire hogs. "It is rare that we find scrubby hogs in this county," boasted an 1878 county history that mentioned Berkshires as a leading breed.[43] Champaign County farmer Jesse Cloyd won premiums for his Berkshires at the state fair in the 1860s and 1870s.[44] A. M.

Fanley, also of Champaign County, recommended Chester Whites for families that wanted a single pig to eat the kitchen slop. But for those who wanted hogs to glean amid their cattle, he advised Berkshires, which, for all their refinement, were still sprightly enough to avoid being trampled underfoot.[45]

ANGLOPHILIA IN THE PORCELLIAN CLUB

It may seem that the popularity of the Berkshires was a straightforward business proposition, in which the Britishness of the animals was just an incidental attribute. Insofar as the Berkshire hog tells us anything about transatlantic connections, the important players would be the English emigrants who introduced the breed to the United States and the handful of breeders who crossed the Atlantic to purchase choice animals. Yet the Britishness of the animals did matter considerably to the farmers who invested in Berkshire hogs, judging from the amount of ink spilled over their origins.

The breeding industry was obsessed with lineage, and Berkshire backers were no exception. Some ostensible experts, including Benjamin F. Johnson of Champaign, described the Berkshire hog as a "native of the South Sea Islands," introduced into England "by Cook or his contemporary discoverers."[46] A piece in the *Prairie Farmer* traced the Berkshire's origins to a cross between Chinese and Portuguese swine and the "original hog of Berkshire."[47] Six months later, the *Prairie Farmer* published another piece tracing the line to a cross between a Siamese boar and "old unimproved Berkshire sows."[48] Professor W. J. Fraser of the Agricultural College in Champaign tried to settle the matter of Chinese or Siamese ancestry by claiming both.[49]

The confusion about the Berkshire hog's origins led farmers to dig deep into English agricultural writings, for their prize essays on the hog cite a variety of English agricultural guides. Berkshire devotees also tried to settle the matter by traveling to England, where they sought out "aged men in different parts of Berkshire" for information on the history of the breed.[50] Such travels help explain why an English farmer reported that he sometimes thought American farmers "were much better informed upon English subjects than the English farmer himself." (His audience greeted this statement with laughter and cries of "hear, hear.")[51] Although the ostensible purpose of such travels was to gather more evidence for the Chinese, Siamese, or South Pacific question, these travels yielded an emotional return. Expeditions to England fostered feelings of affiliation—and in some cases, firsthand connections—with English breeders, whose role in producing the Berkshire was beyond doubt.

These English breeders were not ordinary farmers. The membership lists of the British Berkshire Society include names like the Countess of Camperdown, Lord Arthur Cecil, and Lord Chesham. Merely basking in their aura conveyed cultural capital, for these were the kind of people that those at the pinnacle of the American meat complex aspired to become. Meat magnates revealed their aspirations in the 1913 American Meat Packers Association Dinner. After donning red coats with brass buttons, the assembled men followed the Master of the Hounds and his pack of dogs down to the Elizabethan Room, where long tables were "set in the style of an English country house hunt breakfast." Waiters in knee breeches with "typical English mutton-chop whiskers" served an eight-course meal, starting with "English Savoury Fantasie" and proceeding on through filet of English sole, Yorkshire pudding, and cheddar cheese to glasses of Scotch whisky.

Though far from the red-coated pinnacles of the packing elite,

The "English Hunt Dinner" given by the American Meat Packers'
Association in Chicago in 1913. Telling though this photograph is,
it fails to capture the baying of the pack of foxhounds at one end of the
room and the horns that sounded the hunter's call "ever and anon."

"The English Hunt Dinner," The National Provisioner 49 *(Sept. 27, 1913), 109.*

pig breeders and their customers also strove to associate themselves with the British landed gentry, through their acquisition of
high-class pigs.[52]

These pigs did more than mark the distance traveled from the
hardscrabble times of savage woods hogs to the prosperous times of
well-fenced fields. More than mere symbols of gentility, they were a
means to increasing affluence. Whereas the earliest settlers had lived
the threadbare existence of a largely subsistence economy—wearing
straw hats and buckskin overclothes, living in notched log cabins
caulked with mud, devoid of window glass—their descendants
stitched their farms more thoroughly into wider markets. By the
1850s, residents of Champaign County could purchase Castile soap,
gum arabic, oil of cloves, oil of cinnamon, opium, Peruvian bark,

Columbo root, fine silks, satin vestings, and Cuban hats on their trips to town.[53] Young ladies of good fortune could study English history, geometry, Latin, Greek, piano, embroidery, the making of crepe flowers, and the molding of wax fruit (among other subjects) at Mrs. Fletcher's Female Institution.[54] As time marched on, the upper-crust residents of the county continued to bridge the gulf between themselves and the Berkshire breeders of England, thanks in part to the profitability of their hogs.

As the role played by the Berkshire in regional economic development suggests, enthusiasts who crossed the ocean were driven by more aspirations than just rubbing shoulders with country gentlemen. They also traveled to England to research porcine genealogies because of the financial stakes. Farmers stood to make—or lose—considerable money by favoring a particular breed. If the breed seemed to be on the rise, animals sold at a premium. If it seemed overrated, the value of the animals fell. Berkshire breeders' investments in animal stock brought them together across national lines due to their common economic interests. Thus when the American Berkshire Association met in Springfield, Illinois, in 1885, delegates from Londonderry, Ireland, and Abingdon, England, joined presidents from seven U.S. state associations to formulate Berkshire policy.[55]

The widening networks of interpersonal connections extended beyond research expeditions and livestock breeding associations to the fair circuit. Whereas farmers without pedigreed pigs found few venues for display, those with certified lines could compete in county, state, and world's fairs, such as the 1893 Columbian Exposition in Chicago, touted as having an unsurpassed display of Berkshires.[56] Breeders met in such places as potential dealmakers as well as competitors. As they inspected the animals on display, they cultivated relationships that crossed national boundaries. But that was not all: they also fostered allegiances to a British-led branch of scientific agriculture and to British-led standards of taste.

The Stock Pavilion at the 1893 Chicago Columbian Exposition, located next to an extensive array of livestock sheds and barns. Livestock breeders from both sides of the Atlantic met in this and similar venues.

Das Columbische Weltausstellungs-Album *(Chicago: Rand, McNally and Co., 1893), np.*

ANGLO-SAXONIST PIGS

In buying Berkshire pigs, U.S. farmers invested in far more than improved meat production; they also invested in a set of aesthetic and cultural values. Prize Berkshires derived their value not only from quantifiable attributes such as fattening ability and fertility, but also from looking well bred. The value placed on aesthetics can be seen in claims that the Berkshire's eyes should be "bright and expressive," their tails "slender and well set, with a handsome curl near the rump," their bones "fine and of an ivory-like grain and hardness."[57] Although fat jowls were fleshier, Berkshire breeders preferred lean ones that "gave their stock a finer and higher bred look in the head."[58] Windsor Castle, a prize pig rhapsodized by the 1894 *Year Book of the American Berkshire Association*, exemplifies the value stemming from the right demeanor. It wasn't anything so prosaic as his hams that caught the viewer's fancy, it was that he "was the only one of this sort of stock he had ever looked upon which had any *poetry* in him."[59]

With their handsome curls, ivory bones, aristocratic names, and poetic graces, Berkshire pigs were upper-crust pigs—so much so that some hog experts began to lament the passing of the hardier "pioneer hog." One critic of pedigreed pigs denounced them for being "so fat that locomotion is uncomfortable," so greedy and indolent as to be "weak, feverish and subject to cholera."[60] By the early twentieth century, the Berkshire had come under fire as the "gentleman's hog," "too fine" to fatten well. Defenders conceded "excessive refinement" in some Berkshire hogs but praised the Berkshire as "the handsomest type of swine ever developed," a pig for idealists, due to its "charm of aspect" and "beauty of form."[61]

Despite insinuations of upper-crust effeminacy, Berkshire mania persisted, and indeed, the breed's cultural associations continued to enhance its value. In this respect, the Britishness of the Berkshire did more than convey its elite status, it also helped paper over its least attractive characteristic: its dark coloring. Refusing to accept an all-black or mostly black pig as an adequate standard, a Berkshire prize essay proclaimed that the pigs should have "white feet, face, tip of tail, and an occasional splash of white on the arm."[62] (Yes, the *arm*—this slip helps explain why attributes such as color mattered so much.) Other breeders worked to whiten the animal as a whole. According to the *American Swine and Poultry Journal*, "Some of our best breeders are now getting their best pigs with a nearly clear or white skin and black hair, which makes them very attractive, much more so than a dull black skin."[63] Since skin coloring had no intrinsic economic value in a dressed animal, Berkshire breeders' efforts to whiten their animals can be attributed to their investments in white supremacy.

Although Berkshires remained stubbornly dark, their proper British breeding could be detected in their forms as well as in their well-documented ancestral trees. Writings on "the best breeds of swine" insisted that "ugly" heads indicated "impure breeding." Low breeds were "too flat on the forehead." Such statements came straight out of the phrenology books that deduced temperament and other attributes from the shape of the human head. The profiles of northern European men that illustrated these texts typically featured the attribute so valued in Berkshires: a bulging forehead, indicating "reason" and "perceptive intellect." Significantly, phrenological depictions of mental defectives, criminals, and savages featured the kinds of backward-sloping foreheads associated with lesser pigs.[64] The idea that flattened noses also indicated a lower state of human evolution helps explain the praise for snouts that curved upward.[65] And racially inflected ideas about human hair added extra layers of meaning to denunciations of coarse bristles and the corresponding praise for "hair fine, soft and silky."[66]

Assumptions about proper male and female attributes factored just as importantly in pig appraisements as those related to beliefs about human racial differences. Pig breeders cast their lot with male supremacy. This stemmed in part from the fact that a stud boar could produce more offspring than a sow. But the men who dominated the breeding industry also believed that boars exercised "prepotency," meaning that their attributes carried more weight than those of their mates. Thoroughbred Berkshire boars supposedly transmitted the breed's qualities to their progeny, even when crossed with different types.[67] That made their selection all the more important. Much as refinement was to be valued among Berkshires, the boars ought to have a "strong masculine expression . . . even at the expense of a little coarseness."[68]

To the extent that sows mattered, it was not for their inferior ability to determine type, but because they could pass on the attributes of prize boars through reaching fecundity early, producing large litters, suckling well, and mothering with care and affection.[69] As the attention to masculine expression, feminine nurturance, racialized appearance, and upper-crust airs suggests, to buy Berkshires was to buy into a set of values that went deeper than mere meat-making and relationships that went beyond money.

Above all, to buy into Berkshires was to buy into empire. Not only had some of their genetic material arrived on the ships of empire from the far pigpens of the East, but having been perfected on English farms, the improved breed had been sent forth to conquer the world as a junior partner to the English emigrant. "They have," as one enthusiast put it, "followed in the wake of Anglo Saxon colonization the world over."[70]

Never mind that the pioneers' pigs had been semiferal animals, not pedigreed pen dwellers, Berkshire enthusiasts cast the Berkshire as a particularly effective tool of American empire, as a "faithful companion to man in the subjugation of the great west."[71] In such anachronistic renderings, the Berkshire pig had helped white settlers colonize the continent. More than the savage woods hogs that had scrounged around the earliest white settlements, the Berkshire represented civilized advancement.

The Berkshire appeared to be a particularly apt agent of empire because of its supposedly superlative ability to thrive in any clime and to fatten on any food. The eastern farmer could feed them the "skim milk of the dairy, the whey from the factory and products of farm and kitchen that would otherwise go to waste"; the western farmer would appreciate their ability to turn grain into meat. In contrast to other breeds with only regional or national potential, the Berkshire met "the requirements of all."[72] Their hardiness was another mark in their favor, for their great muscular power and vitality supposedly rendered them "less liable to accident and disease" than other pigs.[73] Like the British sailors and soldiers deployed across the globe, they had spread across the map, so far so that the 1896 *Berkshire Year Book* described their distribution as "world wide."[74] In contrast to more local breeds with only regional or national potential, the Berkshire was a more universal animal, capable of global domination.

POSTCOLONIAL PIGGERIES

It was not only its capacity for universality that made the Berkshire an exemplary imperial animal but also its capacity for uplifting more benighted pigs. Writing in the *Berkshire Year Book*, Professor Thomas Shaw of the University of Minnesota claimed that the main mission of the Berkshire was not "the production of a fine quality of meat at a minimum of cost," but the mission of racial uplift, "the engrafting of its own splendid qualities upon the common races of swine in Anglo Saxon speaking countries." These countries included the United States. According to Shaw, the Berkshire had "overspread the whole country," filling the land with its descendants, whether purebred or mixed.

The image of Anglo-Saxonist pigs marching out from Britain to overspread the United States seems at odds with Williams's account of U.S. farms as the wellsprings of American empire, for it conjures images of the United States as more colonized than colonizing. Yet Shaw did not see the Berkshire's ascendance as a mark of ongoing dependence. The breed might be imperial, but it was also "cosmopolitan to a greater extent than any other breed of swine." Having "gained free access to many a sty in Continental Europe, in Asia, in Australia, in New Zealand and in South America," Berkshires had established themselves as world-class animals. Their presence in the barnyard signified inclusion among the advanced nations and white outposts of the world.[75] British breeders drove that point home in their claims that the estimation for Berkshires across the "civilized World" provided "evidence sufficient as to their value."[76] To invest in the breed may have meant investing in British superiority, but that investment also brought membership in the larger club of civilization.

To invest in Berkshires meant to invest in the racial purity so valued by British and other European breeders. The *Breeder's Gazette* cast the matter as a "Battle for Live Stock Improvement." It called hog farmers to arms by characterizing the United States as a nation at war against its own mongrelism. To rally these troops to victory over mixed-blooded "scrubs," it urged the enlistment of purebred Berkshire sires from "the Mother Country"—assumed to be Britain, not any of the other places that had helped populate the United States.

Though victory was in sight, it was not in hand. As the *Breeder's Gazette* put it: "Understand that it takes time to stamp out the virile taint of mongrel blood; its perpetuating prepotency gives it stubborn antagonism to gentler blood which would neutralize it."[77] Such claims might suggest that the Berkshire's mix of English and Asian ancestors had contributed to its preeminent prepotency, enabling it to bring both virility and gentility to the race wars of the porcine world. Yet the *Breeder's Gazette* quashed any celebration of race mixing by depicting the Berkshire as thoroughly British. Having faced the same challenges as mongrel America, the Berkshire had emerged in triumph as a pure-blooded sire of the mother country.

All the attention to the Berkshire's Britishness suggests that farmers who invested in Berkshires invested in more than just pigs. Berkshire investments were postcolonial investments in British superiority. Yet even as the Berkshire perpetuated attachments to the British Empire, its eugenic capacities promised to someday raise the United States to the same lofty imperial position as Britain itself, if not a tad higher still. These expectations were not disappointed. By the early twentieth century, the agricultural experiment station in the newly acquired U.S. colony of Puerto Rico was breeding Berkshire pigs for distribution on the island. (Although the cost of corn was prohibitive, U.S. colonial officials reported that the pigs fattened well on kitchen waste, forage crops, and palm seeds, thereby seeming to lend credence to claims of universality.)[78] Government agents also purchased Berkshire boars to head their herd in the Panama Canal Zone.[79] And long after American hog breeders began to trumpet their own varieties as the best in the world, the Berkshire's genetic inheritance carried forward in these new, ostensibly American strains.[80]

It might seem that *The Roots of the Modern American Empire* misses these affiliative impulses because it focuses on the search for export markets. Yet Britain figured largely in market pursuits, too, and not just because it governed some of the Caribbean islands that had long imported American agricultural staples to feed their enslaved workers.[81] Although midwestern pork producers sought South American markets, they understood these much in the way that they saw markets in Caribbean sugar islands: as lower end, less profitable per pound of product. What they particularly wanted in the late nineteenth century was greater access to the more lucrative markets of Europe, those of Britain chief among them. The Berkshire struck them as a promising means to that end.

When it came to pigs, all the attention to racialized and gendered aesthetics played out in relation to another set of tastes: those produced by different types of meat. Prior to the infusion of pedigreed blood, U.S. pork had a reputation for being desirable only for its low price. British housekeeping magazines spread the conviction that American pork "emits a peculiar flavor."[82] Even less choosy buyers spoke ill of it. A Jamaican planter who considered U.S. pork suitable only for menial workers described the pigs from whence it came as "just one Mass of ill-digested Fat." He characterized their meat as disgusting, "more like the Flavour of Train Oil than of fine Irish Pork." When asked "Is there not very good Pork from America?" he replied: "I have never seen any of it."[83]

In addition to being fatty and foul flavored, American pork had the reputation of boiling down to very little meat. There was supposedly so little "proof" in American bacon that it came out of the pot much smaller than English pieces that had gone in at a comparable size.[84] British sailors joined the chorus of those who complained that American pork "will not stand the test of boiling," that it "has not the solidity which our meat has," being so fatty that it dwindled in the pot.[85] Although some British accounts described American pork as "of fine quality, fit for any table," these accounts argued against the general perception of American pork as cheap food for the poor.[86] Prior to the arrival of Berkshire studs, Illinois pork exports fed people who could not afford to be discriminating: plantation laborers, prisoners, and poorhouse inmates among them.

Critics attributed much of the fattiness, repulsive taste, and insubstantiality of American pork to the maize-based diet of American pigs. Although some English farmers slandered American hogs as fattening on rattlesnakes and manure, more reasoned commentators recognized that U.S. farmers fattened their pigs mainly on maize.[87] An article in the *Illinois Agriculturist* characterized the American hog as "a logical deduction from Indian corn—a sort of an automatic machine for reducing the bulk in corn and enhancing its value; a machine that feeds itself, converting ten bushels of corn into one hundred pounds of pork."[88] The president of the Illinois Swine Breeders' Association preferred the metaphor of a mint, saying of the hog: "The yellow corn of our common country is the bullion which he transmutes into golden coin."[89]

But not all hogs were equally adept in turning bullion into coin. The Berkshire won favor as a veritable "corn condensing and pork-making machine" that somehow managed to make palatable meat.[90] In contrast to "the heavy hog, loaded with the carbonaceous burden of the oleaginous corn," corn-fed Berkshires produced bacon that was "pinguid" but not "plethoric."[91] Berkshires were worth the investment because they produced hams that tasted like the ones that had been gaining favor in Europe—tender, juicy, and well

THE AMERICAN
SWINE & POULTRY JOURNAL.
DEVOTED TO THE BREEDING AND MANAGEMENT OF
Swine, Poultry, Pigeons and Pet Stock.

Volume 3.	CEDAR RAPIDS, IOWA.	August, 18 5.

HOOSIER LADY and two of her pigs. Property of I. N. BARKER, Thorntown, Ind.

A Berkshire piglet, waxing on corn, with its equally
chunky sibling and aristocratic mum.

"Hoosier Lady," The American Swine & Poultry Journal *3 (Aug. 1875), 25.*

marbled—regardless of their diet.[92] Their proponents might argue
that Berkshires would fatten on anything, but they took off in the
Midwest because they fattened well on corn, turning a grain developed over the millennia by indigenous North American people
(many of them the women tasked with corn cultivation) into a product that appealed to Europeans.[93]

As Berkshire production caught on in the United States, even
those who complained about the poor quality of U.S. pork conceded
that the Berkshires made a relatively leaner meat, preferable to that
of rival breeds.[94] The Berkshire's supposedly superior hams and bacons offered midwestern farmers the means to expand beyond the
low-end markets of the plantation South, whether in the United

States or the Caribbean. Especially after Britain reduced tariff barriers in the 1840s, Berkshire boosters used their investments in British breeding to produce pork products with the capacity to sell well in Britain.

TO MARKET, TO MARKET

The problem was how to get the pork to market. Before the coming of the railroad, it took from six weeks to three months to travel from Illinois to the East Coast.[95] Since hogs were not as easy to drive as cattle, the hog producers of central Illinois preferred to drive them to nearby packing plants. After slaughtering and packing the animals, the workers in these plants loaded the salted meat onto flatboats to be floated downstream to New Orleans.[96] Those who wanted to sell their bacon in the infant city of Chicago had to brave unpaved prairie roads by day and keep vigilant watch by their fires at night.[97]

Given these difficulties in getting their products to distant markets, downstate Illinois farmers clamored for a railroad line. Congress responded to their pleas in 1850 by giving Illinois the right-of-way through public lands stretching from Chicago to the southern tip of the state. The Illinois legislature chartered the Illinois Central Railroad Company the following year. By granting the corporation the 2.5 million acres of public land ceded by Congress, it made the Illinois Central the first land-grant railroad in the country. Though rich in land, the Illinois Central still lacked the cash necessary to lay tracks, build stations, and purchase engines and cars.[98] It needed money up front, not just mortgage payments down the road, in a time when the United States could be labeled a developing nation and investment capital was hard to come by.

Unable to raise enough money from New York investors, the ICR did what other transportation companies—whether turnpike, canal, or railroad—were doing: it sent agents to London.[99] The agents quickly raised a million pounds sterling through bond sales at 6 percent interest—a percentage less than they had offered in New York. By the following year, they had raised another $4 million in London from bonds at the more costly (for the ICR) New York rate. They also sold stock to British investors, who were allowed to purchase five shares for every $1,000 bond. Before going home, they placed orders with rail manufacturers, some of whom accepted bonds instead of cash for their rails.[100] Thanks to British capitalization and British-made rails, the Illinois Central began construction in 1852. It reached Champaign County in 1854 and continued south from there.[101]

Unfortunately for the British investors, a corruption scandal engulfing the ICR president (who had fraudulently issued $1 million of stock for another railroad that he directed) and the financial panic of 1857 (which prevented the farmers who had purchased land from the company from paying their mortgages) frustrated hopes of easy riches. The company coped with these setbacks by exercising its right to demand additional payouts from its shareholders—meaning that London investors had to pony up an additional $35 per share (totaling about $5 million in the higher-value currency of the time).[102] Closer to home, the ICR gave extensions on the notes that were due to it from settlers. It also accepted payment in kind, which generally meant corn. So many farmers took them up on this offer that the ICR had to construct cribs to hold the two million bushels of payments. That policy enhanced the ICR's popularity in the state, but it won them few friends in England, especially after the stocks fell in value to below par.[103]

Unhappy with their losses, the British stock and bondholders selected two delegates to investigate the company's management. After meeting with ICR officers and going through the company's books, the investigators won some oversight.[104] But their most important discovery did not come in the boardroom, it came on the train itself, as the agents inspected the initial stretch of rails.[105] Looking out at the prairie, one of them had an epiphany: "This is not a railroad company; it is a land company."[106] Upon realizing that the path to profitability lay in land sales, British investors turned into real estate agents.

They were helped in this endeavor by James Caird, a member of Parliament with agricultural expertise who sang the praises of the ICR lands following a trip to the United States and Canada in 1858. In *Prairie Farming in America*, Caird marveled at the amount of land granted to the ICR: "nearly equal to the fourteenth part of all England." It had sold half of that already and could sell the remainder at much higher prices, but since its goal was to create traffic for the railroad, it was offering bargain rates. And what land it was! The rich prairie soils "excel our best lands," wrote Caird. Although only a tenth of Illinois was cultivated, the state already produced more grain than both Ireland and Scotland and twice as many pigs.[107] Caird promised sure riches to large-scale investors, writing that lots placed under "prudent skillful management . . . could not fail to return a handsome annual dividend; and, in the course of a few years, by the mere lapse of time and the progress of wealth and population, to double in value."[108]

William Scully took the bait. The younger son of an Irish landed family, Scully purchased tenant farms in Illinois, Nebraska, Kansas, and Missouri in the 1850s. At the height of his career as an American landowner, he held almost 220,000 acres, worked by over twelve hundred tenant families. Scully managed his holdings from London, with visits to Illinois about every other year after 1855. Though reviled in Ireland in the 1860s for "all that was evil in landlord-tenant relations," he escaped protest in the United States prior to the 1880s.[109] When a movement arose against alien land ownership in the 1890s, Scully obtained U.S. citizenship. This financial move notwithstanding, he and his heirs continued to live mainly in London.[110]

Besides pitching Illinois to potential landlords, Caird strove to entice emigration. To "young farmers of activity and intelligence . . . with some capital at their command" and to "intelligent, hard-working farm laborers," Caird forecast a prosperous future on the prairie.[111] Sharing his goal of settlement and sales, the Illinois Central distributed tens of thousands of copies of Caird's puff piece in Great Britain and Canada.[112]

Caird talked up the promise of emigration as if he had discovered Illinois himself, but there were already plenty of emigrants from the British Empire in the lands traversed by the ICR. Irish laborers had laid much of the track that Caird traveled. The ICR trolled for workers in the port cities where Irish immigrants landed, and at least one of its contractors recruited workers in Ireland.[113] Although Irish track layers were not as likely to turn farmer when the line was completed as their German coworkers, some did take up the plow. Even after the completion of the railroad, Irish emigrants continued to flow into central Illinois, driven by a desire to escape famine-inducing British imperial policies as much as by a desire to make their fortune in a new land. Among these post-railroad-boom emigrants was Champaign County resident Bernard Hannan, born near Dublin in 1845 and later known for his Berkshire hogs.[114]

RECIPROCAL REPLENISHMENT

Following along on the rails laid by Irish workers came settlers from other points in northern Europe, so many so that shortly after the line went through, the *Urbana Union* noted that "our town does not appear as of yore; its once vacant streets are being thronged with strangers, who have come among us to seek an abiding place."[115] The 1850 census identified 19 percent of the immigrants to Champaign as English (with no Scots or Welsh reported) and 34 percent as Irish.

The 1870 census identified about 22 percent of foreign-born immigrants to Champaign County as English, Scottish, and Welsh and 36 percent as Irish. (In 1850, the immigrant population was less than 2 percent of the county total; by 1870 immigrants constituted nearly 10 percent of the county's inhabitants.)[116] If Irish emigrants came in part to escape English power, those from England, Scotland, and Wales had reason to see their emigration as a means to advance it.

In the 1880s, proponents of Greater Britain worried that the outflow of emigrants to the United States drained the lifeblood of the British Empire. With such concerns in mind, they tried to redirect emigration to imperial outposts. But in the 1850s, the United States struck British emigration advocates as a kind of imperial outpost, never mind the nation's political independence.[117] This view of the quasi-colonial status of the United States can be seen in emigration tracts that emphasized the benefits that would accrue to England. An 1859 guide to Illinois Central lands told would-be settlers from England that they could "profitably contribute to supply the wants of the old country, whose land can no longer meet the demands of her dense population." After pointing out that England "consumed each day the produce of ten thousand acres of foreign land," it called upon Englishmen "to take their share in its supply."[118] Emigration, in other words, would not necessarily mean a break from England; it could be a way to nourish it.

The disastrous harvest of 1845 added to the persuasiveness of such arguments. In the aftermath of that harvest, Britain repealed the agricultural tariffs known as Corn Laws, with *corn* in this context meaning the common grain of the country.[119] Over the next three years, the importation of cured beef, bacon, and pork increased sixfold.[120] Further tariff reductions came in 1853 before being eliminated altogether in 1860.[121] In addition to reducing hunger among the working classes, these imports enabled Britain's poor to eat more meat. As meat consumption rose, so did expectations that even the poor should eat meat on a regular basis. To maintain this standard of living, Britain needed to import more food.

It was not only the poor who needed American imports to thrive—the entire nation needed them in times of war. With the closure of the Baltic and Black Seas to British shipping during the Crimean War (1853–1856), Britain turned to Canada and the United States to make up the resulting grain deficits.[122] Illinois farmers increased their wheat production to meet the heightened British demand. The wheat crop of 1855 was triple that of 1850; by 1856, the value of Illinois wheat outstripped that of Illinois corn. Emigration tracts did not mention that as the end of the conflict brought the midwestern wheat boom to a close it also ushered in the financial panic of 1857.[123] Instead, they reminded British readers that American agricultural production contributed to British security.

British emigrants may have had their own nationalistic reasons for seeking British export markets, but Illinois farmers did not need to hail from England, Scotland, or Wales to share aspirations of feeding the British people. From its formation, the Illinois Central insisted that it would be the vehicle for crowding the quays of Liverpool with Illinois beef, pork, and lard.[124] This promise implied two major changes: lower transportation costs and more northerly trade. The railroad delivered on both. When farmers complained about the rates in 1856, the ICR catered favor by reducing them, from $33 to $15 per carload for cattle, and down to $12 per carload for hogs.[125]

Along with reducing the expense of getting pigs to market, the ICR changed the location of the market. Before the 1850s, the reliance on downstream river transportation directed midwestern pork toward the lower-end markets of the South or necessitated its reshipment through eastern ports. The railroad, in conjunction with the halt to southern shipping during the Civil War, redirected these older patterns of trade northward to Chicago.[126]

As rail connections expanded its hinterland, Chicago became the

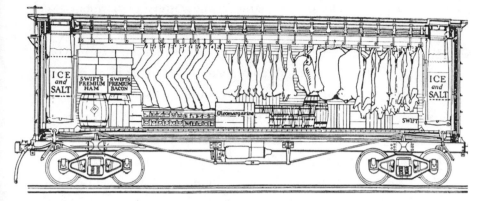

SECTION OF AN AMERICAN REFRIGERATOR CAR, SHOWING THE METHOD OF
LOADING

Thanks to British capital investments in U.S. railroads and the invention of
refrigerated cars, Corn Belt livestock fatteners could export fresh meat to
the high-end British market. This rendition of a loaded American
refrigerator car comes from a volume on Britain's meat supply.

George E. Putnam, Supplying Britain's Meat *(London: George C. Harrap and Co., 1923), plate after 92.*

nation's leading meat-processing center. By 1890, Chicago packers
prepared over a third of all meat produced in the United States.
They slaughtered over 8.5 million hogs in 1891, as many as 74,551 in
one day.[127]

In addition to shifting the meat trade to the north, the railroad
infrastructure financed by British capital and built of British iron facilitated transatlantic trade. Whereas recent U.S. pork exports have
gone mainly to Latin America and East Asia (with the U.S. with-
drawal from the Trans-Pacific Partnership, efforts to renegotiate
NAFTA, and the onset of a trade war with China causing concern
for present-day pork exporters), earlier exports flowed mostly across
the Atlantic.[128] Buyers from England, Scotland, Germany, France,
Belgium, and "nearly every other important country on the globe"
coursed through the Chicago stockyards.[129] Upon placing their orders,
they could rely on Chicago's transportation links to carry the goods
to docks of the Northeast, where Europe-bound ships lay in wait.

In their quest for export markets, midwestern pig farmers owed debts not only to British railroad investors and manufacturers, but also to the British merchant marine. In 1870, U.S. vessels carried only about a third of the country's commerce by sea. That proportion fell in the ensuing years. In 1880, the commercial journal *Bradstreet's* counted 160 to 175 cargo vessels departing weekly from northern ports, most of them British, followed by German, Belgian, Dutch, Danish, French, and Spanish vessels. "It is a foreign fleet," noted *Bradstreet's*, "that carries the whole, almost, of the flood of western produce, grain and provision which is now the daily necessity of Europe."[130] By the mid-1890s, U.S. vessels carried only 8 percent of U.S. seaborne trade. The ships that ferried U.S. pork products to foreign shores flew, more often than not, British flags.[131]

SALT PORK FOR DINNER

In the aftermath of the Civil War, the United States became a pork-exporting powerhouse—a status it has retained to this day, with annual exports of several million metric tons bringing in billions of dollars to farmers. In 1896, the president of the Illinois Swine Breeders' Association estimated that the United States exported over 6.4 million hogs, basing this amount on the assumption that 175 pounds of pork products equaled a hog.[132] The *Illinois Agriculturist* marveled at the magnitude of this trade, finding that "if we count all of the exported horses and mules, all of the cattle and fresh and salted beef products, all of the sheep and mutton and all the butter and dairy products sent to alleviate the hunger and wants of the people in foreign lands, they foot up to a total less than we realize from our surplus hogs, and their products which we send abroad."[133]

Where did all that pork end up? The president of the Illinois Swine Breeders' Association boasted that the United States sold its hog products in "nearly every country in the world."[134] Although American pork did circulate widely, such sweeping assertions hide geographical patterns. The first lay to the south. Midwestern farmers had a long history of exporting pork to the West Indian sugar colonies, especially Cuba.[135] Their product also traveled to a range of other imperial outposts. But in the late nineteenth century, American pork bound for export mostly traveled east, to Europe.

Whereas the United States had about eighty hogs for every hundred people, Europe had only fifteen, a discrepancy full of possibilities for U.S. pork producers.[136] Prior to 1879, about 9 percent of U.S. pork exports went to Belgium and the Netherlands (which reexported most of this to other destinations on the continent). Another 8 percent went to France and 10 percent to Germany. Sales to Germany collapsed, however, in 1879, when Germany banned the import of U.S. pork, ostensibly due to the discovery of the deadly parasitic worms known as trichinae.[137]

Midwestern pork exporters were quick to point out that no German trichinosis deaths had been traceable to American pork. They also downplayed the threat, noting that the worms could be killed by thorough cooking. If only German housewives would be a little more careful, nobody would sicken. With the insinuation of bad housekeeping to back them up, they claimed that it wasn't so much health considerations that underlay the restrictions, but the trade imbalances favoring the United States.[138] Not wanting to anger working-class consumers by passing more protectionist tariffs, the German government had seized on trichinosis as the excuse to exclude American meat.[139] If heated complaints could cook meat, the Germans would have had no need to worry. But they maintained the restrictions.

The combination of health fears and economic anxieties that had led to German prohibitions soon led to restrictions in Italy, Portugal, Greece, Spain, France, Austria-Hungary, Romania, and Turkey. Denmark eventually excluded American pork as well, lest it lose the German export market for its own pork products. (This followed the discovery that some of the "Danish" product had actually originated in the United States.) Exclusionary measures lasted until the U.S. government began inspecting slaughterhouses and forcefully retaliating against nations that continued to discriminate against American pork.[140]

Despite claims of English farmers that American pork was "to a large extent, infested with noxious insects capable of destroying human life," Britain did not join the list of nations that banned it during the trichinosis scare. Britain's larger commitment to free trade militated against restrictions. Health inspectors admitted that restrictions would have been ineffectual because "a large proportion of the objectionable meat would have been sent to this country by a circuitous route."[141] The decision not to restrict U.S. pork was a major boon for midwestern hog farmers, because Britain absorbed close to 60 percent of American pork exports even before the trichinosis restrictions on the continent increased its share.[142] Britain's unparalleled appetite for U.S. pork continued through the 1890s, by which time Britain was absorbing three-fourths of the U.S. ham and bacon exports.[143] These exports were considerable: in 1895, for example, the United States sent to Britain roughly 346 million pounds of bacon, 90 million pounds of hams, and 15 million pounds of pork.[144]

One of the companies most bent on suiting the British taste was the Anglo-American packing company of Chicago, the third-largest pork packer in the United States. With a killing capacity of eight thousand hogs a day, it slaughtered over a million hogs a year. This gave it the "proud distinction of being the largest exporters of American hog products to England." Owned by the Fowler Brothers of Liverpool, the company had the advantage of agents in all parts of England.[145] The British grocery magnate (and later tea baron) Thomas Lipton, who had started in the business by selling American hams and bacons in Glasgow, also invested in U.S. pork processing, by purchasing an

Omaha packing plant in 1887 and the Myer Packing House in Chicago shortly thereafter. The Myer plant disassembled over two thousand hogs a day, shipping some to Lipton's chain of British stores.[146] Other U.S. pork packers developed relations with British commission agents such as William Simpson, Ltd., of Liverpool. Simpson sold U.S. hog products throughout the United Kingdom, promising to "handle these goods to the fullest advantage and benefit of consignors."[147]

The major selling point was price. Despite Berkshire breeders' insistence that Berkshire ancestry produced a product indistinguishable from the British product, even if fed on corn, the struggle to fully crack the upscale British market persisted. Meat products known to be American continued to sell at lower prices than those known to be British. The preference for the home product was so pronounced that butchers reportedly cut American hams in half, marking one part as "home cured" for 10 d (the denotation for ten pennies in the money system of the time) and the other as "American" at half the price. Even more tellingly, they claimed that "the 'home cured' is speedily bought up, while the same article with a different name, and at half the price, is left untouched."[148] In various hearings over legislation requiring foreign meats to be marked as such, witnesses testified that consumers preferred British meat.

Some of this preference can be attributed to concerns about food safety, extending beyond trichinosis to a disease known as hog cholera.[149] Occasional reports that people who had eaten American pork had fallen violently ill—like the ham eaters seized with colic, diarrhea, and vomiting so severely that eventually "four or five" of them died—did little to foster consumer confidence.[150]

Consumers were so suspicious of imported animal flesh that in the 1840s a British patent medicine company concocted a remedy for the side effects deemed likely to follow from the "American pork and other kinds of Foreign Food being now freely imported into this country." Its ads counseled those whose stomachs had suffered "serious derangement" to turn immediately to STIRLING'S STOMACH PILLS. These could be safely administered to "sufferers of all ages, whose lives might, without their immediate aid, be lost, or placed in imminent danger, before medical assistance could be procured." Doubters could see evidence of their efficacy in the "good effects . . . daily experienced by thousands who have been tormented with windy spasms, head-ache, indigestion, giddiness, nervous debility, and other complaints arising from a disordered state of the digestive organs."[151]

The lingering nature of this disrepute fortified efforts to pass U.S. pork off as Canadian. This enterprise can be tracked back to the era of British protective tariffs, when colonial hams entered at a lower rate than ones considered "foreign." It did not take U.S. farmers long to figure out that by exporting their "productions" to the Dominion of Canada "at a small rate of duty, in a raw or unmanufactured state," they could gain favorable access to the British market. Even hams that had been pickled in the United States could be considered colonial produce, so long as they were then smoked in Canada.[152] Tariff reductions pulled the rug out from under Canadian processors, but they did not eliminate the Canadian export route altogether. In the 1860s a reciprocity treaty between the United States and Canada enabled packers in Toronto and Hamilton to import hogs duty-free from Chicago. The Canadian packers then sold the meat to Britain as Canadian, thereby reaching consumers who favored products from the empire and those who thought that pea-, barley-, and rye-fed Canadian pork tasted better than the corn-fed U.S. product.[153]

METAMORPHOSING MEAT

Besides justifying the extra expense of transshipment through Canada, British consumer preferences can explain the curious dynamics of the English-Irish pork swap. Starting in the 1860s, Liverpool merchants shipped U.S. bacon from that city on to Ireland. This freed up Irish bacon for the English market. Though roughly the same amount of meat traveled each direction, the scales of value favored the Irish product.[154] This early foray into meat exchange grew over time into an Irish industry devoted to laundering American pork.

Limerick dealers in particular developed a reputation for reselling American pork as Irish bacon and hams. By putting American hams on the market as the Irish product, they could charge as much as 24 cents per pound, at a time when American hams were selling for less than 18 cents per pound.[155] As the London *Echo* reported: "It is esti-mated that 3,000,000 American pigs will be manufactured this year into many more millions of American hams for sale in England; but these hams are seldom sold by retailers for what they are. They are carefully selected and 'dried' in England or Ireland, returning from the latter country in the form of the well-known Belfast hams . . . The American 'long rib' is transmuted into 'Irish rolled' bacon . . . Wholesale dealers sell what is known as clear middles at 3d. a pound, and find it marked on the counter of a retailer who keeps 'no Yankee rubbish' at 8d. per pound."[156]

As the reference to duplicitous retailers suggests, Irish dealers were not alone in naturalizing American pork. In 1880, *The Illustrated House-hold Journal and Englishwoman's Domestic Magazine* claimed that Amer-ican pork products were "sold under many *aliases* . . . in Bond-street and other fashionable London shops, where their Chicago origin is not conspicuously set forth."[157] An 1893 parliamentary investigation sub-stantiated these accusations. It turned up ample evidence that British dealers falsely marketed American bacon, lard, and hams as domestic. Witnesses produced wholesale price lists that "gave evidence of a sys-tematic and quite open practice of consigning to retailers articles of food received from shippers in the United States and Canada, desig-nated as 'prime Wilts,' 'best Irish,' 'best Waterford,' &c."[158]

More evidence of this nature emerged in an 1897 suit, brought by

British breeds of animals packed according to British methods
could be passed off by British provisioners as the pricier domestic product.

W. H. Simmonds, The Practical Grocer: A Manual and Guide for the Grocer the Provision Merchant and
Allied Trades, *vol. 3 (London: The Gresham Publishing Company, 1906), 246. The New York Public Library.*

the Bacon Curers' Association of Great Britain against the Junior
Army and Navy Stores of London. The Stores manager (who had
since procured other employment) testified that the company was in
the practice of rubbing American hams with oil or holding them over
a gas jet and rubbing them with pea meal to sell them as Wiltshires.
"Was that often done?" asked the prosecution. The witness: "Yes,
practically whenever we required a Wiltshire ham." The ex-manager
went on to report that if the customer wanted a York ham, they
brought up a genuine York ham, but if the customer asked for a
smoked York ham, they forwarded an American one instead, though
billing for the more expensive British product.[159] The Stores company used similar stratagems to turn midwestern animals into Irish,

Yorkshire, Scotch, and Cumberland hams. The Bacon Curers' Association won the case.[160]

It took more than a little ingenuity and a flexible sense of ethics to pass American pork off as the British product—it also took a chunk of meat packed according to British practices. Irish and other tricksters could sell U.S. pork as the British product because U.S. meat-packers—many of them Irish in origin—separated joints and preserved the flesh in English and Irish styles.[161] Making the most of their familiarity with British markets and methods, they cured cuts named after northern cities (Cumberland, Yorkshire, Stafford, and Wiltshire) known for fattier bacons and hams.[162] The Chicago Board of Trade aided this business by providing guidelines for cuts such as "Birmingham Sides."[163]

After cutting hogs up with British markets in mind, Chicago preserved the meat with British methods. These included smoking and pickling in a brine composed of salt, saltpeter, and sugar or molasses. Meat-packers seasoned some of their products with red Zanzibar pepper, allspice, cloves, mace, nutmegs, and Jamaican and African ginger—all of which suggest some reliance on the imperial trade networks in which Britain figured largely.[164] (The Chicago-based manufacturer of a powder used in meat products thought British imperial connections so desirable that it faked them, naming its product "Zanzibar carbon" and advertising it with images of scantily clothed hut dwellers in that British colony.)[165] Chicago packers also produced singed bacon, in imitation of a British cure.[166] Even the low-cost salting method referenced Britain, because packers preferred Liverpool salt—much of it actually mined in Upstate New York, but named after the world-renowned British product. The practice of rubbing pork with salt and then stacking the pieces in a salt-filled box, where they would continue to cure while in transit, gained ascendance over wet-barreled pork by the end of the nineteenth century.[167]

Despite its growing popularity, this method had some problems.

The longer that bacon packed in layers of salt stayed in its box, the more salt it absorbed, which meant that the longer the voyage, the saltier the meat. English critics had this method in mind when they denounced American pork as "intolerably salt."[168] To reduce the salinity, some retailers soaked the meat in large butts of water for four or five days, after which they beat it into shape and hung it up to dry.[169] The most successful of these grocers then smoked the bacon and sold it at a handsome profit as "Prime Wiltshire" or "First-class Yorkshire." But other grocers complained that no matter how long they steeped it, they could not adequately desalt it.[170]

To reduce the saltiness, U.S. packers started using borax (a compound now widely used in detergents) as a preservative and color enhancer for bacon and ham. They dusted it on the meat in order to prevent it from becoming flyblown (a euphemistic reference to fly eggs and maggots). The borax treatment also helped absorb moisture, thereby making the meat less slimy. And finally, it reduced the amount of salt needed as a preservative. British bacon curers had pricier methods for the long-distance trade, involving extra drying and canvas cases to buffer their hams from the surrounding salt. Suffering from the American competition, they sent borax-cured bacon out for analysis. Their chemists found that, contrary to claims that the borax could be pared off the surface, it penetrated the meat. Although American pork products had been gaining a better reputation in some quarters (perhaps aided by the realization that consumers had been buying them inadvertently all along), the resulting scandal stoked the lingering conviction that U.S. pork was inferior to the domestic product.[171]

BRITISH ORDERS

The repeated investigations into American meat reveal a certain vulnerability on the part of U.S. exporters, whose ability to sell pork to the British market depended not only on British breeds, rails, bottoms, packing methods, merchants, and tastes, but also British tariff policies and public health measures (or lack thereof), and the British inability to purchase comparable products for lower amounts from other suppliers. By the end of the nineteenth century, the consumption of American preserved meats fell off in Britain, as rising U.S. demand inflated prices and cheaper meats flowed in from places such as Australia and Argentina.[172]

The realization that Britain was turning to other suppliers for meat made U.S. hog raisers anxious. Illinois farmers fretted about competing in the Liverpool markets with the "millet-fed wheat farmers of India, the lately emancipated serfs of Russia, and all the other poorly fed and poorly clothed farmers of creation."[173] They expected that this competition would only get worse, given imperial railroad-building projects in Russia, Australia, India, "the Turkish dominions in Europe," and Egypt. Making matters worse, British capitalists had begun investing in Argentinian and Chilean lines too.[174] "Lower prices are coming," warned the *Prairie Farmer*.[175]

In presenting the vast supply chains of the British Empire as a dangerous threat to their own interests, midwestern pork producers overlooked the importance of the empire for their British trade. In the nineteenth century, Britain typically ran trade deficits with the United States. What enabled Britain to pay for all the pork was U.S. trade with India. In this circle, the United States purchased Indian products and India used that money to pay for British investments and the charges that Britain levied on India for the privilege of pertaining to the British Empire. Britain, in turn, relayed some of these monies to the United States, in its purchases of agricultural goods.[176] By casting India as a threat rather than an enabler, the U.S. agricultural press hid the extent to which hog farmers depended on Indian subordination for the bulk of their export trade.

Although midwestern farmers did not acknowledge their dependency on Indian payments, they did worry about their dependency on British markets. The British press stoked such fears by claiming that if there were ever a war with the United States, Britain would procure its meat from its colonies. Once they had lost their major export market, U.S. farmers would not be able to regain it. When the United States and Britain clashed over a Venezuelan boundary dispute in 1895, the *Mark Lane Express and Agricultural Journal* issued a stern warning: "Should a great commercial country deliberately go out of its way to seek a quarrel with its best customer it must be prepared to take the consequences."[177]

The costs of this dependency could be seen in the cases of other agricultural nations that had supplied Great Britain with food. According to Illinois Department of Agriculture reports, Russia, "the granary of England," had received so little for its breadstuffs that it depended on British loans. The same held true for Ireland, plagued by "suffering, famines and horrors unknown to any other Christian people on the face of the earth." Egypt, India, Italy, and Spain had also poured forth their agricultural goods, receiving so little in return that they, too, depended on foreign capital. Grain-exporting India was so immiserated that it suffered from famine one out of every four years in the century before 1900. Midwesterners wary of such a fate saw their salvation in rail connections to the Gulf of Mexico, from whence they could end Britain's dominant role in setting the terms of trade.[178]

The Illinois Central, now largely under U.S. ownership, heeded these calls. It built docks, elevators, and warehouses at its southern terminus in New Orleans. By the 1890s, it had become a leading carrier of bananas and coconuts—more than three million bunches and fifteen million woody balls each year. It also invested in Cuban American Sugar Company stocks and bonds. With the construction of the Panama Canal, it found itself well positioned in the Pacific trade.[179]

Bananas waiting to be loaded onto an Illinois Central Railroad car in New Orleans. The British capital investments that had gotten the Illinois Central going later helped connect the Midwest to the Caribbean via rail.

Cargo of Bananas, item fbm000313, Frank B. Moore Collection, Louisiana and Special Collections, Earl K. Long Library, University of New Orleans.

Embracing U.S. expansion into the Caribbean at the turn of the twentieth century, the Illinois Central positioned itself as the main north–south conduit between the tropics and the vast interior of the United States as well as the main carrier for imports through the Panama Canal from the Pacific and East Asia.

Poole Brothers, Aero View of the Panama Canal, Looking Southwest, the World's Greatest Engineering Feat to be Realized 395 Years After First Proposed *(Chicago: Poole Bros, 1912), Library of Congress, Geography and Map Division.*

These new connections are the kinds of relationships that William Appleman Williams alluded to when he spoke of the modern American empire. Yet these investments did not *introduce* the Midwest to empire. To the contrary, they built on an older imperial infrastructure—the British-financed line from Chicago that had assiduously recruited settler colonists. Nor did these connections displace older imperial relations, for even as the Illinois Central became a leading banana distributor, it continued to carry pigs with Berkshire blood to Chicago, there to be slaughtered and packed, with Britain as the leading export destination.

Thanks to U.S. farmers, British consumers ate more pork products than they had previously. But they also ate different pork products, and the wide availability of lower-cost U.S. hams and bacons ended up driving down the prices of farm products in Britain. Falling commodity prices combined with the advent of more labor-saving devices to lower wages among agricultural workers. This in turn prompted young people from lowland Scotland and Northern England to leave the countryside for English cities and overseas destinations, foremost among them Canada, Australia, and New Zealand.[180] In this respect, midwestern farmers had unleashed some of their main rivals.

Yet they also fed those rivals, even as they ventured to the far limits of empire. Emigrants bound for the antipodes on British ships were entitled by law to a pound of pork every week. Given that in practice they often got more, a typical ship took on board ten tons of ham and bacon every year.[181] Salted pork products fed the merchant marine as well as passengers. In 1852, a man connected with the naval victualing department reported that London merchants "provision their ships entirely with American meat."[182] That tendency persisted over time. In a 1903 hearing, a ship's cook with fifty years' experience reported that all his beef had "the American stamp on it." When asked whether Lipton's sold American beef, the cook replied:

120

"Yes, American beef, American pork—he supplies vessels with anything—and if you went to Lipton's and asked for English cured beef or pork you could not get it."[183]

The same long shelf life that made preserved pork suitable for distance shipping also made it a significant food item for explorers. Polar and tropical expeditions alike relied heavily on American bacon and salt pork.[184] And so did the British military. Pork was such a staple in the military that one of the leading types of barrel-packed pork was known as "Mess" pork, in reference to the military market.[185] Another variety, known as India or navy pork, likewise suggested, by its name, military use.[186]

Although the British military preferred beef—to the extent that military personnel sometimes used the word *meat* to refer to beef alone—it also relied heavily on pork, spurred on in part by pork packers who insisted that "pork can be transported more readily and economically to troops in the field than can any other meat."[187] In the 1860s, troops in New Zealand ate salt pork from England and the United States as well as more proximately sourced pork. (The latter gave "occasional trouble to the Commissariat," having been fed mainly on fish. While in the cask it looked excellent and smelled inoffensive, but when cooked it emitted a powerful fishlike odor.)[188] The soldiers in the 1868 Abyssinian campaign ate "salt beef and pork, and preserved potatoes."[189] Even the Royal Engineers stationed in the country outside of London ate American bacon and ham as part of their rations.[190]

Despite accusations that Chicago packers had sold embalmed beef to U.S. troops serving in Cuba in 1898, the British government looked to American packinghouses to supply Her Majesty's troops in the Boer War.[191] During the Boxer Rebellion, Chicago packers shipped about ten carloads of barreled pork and various beef products to the Far East for the Allied troops. They shipped another seven carloads of canned goods (mostly corned beef) to England for army use.[192]

It was not just men on the march who got their protein from salt pork. In an article on the supremacy of the American hog, the Chicago meat-packing magnate J. Ogden Armour boasted that the American hog had "provisioned the navies of the world." Armour undoubtedly knew what he was talking about when he spoke of naval provisioning, but he would have characterized the situation more accurately if he had pointed out that U.S. pork toured the world on *British* naval vessels in particular.[193]

Sailors in the Royal Navy had to put up with what one article on "sea-fare" described as "an unvaried diet of salt beef and salt pork, accompanied by hard biscuit or dried peas."[194] Through the latter part of the nineteenth century, British naval vessels unable to obtain fresh meat typically issued salt pork every other day and salt beef on the alternate day.[195] Long after refrigerators had become common on passenger liners, the sailors on Her Majesty's ships continued to eat "salt junk" except for a day or two after calling at port.[196]

In the early 1840s, British naval contracts stipulated that the salt meat should be the cure of the United Kingdom. But following the repeal of the Corn Laws, its contractors sold the Admiralty U.S. pork, which they had repacked and branded as Irish. Upon discovering this deception, the Admiralty "immediately gave directions to their officers at the different depots, to be very particular in the examination of this meat." The resulting investigation confirmed that "a great quantity" of it was American.[197] This discovery struck *Blackwood's Edinburgh Magazine* as scandalous. "We believe that the British navy, which is victualed by contract, is at this moment supplied from foreign, and not British produce!"[198] Following further discoveries that "American cured salt meat" had been passed off as Irish, the navy authorized the purchase of some American pork for experiment. The meat experts at the Deptford depot found it to be of "a superior quality."[199] The Admiralty rewrote the contracts so that the salt meat need not be British cured.[200]

The legalization of American meat makes it harder to trace its consumption, since nobody needed to file reports. Yet passing references to American pork continued to surface in parliamentary papers. Navy doctors attributed the diarrhea that "prevailed almost epidemically" on a ship stationed in the tropical division of the Pacific station (along the west coast of the Americas) in 1869 to the "coarse character of some American pork which had been supplied to the ship."[201] The Admiralty reported in 1873 that its store receivers opened 10 percent of the casks of American salt pork, to examine them for weight, quality, and cure.[202] By the 1880s, however, the director of victualing for the Admiralty reported that although its beef came mostly from America, the navy had stopped purchasing American pork. "They found that it was not so good, so I was told."[203]

Despite this official shift away from the American product, it is still probable that some made its way into shipboard messes, due to inappropriate marking (as in passing off the U.S. product as Irish) and the reliance on contractors, who were frequently charged with dishonest reporting.[204] The need for resupply while en route makes the presence of American pork on British naval vessels seem all the more likely. At each port of call, ships took on more provisions, including live animals, "dead-meat," and tinned meats.[205] Naval officials admitted that they could not identify the origins of the meat loaded onto British vessels in colonial ports.[206] But if they had read U.S. export records, they might have ventured some guesses.

In 1870, the United States exported over 6.3 million pounds of pork to the British West Indies (Jamaica and Barbados), over 142,000 pounds to British possessions in Africa, and over 59,000 pounds to China (including Hong Kong) and Singapore.[207] In the year ending June 30, 1883, it exported over 244,000 pounds of bacon to the British West Indies and lesser amounts to British Guiana, British Honduras, Hong Kong, and "British Possessions in Africa and adjacent islands."[208] In 1897, the Cape Colony imported over two million pounds of preserved meats from the United States and another 220,000 pounds of salted and canned meat.[209] Treasury Department records list other British imperial destinations for U.S. pork, bacon, and hams, among them Gibraltar, ten Canadian provinces, the British East Indies, "British possessions in Australasia," and "British Possessions, all other."[210]

If it was true, as the military commonplace had it, that the success of a campaign depended on the feeding of the forces, then the hog farmers of Champaign County deserved some of the laurels of war.[211] They were from the start agents of empire, if not always directly their own.

LARDING IT OVER THE BRITISH EMPIRE

The U.S. agricultural press followed British imperial affairs with an eye on the bottom line. When Britain went to war with Egypt in 1882, the *Breeder's Gazette* anticipated a rising demand for American farm products. It claimed that although Egypt was a "comparatively unimportant country," it might yet become a significant factor in the lives of its readers.[212] "It is an ill wind that blows nobody good," observed the *Illinois Agriculturist*. "American farmers generally receive their share of the spoils from foreign wars."[213]

Midwestern farmers' tendency to profit economically from imperial wars held true for World War I. After peaking in 1900 and 1903, U.S. pork exports had declined almost continuously from 1903 to 1913, due to the demands of the domestic market and the resulting spike in prices that U.S. pork products commanded. The world war reversed this course. Not only did the war cut Britain off from some of its staple providers—including Russia—but the shift of labor from the field to the trench reduced its domestic production.[214] Wartime demand caused pork production to shoot upward and European exports to rebound.[215]

The increased pork exports of the World War I era helped the Allies win the war. In contrast to Germany, which suffered from demoralizing shortages of food, most notably a food crisis in the winter of 1916–1917, the British people and military did not go hungry. The United States was the main provisioner, supplying over half of Britain's flour and about 80 percent of its fats and meats—primarily from pigs—from 1917 to 1918.[216]

Food exports helped Britain win the war in a second way as well: they helped turn the United States into an ally. In the early years of the war, American exporters tried to make the most of neutrality by selling to all parties. The more they sold, the more difficult it became to stay neutral. Food exports led to conflict with Britain when the British navy detained U.S. ships carrying food to Germany and to neighboring countries (the Netherlands, Denmark, and Sweden) that reexported goods to Germany. Representatives from the U.S. meat industry joined the chorus against British interference in neutral shipping, calling on Secretary of State Robert Lansing and the British embassy to protest.[217] Yet food exports led to even greater conflict with Germany, which let its U-boats loose on merchant vessels bound for Britain. Realizing the importance of grain imports for British food security, the Germans continued their U-boat campaign even in the face of heated U.S. denunciations. Their efforts to starve their enemy into submission failed. The United States continued to ship food to Britain, and ongoing German predations brought the United States into the war.[218]

As a belligerent, the United States upped its efforts to keep Britain from hunger. In response to the Allies' calls for lard and meat, and recognizing that pork production could be ramped up more quickly than beef, the U.S. Department of Agriculture encouraged farmers to raise more hogs. The Food Administration, established following the United States' entry into the war in 1917, set a minimum price of $15.50 per hundred pounds (later raised to $17.50) for droves of hogs in Chicago. These measures produced the desired result: hog production skyrocketed. In February 1918 the Allies urgently demanded more pork shipments, claiming that the further prosecution of the war depended on immediate shipments of meat and wheat. The following month, the United States shipped over ten million pounds of pork daily, a figure equivalent to 66,000 hogs.[219] Exports of pork and lard rose from a prewar annual average of slightly under a billion pounds to over 2.2 billion pounds in 1918.[220]

The sheer magnitude of these exports seems to substantiate claims that U.S. food mattered more to the Allies than U.S. troops, munitions, and ships. Yet regardless of their comparative significance, it is clear that U.S. grain and pork exports contributed to the Allied victory. This, in turn, helped preserve the British Empire, which extended its reach even farther through the mandate system established by the League of Nations at war's end.[221]

The recognition that Britain relied on U.S. pork and other food products led to very different assessments of British-American relations than those concerned with U.S. dependency. Even before World War I, U.S. farmers pointed out that Britain could not feed her own people without imports.[222] Agreeing with this assessment, the British Navy League had clamored for a stronger navy to protect Britain's food supply.[223] Much of the talk about food security focused on grain, but pork also merited mention. As one article in the *Journal of the Royal Agricultural Society* phrased the matter: "It has become an accepted truth that we in England cannot produce enough bacon to supply our demand."[224] One turn-of-the century investigation characterized around 90 percent of the bacon sold in Bristol as the U.S. product.[225] After noting that Britain had imported over 200 million pounds sterling of food in 1898, the British publication *Mark Lane*

Express and Agricultural Journal remarked: "We are to depend on the eternal friendship of the United States." This struck the author as a dangerous prospect. If Britain were ever in a tight corner, the United States might make a grab for Canada and the West Indies, and hungry Britain would be in a pinch.[226]

Such assessments provided a very different perspective on dependency, one in which the power relationships were reversed. Illinois farmers fueled such anxieties by alluding to their own growing power. As early as 1856, the *Illinois Farmer* pointed out that war with Britain would be "fratricidal." Yet much as U.S. farmers would suffer from their loss of markets, Britain would suffer even more because it "depends on foreign countries for many of her necessities."[227] As they provided vital foodstuffs to the British Empire, U.S. pork producers often concluded that the greatest accrual of power was to themselves. Britain might still be the greatest empire on earth, but well before World War I, midwestern pork producers had begun to assert that British strength and vitality came from the United States.

PIGGYBACKED POWER

The heartland is certainly not the only brick in the edifice of U.S. imperial denial, but it has occupied a central, keystone role. William Appleman Williams recognized as much when he trained his sights on midwestern farmers. His *Roots of the Modern American Empire* was never just about export markets—its larger goal was to critique exceptionalist claims of anti-imperial virtue. By aiming at the American pastoral, Williams intended to take down the myth of an innocent heart. But in insisting that the United States was thoroughly imperial, Williams suggested that it was exceptionally so. In dismantling one conceit, he laid the foundation for another.

The United States did not become imperial by expanding its

markets in Latin America and Asia, as Williams claimed, because the United States had been imperial all along. Not only did midwestern farmers—many of them emigrants from Great Britain and its Irish colony—advance settler colonialism, they were also deeply entangled in British imperialism. Whereas U.S. manufacturers pushed for anti-British tariffs and U.S. cotton and wheat producers complained that Britain kept them in a condition of colonial subordination, akin to those of Ireland and India, the hog farmers of the Corn Belt piggybacked on the British Empire.[228] Through their livestock investments, connections, and values, they revealed a sense of affiliation with the leading empire of the day. By exporting cheap and durable pork products, they fed the British Empire, most notably in time of war. The tale of the Berkshire hog reveals that roots of the American empire were not as exceptional as Williams suggested—nor were these roots even always American.

To the extent that the United States was beginning to surpass the British Empire by the early twentieth century, it was in part because of its long history of connections to that empire.[229] Midwestern pork producers depended on British genetic material, British capital, British goods, British know-how, British transportation infrastructures, and British export markets. Those who pushed for naval building did so not only to open up new markets, but also to protect their shipping lanes to their leading customer, Great Britain.[230] When they joined with other midwestern farmers to pursue economic empire in Asia and Latin America, they built literally and figuratively on their British ties.

Williams missed out on the wider imperial context, in which the United States simultaneously benefited from and supported the British Empire, because of the tendency to see empires more as rivals than as interconnected and mutually supporting entities. This view of imperial rivalries explains why the shooting of a pig on a disputed island in Puget Sound in 1859 has received far more attention in historical accounts than the tale of the Berkshire hog. Whereas the 1859 pig imbroglio nearly led to an interimperial war over the U.S.-Canadian border, the Berkshire hog reveals interimperial solidarities well before the fabled Anglo-American rapprochement of the 1890s.[231] Although the decolonization struggles of Williams's time had made it clear that a nation could be seen as imperial because of the company it kept, the Cold War context did not invite much thought on the ways that competing empires might have owed great debts to each other or that rising empires might be less exceptional than they liked to think.

If the *post* in *postcolonial* can be construed as referring to a place (as in an outpost or a base) as well as a time and a politics, then the heartland can be seen as unexceptionally postcolonial indeed.

ARCHIVAL TRACES

A missionary among her own people

New Guide for Emigrants to the West, 1836: "Probably one half of the earth's surface, in a state of nature, was prairies or barrens. . . . Mesopotamia, Syria, and Judea had their ancient prairies, in which the patriarchs fed their flocks. Missionaries in Burmah, and travellers in the interior of Africa, mention the same description of country."[1]

H. J. Dunlap Scrapbook, 1890: The clock in Strasbourg is "wholly unworthy its great notoriety. The model of it shown in Champaign a few years ago was a much finer thing than the real. In the audience to see it strike, the day of my visit, there were Caucasians, Japanese and Indians, these latter a part of our celebrated fellow citizen's show, Buffalo Bill . . . Strange, yet true, a young lady of my party, born in Champaign, had never seen an Indian until that day, and also saw a buffalo for the first time a few months ago at Breslau."[2]

History of Champaign County, 1905: "Mrs. Mary Elizabeth (Bowen) Busey, wife of Gen. Samuel T. Busey, Urbana, Ill., was born in Delphi, Ind. June 21, 1854, the daughter of Aber H. and Catherine J. (Trawin) Bowen, the former born in Dayton, Ohio, and the latter in Calcutta, India."[3]

Urbana Courier, 1912: On the Busey family's trip to Cuba: "Mr. and Mrs. F. E. Earle were the hosts of the Buseys, their friendship dating back to the days when Mr. Busey was on an Indian reservation as an Indian agent. Mr. Earle is a former college professor having held chairs in several American institutions and went to Cuba on the invitation of ex-president Palma for the purpose of making certain agricultural experiments."[4]

Urbana Courier, **1915:** "Word has been received of the death from heart disease of Andrew Rutherford, a graduate student of this University in 1911. Mr. Rutherford was a graduate of Edinburgh university, and spent the years 1911 and 1912 in this country as a Carnegie fellow on entomology. In 1913 he was appointed as Governmental Entomologist of Ceylon, one of the most important positions in the English entomological service."[5]

Urbana Courier, **1915:** Miss Mali Lee will return to China after her graduation to "become a missionary among her own people." Had it not been for Christian missionaries in China, "she would no doubt still be living in China the way many other Chinese girls do."[6]

Urbana Courier, **1916:** "Dr. Fanny C. Gates, former dean of women at Grinnell college, will succeed Martha Kyle as dean of women at the university . . . From 1895 to 1896 she was a graduate scholar at Bryn Mawr college and a graduate fellow in 1896 and 1897. She then accepted an appointment of European fellow in the association of collegiate alumnae at the University of Gottingen, Germany and Zurich Polytechnic. Moreover she has studied at the University of Chicago, McGill university, Canada, and received a Ph.D. degree at the University of Pennsylvania. At the University of Cambridge she studied in the celebrated Cavendish laboratories."[7]

THE ISOLATIONIST CAPITAL OF AMERICA

Hotbed of Alliance Politics

DOWN ON THE MIDWESTERN FARM

Although many urban legends sprout from urban concerns, they are not all about urban places. This can be seen in the most stubborn urban legend of all, one that still circulates today, though debunked from the time of its creation: the legend of American isolationism.

This legend took root at the end of World War II. For evidence, its proponents sometimes reach back to George Washington's warnings against entangling alliances, but they more commonly alluded to noninterventionist sentiments espoused in the interwar years.[8] From the beginning, critics pointed out that, apt as characterizations such as "anti-League" might be, the blanket term *isolationism* misleadingly implied a desire to cut ties with the rest of the world. Turning the League of Nations vote into an "ism" was more than an exaggeration, it was a distortion, for it deflected attention from interventions in the Caribbean, involvement in European affairs, participation in international organizations, and cross-border mobility, culture, and commerce.[9] In dismissing isolationism as "no more than a legend," diplomatic historians have pointed out that the United States actually expanded its reach in the 1920s and 1930s. Bankers, sales reps, purchasing agents, diplomats, marines, missionaries, tourists, and workers continued to cross U.S. borders in significant ways even after the Senate had nixed membership in the League.[10]

Despite an abundance of scholarship denouncing isolationism as a misleading myth, the term refused to die.[11] Efforts to debunk the isolationist legend by parsing policy preferences and tracing private sector ties have lacked traction because this legend was never only about ideology and practice; it was always just as much about place. Those who made the case for American isolationism claimed that in its earliest incarnations it referred to the nascent nation as a whole, separated from Europe by an oceanic moat that took more than a month for wind-powered vessels to cross. Proximate neighbors, whether indigenous, Mexican, Canadian, or Caribbean, fell off the map in this Eurocentric geography. With the advent of telegraphs, cables, and steamships, such a sweeping appellation made even less sense. To label a place like New York City "isolationist" would have been manifest nonsense. But rather than retiring the misleading concept, its proponents merely relocated it, from the nation as a whole to the rural Midwest, the so-called isolationist capital of America.[12] Even in an age of American global ascendance, the heart of the nation remained stuck in a more local past.

The isolationist capital of America won its title by seeming quadruply insulated from the rest of the world: through vast oceans, a mass of land, distance from urban centers, and historic proclivities. One historian characterized isolationism as "an idealized vision of small-town and rural America applied to international affairs."[13] Though insisting that "the isolationist movement was by no means exclusively rural and small town," another described it as "rooted in the interests and values of agriculture in the upper

Missouri-Mississippi-Ohio river valley."[14] Stretching far beyond particular policy choices, the term "isolationism" came to evoke an inward outlook that made sense only if anchored to a seemingly isolated place with a long history of going it alone. The heartland myth took root in such soil, with offshoots that sprout to this day.

The idea of the heartland as the home of isolationism remains so entrenched in nationalist imaginaries that we mistake it for an apt characterization of core convictions, if not a timeless truth. But history suggests otherwise. Keyword searching small-town newspapers prior to 1945 reveals that rural midwesterners did not use terms like *isolationist* or *isolationism* to refer to themselves or their politics.[15] The term *isolation* mostly turns up stories on medical quarantines, with scattered hits for stranded polar expeditions and Indian Ocean islands.[16] On the occasions when rural midwesterners did refer to their own "isolation" (note the lack of an *ism*), they presented it as a liability, fortunately in the process of being remedied by railroads, paved roads, automobiles, telephones, Grange meetings, newspapers, telegrams, and rural free delivery.[17] A report on a convivial Commercial Club meeting captures the connotations of the word: "Isolation means death. Hermits are abnormal people." No wonder, continued the report, that women constituted a majority in insane asylums, for confinement at home was stultifying.[18] Although calling oneself a local could be a means to claim place-based entitlements, to be called isolated was no compliment, as the allusion to disturbed housewives indicates.

From its inception, the word *isolationist* was not so much a description as an insult—the kind of insinuation of inferiority that continues to rankle the region. By associating particular policy perspectives with hayseeds, it misrepresented both politics and place.

SWORDS AND PLOWSHARES

If the isolationist legend had been rooted in evidence and logic, it would have withered from the start, for historians have long realized that the settlers who forged the heartland hankered after foreign markets. From the nation's founding to 1911, agricultural goods constituted the majority of U.S. exports. Pick up a musty old farming journal, rural newspaper, or agricultural report from the Midwest, and you will find aspirations of conquering the globe.[19] An early dean of the Agricultural College at the University of Illinois made these ambitions clear: "we shall never rest satisfied . . . until we have attained commercial supremacy in the agricultural markets of the world."[20]

Farmers called for greater market access so vociferously that the biggest boundary enforcers of them all, the protective tariff proponents of the Republican Party, reassured them that agricultural exports would continue to flow out even as imports faced more obstacles to entry. Democrats, Grangers, and other tariff opponents doubted the feasibility of that Gore-Tex-like scenario, insisting that their exports would rise and cost of living fall only if the tariff barriers that advanced the interests of urban manufacturers were removed. Speaking on behalf of the "agricultural classes," one Champaign resident claimed that "the farmers of Illinois can supply the world, if need be, with meat and grain—with wheat, corn, hogs and cattle, and why they should not be suffered to buy as freely as they are allowed to sell in the markets of the world, is one of the infamous outrages of the age."[21] In response to manufacturers' nationalist arguments, this Champaigner against the tariff prioritized profit and economy over the coinage of the trade.

Though seemingly motivated by a sense of unbounded productive capacity and taste for imported goods, ambitions of feeding the world sprang from anxiety as well. Undercurrents of concern were particularly strong between 1865 and 1894, when foreign competition drove down U.S. grain prices in international markets. Increasing competition also affected prices closer to home. Earlier in the century, farmers could hope to weather poor harvests through high commodity prices nearby. But by the late nineteenth century, cheaper grains from elsewhere flooded in whenever their own harvests were poor.[22] As consumers suffered less of a wallop, growers suffered more. The threat that foreign rivals posed to profits focused farmers' attention on competitors.

Much of this attention zeroed in on the temperate agricultural regions stretching from Argentina to Australia and Canada to Russia. Federal Department of Agriculture reports warned of the European immigrants pouring into the "vast areas of productive lands" of South America, bringing with them knowledge of modern agricultural methods and a "good degree of enterprise and ambition." The realization that U.S. manufacturers were selling these settlers cutting-edge agricultural implements heightened the sense of threat, as did news that these "agricultural colonies" would have ready access to markets thanks to expanding railway lines.[23]

Accounts of rising threats prompted midwestern farmers to regard foreign rivals as antagonists. Though by no means isolationist, the farmers bent on export markets do not appear collaborationist. They seem to exemplify an us-versus-them mentality, a desire to dominate in a win-or-lose world. A drawing published in the *Illinois Agriculturist* in 1898 captures this stance—under waving flags and an arrow-clutching eagle, a cannon bombards the world with corn.[24] Such aspirations provide a powerful rebuttal to the isolationist legend. But militant unilateralism is not the whole story.

The career of Congressman William Brown McKinley hints at a more collectivist outlook than that suggested by cannonades of corn.

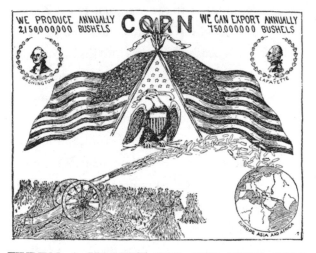

FINDING A MARKET FOR OUR CORN CROP.

The *Illinois Agriculturist* proposed rendering this image in ears of corn at
the Paris Exposition of 1900, so as to "excite the curiosity of the foreign people
long enough to convert them to the use of corn products." Although the artist
meant to signal hereditary friendship through the depiction of Lafayette, he
seemed unconcerned with the ways that European audiences might regard
the reach of the American flag or the threat posed by the cannon.

*E. S. Fursman, "Finding a Market for Our Corn Crop," Illinois Agriculturist 2 (1898),
81, University of Illinois Urbana-Champaign Archives.*

This William McKinley should not be confused with the Ohio congressman William McKinley, who won the presidency in 1896 and
subsequently took Puerto Rico, the Philippines, and Guam as spoils
of the Spanish-American War, annexing Hawai'i along the way. The
Illinois McKinley represented Champaign and neighboring counties.
The son of a Presbyterian minister, he made big money in public
utilities. Financed in part by capitalists in Montreal and England, his
business empire grew from the waterworks of Champaign to electric,
gas, and streetcar lines and interurban trains in several states.[25] Having amassed a fortune from downtown infrastructures, McKinley
turned to agriculture as a hobby.[26]

He also turned to politics, winning election to the U.S. Congress in

1904. He served until 1921, with the exception of the Sixty-Third Congress (1913–1915). In 1921, McKinley took up a seat in the U.S. Senate, which he held until his death, five years into his term. Given the composition of his district and his investments in railroading, his service on the House's Agriculture and Pacific Railroads Committees comes as no surprise.[27] His third major committee assignment, on the House Foreign Affairs Committee, may seem less apt, but it enabled him to advance his constituents' trade-related interests.[28] Yet protecting U.S. farmers from competition and extending their markets were just two of the issues that animated McKinley.[29] As he rose to become the ranking minority member on the Committee on Foreign Affairs, he also embraced the movement for global governance.[30]

McKinley did so primarily through his membership in the Inter-Parliamentary Union. Founded in 1889, this organization brought legislators from different nations together on behalf of international arbitration treaties and the judicial resolution of international disputes. In pursuit of this larger mission, it took up related issues such as the protection of private property at sea and "interdicting the use of aeroplanes in war." As of 1912, eighteen European nations belonged, joined by Australia, Canada, Japan, Liberia, Turkey, and the United States. By 1914, the union had held eighteen conferences, mostly in European capitals but on one occasion in St. Louis. Although its efforts to promote world peace failed spectacularly in 1914, members held on to that vision, endorsing the League of Nations at the close of World War I.[31]

In 1904, the U.S. affiliate of the union had about forty members from the two chambers of Congress.[32] McKinley threw himself energetically into the work, rising to become leader of the global organization shortly before his death. His participation in the union's congresses added to his tally of transatlantic crossings: fifteen round-trips, thirty crossings overall.[33] In 1911, he brought over a dozen men from Champaign County with him to the union's congress in Rome.[34] McKinley denounced the millions of dollars expended "for the purposes and machinery of war" as a waste. He regarded peace advocacy as the means to shift these investments to "the betterment of human conditions."[35]

The *Urbana Courier* joked at the congressman's expense when Italy started a war around the time of the peace conference in Rome, but it more generally praised McKinley's efforts. As a Republican paper, the *Courier* stood behind its Republican representative, claiming that McKinley "may justly be regarded as one of the foremost exponents of universal peace in this country." It lauded his service on the Foreign Relations Committee as a credit to his district and indeed the entire "middle west" and proudly reported that the noted Chautauqua orator Reverend John Wesley Hill had praised McKinley's peace advocacy as an exemplification of Christian principles.[36] Along with endorsing the kinds of economic self-advancement that McKinley supported, the *Courier* also endorsed McKinley's efforts on behalf of international cooperation. Positioned in the midst of two sets of politics—self-interest and collective well-being—McKinley and his backers chose both.

Competition or cooperation? Struggles for global domination or world peace? How to strike the balance and with whom? McKinley and his largely rural constituents faced the same questions as the nation as a whole. In refutation of the isolationist legend, they had no particular proclivity for walls. Having so egregiously misrepresented their stances on the major foreign policy debates of their day, the legend proceeds to overlook a more intriguing story: the particular relations that unfolded on the ground. As an urban legend in more than one sense, it completely misses the possibility that the isolationist capital of America was a veritable hotbed of alliance politics, with a specifically agrarian bent.

IMPORTING THE MEANS
OF PRODUCTION

The farmers who colonized the Midwest in the nineteenth century did not export indigenous coneflowers or big bluestem grass; they plowed them up instead. Nor did they export the varieties of Indian corn that they encountered upon arrival. To the contrary, they mixed eastern flints (traceable back to ancient strains developed from Canada to Georgia) and southern dents (traceable back to strains imported more recently from Mexico) to develop the signature grain of the Corn Belt.[37] Just as they applauded themselves for improving on Indian corn, they saw the extent of their cultivated fields as a sign of civilizational advance. Where once small plots of cultivated land had dotted the prairie, small parcels of untilled prairie became lonely holdouts against furrowed fields. The pioneers often praised themselves for forging homes from the wild. But the more familiar they made their fields, the less domestic those fields became in ecological terms.[38]

The extent of the environmental transformation wrought by these farmers can be glimpsed in an 1859 guide to what was then known as "the American West." The guide reported on the staples to be found there: wheat, oats, Irish potatoes, hay, butter, and cheese. With the possible exception of hay (depending on its composition), none of these things were found in Illinois prior to European colonization. A few exceptions—maple syrup and some nuts and berries—aside, this guide trumpeted products new to the prairie.[39]

As ever more settlers packed up their seeds and went west, ever more exogenous plants took hold. With the important exception of maize, all the pioneers' major grains came via Europe, tracked back much farther by agricultural writings of the time. According to an

1853 article in the *Urbana Union*, wheat originated in the central ta-bleland of Tibet, "where its representatives yet exist as a grass, with small, mealy seeds." Rye grew wild in Siberia; oats in North Africa; barley in the Himalayas. The article traced garden beans to the East Indies, onions to Egypt, potatoes to Peru and Mexico, pears and ap-ples to Europe, cherries to Asia Minor, walnuts and peaches to Per-sia, and radishes to China and Japan.[40]

Other publications played the origins game, too, in this time of radical biological change. The *Prairie Farmer* claimed that Duchess apples, though native to Russia, disembarked from England and Ger-many.[41] The *Illinois Farmer* attributed a rival, the red Astrachan ap-ple, to Sweden, by way of England.[42] It reported that the Chinese sugarcane (sorgo) had arrived via Europe, whence it was brought in 1851 by the French consul to Shanghai. It tracked the travels of im-phee from Port Natal (now known as Durban, South Africa) to En-gland, France, Belgium, the West Indies, Mauritius, and Brazil.[43] Attention to origins helped farmers evaluate the likelihood that a new plant would prosper in their clime and soil; attention to previ-ous migrations suggested that, having adapted to new lands already, these plants could thrive elsewhere as well.

The histories of well-traveled plants conveyed a third important message: desirability. Before the nineteenth century, American farm-ers typically planted seeds that they had saved from the previous year's harvest. When they moved, they brought their own starter seeds along. To broaden their plantings beyond the seeds from their own plots, pioneers traded with their neighbors and exchanged seeds within agricultural societies.[44] This meant that much of what nineteenth-century colonists grew could be traced to eighteenth-century importations, and some back as far as the "Columbian ex-change" of the early colonial era.[45] Important though these older strains were, the colonization of Illinois in the nineteenth century coincided with a new wave of botanical importation, stemming from a desire for world-class plants.

This wave reached Champaign later than less swampy parts of the state, but the inexorable advance of drainage efforts in the aftermath of the Civil War led to the ascent of mixed farming—meaning farms with a variety of crops and animals. Even farmers who did not specialize in stock typically raised some animals on the side and most farmers kept draft animals before the advent of mechanical tractors. The need to feed these animals led to even more importations. Rather than rely on native prairie grasses, the farmers of Champaign began planting exogenous grasses and fodder such as timothy. Among the seeds hawked by a Champaign County hardware store in 1913 were ones for millet, soy, rye, rape, clover, redtop (a Eurasian grass), and alfalfa.[46] A 1917 Champaign County directory reveals the effects of these purchases. It listed over twenty-nine thousand acres of "tame or cultivated grasses," but none in the category of wild prairie grasses.[47]

Farmers' transformational efforts extended to the farthest margins of their land. To establish boundaries, farmers planted hedgerows like those of Europe, many grown from Osage orange seeds obtained in Arkansas and Texas.[48] To block winter winds, they grew timber breaks of Norway spruce, Austrian pine, Scotch pine, European silver fir, Siberian arborvitae, cedar of Lebanon, and English yew.[49] For ornamental purposes, they purchased black European mulberries, English bird cherries, and Siberian crab apples.[50] The biological transformation of the wet prairie was so thorough that less than a tenth of 1 percent of its original sweep remains in Illinois, the so-called Prairie State.[51]

NON-NATIVIST DEVELOPMENT AGENCIES

The U.S. government played a significant role in these importations. In the 1830s, the commissioner of patents, Henry Leavitt Ellsworth, started collecting seeds from consuls and naval officers, even though he had no legal authority to do so. He distributed them through congressmen—who mailed thousands of packets of free seeds to constituents—and through agricultural societies.[52] In 1839, Congress began budgeting money for such work and the Patent Office ramped up its efforts. In the 1850s, it sent agricultural explorers to Europe, South America, and Japan. The U.S. Department of Agriculture, founded in 1862, carried on the efforts to improve and broaden the genetic stock of grains, grasses, fruits, legumes, and vegetables through importation.[53]

Most of the seeds brought ashore in this wave did not take hold, due to differences in soil and climate. Quality, too, played a role. As members of Congress passed out ever more packages of free seeds to their constituents—as many as forty-nine million packets of vegetable seeds in a year—the reputation of those seeds declined.[54] Though many seeds did not catch on, those that did provided the foundations of modern American agriculture, with later introductions being used mainly to improve particular characteristics of established varieties.[55] Some nineteenth-century importations now carry on of their own accord, such as the chicory (imported as a coffee substitute) that now graces the margins of rural roads.[56] Yet to understand why so many seeds took root in this period, we need to look beyond their adaptive capacity. So many seeds took root because so many were planted. Farmers willingly took a chance on the next big thing, encouraged by the burgeoning agricultural press.

Between 1819 and 1860, at least 259 agricultural magazines were published in the United States. Much of the writing in these publications focused on exciting new seeds and plants.[57] The *Prairie Farmer* ran many such articles, including one recommending Japan as a good place to look for "tender varieties of fruits," because the Japanese had been working for more than two thousand years to bring southern varieties "degree by degree to their northern limit."[58] The *Illinois Farmer* also saw a bright future for European plants such as Red Dutch currants and English Red Cane raspberries.[59]

Government-supported exhibitions and fairs underscored the prospecting message of the agricultural press. The 1876 International Exposition at Philadelphia yielded a variety of foreign seeds for the Agricultural Museum in Springfield. Official reports boastfully alluded to the wide range of places that had yielded seeds: Canada, Cuba, Jamaica, Brazil, Spain, Russia, Sweden, Italy, Egypt, Queensland, Tasmania, Victoria, and New South Wales.[60]

The search for the next big thing grew so frenzied that some novelty seekers urged caution, Matthias Lane Dunlap among them. Dunlap was a fruit grower in Champaign County who wrote under the pen name Rural. After expressing some skepticism on the virtues of *Dioscorea batatas*—a Chinese yam said to have roots two feet long and two inches wide—Rural got a suspicious pine box in the mail in 1856.[61] "We debated some time, considering whether it was safe to open it. It was too light to contain fire-arms, and had too expensive a finish to contain plants." Curiosity overcame prudence, and Rural opened the lid. He found, nestled in moss, "a vegetable product twenty-two inches long." After cutting off the last six inches, he boiled and ate it. Rural reported that it was "equal to the common potato in some respects" but not as good as the sweet potato. Though still skeptical of claims that the yam would someday equal cotton in value, that in fifty years its roots would be so huge that they would have to be "excavated by steam," Rural planted some sets, which he promised to distribute gratis to his readers.[62] Three years later he concluded his report: the "celestial plant" was a bust. Despite its reported success in Europe, it had flopped on his farm. There was no need to "raise a monument to the memory of those great men who have rescued this plant from the Chinese."[63]

Dunlap's dismissive report may have downed the prospects of the Chinese yam, but it did not put a stopper on the larger pattern of biological innovation. Commercial nurseries joined the agricultural press and exhibition circuit in stoking interest in new plants. Especially after the spread of rural delivery services after the Civil War, commercial purveyors hawked their wares through illustrated catalogs.[64] These tempted readers with drawings of shiny peppers and luscious tomatoes and exotic names such as Asiatic cauliflowers and Belgian green top carrots.[65]

Although most of the catalogs that circulated through the rural Midwest came from U.S. nurseries, farmers in search of a competitive edge could buy their seeds direct from Europe. The British seed purveyor William Bull claimed to send its product "to any part of the world," using the best routes, mail steamers, clipper ships, and railways.[66] German companies likewise published English-language catalogs with shipping information for American customers.[67]

By the late nineteenth century, the agricultural programs and extension offices of land-grant universities had become leading champions of agricultural innovation.[68] Pathbreaking though these institutions were, they built on the prior efforts of government prospectors, publicly supported expositions, the agricultural press, and commercial nurseries. By persuading farmers to adopt a wide variety of exogenous plants, these plant purveyors served as nonnativist development agencies. Thanks to their efforts, the roots of midwestern prosperity could be traced to far corners of the world.

NEW MAMMOTH SILVER KING ONION.

This immense, large, beautiful and excellent Onion, which was introduced last year for the first time is rightly named, and is the king of all Onions. It is without doubt the largest onion in cultivation in this or any other country.

It frequently attains the weight of 2¾ to 4 pounds the first year from seed, and will measure from 18 to 20 inches around. The bulbs are of a beautiful and attractive form, flattened, but thick through as shown in the illustration above. The average diameter of this beautiful onion is from 5 to 7 inches. No other onion attains such mammoth size, nor will any other variety grow uniformly so large. The skin is a beautiful silvery white, the flesh is snow white, of a particular mild and pleasant flavor. So sweet and tender is the flesh, that it can be eaten raw like an apple.

The Silver King, being an Italian onion, will mature as early as the large white Italian, or the large Mexican, attains a much larger size than any other variety, either foreign or home grown.

Before offering this new onion to our customers, we had it fairly tested on our own grounds, and also in various parts of the United States and Canada, and found it to do uniformly well in almost every climate, both warm and cold.

It cannot be too highly recommended, either for family use, for exhibition purposes, at fairs, or in restaurants. Onions of larger size can be grown from seed of the Silver King, quite as easily and much less trouble than from sets of other varieties. One package will contain seed enough to supply onions enough for an ordinary family. The seed should be sown as early in the Spring as possible, in rich

Seed catalogs often heralded foreign origins, as seen in this ad for the "Silver King" onion, an Italian onion promised to "mature as early as the large white Italian, or the large Mexican." The company claimed to have tested it widely on its own ground as well as in "various parts of the United States and Canada," finding that it did "uniformly well in almost every climate, both warm and cold."

Wilson's Seed Catalogue for 1885 (Mechanicsville, Pa., 1885), 9.

BEET.

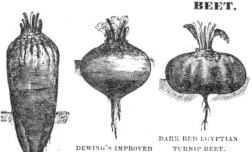

DEWING'S IMPROVED BLOOD TURNIP.

DARK RED EGYPTIAN TURNIP BEET.

BRIGGS'S PREMIUM LONG RED.

Young Beets make excellent greens for the dinner table, in early spring. These are obtained by thinning the plants where they are too thick in the rows. In garden culture, sow in drills fifteen inches apart, and one and one-half inches deep, and thin to six inches apart. The New Egyptian is the most profitable early market variety, and has now become very popular. The Beet makes excellent and superior feed for stock, and considering the ease and certainty of its success, should be very largely grown for the purpose. In Field culture, well manure and deeply plough the soil, thoroughly working it until it is well pulverized. Sow the seed in drills thirty inches apart, and thin to six or eight inches. Keep clean and loose with the cultivator and hoe as often as is necessary.

PAP. CTS.

Dark Red Egyptian Turnip—New and excellent sort, from EGYPT; in form like the Dutch Early Turnip. Good form; *early, very dark*, and of *fine flavor*, - - lb. $2.50; ¼ lb. $1.25; ¼ lb. 65c.; ⅛ lb. 35c.; oz. 20c. 10

Dark Black Red Erfurt, finest Long—*Imported*. New here, and for the fourth time offered. This is, no doubt, a very *tender, long* and *very dark* blood beet, - - - - - - - - - - - oz. 20c. 10

Round Early Red Blood—A fine French, tender Turnip Beet, lb. $2.00; ¼ lb. $1.00; ¼ lb. 50c.; ⅛ lb. 30c. oz. 20c. 10

Dewing's Improved Blood Turnip—A very early, tender and delicate Turnip Beet, of fine form and smooth skin; very desirable for either family use or the market gardener. Regarded as earlier but not so solid as the common Early Blood Turnip Beet, - - - - lb. $1.00; ¼ lb. 50c.; ¼ lb. 25c.; ⅛ lb. 20c.; oz. 15c. 10

Crapaudine, or Bark—French sort, remarkable for its shagreened and somewhat scaly bark that covers its skin; flesh intense red, sweet, fine flavor, tender and delicate, lb. $2.00; ¼ lb. $1.00; ¼ lb. 50c.; ⅛ lb. 30c.; oz. 15c. 10

Extra Early Bassano—Flattish, good size; flesh white, circled with bright pink; sugary and well flavored. Fine for summer or winter, - - - - - - - - lb. $1.00; ¼ lb. 50c.; ¼ lb. 25c.; ⅛ lb. 15c.; oz. 10c. 5

The *Briggs and Bro's.* seed company of Chicago and Rochester marketed its beets with allusions to Egypt, Erfurt, and France. Horticultural experts would have recognized Erfurt as a major center for German seed production and its export-oriented nurseries as the sources for many imported seeds.

Briggs and Bro's. Quarterly Illustrated Floral Work *(Chicago and Rochester, Jan. 1876), 65.*

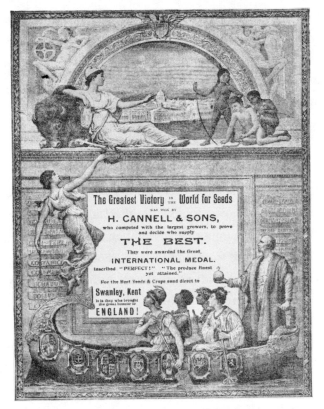

H. Cannell and Sons of Kent, England, hawked its product
through imperial imagery. To buy its seeds meant to be world-class,
to share in the laurels (and other plants) offered to England by
diminutive and seemingly more localized peoples.

H. Cannell and Sons, Complete Catalogue of Golden Seeds
(Swanley, Kent: H. Cannell and Sons, 1898).

ECOLOGICAL UN-AMERICANISM

The alacrity with which the pioneers introduced new plants should
not come as a complete surprise because they had, after all, transplanted themselves. For newcomers from Europe, the truly foreign
plants were the American ones they discovered on arrival, not the
ones that were being introduced. And yet these newcomers also experimented with plants such as imphee and sorgo that they did not

know from home. As newcomers in a strange land, nineteenth-century arrivals sought both familiarity and possibility. Given their diverse backgrounds and investments, this led to plenty of cross-pollination in agricultural practice.

The desire to duplicate departed lands and the openness to opportunity that characterized the first century of settlement extended to other means of production besides plants. Fields of fodder fed imported strains of cattle and pigs, Shorthorns and Berkshires prominent among them. Oats fed draft horses, some with a Percheron influence, following importations from the La Perche region of Normandy. Breeders also imported a number of sturdy English Shire horses and Clydesdales from Canada and Scotland.[69]

Ongoing imports also affected sheep and poultry lines. In the 1870s, the Illinois State Fair offered prizes for Cotswold rams and Spanish, Hamburg, Polish, and French Houdan chickens. It also ran an "Asiatic" poultry competition, with prizes going to "light Brahma," a Chinese breed with some South Asian admixture.[70] Breeders advertised Rouen ducks, Pekin drakes, and blue Andalusians in the *Prairie Farmer.*[71] Ads in the *American Swine and Poultry Journal* hawked Toulouse geese, Java sparrows, "French fowls," and Spanish Merino sheep "from the most celebrated and tested strains."[72]

Then there were the Italians that swarmed across the Illinois countryside—countless millions of them, descended from imported queens. Queen bees, that is. Whereas Italian people struck nativists as undesirable in the late nineteenth century, Italian bees had a warmer reception. Beekeepers found the offspring of these pollinators to be superior honey gatherers, quieter and more peaceable than native bees, more prolific, and less susceptible to moths.[73] Enthusiasts also preferred the Italians' golden bands to the dull black color of native bees.[74]

Not even subsequent introductions of Syrians, Cyprians, Punics,

New Specialty Advertisements.

For first-class chickens, poultry producers turned to varieties with
Asian ancestors (among them Brahmas and Cochins), the Houdan
breed that originated in France, Leghorns traceable back to
Italy, and the Plymouth Rock breed, developed in the
United States from a range of immigrant ancestors.

American Swine and Poultry Journal *3 (Nov. 1875).*

Holy Lands, and Hungarians dislodged the Italians from their hives.
"Italians Are the Best," claimed a report on the various "races" of
bees.[75]

As imported bees brought new pollination preferences to Illinois
flight paths, new underground organisms changed the composition

Italian queens, shipped by rail, established gold-banded colonies of pollinators across the Midwest in the late nineteenth century.

American Bee Journal 10 (March 1874), 74.

of the soil.[76] The worms that wiggled out of the root balls of introduced plants found a virgin land, at least in terms of rival worms, because Ice Age glaciation had frozen competitors out. These largely unremarked newcomers began to change soil structure and chemistry through their digging, defecating, diet, decay, and impact on microarthropods.[77] If worms arrived mostly as stowaways, new bacteria strains debuted under the watchful care of chaperones. The Illinois Agricultural Extension service shipped what it referred to as "infected alfalfa soil"—containing nitrogen-fixing bacteria derived from German cultures—to farmers across the state.[78] In conjunction with the spread of European pollinators, the new soil makers and nitrogen fixers helped Europeanize the land. And since Europeans had long histories of introducing African and Asian plants, to become more like Europe meant to become more global.

The process of making the midwestern countryside ecologically un-American was hardly isolationist. Nor was it even unilateralist. Although farmers certainly wanted to advance their own competitive advantage through their importations of exogenous plant and animal lines, these importations also fostered cross-border business relationships. By crediting other farmers with domesticating and improving various plants and animals, Illinois farmers acknowledged their indebtedness to agriculturalists elsewhere. Even as they tried to locate their own place in space by figuring out what would prosper on their fields, their efforts to acquire the world's best germ plasm also taught them about global threads of connection.[79]

DUNLAP GOES TO GERMANY

By the late nineteenth century, falling prices competed with seed catalogs for farmers' attention, turning them into a vociferous foreign policy constituency. In hopes of reaching wider markets, they called for low tariffs, an isthmian canal, and other transportation improvements. Less known are their demands for foreign relations representation through commercial agents focused on agricultural markets, agricultural attachés attached to embassies, and, most importantly, consular appointments.[80]

In the early 1890s, the United States employed about 775 consular officers in foreign posts. These officers did most of the daily work of U.S. foreign relations, issuing passports, administering the estates of U.S. citizens who died overseas, tracking down heirs and fugitives, verifying invoices for tariff purposes, and serving as the U.S. government's overseas eyes and ears (among other responsibilities). In hopes of advancing production and trade, the Department of State charged consular officers with filing dispatches on about fifty subjects, including agricultural matters.[81] Appreciating the value of this large pool of area experts, the U.S. Department of Agriculture asked consular officers to relay promising seeds and plants, and it disseminated their written reports in its own publications.[82]

From the early nineteenth century, party hacks regarded consular posts as political plums. Despite the establishment of an examination system in 1895, patronage remained pervasive until President Theodore Roosevelt broadened the merit principle a decade later.[83] The desire to reward political allies and build party loyalty explains why places like east-central Illinois became nurseries for consular officers. President Rutherford B. Hayes appointed George Scroggs, of the Champaign *Gazette*, consul at Hamburg in 1879.[84] Dr. L. S. Wilcox, a former mayor of Champaign, served as consul general in Hankow, China.[85] William R. Grant left a managerial post to serve as a deputy consul in Calgary.[86] John M. Gregory, the onetime president of the Illinois Industrial University, was not as fortunate, for his many pleas for an appointment came to naught. Rejected for the post of U.S. minister to Italy, as well as for that of minister to Switzerland and a position in the mission to Belgium, he became a tour guide instead, joining with his wife, Louisa, to offer an exclusive ten-month study trip to Europe for a "select party of ladies."[87]

Hiram J. Dunlap, known as H. J. Dunlap, had better connections and luck. Born near Chicago in 1841, he moved at age fifteen with his parents to Savoy, a village southwest of the Champaign County seat. Dunlap's father, the Dunlap who tested the Chinese yam, had established a nursery and orchard in Savoy, continuing to write on the side.[88] H. J. followed in his father's footsteps. For fourteen years, he ran his own farm, with the help of his wife, Nellie Baker Dunlap (born in Michigan, she had taught in Mississippi during Reconstruction before moving to Savoy).[89] In 1874, H. J. Dunlap became the associate editor of the *Champaign Gazette*. Five years later, he assumed the editorship.[90] He proved himself to be a stalwart Republican, including on the protective tariffs so dear to Republican hearts. In 1889, through his connections with Congressman Joseph Cannon, Dunlap won a presidential appointment as the U.S. consul in Breslau (now Wrocław, Poland, but then part of Germany).[91]

In the early twentieth century, as merit reforms passed during Theodore Roosevelt's presidency took hold, the University of Illinois began to offer consular service courses in its business administration program.[92] Dunlap, however, had no such formal training. (This may help explain why his superiors admonished him for his sketchy report on "injurious beer mug covers.") Nevertheless, Dunlap did have several qualifications.[93] Besides his Republican Party bona fides and expertise with a pen, Dunlap spoke German, having learned it as a child from his family's hired help and his attendance at a German-language school.[94] According to the press reports, when his friends gathered to bid him goodbye, "Herr Dunlap responded in a German speech."[95]

After accepting the post, H. J. traveled to Washington, D.C., for a predeparture briefing. He and Nellie stayed ten days, with friends.[96] H. J. called at the State Department, which referred him to the consular bureau. Dunlap reported that "the experience was rather disappointing, for they give you the last few months' correspondence with your predecessor to read; and as my predecessor, who was spoken of in the Champaign *Times* a few weeks ago as being so lonesome, died last April, there wasn't much from him." Before leaving Washington, he stopped at the White House, to shake hands with the president.[97] From there, he and Nellie set forth to New York, and onward to Hamburg. En route to Breslau, the Dunlaps visited Berlin, where H. J. called on W. W. Phelps, the U.S. minister, who has "frequently been in Champaign and made many inquiries about the place."[98]

Having assumed his post (and hired Nellie as the consulate's clerk), Dunlap wrote home to say that the nation's newest consular officer had never dreamed that he should "represent in an humble manner the greatest nation on earth in one of the chief cities of Poland; but nevertheless, by the grace of Providence and the republican party, here he is."[99] Marveling at his own accomplishment, Dunlap knew he owed his job to his political connections. But in the larger sense, he won his post because his fellow midwestern farmers demanded international representation. With their interests in mind, Consul Dunlap did his best to provide that.

FARMERS FIRST

Then the second city in size in the German Empire, Breslau did not seem an obvious posting for a farmer turned editor of a small-town Illinois newspaper. It was the seat of large manufacturers of woollen, linen, silk, and cotton goods, not a center of agricultural production.[100] But this did not keep Dunlap from pursuing his abiding interest in farming or serving his fellow citizens with interests in this topic. In addition to submitting the required crop reports to the U.S. Department of Agriculture, Dunlap investigated the undervaluation (for tax purposes) of German sugar shipments.[101] He wrote favorably of the cooperative efforts he saw in Breslau, seeing them as a model for U.S. Granges, Farmers' Alliances, and "kindred associations."[102] On trips into the countryside, Dunlap paid sharp attention to plowing and ditching, the composition of the soil and the size of the plats.[103] He noted the economy practiced by Prussian farmers, which he urged farmers at home to emulate. He took a more critical view of labor conditions, and especially of the frequency with which he saw women in the fields with hoes.[104]

Dunlap lasted less than a year in Breslau. He resigned his position upon being appointed U.S. commercial agent at Fürth, a Bavarian manufacturing center considered a more pleasant and lucrative post.[105]

As in his prior post, Dunlap escaped the city for the countryside, keeping a keen eye on farming practice. A sample dispatch: Bavarian farmers kept their manure heaps wet, which destroyed the seeds they contained, thereby preventing the propagation of weeds. From a trip to Strasburg: the soil was rich, the country a "good deal like our Illinois prairies," only without a foot of wasteland and no weeds anywhere.[106] On market conditions: Germans were afraid to buy American hams, even though cheaper, because they were afraid they would not taste right. Horse meat was abundant in German cities.[107]

In 1891, H. J. had terrible news to report in the column he regularly dispatched to Champaign: Nellie had died. He brought her body home for burial. After the funeral, he returned to his post, but not for long.[108] In 1893, H. J. moved to Kankakee (about sixty miles north of the Champaign County line), where he published the *Kankakee Republican News* and courted Elizabeth Frith, known as Bessie. The two married in 1894.[109] Dunlap's experiences as consul appear to have enhanced his political prospects, given that he became a state senator and served as president of the Illinois World's Fair Commission.[110] Yet whatever the attractions of Kankakee, either H. J. missed the life of a consular officer or Bessie keenly wanted to see the world. Maybe both. In 1905, the Dunlaps packed up for a posting in Cologne. They stayed in that city for eight years.[111]

As the U.S. consul in Cologne, Dunlap continued his efforts to advance U.S. interests. He offered marketing advice to U.S. firms and aid to the impecunious Americans who had traveled to Europe as stock tenders on cattle ships, only to find they had no means to return.[112] He provided valuable information to his apple-exporting relatives in an official report on bruising in transit.[113] His descriptions of crude instruments and backbreaking farming methods alerted U.S. farm implement makers to export opportunities.[114]

Yet for all these efforts to advance U.S. interests, Dunlap could not hide his feelings of sympathy toward farmers. In multiple dispatches, H. J. expressed solidarity with their struggles against leechlike merchants, bankers, and shippers. Writing from Breslau, he complained that Germans regularly satirized farmers along with old maids and mothers-in-law. Feeling the "unjustness of such flings," Dunlap rose to the defense of those who worked the soil.[115]

From his post in Fürth, Dunlap deplored the poverty of the peasantry, characterizing it as so extreme that would-be emigrants could not afford passage.[116] Although he advocated the free entry of American agricultural goods into Germany, he confessed that the prospect caused him some concern. "What will become of the farmers of this great country, once the gates are opened, is something I cannot predict. They stand in the same relation to the farmers of Illinois, that the manufacturers of the United States stand to those in Europe." That is, they were at risk of being crushed by foreign competition. Chatting with rural people as they dug their potatoes made him appreciate their vulnerability. When they complained that wealthy manufacturers would use cheap foreign food to keep their operatives' wages low, shafting German farmers in the process, Dunlap felt the injustice.[117] However much Dunlap wanted his associates from home to outcompete their German rivals, he did not want farmers to live in misery, no matter their nationality. Years before the United States entered World War I as an associated power, H. J. Dunlap had begun to imagine a kind of alliance politics that tempered commercial competition with agrarian solidarity.

ALLIANCE POLITICS

Consular agents like Dunlap were not the only government agents susceptible to feelings of agrarian solidarity. Such feelings also flowered in the International Institute of Agriculture, founded in 1905.

This institute built on the earlier International Commission of Agriculture, established in Paris in 1889, to foster the exchange of data on crop production collected by national statistical offices.[118] The institute can also be seen as a response to Grangerist calls for agrarian cooperation.[119] As they gathered information on comparative practices, such as the cooperative stores that were spreading across England, Grangers drew attention to farmers' common interests as a class.[120] Grange members were so deeply committed to cooperation across national lines that they endorsed international arbitration and, in 1916, the League of Nations.[121]

The instigator behind the International Institute of Agriculture was David Lubin, a California department store magnate turned farmer on the side. Inspired by European cooperative and credit bank movements and Grangerist efforts to organize against the monopoly interests of shippers, bankers, tariff advocates, and commodity traders, Lubin advocated a Chamber of Agriculture that would unite the agricultural classes of all countries in defense of their common interests and human food security.[122] The Italian king made the first bid, so the founding conference and subsequent proceedings took place in Rome. Forty-one nations sent delegates, motivated in some cases more by a desire for good relations with Italy than a particular commitment to Lubin's vision. The United States signaled its support for the cause by signing the treaty and then appointing the determined Lubin to its seat.[123]

Although the resulting organization fell short of Lubin's vision of a unifying world congress of farmers, its charter did reflect his commitment to transnational organization on behalf of rural people. It called for the collection, analysis, and publication of statistical, technical, and economic information on farming, the commerce in agricultural products, and prevailing prices. The charter also charged the organization with tracking farm wages, studying agricultural

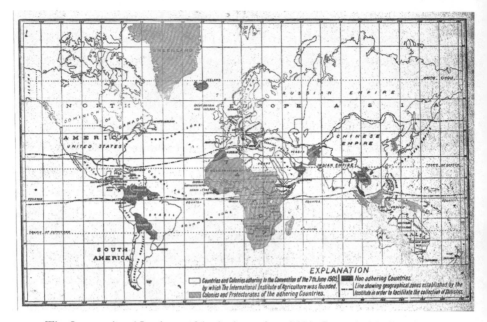

The International Institute of Agriculture, founded in Rome in 1905, gathered
statistics from much of the world. The adhering nations and colonies are
depicted without shading; additional colonies and protectorates represented
under their auspices are depicted by light shading. Only a smattering of
darkly shaded nations—stretching from Haiti to Liberia and
Siam—fell outside its reach.

International Institute of Agriculture, Bulletin of Agricultural Statistics 1 (Nov. 1910), back cover.

cooperation, insurance, and credit, and investigating vegetable diseases. Besides the United States, its top-tier contributors by the
1920s included Germany, Argentina, Brazil, China, Turkey, Spain,
France, Great Britain, Italy, Japan, Romania, and Russia. Fifty-eight
other states contributed, some of them colonial regimes in places
such as Hawai'i, Puerto Rico, French Morocco, Italian Somaliland,
and the Belgian Congo.

The institute's reach extended to central Illinois, where the *Urbana Courier* took note of its proceedings and the University of
Illinois subscribed to its *Bulletin of Agricultural Statistics*.[124] If the

United States participated in the International Institute of Agriculture largely to advance U.S. farmers' particular interests, its participation drew the readers of institute reports into collective security matters, for these reports made it clear that plant diseases had implications for food security and little respect for borders.[125]

This mix of self-serving financial motives and collective security commitments gave rise to another alliance of particular interest to agriculturalists: the alliance against bad weather. Recognizing the value of accurate forecasts to farmers, the U.S. government created the Weather Bureau in 1870 with about fifty stations. Telegraphic reports from Canada, Mexico, the West Indies, the Azores, and western Europe soon arrived in the Bureau's Central Office in Washington, D.C., from whence agents distributed them across the country.[126] Following the demands of a state farming convention, the Illinois Department of Agriculture called for a "pan-national conference" that would implement a "systematic plan of observation and reports." The payoffs, it claimed, would be huge: millions of dollars for a few days' foreknowledge of the weather, "at particular stages of the crops."[127]

In response to such calls, the United States negotiated more bilateral weather information exchanges.[128] It also sent delegates to international meteorological conferences, starting with Vienna in 1873. Other international conferences followed: St. Petersburg in 1886, Munich in 1891, Uppsala in 1894. The U.S. Weather Bureau, which had moved from the Army Signal Corps to the Department of Agriculture, hosted its first international conference in 1893.[129]

Whereas Dunlap imagined himself to be part of a farming fraternity that extended across national borders, the farmers who pushed for more cooperative efforts did more than profess solidarity. They pioneered tangible forms of alliance politics, justified not only in terms of self-interest, but also in terms of humanity's need for food.

IMPERIAL OVERSIGHT

Taking a closer look at the kinds of alliances of particular interest to rural midwesterners reveals that the supposed isolationists of urban lore were no more neutral than they were go-it-aloners. Although they professed feelings of solidarity with farmers as a class, united in common cause against hunger, they also worked hard to ally themselves with the great imperial powers of the time. In part this was a matter of markets, for European powers, and especially Britain, were the leading purchasers of their exports. Yet midwestern farmers became entangled with European imperialism well before the point of sale.

We can glimpse some affinities with European imperialism in Dunlap's bid for one last post. After five years in Cologne, Dunlap wrote to his congressman, Joseph Cannon (then the Speaker of the U.S. House of Representatives), to say that he was "thoroughly tired of Germany" and wanted to be "transferred to some English speaking place, where the salary is larger." Admitting that $3,500 might be considered a good salary in some quarters, he insisted that it was not adequate for Cologne, where the price of living was high and "we have out of respect to the office and the country we represent to put on a little style, though I assure you in my case it is very little." He mentioned the Cape of Good Hope as a preferred choice, followed by "some place in Canada like Winnipeg or Vancouver."[130]

Dunlap's attention to the money to be made by men such as him in places such as the Cape of Good Hope shows that he kept an eye on more than just North Atlantic trade. Looking out on the wider world, he saw European imperialism—with its footholds in South Africa and the Canadian West—as a means to advance his own prospects. He identified more with the Europeans who profited from their overseas holdings than with the non-Europeans they ruled over. These colonial subjects included the Hereros. From 1904 to 1908, the German army killed over sixty thousand indigenous Hereros in southwest Africa, as part of a campaign to open up their land to settlement by German agriculturalists. However sympathetic to German farmers, Dunlap never wrote a word about their empire's rural victims.[131] Out of sight, out of mind, and not one of his responsibilities anyway. His job at the time was to advance U.S. commerce in Cologne, and he stuck to his commercial mission so faithfully that he paid little heed to political matters of any kind, including even Prussia's rule over Polish subjects, many of them peasants.[132] But even if we pardon Dunlap by attributing his oversight more to his position than his politics, his eagerness to rope his own fortunes to European imperialism tips us off to something larger. Dunlap's feelings of affinity with European empires outpaced his empathy for farmers subject to colonial rule.

In this respect, Dunlap was not alone. Indeed, while Dunlap focused on what the British Empire might offer specifically to him, bioprospectors and scientific agriculturalists took a larger view as they built selective alliances on the grounds of agrarian solidarity.

Bioprospecting may not immediately appear to be a form of alliance politics, since it largely involved efforts on the part of government plant prospectors, tourists, missionaries, and consular officers to identify and ship seeds and cuttings. The Department of Agriculture formalized these efforts by establishing a Section (later labeled an Office) of Seed and Plant Introduction, which published its first report in 1898. After screening introduced plants for disease and desirability in test gardens on the East and West Coasts, the Department of Agriculture's plant propagators distributed them to state experiment stations, agricultural extension offices, and thousands of experimenters and breeders across the country.[133] University of Illinois faculty participated in the experimentation movement, testing the suitability of plants such as Turkestan alfalfa on the university's "curiosity strip" and others in the university's arboretum.[134]

HAND WARDIAN CASE OF LIVING TROPICAL PLANTS PACKED FOR A JOURNEY OF SEVERAL WEEKS' DURATION.

Each plant must be securely fastened in the case by means of cross slats. Ventilators in this case large ones, must be screened, and the glass roof must be protected from breaking by slats or heavy wire. This case should be carried on deck in a light but not sunny situation, sheltered from salt spray and from salt water used in scrubbing down the deck. The plants require watering once a week.

To aid the bioprospecting frenzy, the U.S. Department of Agriculture provided instructions on transporting plants, cuttings, and seeds.

David Fairchild, "How to Send Living Plant Material to America," United States Department of Agriculture, Bureau of Plant Industry, Office of Foreign Seed and Plant Introduction [1913], plates I and VI.

PACKAGES SHOWING METHODS OF PREPARING SEEDS FOR SHIPMENT BY SAMPLE AND PARCEL POST.

Short-lived seeds are packed in moistened charcoal or sphagnum moss, whereas grains and other long-lived seeds can be sent in seed packets, envelopes, or strong cloth sacks and these assembled in packages. (Examples of packages as received at Washington.)

Most of the plant material tested on such plots did not come from lonely wandering in the woods. It came from networking capacities. Acquisition records credit seeds and plants to foreign horticultural schools, agricultural expositions, experimental stations, private residences, and botanical gardens; to societies, scientists, officials, and military personnel.[135] Even the plant prospectors employed by the Department of Agriculture spent most of their time tracking down plants of known commercial value, rather than ones from the wild. Such networking efforts played out in a thoroughly imperial landscape. In their travels through colonial terrain, professional bioprospectors relied on the assistance of European as well as U.S. expats.[136] Reporting on the help offered to him in China by missionaries, plant explorer Frank Meyer wrote that "their homes are like oases to me in this yellow land."[137]

Plant prospectors acknowledged their dependence on European imperial power. Reporting from around Hankow on the Yangtze River, Meyer told of taking refuge in the foreign quarter after some toughs attacked him. Despite the uncertainty in the air, he decided he did not need to seek safety in Nagasaki because "there are twelve foreign warships in the harbor and many more along the coast. . . . The last time 100 rowdies were killed here by the foreigners and they got a pretty good lesson. Whenever I come in contact with Chinese I tell them to be very quiet with the foreigners for the next time they would smash China."[138] The defeat of the Russians in the Russo-Japanese War dispirited Meyer, for it shook up the power relations he relied on in his travels: "As you know, the Chinese consider us as rather uncivilized and especially after this ever-to-be-regretted war between the best branch of the yellow and the poorest of the white race, they have lost considerable respect for us. When I walk through the streets like here in Kaiyuan, they even call me nicknames and laugh and sneer."[139]

As the reverberations of the Japanese victory reveal, Meyer and other prospectors were able to search for plant material developed over the millennia by indigenous people because of their privileged status as white Westerners. They gathered even more specimens from colonial agents, traders, and missionaries and, in the independent republics of Latin America, from Spanish-speaking officials. Meyer obtained Siberian tree and shrub seeds from the head forester of the Imperial Russian Domains and still more seeds of "economic plants" from a Russian government agronomist.[140] Many of the agricultural schools and botanical collections that he and his colleagues benefited from were colonial institutions. "Wherever the British settle, they seem to create a public garden of some kind, and Karachi was no exception," noted Fairchild.[141]

Bioprospectors did not have to travel to colonies to access imperial collections, for the metropolitan botanical collections started in the eighteenth century offered choice pickings, too. Along with stocking public collections such as the Royal Gardens at Kew, Europeans turned private gardens and fields into experimental plots, from whence U.S. prospectors could procure promising plants.[142] Though native to Mesoamerica, the tomato varieties cultivated in the Midwest can be traced back mainly to England.[143] To acquire Turkestani, Uzbeki, Afghan, Chinese, and Korean seeds thought to be climatically suitable for the Midwest, bioprospectors in search of a shortcut scoured western Russia.[144]

Imperial infrastructures facilitated transport as well as acquisition. "Economic plants" journeyed to the United States the same way that bioprospectors had traveled to them: on imperial steamship routes. When the United States did not have parcel-post agreements with specific countries, bioprospectors routed some specimens through a dispatch agent in London and others from China through Siberia by the Russian postal service.[145]

Bioprospectors might write of their "philosophy of a free

exchange of plant varieties between the different nations of the world," but they knew full well that these exchanges were uneven. The only true exchanges that Fairchild noted were the ones he established with other white men, such as the missionaries he met at Canton Christian College. Such exchanges did contain the possibility of enhancing agricultural production in South China, but only through the enhancement of missionaries' influence.[146] Tellingly, the European and U.S. botanists who mined Latin America for plants directed their publications to North Atlantic scientific audiences, not to farmers or scientists in Latin America.[147] The Americans who curated plants from around the tropics in a new nursery on the outskirts of Manila published their catalog in English, the language of the U.S. occupation.[148]

The connections that U.S. plant prospectors forged with European imperial agents stand out in even starker relief when contrasted with their relations to the people who had actually developed the plants they sought. Collectors in metropolitan centers looked down on European peasants and they disdained non-Western agriculturalists as lowlier still.[149] Their rare acknowledgments of non-Western expertise reveal unabashed surprise: "As I learned a little Malay," wrote Fairchild, "I was astonished when chatting with the Javanese, Sundanese, and Madurese working in the garden to realize their knowledge of the plants."[150] Regarding farmworkers as mere menials, prospectors credited place, rather than people, for producing plants of value. In praising North China as "a veritable Klondyke of vegetable gold," Meyer made it seem as if the land alone had produced the nuggets he sought.[151] If anyone deserved to profit from this Klondyke, it was the prospector. "The whole world is mine!" exulted Meyer from the field in China.[152] And from Manchuria: "I, here in my solitudes, love to call myself a builder of an empire."[153]

That empire extended to Champaign, where prior to World War I, about five hundred farmers had begun to plant soy from Japan for hay, seed, silage, hogging down, lambing down, and green forage. As early as 1902, a student essayist at the University of Illinois was urging soy as a "profitable ration" for hogs, as a protein-rich adjunct to corn. Within a generation, central Illinois had become a biculture commodity zone, its miles of corn checkered by soy.[154]

NORTH ATLANTIC CROSSINGS

The selective affinities grafted onto genetic importations fit into the larger politics of scientific agriculture. Along with serving as a means for self-advancement, scientific agriculture can be seen as a kind of alliance for progress that brought agricultural competitors together in opposition to the dread common enemy, hunger. Though potentially a universal alliance, scientific agriculture knit some farmers together more closely than others. It stitched the fortunes of midwestern farmers to those of northern Europe in particular, for despite the kinds of disparaging reports that Dunlap sometimes sent, midwestern farmers generally regarded Europe as the place to turn for the latest, most scientific practice.

On occasion, their search for best practice took midwestern agricultural experts farther afield. The Wisconsin professor Franklin H. King traveled to Korea, China, and Japan to study farming methods, believing these countries to be the only ones "where self-maintaining systems of agriculture have ever been developed." In his resulting book, *Farmers of Forty Centuries* (which he lectured on at the University of Illinois), King insisted that East Asian farmers' seemingly "crude and unprogressive" methods were "by no means unscientific."[155] Professor O. H. Peabody also spread knowledge of Japanese farming methods among the farmers of Champaign County through extension lectures derived from his three-year posting to the Royal Agricultural College in Japan.[156] Following a trip to Hong

Kong, Burma, Singapore, and India, Congressman McKinley offered thoughts on farming in a newspaper interview: "the American farmer has a great deal to learn from the Chinese farmer in regard to the careful cultivation of the soil. In some of our states in America . . . the crop supply has diminished after a cultivation of fifty years; while in China I find that as high as three crops a year are in some instances raised and gathered from land which has been farmed for about 3,000 years."[157]

Such attention to East Asia was more the exception than the rule, however, especially before the twentieth century. More commonly, midwestern farmers regarded Europe as the place to turn to for model scientific practice. In 1898, the *Illinois Agriculturist* identified Germany, Belgium, and England as particular leaders in scientific farming.[158] These nations reportedly had embraced scientific practices from necessity, as relative land shortages and earlier industrialization had made increased yields imperative for agricultural self-sufficiency.[159] Scientific agriculturalists insisted that if the United States were to follow Europe in its population growth and industrial development, it, too, would need to invest in scientific agriculture to ensure short-term profits and long-term survival.

Enticing readers with prospects of European-style advancement, U.S. agricultural publications relayed European agricultural discoveries.[160] Readers of the *Illinois Farmer* discovered not only that parasitic mushrooms could trigger bovine abortions, but also that the Belgian *Annals of Veterinary Medicine* had first printed these findings.[161] The *Illinois Agriculturist* kept readers up to date on German experimental stations' ration guides for dairy cows.[162] In addition to learning about cutting-edge European practices through academic channels, midwestern farmers learned about them from their immigrant neighbors who had studied agriculture—and related fields such as chemistry, botany, and veterinary arts—prior to leaving for America.[163]

The search for the most advanced agricultural knowledge led a select group of midwestern farmers to study agricultural science in Europe.[164] These travelers included one of the founders of the Illinois Industrial University, Willard C. Flagg, who had studied agriculture in Württemberg. His papers on agricultural education contain notes on *Agronomie* (agriculture), *Feldbau* (productive land culture), *Blattfrüchte* (leaf fruit), and *Ölgewächse* (oil plants).[165]

More than just knowledge came from Europe: the very structures of knowledge creation and dissemination had European inflections. The Illinois State Agricultural Society, founded in 1853, can be fit into a longer genealogy of such organizations, traceable back to the Highland Society of Scotland, instituted in 1784, and the Royal Agricultural Society of England, established in 1837. The founding of land-grant colleges likewise owes a debt to European agricultural education. Citing the 350 agricultural schools in Europe as of 1851 (three royal academies of agriculture in Prussia alone), the Illinois State Agricultural Society became an early supporter of comparable schools in the United States.[166] As the executive committee of the Illinois State Agricultural Society put the case: "We have not one state school of agriculture in the whole Union! . . . While in Great Britain and on the continent of Europe there is no lack of them."[167] "Why should not we profit by these examples?" asked the *Illinois Farmer* in reference to European agricultural schools.[168]

Heeding such pleas, the Illinois legislature petitioned Congress to grant land from the public domain for industrial universities.[169] Congress got the message. It passed the Morrill Act establishing the land-grant college system in 1862.[170] The Illinois Industrial University (which changed its name to the University of Illinois in 1885) was one of the outcomes of this act. Upon its founding in 1867 it consisted of four colleges: Agriculture, Engineering, Natural Science, and Literature.[171] Into the 1880s, more than half its students came from farms.[172] Illinois faculty reached even more farmers through their agricultural extension programs. Inspired by European models, these programs and related experiment stations strove to publicize the "researches of this country and of Europe in the line of agriculture."[173]

Scientific agriculturalists in the United States did not copy European plans word for word. Eugene Davenport, an early dean of the Agricultural College at the University of Illinois, critiqued the exclusively technical nature of leading European programs. Yet his admiration for the ways that European institutions pursued scientific discovery and education affected the way he structured his program, starting with the blueprints.[174] For his college's farm buildings, Davenport chose modern English architecture.[175] Faced with the task of furnishing one of these buildings, agronomy professor Cyril G. Hopkins wrote to his contacts at the agricultural research station in Rothamsted, England. Could the researchers there send photographs of themselves "which we could have enlarged and placed in suitable frames and hung upon our walls"? He also solicited a painting "for the ladies' parlor of our Agricultural Building," promising that such a painting would be "held in the possession of the University of Illinois as a sacred trust." Though proud of the new Agricultural Building, and the future research and education it portended, Hopkins hoped to visibly commemorate its debt to England, and, indeed, to increase that debt through soliciting gifts of symbolic value.[176]

NODES OF EXCHANGE

It did not take long for agricultural universities to become nodal points of informational exchange. In 1877, just a decade after its founding, Illinois trumpeted its "large collection of the best works, both of Europe and America, on all branches of Husbandry, and the best Agricultural Periodicals from both continents." As titles such as *Agronomische Zeitung* (agronomic newspaper) and *Annales de*

Pomologie Belge et Étrangère (annals of Belgian and foreign pomology) reveal, many of the journals trickling in were written in German and French—so many so that Hopkins told prospective students that they should have a reading knowledge of German to study for a master's degree and of French as well for the PhD.[177] For handy reference, Hopkins kept books such as *Die Rationelle Dungung* (rational manuring) and *La Question Des Engrais* (the fertilizer question) in his office.[178]

To supplement his library of printed works, Hopkins developed a library of seeds. As an armchair bioprospector, he wrote the Toronto seed purveyor William Rennie for Canada field peas and Black Tartarian, Siberian, and Danish White oats.[179] He ordered New Zealand seed oats from a Minnesota company and Chinese Poor Land Corn from a grower in Centralia, Illinois.[180] From Burpee & Co. he ordered White Dutch Clover, Japanese Buckwheat, Australian Salt Bush, and Hungarian Millet.[181] He procured some of his Klein Wanzleben sugar beet seeds from a grower in Nebraska, from whom he also requested the pamphlet "A Visit to Klein Wanzleben," about the German village where the seeds had originated.[182] In search of more seeds to test, he ordered "a very good stock" of Braun's Elite Klein Wanzlebener direct from Germany.[183]

Although seeds, like publications, frequently arrived through the kinds of straightforward orders that Hopkins placed, they also reached Illinois faculty through social networks.[184] Hopkins worked hard to build such relationships: "I have read with very much interest an abstract of your address, 'Das Nährstoff-Kapital west-deutcher Böden . . .'" (the nutrient capital of west German soil), he wrote to a would-be colleague in Bonn. "I shall be very much pleased to have a complete copy of this publication." Then a further request: "I wish to ask also if it would be possible to have my name put upon your permanent mailing list . . . In return, I shall be very glad to put your name upon our mailing list so that all of the bulletins which are issued by the

170

University of Illinois Agricultural Experiment Station will be sent to you as they are published."[185]

Illinois faculty members developed relationships through face-to-face meetings as well as correspondence. Professor George Espy Morrow traveled to Europe in 1879 to visit the Royal and Highland Agricultural Shows.[186] Parasitic fungi expert Thomas Jonathan Burrill held fellowships in several European organizations.[187] In 1903, Hopkins apologized for delays in answering the mail, saying in justification that the instructor in farm mechanics was traveling in Europe and his assistant was traveling in Canada.[188]

Travel begat more travel. Seasoned agronauts brought colleagues along on subsequent trips and offered valuable advice to associates who did not know where to begin.[189] Hopkins offered the following counsel: "I believe that you would find the University of Halle or the University of Göttingen the best place for the study of practical and scientific agriculture in Germany, but, unless you are quite familiar with the German language, it would probably be of greater value to you to go to the Durham school of Science or to the Agricultural College at Redding, England."[190] Other seasoned travelers proffered names. Professor Louis H. Smith, an expert in crop production, recommended visits to Prof. von Seelhorst at Göttingen, Prof. Schneidewindt at the Experiment Field at Lauchstedt, Prof. Ramey at Bonn, and Prof. Früworth at Vienna. Smith knew at least some of these scholars personally. "If you go to Halle, I would advise you to call on Prof. F. Wohltmann, who is in charge of the Agricultural Institute . . . It was my privilege to sit under Prof. Wohltmann's lectures for some time, and also to take a part of my final examinations under him, so that probably he will recall me if you mention my name."[191]

The networking carried on in Champaign as well as in Europe. From its early days, the College of Agriculture brought in experts from outside the United States. Some of these experts came to fill faculty positions, including animal husbandry professor W. J. Kennedy, a

Canadian who had studied at the Ontario Agricultural College in Guelph, Dr. Heinrich J. Detmers, a graduate of Berlin's Royal Veterinary College, and Donald McIntosh, a graduate of the Toronto Veterinary College.[192] The German army was able to draft "bacteriological" expert Professor Otto Rahn when he visited Prussia in 1914 because he had grown up there.[193]

Foreign-born agronomists also came for shorter terms. Celebrated scientists such as Dr. E. von Tschermak of the University of Vienna and Dr. Ruemecker of the University of Breslau visited the College of Agriculture while on U.S. tours.[194] Canadians cropped up so frequently in university-sponsored farmers' institutes that they hardly seemed foreign.[195] Their insider status contrasted with that of the Mexican agricultural expert señor Zeferino Dominguez. A prominent landowner, Dominguez had traveled in the United States before the Mexican Revolution, studying midwestern methods of corn raising.[196] During the Revolution, he fell into trouble with the dictatorial president, Victoriano Huerta, and landed in jail. According to the *Urbana Courier*, "All of his scientific manuscripts which were written in Mexican were destroyed." Thirty years of exhaustive research aimed at aiding Mexican corn growers, gone. In 1916, he escaped from prison and fled to the United States. And then a glorious surprise: he discovered translations of his work in San Antonio. At Davenport's invitation, Dominguez spoke at the University of Illinois, showing five reels of pictures on corn raising in the United States and Mexico.[197]

All these investigations and talks and library collections may not seem to be anything extraordinary—that is, after all, what we expect professors and universities to do and enable—but they counter perceptions of midwestern farms as far from the beaten path and of midwestern farmers as guarded against all rivals. In their classrooms, publications, tours, and lectures, scientific agriculturalists exchanged information with considerable commercial value. They did so not only with farmers from Iowa and Michigan, but also with those from other nations, in a cross-border alliance against hunger.

PREPPING FOR THE RACE WAR

Scientific agriculturalists often depicted their alliance as being above politics insofar as it aimed to benefit humanity. Food for all meant peace, not war.[198] Since agriculture provided the foundation of civilization, the source of the comfort, happiness, and even existence of "nearly the whole earth's population," then advances in agriculture would benefit humankind.[199] As the *Breeders' Gazette* phrased the matter: "Upon the prosperity of agriculture all human progress is predicated."[200] With such thoughts in mind, a Nova Scotian speaker at the Illinois Farmers' Institute invoked the "unity and fellowship throughout the entire farming brotherhood."[201]

But the "entire farming brotherhood" encompassed by scientific farming did not include all farmers. Indeed, proponents of scientific agriculture believed that agricultural practice revealed civilizational hierarchies. Following the Mexican-American War, the *Prairie Farmer* claimed that the people of Mexico had fought "just about as well as they plowed, and cultivated"—in other words, not well. Their fields corresponded with their arms. This was more than a coincidence; it evinced a law—that a nation would not advance in civilization much beyond the condition of its agriculture.[202] The corollary to the law was implicit: better farming meant greater strength, as demonstrated by military power.

The conviction that agriculture served as a prime benchmark for development maintained its hold as the nineteenth century progressed. Agricultural reports near the end of the century insisted that scientifically minded Anglo-Saxons had taken the lead in agricultural progress, with the "Latin races of Southern Europe" progressing more slowly and Russia lagging further behind.[203] The rest of the world rarely surpassed the output of Russian serfs, as seen in the case of the Indian ryots who purportedly clung to antiquated methods, like heathens to their false religion.[204]

Given the role of agriculture in marking difference and its importance to the exercise of power, scientific agriculture did not stand as aloof from politics as references to human progress implied. Benevolent though an alliance against hunger might appear, in practice it often meant allying with imperial powers and on occasion directly with their colonial agents. Embracing the project of imperial uplift, Hopkins corresponded with the Hope Botanical Gardens in Jamaica and the imperial commissioner of agriculture in Barbados.[205] Illinois hosted visitors—such as Bob Bartholomew, an American agricultural missionary in India—who spoke on colonial agronomy.[206] By adding publications such as "Fertilizing Sugar Cane in the Hawaiian Islands" to its growing library collections, the College of Agriculture prepped Illinois students for careers in the tropics.[207] With their scientific credentials and networks to back them up, Illinois agronauts could join in the great work of plantation management in distant, white-dominated, ecologically different colonies.

An earlier generation of historians would have labeled the ties that scientific agriculture fostered as *international;* more recent scholarship would suggest the word *transnational,* since the relationships were not state to state. Both these terms suggest the horizontal relationships of commensurate players, on the fairly level field of independent nations. Recognizing the vertical roots of agricultural expertise suggests that *transimperial* may be a better description for these types of alliances. Though centered in the North Atlantic, the alliances forged through scientific agriculture stretched from Tasmania to Barbados and Hawai'i. For all their pretensions of universality, scientific agriculturalists networked along imperial circuits, in ways that benefited alliance partners more than the "colored" laborers who cut the cane.

Among those who expounded on the political stakes of agricultural alliances was the College of Agriculture dean, Eugene Davenport. Writing against the backdrop of Malthusian concerns, Davenport insisted that agriculture would determine "the final supremacy of races."[208] He elaborated on these convictions in a 1902 speech, one of a number on the topic: "The stubborn fact is, that mankind as a whole has never yet learned how to get enough to eat; that those people who have grown careless of their food supply have somehow dwindled and disappeared from off the earth; and that those who have possessed themselves of good land and have made the most of it have in some way prospered and have gradually possessed themselves of a large share of the earth."[209] Davenport believed that farmers were smack in the center of global struggles for dominance, struggles that over the *longue durée* would determine the fate of mankind. Without food, there would be no nation, or civilization, or race, and without farmers, no food.

According to Davenport, the day of racial destiny was coming ever closer to hand. "There is to be, in the very near future, a struggle for land and the food it will produce, such as the world has never yet beheld. He who knows where and how to look can see it coming." Evidence for this coming could be found in "the African activity among western European nations" and European investments in Latin America.[210] Illinois might seem to be far from these struggles, but it, too, was at risk. If the "human animal" persisted in doubling "his" numbers every twenty-five years, within a hundred years the United States would hold 1.2 billion people, a hundred million of them in Illinois. The dread prospect of race suicide would not result from a failure in the birth rate—as those who wanted white women to bear more children foretold—but from farmers' inability to keep up with population growth.[211]

In the past, the United States had coped with population pressures through expansion. Driven by the same racial imperatives as their ancient Aryan forebears and contemporary adventurers in Africa, white Americans had moved ever westward, "preferring the conquest of inferior peoples to the more difficult problem of a permanent agriculture."[212] But now there was no more proximate land to be had. "We have been great pioneers," pronounced Davenport, "but our pilgrimage is over . . . We cannot as before move on."[213] The Europeans might be fighting for Africa, but "for us there are no more 'new worlds.'"[214] True, a few "wanderers" had gone to Hawaiʻi and the Philippines, but these islands could hold only a fringe. "We are done with moving," wrote Davenport. "It is here we rest. It is here if anywhere that we shall work out our racial destiny and that future will depend in the last analysis upon our food supply."[215]

With no more moves on the horizon, would Illinois follow the path of once great civilizations like Carthage, Egypt, Palestine, Babylon, India, and China, all of which had failed to feed their people?[216] Davenport thought not, due to scientific agriculture. In the short term, sharing information with market value might nick at the competitive advantages earned through scientific breakthroughs. But in the longer run, an alliance of agriculturalists would forestall the horror of an all-out race war. And if, despite the best efforts to avoid it, that race war ever came, the scientific agriculturalists who heeded Davenport's words could hope that their web of contacts and exchanges would at least place American farmers and their northern European associates together on the well-fed winning side.

AMERICAN EMPIRE

Their transimperial alliance building does not mean that people such as Davenport had no particular commitments to American power. To the contrary, Davenport construed agricultural alliances as a means to advance American empire. Born in a log cabin in Michigan in

1856, this son of settler colonists graduated from the Michigan Agricultural College (now Michigan State University). After several years working the family farm alongside his father, he returned to his alma mater as a professor.[217]

Davenport's life took an unexpected turn in 1891, when Louis Queroz came to Michigan from Brazil in search of a man to establish an agricultural college in Piracicaba (in the state of São Paulo). Relying on his English-speaking wife as his translator, Queroz beseeched Davenport to found a "Leetle Lansing" in his country. Davenport demurred. Queroz offered Davenport $6,000, three times his current salary. That did it. Davenport said he would go for a year, even though Michigan said there would be no job waiting for him upon his return.[218]

Eugene Davenport and his wife, Emma, found Brazil to be a land of wonders. "It was a land of coffee, cotton, cane and cattle," reported Eugene. He characterized most of the laborers as "negroes." The farmers fattened their hogs on sugarcane; they butchered their cattle in the cooler hours of the evening, knowing that whatever beef had not been sold by six the next morning would have to be destroyed. The people subsisted largely on black beans and rice. Distanced from most of their neighbors by gulfs of race, class, and language, the Davenports socialized with elites such as the Querozes, with fellow U.S. citizens, and with expatriates from Ireland, Spain, and Germany. They returned from their outings to a house full of chickens, kept inside to combat roaches.[219]

With the help of his interpreters—the first a Dane, the second from Switzerland—Davenport set to work. His initial task was to build a house for the *presidente* of the college and to design the campus. The larger goal was more daunting: to spread the principles of scientific agriculture. The surrounding political context made his later institution-building struggles in Illinois seem like a cinch. "Revolution was the order of the day," recalled Davenport after the fact. In subsequent letters to colleagues in England, Davenport also complained about the "indolence of the people": their mental makeup, refusal to learn, and lack of honesty and moral perception.[220] When the promised funding from the state of São Paulo did not materialize, the Davenports packed their bags.

Rather than return to the United States straightaway, they traveled first to England. There they visited the famous agricultural station at Rothamsted. They arrived at a moment of great excitement—the researchers there had just solved the mystery of fixing nitrogen in the soil. Just as exciting for the Davenports was the warm welcome they received. They were thrilled to see the inside workings of the oldest agricultural station in the world and to talk farming with its leading figures.[221]

If Davenport had been a source of scientific knowledge in Brazil, his time in England reminded him that he was still on the periphery of scientific agriculture circuits. Following his arrival in Illinois, he wrote deferential letters to his esteemed Rothamsted contacts, thanking them again for their kindnesses and telling them that his students were studying their experiments closely, regarding them as a model. When his students ventured "a little publication," he solicited a few lines of encouragement to be included therein.[222] But even as Davenport played the part of a postcolonial supplicant, he set to work building an empire of his own.

As dean of the College of Agriculture, Davenport attracted students from fifteen countries to come to Illinois to study. A 1909 report mentioned agriculture students from China, Japan, India, Norway, Argentina, Brazil, Mexico, and the Philippines.[223] These students tended to come from privileged backgrounds, as seen in the example of George M. Yankovsky, of Vladivostok, Eastern Siberia. Yankovsky wanted to learn "improved methods of farming" to increase production on his family's land—amounting to 21,800 acres—bordering the Japan Sea. Given that Vladivostok had been founded as a far outpost of the Russian Empire only in 1860, Yank-ovsky struggled with the same issues as the settler colonists of Illinois—how to establish profitable commodity production on newly acquired land.[224]

Davenport praised these recruits for bringing to the university "a rich variety of agricultural practices from other parts of the country and the world."[225] In making such claims, he may have had a student like Camili R. Lopez in mind. Born and raised in Mexico, Lopez had studied two years in Spain, two years in Alabama, and one year at Notre Dame before coming to the University of Illinois to complete his undergraduate work. True to Davenport's claims, Lopez brought agricultural expertise to Illinois, which he shared in an article on coffee growing that he published as a student.[226]

Local business leaders agreed with Davenport's claims that foreign students could serve as a resource. The Chamber of Commerce invited students from Chile, Brazil, Peru, Mexico, Cuba, Canada, China, India, Turkey, and several European countries to speak on ways to reach prospective customers in those lands.[227] In addition to speaking about markets, the students provided tips on investment opportunities. In 1920, J. J. Mirasol, a graduate student in agronomy from the Philippines, spoke of the small proportion of the land under cultivation and the opportunities that afforded.[228]

Yet despite claims that foreign students should be regarded as resources, they had come as students, not teachers. They did not hail from places known to be at the forefront of scientific agriculture. Whereas the faculty in the College of Agriculture turned to Europe for the latest lab equipment, it imported "old agriculture implements" from Mexico for "museum specimens."[229] In a reference letter for S. Sinha, who had come to Illinois to study agriculture "as it can be applied to the development of his native country," his faculty adviser made no mention of the knowledge he had brought with him. Instead, he commented on Sinha's earnestness, energy, and industry.

The herbarium specimens, bulletins, and lantern views that Sinha would bring to his new post had all been collected in Illinois.[230]

Davenport's efforts to educate students such as Mirasol and Sinha fit with the larger politics of colonial uplift through agricultural education. Dean C. Worcester captured some of these politics in his 1914 account of the U.S. occupation of the Philippines. This book, which drew on Worcester's extensive experience as the secretary of the interior of the Philippine Islands and member of the Philippine Commission, featured a photograph of a cornfield as the frontispiece. In front of the corn, next to a U.S. educational official, stood the vanquished revolutionary leader turned U.S. collaborator General Emilio Aguinaldo. The caption described the corn as having been raised by Emilio Aguinaldo, Jr., for a school contest. According to the caption, the scene typified "the peace, prosperity, and enlightenment which have been brought about in the Philippine Islands under American rule."[231]

The *Illinois Agriculturist*, published by the Agricultural Club of the university, celebrated the college's role in imperial uplift in a piece on Antonio Bautista, an agronomy student in the class of 1906. In the interview, Bautista played the part of the appreciative colonial subject: "the outlook for agriculture in the Philippines seems dependent upon the efforts of the United States government, which is doing its best to make the people understand some of the more important principles of crop production." In reviewing the importance of agriculture for colonial incorporation, Bautista did not condemn U.S. efforts, but he did not really praise them either. "By the establishment of experiment stations, the founding of schools of agriculture in different parts of the Archipelago, the introduction of seeds of plants from the temperate zone, and the survey of soils, the resources of the islands are becoming known." Known to whom, he did not say. But he did say who would benefit: agricultural development would make the islands "a most valuable addition" to the United States.[232]

Dean Conant Worcester, the secretary of the interior of the U.S.-occupied
Philippine Islands, began his account of the Philippines with this photograph
of the defeated nationalist Emilio Aguinaldo alongside the U.S. colonial official
in charge of education. This field of cultivated corn—grown by Aguinaldo's
son for a school contest —signaled the important role of scientific
agriculture in the U.S. program of "benevolent uplift."

*Dean C. Worcester, The Philippines Past and Present, vol. 1
(New York: Macmillan, 1914), frontispiece.*

Near the end of his career, Davenport recalled some of the international students he had taught, starting with three "high class
Hindu" students in agriculture: Rathindranath Tagore, Nagrenda-
nath Gangulee, and Santosh Chandra Majumdar. Then there was
Saleem Raji Farah, a Nazareth Palestinian. "An Arabian but a fine
student. We exchange cards every Christmas." The recollections go
on: Diego Aguilar Sevilla, "A Philippino who after doing excellent
work with us at Illinois was found to be a leper." Yoshifusa Iida, "Japanese, now in Imperial College of Agriculture in Tokyo." George
John Bouyoucos, "Greek student specializing in soils."[233]
With the exception of Bouyoucos, from the bankrupt nation of

Greece, these were not European students. With the exception of Iida, they hailed from the imperial periphery. Their decision to study scientific agriculture in Illinois put Davenport in an imperial center. Having adopted the structures of scientific agriculture from the European powers, his agricultural college could elevate its own position by propagating those structures elsewhere—including in Europe. Davenport's greatest coup came with Don Demetrius Andronescu, minister of agriculture in Romania. He came to Illinois with a government commission to study corn. According to Davenport, the minister was humbled by what he saw: "In my country I am Professeur. Here (holding his head down) I am estudiente; I am as nothing."[234]

Davenport gloried in the humbled professeur's decision to stay and take a doctorate in Illinois, for it seemed to prove that Illinois had moved to the center of a wide set of relationships from what had once been the western edge. The teacher-student nature of these relationships encapsulated Davenport's ambitions for leadership in the expansive world of scientific agriculture. As these reminiscences show, Davenport was more empire builder at heart than isolationist. He dreamt not only of bombarding the world with Illinois corn but also of transforming the world along Illinois lines. Rather than fencing his cornfields off from the world, he aimed to make his college a seedbed for a new strain of empire.

GLOBAL GOVERNANCE

In hoping to make Illinois an imperial center, Davenport had a lot in common with his congressman. Along with crisscrossing the Atlantic, McKinley circled the globe three times and went on several Caribbean cruises.[235] He traveled for pleasure, for business, and to gather information that would help him make policy. Crowds numbering in the hundreds turned out to hear him speak when he returned.[236]

The Secretary Taft Party Aboard the Manchuria

Congressman William B. McKinley of Illinois (not to be confused with President William McKinley) en route to the Philippines with a congressional party conducted by Secretary of War William Howard Taft. McKinley is seated third from the right in the second row. First daughter Alice Roosevelt is seated fourth from the left in the front row and Taft stands directly behind her.

"The Secretary Taft Party Aboard the Manchuria," The Urbana Courier, *Oct. 3, 1905.*

In 1905, McKinley sailed to the Philippines as the guest of the secretary of war, in a party that included other members of Congress and first daughter Alice Roosevelt. Based on the party's sightseeing trips, McKinley considered himself an expert on the islands. Speaking at the First M. E. Church in Urbana, he reported that the soil of the Philippines was fertile, but graft was rampant and "the farmer pays the freight." Disregarding the Filipino independence efforts that had led to a full-blown war against the United States from 1899 to 1902 and a guerrilla war thereafter, McKinley praised U.S. efforts "to educate the people, so that they will know their rights and will have the ability to assert them." Comparing the Filipinos to children, he commended the U.S. regime's efforts to "instill into them some ambition to work and to save."[237]

The *Urbana Courier*, which praised McKinley's portrayal of the islands for its faithfulness and accuracy, wrote that "Mr. McKinley showed that there is no standard of right among the people he visited, for they conscientiously do things which would shock our conception of at least the proprieties." McKinley's claims that "American civilization must act as a lever to raise them to a higher and nobler plane of living" seemed indisputable. To top things off, the congressman known as an advocate of peace told his audience that since many tribes in the Philippines were "far from conquered," a "tremendous work" lay ahead for the American people. After an hour and thirty-five minutes, he stopped, but according to the *Courier*, his audience, so "glad that their lots have been cast in this God-blessed land," was "anxious to hear more."[238]

Two years later, the newspapers covered another trip, a month-long cruise around the Caribbean with the Speaker of the House, Joseph Cannon. On this expedition, the party stopped in Venezuela and "all the important points in the West Indies," including Puerto Rico. The group also spent a few days looking over the work on the Panama Canal, "and all seemed pleased with what they saw there."[239]

Just as scientific agricultural alliances did not quite extend to colonial plantation laborers, the principles of the Inter-Parliamentary Union seemed less universal from a Caribbean cruise. Just as for Davenport, McKinley's solidarities with Europe undergirded hierarchies elsewhere. The more he hobnobbed with parliamentarians from European empires, the greater his own will to rule. His two sets of commitments—to interparliamentary cooperation and U.S. expansion in the Caribbean and Pacific—were not as oppositional as they might seem. As with the scientific agriculturalists in his district, the former helped prep the ground for the latter.

ANTICOLONIAL STRUGGLES

Not everybody in Champaign County shared these northward-skewing alliance politics and southward-skewing imperialist impulses. Important veins of dissent can be found in the county's sanctum of scientific agriculture, the College of Agriculture at the University of Illinois. Yet even these countervailing currents do not give credence to the isolationist legend. To the contrary, they reveal a different kind of alliance politics sprouting among the grass roots, planted by foreign students such as Rathindranath Tagore.

Born into a landed family in British-ruled Bengal, Tagore was educated by an English tutor who had a bungalow in his family's compound.[240] Believing that a technical education would enable him to benefit his people as well as himself, Tagore set forth from Bengal in 1906 at age eighteen to study agriculture in the United States. After chugging from port to port along the Malay coast and China, the ship docked in Japan in the midst of the celebrations for the Japanese victory in the Russo-Japanese War. Being "fresh from the political battleground of the Swadeshi movement" (a movement to oppose British rule through the use of Indian-made goods), Tagore and the other students in his party joined in the celebrations. "We looked upon every Japanese as a hero," Tagore later recalled, for the Japanese had killed the specter of the "foreign devil" in the Orient. The Japanese they encountered treated them in turn with respect, offering up their tram seats when they realized that the travelers had come from the land of Buddha's birth.[241]

Denied passage on a ship to California, ostensibly due to an eye disease, Tagore sought advice from a Japanese specialist. The doctor laughed aloud, telling Tagore that he did not have an eye problem, he had a mathematics problem—anti-Asian quotas. The doctor had a mathematical prescription, premised on the realization that U.S.

officials could not tell one Indian from another, especially when charged with evaluating so many. He counseled Tagore to return day after day until the odds came up in his favor and he was included in the 10 percent quota. Tagore followed his advice and was approved on his third try.[242]

He traveled to the United States in steerage, squished in a cabin with five tiers of bunks. "But," he wrote, "the worst torture that we suffered during our seventeen days' passage across the Pacific was the type of American men and women . . . whom we had to associate with"—the type that pulled knives if a Japanese man dared take their seat. This seething ship pulled into harbor the day after the San Francisco earthquake and fire. Shocked by the discovery that their intended destination, the University of California at Berkeley, had just been "raised [sic] to the dust," Tagore and his comrades boarded a train for Chicago. Somebody, Tagore later wrote, had told them "that there was a good agricultural college at the University of Illinois. Chicago being in the state of Illinois, we thought the University could not be too far from it." In Chicago, they asked a telegraph girl to wire the YMCA to have someone meet them in the Champaign station. Nobody came. Several days later, they figured out why: the operator had never heard of a place called India, so she had typed *Indiana* instead. The YMCA agent had seen no need to go to the station to meet students from a neighboring state.[243]

Though appreciative of the technical aspects of his education, Tagore was unimpressed by the social components. "The United States in 1906 cared little for the outside world. We found in our university just a handful of foreign students, mostly from the Philippines and Mexico. All of them felt ill at ease—their American fellow students being either too inquisitive or too indifferent." Somewhere between the curiosity and the aloofness, Tagore found something he characterized as small-mindedness: "The general outlook of the students—I can speak only for the period I was there—was

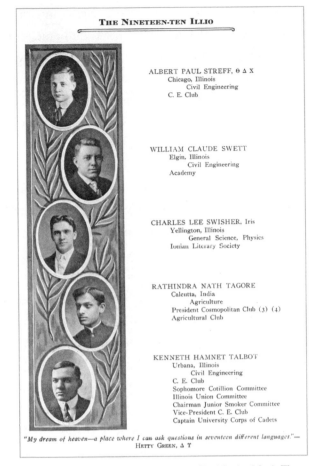

THE NINETEEN-TEN ILLIO

ALBERT PAUL STREFF, Θ Δ Χ
Chicago, Illinois
Civil Engineering
C. E. Club

WILLIAM CLAUDE SWETT
Elgin, Illinois
Civil Engineering
Academy

CHARLES LEE SWISHER, Iris
Yellington, Illinois
General Science, Physics
Ionian Literary Society

RATHINDRA NATH TAGORE
Calcutta, India
Agriculture
President Cosmopolitan Club (3) (4)
Agricultural Club

KENNETH HAMNET TALBOT
Urbana, Illinois
Civil Engineering
C. E. Club
Sophomore Cotillion Committee
Illinois Union Committee
Chairman Junior Smoker Committee
Vice-President C. E. Club
Captain University Corps of Cadets

"My dream of heaven—a place where I can ask questions in seventeen different languages." —
HETTY GREEN, Δ Υ

Rathindranath Tagore, identified as Rathindra Nath Tagore
of Calcutta, India, alongside four in-state University of Illinois
classmates, in this page from the 1910 yearbook.

*Nathan L. Goodspeed, ed., The Illio (Urbana, Ill.: University of Illinois, Urbana-Champaign,
1910), np. Image courtesy of the University of Illinois, Urbana-Champaign Archives.*

extremely narrow and parochial in this Middle West University. There was nothing of the freedom of mind and spirit of adventure which is generally associated with Universities. It seems strange to us that the University should be considered a congenial ground for the propaganda of missionaries and even evangelists."[244]

Tagore eventually found a friend in Romance language instructor

Dr. Arthur R. Seymour, who served as an adviser to foreign students. Seymour's wife, Mayce, welcomed him into their home with "motherly affection, when I was most in need of it." He later recalled his time with her as "a bright spot in an otherwise dull existence during the three years of my stay at this mid-West University." Tagore read translations of Indian classics to Mayce as she washed the dishes, and she in turn read him poems that she composed.[245]

Some of the dynamics of this relationship can be deduced from Mayce's recollections of her first encounter with Tagore and his classmate Santosh C. Majumdar at a Unitarian reception: "Hindus! India! Up to that moment our idea of India was of a land as remote and visionary as a province of the moon. A word in the dictionary, a tinted area on the map, caste, elephants, tigers, typhoons. And here before us, like planetary visitants from the skies, were young men to whom all that was home! 'Are you really from India,' I asked. And in merry tones they assured us that they had come from that fabulous land." Mayce's warmth and enthusiasm were such that Tagore corresponded with the Seymours for fifty years following his student days.[246]

Much as he valued the Seymours' friendship, Tagore continued to search for a place to call home. Finally, with the Seymours' encouragement, he and some fellow students created that place by founding a Cosmopolitan Club. As a Filipino member, H. Silvilla, told the *Urbana Courier*, the club aimed to furnish a means whereby students from different countries could get acquainted with one another. Members hoped to dispel prejudice and advance peace.[247] By 1907, forty students had joined, hailing from Mexico, Spain, Argentina, India, Germany, China, Japan, Scotland, the Philippines, and the United States. When Tagore became president two years later, membership had risen to fifty, representing twenty-one countries.[248]

In their meetings, the Cosmopolitans taught each other about their languages, costumes, foods, and other "peculiarities."[249] Club members also hosted national nights, open to the public, with musical performances, stereopticon slides, and presentations on topics such as "The Hindu Life."[250] Although the students had, as the campus paper put it, "come to America to learn our ways," they turned the tables in their public entertainments, assuming the position of teachers.[251] If the campus newspaper saw this as political, it did not mind: "May the cordial relations between Cosmopolitans and Americans continue for all time to come."[252]

The politics of amity and celebration soon shaded into a different kind of politics. In some of the club's public events, members spoke on matters such as reforms in China.[253] The club's secretary, Sudhindra Bose, denounced British oppression of India. He blamed the prevalence of famine in South Asia not on backward agricultural methods but on the "burdensome taxes which are imposed by government." "The people are awaking," said Bose, "and a free India is not a visionary thing; now it is a practical thing."[254]

Students from the U.S.-occupied Philippines also weighed in on colonial politics. After presenting "a true picture of life and customs in the Philippine islands," the Filipino students in charge of one public event discussed "their country life and aspirations." In its announcement of the gathering, the student newspaper emphasized the value of such talks for colonial administration: "Since these islands are under the control of the American flag, an exceptional opportunity will be offered to learn more of our insular interests."[255] But the reference to "country life and aspirations" suggests a different kind of politics, more focused on national independence than on control by the American flag.

In a later meeting, Vicente Ylanzan Orosa spoke to all those who had ever asked him "Do you eat dog?" and "Do you wear clothes?" To refute the assumption of savagery, he pointed out that the Philippine Islands had universities older than Harvard and Yale (and thus, implicitly, older than Illinois, too). Orosa told the would-be colonial agents in his audience that Filipinos wanted to be taught in their own tongue, "as we can never be made into [an] Americanized nation." His classmate, Angel Severo Arguelles, followed him with a talk on "Some Aspects of the Philippine Problem," making a "stirring appeal" for immediate self-government. "This is a vital problem," he said, "for on it depends the liberty of 8,000,000 souls and the preservation of the principle upon which the American nation rests, that government derives its just powers from the consent of the governed." The campus paper noted that the students in the audience liked the musical numbers and native dances. It did not say what these students thought of Arguelles's statement that if Americans were true to their ideals, "your sense of justice must tell you that immediate self-government is the only solution of the Philippine problem."[256]

Cosmopolitan Club members' connective efforts soon took them beyond the Illinois campus. Starting in 1907, the club sent delegates to the National Association of Cosmopolitan Clubs.[257] As these connections grew, the Illinois student newspaper began reporting on other chapters' doings, covering events such as a debate between Turkish and German students over Germany's interference in Turkish affairs.[258] Adopting as its motto "above all nations is humanity," the national association proclaimed its desire for world peace.[259]

THE COSMOPOLITANS' PEACE BURLESQUE

Tagore relinquished his presidency upon completion of his studies in 1909. He traveled home via Britain, where he, like Davenport before him, visited the famous experiment station at Rothamsted. Not finding "much opportunity in England at that time to improve my knowledge of agricultural science," he headed on to Germany, where he attended lectures at the University of Göttingen for a term.[260]

Following his return to India, Tagore settled on family land. Although he described himself as leading "the life of a country gentleman," he patterned himself as much after the scientific agriculturalists he had known in Illinois as those he had met at Rothamsted. He imported maize, clover, and alfalfa seeds from the United States and cutting-edge implements to cultivate them. He fitted up a laboratory to test the soil and relished U.S. visitors' assertions that he had created a genuinely successful American farm. Davenport would have been proud. And yet Tagore felt that something was missing in this life. Taking stock of himself, he discovered "a raw youth fresh from a technical college in the corn-belt of the United States, with no pretensions whatever to aesthetic sensibility." Concluding that the "pragmatic philosophy of America" had stifled a sense of higher purpose, he left his farm for his father's school and its "atmosphere of literary and artistic endeavor."[261]

That apparently did not sit well either, because in 1912, Tagore returned to Illinois, via London, to earn his doctorate.

Back in Champaign, Tagore rejoined the Cosmopolitan Club. It had been busy in his absence, hosting more national nights and events backdropped by flags from all nations.[262] It had also continued its political activities. In 1909, the National Association of Cosmopolitan Clubs had associated itself with the Corda Fratres student movement in Europe. Through that affiliation, the U.S. Cosmopolitan Clubs sent a delegate to a peace conference at The Hague.[263] In keeping with its associates' emphasis on peace and arbitration, the Illinois chapter toasted "international spirit" and "international comity" at its meetings.[264] But that was just a starting point. The national association president, George W. Nasmyth, insisted that "the cosmopolitan ideal is far larger than the peace ideal. Long after peace has been assured through international arbitration agreements and the reference of all disputes to the world's court of justice, there will remain work for cosmopolitanism to do in bringing about a better understanding and a deeper sympathy between man and man." The movement's work would not be done until there was, on the whole earth, only one country.[265]

As Nasmyth's statement suggests, the Cosmopolitan movement sought something more radical than the European meetings and North Atlantic arbitration treaties that Congressman McKinley fancied. It sought a more universal understanding and justice. In pursuit of these ends, the Illinois club joined with the Political Refugee Defense League of Chicago to oppose the deportation of Christian Rudowitz, a political activist wanted by the Russian tsar for his pro-democracy activism.[266] It subsequently put on a "peace burlesque" that poked fun at the kinds of politics that McKinley held so dear. In the opening scene, ambassadors representing the United States, Russia, Japan, Turkey, England, Mexico, China, Germany, and the Philippines proceeded to the Palace of Peace at The Hague. Eye-catching in "shining uniforms and brilliant robes of state," the delegates competed for the most bombastic declarations of worldwide peace.

Yet all this talk rang hollow. The conference expelled the Japanese delegate (and only the Japanese delegate) for his bellicosity, and it refused to let a suffragette speak. Near the end of the burlesque, the delegates debated the selection of an international capital. After much discussion and wrangling, they chose their current home, the town of Urbana.[267] The performers and audience alike appear to have laughed at that joke, as they had at the earlier nonsense. The next day's headlines applauded the event: "World's Peace Burlesque True Cosmopolitan Success." And yet, for all the lighthearted humor, the burlesque had a sharp edge. The performers had mocked some of the noblest pretensions of the Western statesmen who spoke of peace while building empires. If Urbana was really an international capital, at the true forefront of peace, it was because the students on the stage had made it so.

Although Tagore renewed his association with the Cosmopolitan Club, he did not move into its newly established residence because his wife and father had accompanied him this time round. The younger Tagore was happy to see his father settle into writing, believing that this would keep him from wanting to leave. "But," he wrote, "the backwaters of a provincial place like Urbana could hardly be expected to hold him long." His father, feeling restless, began traveling around the United States, giving talks. Instead of studying agriculture, Rathindranath Tagore spent most of his time arranging for these travels. Unable to make progress toward his degree, he gave up his postgraduate studies, "not that I regretted it much." The Tagores returned to India via England in September 1913.[268]

The Tagores may have regarded Champaign as a kind of backwater, emblematic of the worst kinds of provincialism, but they did not refer to the Midwest as isolationist. Given their own multiple comings and goings and cosmopolitan clubbing, that would have made no sense. The provincialism they found in east-central Illinois was not that of an isolationist capital, but rather, the kind found in an imperial metropole. The Tagores knew Champaign as a hotbed of missionary aspirations and colonial commitments and as a hub for anticolonial activists. They had seen these two sets of politics come together in Cosmopolitan Club talks. The Tagores may have deplored the small-mindedness they encountered, but they also valued the world-class education in scientific agriculture that Illinois could offer. And they could take tremendous pride in Champaign's status as a center of culture. It had, after all, nourished a Nobel Prize winner: Tagore's father, Rabindranath Tagore, who won the award for literature in 1913.[269]

The Nobel laureate returned to the United States two more

times. On a 1916 trip, he spoke to a large audience at the University of Illinois on the need for humanity to catch up with advances made in science. That, he argued, meant embracing the anticolonial cause. After speaking of the harm done to India by European imperialism, Tagore alluded to the global politics of the Great War. Agreeing with the Cosmopolitans' one-world aspirations, he claimed that "the principle of barbarism is isolation and of civilization unity."[270] The world's people—*all* the world's people—must join together as select groups of scientists had.

On the eve of his return to India, the prizewinning poet offered a prophecy, reported in Urbana papers. "On your soil will be the greatest nation in the world."[271] The nature of that greatness and whether it would emerge because of or in spite of the cosmopolitan seeds that his son had helped plant, Rabindranath Tagore did not say.

ISOLATIONISM AS SEEN FROM THE GRASS ROOTS

Approaching the matter of isolationism from a grassroots perspective reveals that even the heartlanders thought to exemplify isolationist leanings were never autarchic, unilateralist, or even neutral. To the contrary, although they sometimes claimed to be local, they regarded isolation as a liability, strove to develop cross-border alliances, and were deeply committed to empire, meaning both to a European-dominated global system and to their own nation's increasing influence and power. Their cultivation of cross-border relationships prepared the field for the security commitments of the century to come. Yet they were also, in themselves, meaningful forms of engagement with the world. This history of the supposedly most isolated of places in the supposedly most isolated of times can thus help us appreciate the extent to which the denigratory label "isolationist" has

deflected attention from a long history of selectively collaborative relationships aimed at comparative advantage and collective security.
And if we dig deeper than the attachments of those thought to exemplify isolationist politics, unearthing the political commitments of the
colonial subjects who called the Midwest home, we find the subter-
ranean entanglements of liberation politics.

Countless aspirations shaped midwesterners' engagements with
the world on the eve of the American century, but to be isolated was
not one of them. The very idea was a slur, and they were connected
enough to know it.

ARCHIVAL TRACES

We are just like the birds

Urbana Courier, 1911: "Bird vendors with a large assortment of canaries and parrots made the rounds of the business district today."[1]

Urbana Courier, 1912: The Ringling Brothers will have a parade in town, with camels, elephants, llamas, deer, and zebras "hitched to an Oriental throne car in which rides an Indian potentate with his retinue." The nearly three hundred men, women, and children who will appear in the parade "have been gathered from the nations of Europe and Asia and from the remotest savage lands."[2]

Urbana Courier, 1915: From an F. K. Robeson department store advertisement: "Notions. Ostrich Feather Boas. Large line of these new novelties."[3]

Urbana Courier, 1917: "Few towns the size of Homer can boast of having as many soldiers in the army, in its various branches as does this little city. Twenty-one men have answered the call to duty thus far."[4]

Urbana Courier, 1917: "A. Santiago, a Filipino student of the University of Illinois, . . . is awaiting a passport to return to his island home after having been informed of the illness of his mother. He received a cablegram two weeks ago telling him she was ill . . . No passport was required of him when he came to the United States four years ago and he was surprised to learn of its necessity now. Mr. Santiago was a member of Battery A of the University of Illinois but was rejected for border warfare in Texas on account of his [being] underweight."[5]

Urbana Courier, 1918: "Edward Brown, F. L. S. of London England will speak on the vital importance of the hen and her products in winning the war . . . He is not only in a position to point out clearly the necessity of poultry and egg production as a source of food supply, but he can state from personal experience how it feels to be in an air raid, for on sixteen different occasions he witnessed aerial invasions on London by German planes."[6]

Urbana Courier, 1918: Writing from the front, Sergeant H. G. Smith reported on the view from the telephone wires that he was stringing to a lookout post. The Germans below had put up their hands, begging to be captured, but they "died from heart failure, with the help of machinegun bullets."[7]

Urbana Courier, 1918: "The big monarch butterfly, who lives on milkweed, migrates like the birds. . . . One naturalist describes a shower of butterflies that he saw off the South American coast. It extended as far as the eye could reach and even with a telescope it was not possible to find where there were no butterflies."[8]

Urbana Courier, 1920: "Bird fanciers would find it interesting to visit the Renner undertaking parlors and watch the collection of birds . . . The Australian Paraquet and the Brunnette Java Rice bird each lost its mate a short time ago and have mated with each other."[9]

Dallas Morning News, 1977: "We are just like the birds. In the fall we come back. That's the way it's meant to be. Now they'll throw you in jail for shooting a migratory bird. But they won't do nothing when a person practices prejudice and discrimination against a migratory human being."—Margaret Whitewater, a Kickapoo woman living under the International Bridge at Eagle Pass, Texas[10]

FLOWNOVER STATES

The View from the Middle of Everything

FLYOVER COUNTRY

Flyover country. These two words convey a world of meaning. They imply that the American heartland is best regarded through an airplane window; there is really no reason to land, for the rural Midwest is a provincial wasteland in contrast to the cosmopolitan coasts. Cross-country fliers have a lock on mobility; the people below are stuck on the ground, too rooted to soar through the sky. Flyover jokes fit with theories that link heightened perspectives to power. Like the colonial explorers, mapmakers, and military scouts who have positioned themselves on high to capture the landscapes below, fliers-over can grasp entire communities from above. And this is what they see: a land of squares, nothing down there but Flatville.[11] By mixing the cachet derived from mobility with the power of elevated place, the flyover slur packs a double whammy on the status enhancement front.

Yet despite such efforts to claim power and privilege, the view from the air misses much of what is happening on the ground. Even the massive engineering works that undergird the wet prairie evade detection from the air, buried as they are beneath those rectangular fields. The fliers-over who turn Flatville into an insult fail to recognize it as a real place. They overlook the possibility that the people down there might have their own views on how they fit into the world, that they might regard airspace from their own particular perspectives. Such a possibility would demand a different term: flownover states, perhaps.

But how to capture the perspective from the ground, over a century ago? How can we get at the worldviews of people who rarely sat down to write about themselves in the larger scheme of things? What archival collection would even begin to disclose bottom-up geographical imaginings?

The Illinois Digital Newspaper Collection, for starters. Developed by librarians at the University of Illinois, this collection contains well over a million pages of Illinois newspaper content. Among the papers scanned into this database is the *Urbana Daily Courier*, digitized from 1903 forward. Some issues are missing and some of the originals from which the scans were made are torn or otherwise faulty. Speckled text, uneven inking, worn type, variant spellings, line breaks, fading—it's enough to keep a search engine up at night. And yet, keyword after keyword, the *Courier* yields glimmerings into aerial consciousness and so much more besides. It is both a source in itself and a generous provider of leads.[12] The more I delved into it, the more it appeared that coastal areas had no edge on continental centers when it came to connectivity by air. Airspace has offered the heartland direct connections across long and otherwise insurmountable distances.

FLATVILLE

Flatville arose from the muck. Like the wet prairie more generally, its flatness inhibited drainage, contributing to swampy conditions. The firmer lands that had once supported buffalo enabled the first settler colonists to graze cattle, but the land in and around Champaign County was so boggy that in 1840, the area had fewer than two residents per square mile.[13] In contrast to the arid West, where farmers struggled to bring more water to land, in the sodden prairies, farmers worked hard to remove the water from the land so as to enable the cultivation of crops. Health concerns factored into the drying campaign as well. Long before the discovery that mosquitoes carried malaria and yellow fever, the association between swampland and ague added to the desire to pull the plug on wetlands—including about 8.3 million acres in Illinois, or about a quarter of the state.[14]

Thus began the still ongoing engineering project that has turned the wet prairies into some of the most productive agricultural land in the world. Step one was to dismantle the existing engineering works—the beaver dams that blocked the "smaller water-courses." In his 1905 history of Champaign, J. O. Cunningham reported that at first the beavers repaired their dams. But as hunters reduced their numbers, the animals abandoned their homes. The near total eradication of beavers culminated in grand euphemism: "finally the last of this interesting and intelligent animal, with his contemporary, the wild Indian, moved westward."[15]

Step two was to introduce new engineering works. To dry the "inundated lands" that were underwater for part of the year, farmers experimented with mole ditching (dragging a plow that would carve out a tunnel) and, when that proved unsuccessful, using cattle (up to forty head together) to drag larger ditching apparatuses.[16] An even more laborious method was to dig drainage ditches that fed into creeks and streams.[17] This backbreaking work slowly began to yield results. Whereas a traveler who rode through Champaign County in 1873 characterized half the cornfields as being underwater, residents could have pointed out that the other half were not.[18] By 1885, Illinois farmers were beginning to use steam-powered dredging machines that opened canals and cleared the course of creeks. They also straightened these creeks, to speed the flow of water from their fields.[19]

In addition to creating lateral drainage through ditching, farmers with sodden land invested in underdrainage. They dug up their fields to lay clay tiles beneath, four to five feet deep. Typically baked into tubular shapes, these tiles, when laid end to end, fast-tracked the groundwater that seeped into them out of the fields. Reporting from Champaign in 1863, M. L. Dunlap claimed that tile draining had not caught on yet in the county, since the heavy tiles had to be hauled in from afar.[20] By the 1880s, however, county maps show about twenty evenly distributed tile factories, which enabled their widespread adoption.[21]

The expertise for these engineering projects came from Europe, either directly or via more eastern states such as New York, Ohio, and Indiana. Nineteenth-century agricultural writings often credited England—and particularly its eastern fen dwellers—for pioneering modern drainage techniques.[22] They also acknowledged the roles of other European countries—among them France, Scotland, Holland, Belgium, Germany, and Italy—in producing drainage engineers "of no mean ability and reputation."[23] Along with attributing drainage techniques to European inventiveness, agricultural writings cast better drainage as a means of laying the groundwork for European-style agriculture, with European markets in mind. All that digging in the mud and dirt might suggest an entrenchment in place, but settler colonists dug trenches to move themselves closer to Europe.

Knowledge of drainage techniques arrived on immigrant ships as

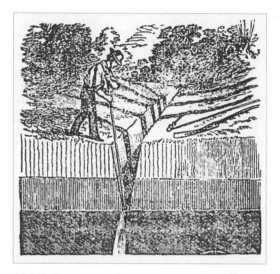

This cutaway illustration shows how to lay clay drainage pipes. After entering through perforations or gaps between the tiles, the water flows briskly downhill, where the farmer has presumably sunk a drainage ditch. Although it is difficult to decipher in the image, the accompanying text describes the tool on the ground to the right as an Irish spade.

Henry F. French, Farm Drainage: The Principles, Processes, and Effects of Draining Land *(New York: Orange Judd and Co., 1859), 245.*

Drainage tiles being emptied from an Indiana kiln.

The Drainage Journal *22 (Aug. 1900), 219.*

well as through published writings and scientific networks. The Frisian people, living on the coast of the North Sea (in what is now the Netherlands and abutting part of northwest Germany), had centuries of experience draining marshlands. From 1845 to 1895, over forty thousand eastern Frisians, known as Ostfrieslanders, came to the United States, fleeing hunger, poverty, and military conscription by the expanding Prussian state. They also came in search of opportunity. After landing in New York, Baltimore, or New Orleans, many headed for the Midwest, where they purchased the cheapest land on the market: marshy land, that is.

In the mid-1860s, when land had become scarce around their first footholds, newcomers and those with dim inheritance prospects looked around Illinois for more. Champaign County caught their eye. Although settler-colonists already owned title to most of the county, there were still bargain-rate swamplands for sale in the north. Surveying reports describing the area as "level wet prairie unfit for cultivation" had dissuaded other would-be settlers, but the Ostfrieslanders saw opportunities below the pond waters. At least there was no need for dikes to keep the ocean out. The earliest settlers moved in by night, so as to drive their wagons on the thinning March ice. They soon commenced the arduous process of digging ditches, laying tile, and sloping their fields.[24]

Within a few years, the Ostfrieslanders of Champaign had established a German-language school and a Lutheran church—led for a while by a Brazilian-born and German-educated pastor. The settlements that sprang up around these institutions became known as Flatville. In the early summers, scummy green water surrounded the settlements' houses. The mosquitoes that bred in this soup had free access to their human blood supply through screenless windows. After a rain, it was possible to row from some of these houses five miles into the country—not a promising start.[25] Yet by World War I, Flatville contained some of the most valuable agricultural land in the state.[26] It had taken a generation, but swampland that had once sold for 25 cents an acre was fetching $250.[27] Its increasingly flush farmers soon won a reputation for generosity in their annual missions fund-raiser.[28]

Draining produced a remarkable transformation beyond the "swamps" and "sloughs" of places like Flatville to "higher prairie lands" as well.[29] By 1900, Illinois farmers had drained hundreds of thousands of acres. By 1930, the state had over ten thousand miles of drainage ditches and a hundred fifty thousand miles of tile: enough ditching, observed one commentator, to stretch from Chicago to Outer Mongolia, enough tiling to circle the earth six times.[30] The noted success of Illinois farmers in turning wetlands into productive farms helps explain why real estate agents hawked the agricultural potential of Louisiana cypress swamps in the columns of Illinois newspapers.[31] If anybody could turn a bayou into a cornfield, farmers from places like Flatville seemed to have the requisite know-how.

Despite measurable successes in separating land from water, the rivulets from the past lingered, as seen in the experience of a tenant farmer in northern Illinois. According to the *Courier*, he awoke one morning to discover his entire field of corn stripped bare. Every leaf and stalk on the twenty acres had disappeared. From nine inches' growth to nothing, overnight. There was no evidence of hogs or cattle, no broken fences or evidence of trespass. The farmer complained to the landowner, who consulted with Stephen Forbes, the state entomologist and a professor at the University of Illinois. Knowing that the ground had been recently claimed from the swamp, Forbes surmised that insects were not to blame. He had the farmer replant the field and set a watch. Sure enough, his suspicions were justified. One night, by the thousands, scritch-scratching crayfish emerged from the soil to scour the field again.[32]

Separating land from water enabled more than agricultural production—it also enabled transportation. Whereas eighteenth-century accounts of the Champaign area describe horses being mired in bogs, so deep that they caused injury, at times "environed on all sides with morasses" so thick as to forbid an advance, by the end of the nineteenth century drained fields supported firmer roads.[33] Railroads, too, benefited from drier land. As they channeled more water into ditches, streams, and rivers, Illinois farmers pressed for improved river routes between the Gulf of Mexico and Lake Michigan. Having removed the water from their fields, they sought more removal of land from water, so as to float their crops "northward to the British possessions, south to the Gulf, to Mexico, the West Indies, and south America; and west to the Pacific; and on until the West becomes the East."[34]

By the dawn of the twentieth century, the farmers of Illinois had wrung substantial connectivity from the land and wrested even more from water. Yet their roads and rivers continued to mean fixed routes. Air, in contrast, seemed qualitatively different in its infinite openness. Well before long-range bombers, intercontinental missiles, radar installations, and fallout heightened aerial consciousness in the Midwest and the overlapping big sky country of the Great Plains, air brought to mind a vast array of long-distance connections.[35] If land and water were the matter of daily toil and set ways, air offered astounding imaginative flights.

FROM WIRED TO WIRELESS ACCESS

Starting in the 1850s, the latest news arrived in Champaign through the air. Following right behind railroad construction, using the railroad right-of-way, high-strung telegraph wires connected Champaign to a network of overhead wires and underwater cables extending as far as Russia and India. Although stories of communications infrastructure often suggest a progression from local to national to global integration, the advent of the telegraph plugged the receiver in Champaign into an increasingly global network without many proximate nodes. As telegraph wires unreeled farther into Latin America and along the routes of empire to Africa and the antipodes, the entire web thickened, with single lines turning into what one history of Champaign described as "the large array of wires which now darken the rights of way."[36] Though far too expensive for routine correspondence, telegraph wires sped up emergency notices and urgent communications. They also revolutionized the gathering and transmission of news. No longer dependent on the publications that arrived through the post, papers such as the *Urbana Courier* got their timeliest items from the press syndicates that pooled resources for wired reports.[37] Reveling in its new connectedness, the *Courier* attributed its coverage of breaking news to the means of transmission: the wire.[38]

The next breakthrough on the communications front, the telephone, also had an aerial dimension as seen from the ground in Champaign, since most of the wiring was strung from pole to pole. At the turn of the century, the Bell System competed with city and township exchanges in a high-speed race for customers.[39] By 1905, more than half the farms in the county occupied by owners and many run by tenants had telephone connections. Whereas the telegraph had connected Champaign to national and global networks simultaneously, the telephone started small, connecting users to neighbors, shops, and the doctor. Yet even from the start, the technology promised the longer-distance connections eventually delivered by the Bell System.[40]

The breakneck competition to erect a new aerial infrastructure led to a rapid proliferation of poles, some erected in advance of the required permits.[41] The pole that appeared one day in the middle of a driveway seemed to stand for the wiring frenzy.[42] And then there was the noise. The buzzing attracted the large brown woodpeckers known as flickers, which pecked at the poles as if insects were humming inside.[43]

In response to anxieties that too many young people were leaving the farm for the city, early telephone advertisements maintained that rural isolation was a thing of the past—that modern wiring had turned the tables, making the farm the place for "good social times."

"Getting Up a Party," The Prairie Farmer, *Dec. 26, 1907, 3.*

Telegraph and telephone poles were more than eyesores and buzzing nuisances, they were also threats to the tractors, cars, and horse teams that crashed into them. In 1903, white residents of Danville, one county to the east, purposefully turned a telephone pole into an instrument of death when they used it to lynch a black man.[44] The wires, too, meant danger, as evidenced by news of fires, "nearly electrocuted" children, linemen who died on the job, injuries befalling people clearing storm wreckage, livestock fatalities, and the harm done to low-flying birds, sometimes "cut almost in two by the force with which they struck the wire."[45] With six hundred poles up and more under way, the frustrated residents of the village of Tolono passed a tax—a pole tax, as it were—to slow the plague, but they never attempted to stop it altogether.[46]

Next came the wireless. The first reports of wireless communications that surfaced in the *Courier* focused on the lifesaving possibilities of maritime messages.[47] Though prairie residents had little need for maritime rescue, they soon embraced the new technology. By 1911, the county had its first wireless plant, installed by the manager of the Urbana Western Union office and a university student in electrical engineering who had been an operator for the United Wireless Company on the Great Lakes.[48] Wireless stations soon spread to other places in the county. Before the year was out, the village of St. Joseph had four wireless telegraph stations, and the *Courier* noted that "the boys are getting a great deal of pleasure out of them."[49]

The appeal of wireless stretched beyond those in the communications business to amateurs. Trendspotters might have noted that something was afoot as early as 1910, the year the *Courier* ran a story of Frank Scroggins's "Thrilling Adventure." While experimenting with a wireless telegraph appliance on the roof of his family's house, Scroggins slipped on the wet shingles and fell two stories to the ground. Remarkably, he escaped injury.[50] It seems likely that his parents forbade him from climbing on the roof, because the next time his wireless efforts made the news, it was for falling from a tree.[51]

By 1915, Champaign teenagers did not have to risk their necks to establish radio connections, because the Champaign High School had established a radio club, "with first class equipment."[52] An amateur wireless club in Urbana soon followed, divided into a group that could take or send eight words a minute and a probationary class.[53]

World War I put the brakes on amateur radio. After the United States entered into the war, the "radio inspector in Chicago" issued an order closing all interior wireless stations for its duration. The shutdown did more than clear the channels for official communication, it also reduced the danger of espionage, a significant concern in the Midwest due to its ethnic German residents. After alerting readers to the closing, the *Courier* ran another article warning resisters that the "chief government spy hunter in the middle west" would send federal agents to demolish the plants with axes. As a further goad to compliance, the *Courier* reported that Boy Scouts were ferreting out illegal radios.[54]

After the war, radio fans collected their confiscated instruments and reassembled their sets. The Urbana High School inaugurated an evening wireless telegraphy class in 1919, open to operators from the sixth grade onward. The Champaign County Radio Association also geared up in 1919, with a whites-only membership rule.[55] Catering to the growing market for wireless supplies, the Swartz Electric Shop advertised that it could equip entire outfits.[56] The Co-op Store competed for market share by building a model station and hiring a "wireless man" to offer suggestions.[57]

Although the number of radio operators was not particularly large (in 1917, the War Department had solicited twenty-four wireless operators from the twin cities of Champaign and Urbana to join the naval reserve), the public footprint was larger.[58] Electrical engineering shows at the university offered the public a chance to see radio equipment.[59] The state weather bureau in Springfield turned to amateur wireless operators to help it disseminate forecasts.[60] Wireless exhibits could be found at the county fair.[61] The *Courier* further spread wireless awareness through various articles on wireless telegraphy.[62] This coverage included tips for do-it-yourselfers, such as using barbed wire to wind the tuners for long-distance communication.[63]

To operate a wireless meant to participate in a world of astounding connectivity, a world in which messages flashed from San Francisco to Japan in 1911; from Australia to Germany by 1917.[64] Though such records remained out of reach for the amateurs of Champaign, the wireless opened up expansive channels. The operators of the Western Union wire picked up messages from Galveston, Guantánamo, Havana, Norfolk, New York City, and Boston; from the Atlantic coast and occasionally from a transatlantic liner.[65] When the Astronomy Department of the University of Illinois set up its wireless apparatus, the listeners told of messages from Atlantic liners, Great Lakes steamships, and Key West.[66] The "boys" of the Champaign High School radio club intercepted messages from along the Atlantic seaboard, Newfoundland to Florida.[67]

These operators could communicate directly with people beyond the thousand-mile mark, indeed, beyond the boundaries of the nation. For these early amateur radio operators, the point was not so much the contents of steamship chatter as the ability to access it. The point was connectivity itself. What else could explain the excitement over Winfield Davis's kite? Entered in a school contest, it received signals through a wire attached to the string.[68] Nobody seemed to care what the signals said, but the spectators cared a lot about getting them.

With the advent of the wireless, the air itself took on new meanings, as a place of boundless possibilities. The president of the Champaign County Old Settlers' Association conveyed this sense of the air when he spoke, in 1908, on the telegraph, telephone, and wireless telegraphy. Together, they had changed the world, making it a better place in which to live.[69] Thinking back on the pioneer settlement they had once known and forward to the new world on the horizon, the old-timers in his audience could take pride in having been part of a process that was moving Champaign from the edge of civilization to the thick of it, or, conversely, from the thickets to the cutting edge. If they could have seen over the horizon, a century beyond their own time, they would have glimpsed satellite-guided tractors, locating themselves to within a fraction of an inch, even as their drivers listened to the radio and fiddled with their cell phones.

CLIMATE CHANGES

In deciding whether to move to a strange new land, settler colonists thought a lot about geography, including questions of climate and weather. In the absence of other geographic texts, many of them turned to emigration guides. James P. Caird's *Prairie Farming in America* typifies the boosterish geographies of this genre. Tackling the question of climate, Caird admitted that Illinois might not be as "equable" as Britain. Like neighboring prairie states, it suffered from severe winters and hot summers. Such variation in temperature made it hard to locate Illinois in relation to England, with its more limited temperature range. Caird positioned Illinois as climatically southern, at least in comparison to the rival destination of Canada, when he alluded to the seasonal prevalence of ague and, more positively, to the relative absence of "many of the fatal complaints which are met with in colder latitudes." But in Caird's geography, Illinois was not strictly southern, for it lay in the temperate zone. And Illinois was moving north. As cultivation increased, the incidents of warm-weather fevers were declining, thereby leaving Illinois more equable (and English) than it had been prior to European settlement.[70]

Whereas emigration guides focused on the specificities of place—on categories and comparisons—settler geographies ventured into the matter of connective currents. Caird's contemporary Matthias Lane Dunlap knew what to expect climate-wise in Illinois, having established a successful orchard in Champaign. The questions that concerned him, when it came to prairie geography, were not so much "what" as "why."[71] Dunlap's efforts to advance farming led him to the weather, and his efforts to understand weather led him in search of its origins. That, in turn, led him to Africa.

In an essay from the 1850s, Dunlap drew on understandings of trade winds to explain the currents that coursed over his orchard. "When we cast our eyes over the maps of the *western world* and examine its air currents, we find the *trade winds* setting in from the coast of Africa, and passing west until they meet an impassable barrier, in the Andes or Cordillery range of mountains." These mountains channeled the "immense stream" of African air northward, to the Gulf of Mexico. From there, the African wind flowed east, "around the capes of Florida," and north, "up the delta of the Mississippi, whence it branches off like a fan up the various valleys and tributaries of this great water course."[72]

Having retained its African character in its long journey to the Gulf of Mexico, the hot wind began to dissipate in the Illinois area, as it mingled with cooler currents. For half the year, its lingering traces produced "a continual season of almost intertropical climate." But in the winter, the current from Africa withdrew. Without the "African simoon" to "check the accumulations of arctic cold," the freezing currents from the north swept down with unrestrained severity.[73] Uncontested, these northern winds claimed the region completely for themselves. Illinois might seem more tropical than temperate in the summer months, when hot and cold mingled together. But in the winter, it became fully arctic. Though the meeting place between African simoons and polar blasts, Dunlap's farm skewed north meteorologically, lying a little closer to the white snows of Canada than to the black field hands in the adjacent slave states.

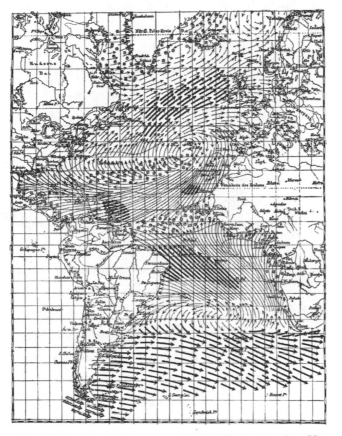

This mapping of Atlantic wind patterns, published in the *American Meteorological Journal* in 1893, echoes earlier mappings that attributed the hot, humid summers of the Midwest to seasonal winds from Africa.

William Morris Davis, "The General Winds of the Atlantic Ocean," The American Meteorological Journal 9 (March 1893), 476–88, unnumbered insert page.

LONG-RANGE FORECASTING

However useful in attracting more settlers and in conceptualizing their new home, writings on general weather patterns had little day-to-day utility. Climate may have been of ongoing theoretical interest, but for residents, a more pressing and perpetual meteorological matter was the forecast. For farmers, accurate weather predictions could mean the difference between profit or loss, abundance or dearth, and, on occasions such as freak freezes and sudden storms, the difference between life and death.

Before the advent of professional meteorology, people in particular places tried to figure out the weather by observing their surroundings. They came up with all kinds of guidelines, some noted by the *Courier*: if pigs pasturing in a field built a nest—expect a storm. "Rainbow at noon, rain very soon."[74] The ways that smoke rose and the ways that clouds streaked foretold some change in the weather "to the man whose eye has been trained to recognize the signs." The "peculiar actions of birds" especially merited watching.[75] When swallows flew low, wet weather could be expected, because that signaled a descent of insects from moist upper regions.[76] Long-distance fliers could also help with forecasts, since "they never venture far from home when bad weather is brewing."[77] All these methods of weather prediction relied on on-the-ground observations. All were relevant only to the surrounding area. And all were utterly inadequate to predicting how the weather would change. Did a red sunset augur clear weather or rain?[78] Each position had its steadfast proponents.

This uncertainty explains some of the appeal of the "weather prophets" who looked for distant signs and larger patterns. These weather predictors continued in the vein of astrological reports long found in farmers' almanacs. They based their reports on analyses of the moon and "star divinations" as well as on observations of animals and plants.[79] Citing the "astronomic outlook" and planetary energy, one popular prophet mentioned in the *Courier* offered forecasts one month out. Even more impressively, his methods enabled him to predict the weather for "the whole world over," barring "a compensating resultant of warring forces that we cannot now see."[80] Though not necessarily wrong in their predictions that the weather would change somehow somewhere, such weather prophets were not very helpfully right.[81]

Barometers provided a more reliable method for predictions, for rapid rises and falls indicated unsettled weather and storms. Yet the *Courier*'s instructions on how to use them suggest that they were not a common tool.[82] Furthermore, barometers were useful only for short-range forecasts. Like pigs and smoke and birds, they warned only of imminent changes. Farmers' ongoing search for accurate long-range forecasts made them a core constituency for meteorological science—so much so that the federal government moved meteorology from the U.S. Army Signal Service to the Department of Agriculture in 1890.

Professional meteorologists tackled the problem of weather prediction by figuring out the fundamental laws of physics that governed the weather, gathering observations, and networking so as to discover patterns as they unfolded in time and space.[83] The *Courier*'s coverage of these efforts underscored the value of imperial outposts, common procedures, and communications networks for long-term weather forecasting.[84] Readers could see the results for themselves, in the changing nature of weather coverage. Whereas weather reportage had once been pointillist and past tense—a matter of site-specific news reports on recent weather events—it broadened in the early years of the twentieth century to encompass the moving lines of fronts and waves with bearing on the future.[85] This way of seeing the weather was so novel that at least one Illinois horticulture society offered lessons in reading meteorological maps.[86]

As meteorological science advanced in the late nineteenth century, advice on predicting the weather shifted from guidance on watching birds to the need to heed the Signal Service. In 1906, the U.S. Weather Bureau issued forecasts thirty-six to forty-eight hours ahead.[87] By 1913, the bureau was able to issue forecasts a week in advance, by monitoring where the weather would come from.[88] Longer-range forecasting promoted geographical awareness, and not just in the pages of meteorological journals. Daily newspapers played a major role in relaying meteorologists' geographic analyses to large audiences.

Much of the *Courier*'s weather reporting positioned Champaign as a place where winds from the more western states passed through en route to the east.[89] This was, in part, an artifact of Weather Bureau politics. Although the Weather Bureau's mappings aimed at crop prediction lumped Illinois and neighboring states in with grain-growing areas in Canada, as a national agency, reporting to a national constituency, it squeezed most of its weather coverage into national maps, with not much more cross-border spillage than one would find in a preschooler's coloring book.[90] On the occasions when the lines extended far into the Pacific, they drew attention to the nation's expanding geographical reach. The *Courier* attributed better forecasts to the Weather Bureau's ability to track storms from the Philippines, Japan, Siberia, and Alaska that traveled to the Midwest on established paths, following particular timetables. "For example," ran one of its articles, "a storm coming from Siberia drifts eastward around the North Pole and reappears in Alaska. It should appear in Washington and Oregon in about two days, should get to the Great Lakes in six days and to the Atlantic coast in seven or eight days." However distant the U.S. colony in the Philippines might seem, airstreams placed it only a week away.[91]

THE POLITICS OF TORNADO MAPS

The sense of being poised between north-south weather wars and west-to-east winds climaxed in the coverage of what were coming to be the defining weather events of the Midwest: tornadoes. At first glance, much of the *Courier*'s tornado news had a local feel. Eyewitnesses reported watching the distinctive funnel clouds emerge in the air before them.[92] Spectators described tornadoes as cutting a short and narrow trail of devastation before dissolving into the surrounding thunderstorms. Accounts of the damage on the ground revealed horrifyingly concentrated damage.

In May of 1917, a tornado killed sixty-two people and maimed six hundred more after hitting the town of Mattoon, about thirty miles south of the Champaign county line. The papers reported a pig disemboweled by the wind; a telephone pole driven though a house. Within seconds, the compacted power of the funnel cloud had turned 120 blocks of cottages into a barren mass of debris.[93] Although it hurtled lumber, bits of furniture, and baby apparel into the surrounding countryside, those who watched it from the relative safety of Champaign, those who read about it in the Champaign papers, and the estimated two thousand sightseers from Champaign who flocked to the scene of desolation saw the tornado as specific to Mattoon.[94]

But in the ensuing days, as wires were restrung, news came in that the Mattoon tornado was one of several that had emerged from a storm that swept from Kansas to Indiana, going as far south as Alabama and as far north as Chicago.[95] This storm system, in turn, fit into a larger regional pattern. Although the *Courier* ran tornado reports from a broad smattering of places—from Mauritius to Russia, Arizona, Manitoba, and New Jersey—most of the tornado news that appeared in its pages covered an area stretching from Oklahoma to Ohio.[96] The *Courier* echoed the latest meteorological findings in characterizing tornadoes as a feature of the "middle west."[97] Positioned in the center of the nation, the tornado belt resembled a conveyor belt that connected the far West to the East.

Yet the tornado belt could be seen another way: as the kind of belt that separated top from bottom. More than just the place where the West turned into the East, the Midwest could be seen the way that Caird and Dunlap saw it: as the line between the North and the South. Plenty of weather coverage in the *Courier* brought such mappings to mind. Especially in the colder months, weather reports drew attention to aerial connections to the North. They traced the "excessive cold" of winter to the "British Northwest Territory," "the British Possessions north of Montana," and to a "great Polar atmospheric wave."[98] Warmer weather drew attention to the South, to phenomena like the Bermuda High, which prevented heated currents from leaving the continent for the ocean.[99] To explain the changes in the seasons, the *Courier* wrote of wind currents emanating from the Antarctic and the Arctic.[100] Reports on the cold fronts and blizzards that swept down from Canada and the heat waves and hurricanes that tore up the Ohio valley from the Gulf positioned Champaign at the point of encounter between the North and the South.[101]

The result was, in many cases, violent clashes. In contrast to Britain, which was comparatively temperate year-round, the skies above Illinois seemed at times to be in the midst of a "titanic war," with "heat invasions" jostling with Goth- and Vandal-like blizzards for dominance.[102] This vein of weather reportage reanimated the issue that had caught Dunlap's attention a generation earlier: Which side was Illinois on? Did Champaign skew more to the North or the South?

Through the early years of the twentieth century, tornadoes appeared to position the Midwest more toward the South, because of the company they kept. Until the teens, weather reporters did not always distinguish between hurricanes, cyclones, and tornadoes.[103] They sometimes used more than one of these terms to refer to a single weather event.[104] The weather coverage in the *Courier* fit into this larger pattern. It labeled a violent windstorm that reportedly plucked seven geese clean a *tornado* in the headline and a *cyclone* in the body of the article.[105] It affixed the word *cyclone* both to the tropical storms that devastated cities like Havana and the whirlwinds that wreaked damage closer by.[106] It labeled a windstorm that dismantled houses in Champaign a *hurricane* and then, further muddling things, "either the forerunner or the tail end of a tornado."[107]

By using the terms *hurricane, cyclone,* and *tornado* interchangeably, weather reports associated Illinois not only with U.S. states on the Gulf and Atlantic Coasts, but also with places like Jamaica, the Caymans, Costa Rica, Nicaragua, Cuba, and the Philippines—that is, with the tropical places featured in its warm-weather windstorm coverage.[108] It was not just the force of the wind that brought these tropical connections to mind, it was also what violent storms left in their wakes. On occasion, powerful windstorms blew in rare birds "from the swamps of the south."[109] They also left the kinds of disarray associated with more equatorial climes. One "full sized cyclone" reportedly made Urbana look "like an African jungle, so thickly did the broken trees fill the streets and yards."[110] Such coverage echoed an earlier tornado report of a storm that killed nineteen people, among them an infant tossed into a slough: "When we review what we have written it seems like a tale of the horrors of the terrible elemental commotions of the tropics."[111] These allusions to jungles and tropics positioned storm-tossed Illinois at the northern limit of the South.

Slowly and unevenly, however, advances in meteorology disassociated tornadoes from tropical storms.[112] By the teens, the *Courier* was associating hurricanes specifically with the East and West Indies.[113] It also began to distinguish between tornadoes and cyclones. Citing the U.S. Weather Bureau, a 1918 article defined cyclones as slower and less violent than tornadoes. They might provide the preconditions for tornadoes, but they were not to be mistaken for them.[114] The disaggregation of twisting windstorms took tornadoes out of the hurricane and cyclone zones, placing them smack in the center of the nation in a category of their own.

Seemingly the most local of storms—with their abrupt origins, concentrated power, and limited range—tornadoes became the signature weather events of the Midwest. And yet even as tornadoes began to define the region at the heart of the nation, the people on the ground realized that these fearsome vortexes, capable of sucking entire dwellings into their craws, did not originate in a vacuum. In redirecting the question that figured so largely in meteorological journals—why tornadoes?—to the more relevant question for its readers—why so many tornadoes *here?*—the *Courier* made it clear that the convergence of equatorial and polar currents was to blame.[115] Meteorologists might place the tornado belt in the middle of nationalist maps, but those who picked through the rubble situated themselves much as Dunlap had before: on the front lines of a boundless north-south weather war.[116]

SCOPING OUT THE SKIES

Rural people had compelling reasons other than weather to look to the sky. Before the United States tilted from rural to urban, hunting figured largely as a provisioning and leisure pursuit and birds figured largely in the chase. An 1837 book on the attractions of Illinois described the state's birdlife as an abundant source of food and feathers: "the ponds, lakes and rivers, during the spring and autumn, and during the migrating season of water-fowls, are literally covered with swans, pelicans, cranes, geese, brants, and ducks, of all the tribes and varieties. Many of these fowls rear their young on the islands and sandbars of the large rivers. In the autumn, multitudes of them are killed for their quills, feathers, and flesh."[117] Even as other objects of the hunt dwindled down to insignificance or disappeared altogether, birds offered the promise of abundant animal protein, there for the taking.

Hunters took nature up on the offer well before the first Europeans appeared on the scene. An archeological excavation of a Kickapoo village in Logan County, Illinois (about seventy miles to the west of Champaign), uncovered bones from fish, turtles, and mammals, and approximately thirty-four species of birds. The most important food bird for the Kickapoos in that village was the turkey, but the excavated refuse pits also yielded bones—some bearing butchering marks—from great blue herons, egrets, Canada geese, ducks, hooded mergansers, greater prairie chickens, woodcocks, sandpipers, passenger pigeons, hawks, woodpeckers, and a swallow-tailed kite. They also turned up bones from small passerine birds such as flycatchers, chickadees, wrens, kinglets, vireos, warblers, and buntings. Though possibly eaten, these birds seem more likely to have been killed for their feathers and skins.[118]

Following often literally in Native Americans' footsteps—on the paths they made through the prairie—the pioneers, too, hunted fowl. Some of their targets lived in the state year-round. Subject to constant assault, these nonmigratory game birds soon declined: the wild turkey, ruffed grouse, bobwhite, and prairie chicken all became increasingly rare.[119] The rapidity of the decline stemmed in part from their commodity value. A single U.S. express company reportedly exported fifty tons of midwestern prairie chickens in a year, helping to explain why the birds sold for as little in London as in Chicago. Along with smoked prairie chicken breasts, settler colonists sold thousands of prairie hen eggs to distant markets.[120]

As resident game birds struggled for their existence, hunters came to rely more on seasonal pickings. Ducks and geese were just the tip of the migratory V, for the category of game bird was a capacious one into the twentieth century. Among the migrating birds classed by the Department of Agriculture as game birds were swans, coots, plovers, surf birds, snipe, woodcocks, sandpipers, and curlews.[121] In contrast to year-round residents, migratory birds seemed relatively more impervious to overhunting. Spring after fall, the rivers and wet bottomlands of Illinois enticed birds to land. Pond-riddled and lakelike fields also attracted waterfowl, all the fatter and more delectable for the grain that they consumed. "Such ducks!" exclaimed a hunter,

Waterfowl and other wild birds had to contend not only with hunters, such as the ones in the foreground of this bucolic scene, but also with significant habitat loss over the course of the nineteenth century.

"Birds-eye view on the (1100 acre) farm of the late Milton Babb," History of Champaign County, Illinois *(Philadelphia: Brink, McDonough and Co., 1878), plate after 170.*

describing his 1890 haul. "Their skins ready to burst with fat." And so many of them, too: in swarms, not flocks, so plentiful that they could hardly be driven away.[122]

The *Courier* provided ample coverage of the hunt. It reported on the arrival of birds from their winter and summer havens and their presence on nearby ponds and puddles.[123] "Duck Shooting Is Good This Year," noted the *Courier* in the spring of 1913, as canvasbacks, mallards, bluebills, wood ducks, and green-winged teals began to alight.[124] In times of nearby scarcity, the *Courier* reported on expeditions to the Illinois and Mississippi Rivers, nearby counties, Indiana, "the wilds of the northwest," and hunting grounds as far as the Everglades.[125]

The popularity of such expeditions grew as the nearby haul declined. Even as Illinois hunters continued to celebrate good seasons and remarkable shoots, by the late nineteenth century, they no longer spoke of inexhaustible flocks, as they had in the 1860s.[126] Take three accounts from 1902. Whereas twenty-five years ago, a "fair shot with a good dog" could secure forty to fifty woodcocks in a day's hunt, only "ten percent of the former bag could now be obtained."[127] An Illinois heronry nearly three miles long and half a mile in width, with two to ten nests every tree: gone.[128] The flocks of wild pigeons so immense that their fall passage shadowed the earth for hours: likewise gone.[129]

Struggling to make sense of quiet skies, some hunters blamed migrations of the permanent kind. These mappings emerged from the discovery that English sparrows were following settler colonists across the continent and that European starlings were drafting a few years behind.[130] "Wherever European civilization has gone this pest bird has gone with it," complained the *Courier* of the sparrow.[131] The realization that these immigrant birds were heading west lent credence to claims that native birds were doing so as well. Hunters trying to explain how onetime shooting paradises had turned into wastelands in which a hunter could go for miles without finding any birds concluded that they had "somewhat changed their course of migration," that they had abandoned their "once tenanted breeding haunts in our Middle and Northern states, for the vast, undisturbed solitudes of the Northwest."[132]

Blame for the supposed westward exodus also fell on farmers, and not just for keeping pigs that ate the eggs of ground-nesting birds and large numbers of cats that crept around farmhouses, living by their wits. The press acknowledged that mowing, plowing, brush

By the early twentieth century, the open prairie that had once
offered diverse habitats for wildlife had been largely plowed
over and planted with corn and secondary crops.

Frank Elmer Wood, "A Study of the Mammals of Champaign County, Illinois,"
Journal of the Illinois State Laboratory of Natural History *8 (1908–10), plate 26.*

clearing, and tree chopping dislodged birds.[133] Retracing a visit to a
birding site in Illinois in 1883, twelve years after an earlier trip, ornithologist Robert Ridgway described the change as "almost beyond
belief"—the open prairie replaced by thriving farms, and no characteristic prairie birds to be found.[134] By 1912, Illinois bird counters
were reporting that cornfields had fewer birds of any kind than pastures did.[135]

And then there was the tiling and draining. After noting that "our
sloughs, swamps and marshes are being ditched and tiled," *The American Field* rued the implications for ducks.[136] Local histories and the
Courier also acknowledged that drainage dissuaded game birds.[137]
Even the *Drainage Journal* admitted the costs: "Drain the bogs, and
what can the woodcock do for a living? Reclaim all the wet lands . . .
but after that look in vain for snipe and duck."[138] This kind of

coverage suggested that hunting alone was not to blame for declining numbers—that some birds were decamping for wetter places. Rather than fully confront the specter of extermination, those who looked out on quiet landscapes imagined birds the ways they imagined Native Americans: as fading to the West. And if not to the West, then to the new "bird reservations" devised by conservationists.[139]

ECONOMIC ORNITHOLOGY

Not every decline in birdlife was lamented, for some of the hunting was exterminationist in intent. This component of the hunt stemmed from the perception of birds as agricultural pests. Bad birds were guilty of a variety of offenses. The bee martin had a reputation for visiting the apiary to suck the honey from bees. Another "pestilent fellow" was the fruit-tree-menacing sapsucker.[140] Although some farmers may have appreciated hawks and owls for keeping mice in check, chicken keepers regarded them as predators.[141] Grain growers had their own particular targets. The land baron Michael Sullivant reportedly hired a hundred gunners every fall to drive waterfowl from his vast array of cornfields in central Illinois.[142]

If any bird merited most-wanted status, it would have been the English sparrow. Antisparrow reports cited the work of Eleanor A. Ormerod, consulting entomologist to the Royal Agricultural Society of England, who found that sparrows drove off swallows and martins, thus permitting an increase in insects destructive to the garden and orchard. By her estimation, the bird caused over $3.85 million per annum in damages in England alone. And England was not the only place to suffer its depredations, for the sparrow's reputation as an agricultural pest reached from Bermuda and Cuba to Germany, Austria, Russia, India, Egypt, and Australia. By the 1880s, the U.S. commissioner of agriculture had joined the ranks of the antisparrow movement, describing the English sparrow as "a curse of such virulence that it ought to be systematically attacked and destroyed."[143] Chiming in to the outcry, the *Courier* said that whoever "first brought these birds to America . . . should have been court martialed and sent to the penitentiary for life."[144]

Such warnings resulted in bounties in Illinois and other states. They also resulted in heavy collateral damage, in many cases from an inability to distinguish sparrows from other small birds.[145] The Flatville twelve-year-old who made the newspapers after accidently killing his brother hints at the common and casual nature of such attempts: the boy had reached for his rifle to shoot a sparrow, and the hammer had caught on his sleeve.[146]

Efforts to kill birds for agricultural purposes gained some scientific justification from the rise of economic ornithology, devoted to evaluating the impact of birds on agriculture. Department of Agriculture reports on stomach and gizzard contents spurred on efforts to kill English sparrows by quantifying the damage they caused.[147] Yet such damning studies of bird guts were the exception. Overall, economic ornithology built a powerful case for protection. In so doing, it affirmed the claims of those who had long insisted on the importance of birds for insect control.

As early as the 1850s, bird-watchers advised Illinois farmers that although birds ate some seeds, they also ate insects.[148] In 1861, the *Illinois Farmer* urged prairie residents to plant trees, "to induce the robin and other birds to breed their young, to keep down the numerous insects that would otherwise destroy the crops."[149] In 1864, the *Illinois Farmer* claimed that injurious insects were overrunning the country because "civilization" had destroyed so many birds. One had only to look in the crop (the pouch near the throat) of a single bird to appreciate the number of bugs, worms, and flies it consumed. Birds ate so many pests that farmers could forgive them the ripe cherries they ate for dessert—especially given the likelihood that their quick eyes had "perceived a worm in the very cherry you grudge them." To check the "teeming millions" of insects, farmers needed to treat birds as "the naturally commissioned sentinels of our fruit trees . . . a standing army—on picket duty—self-marshaled and trained to meet and overpower the invading army of the insect world."[150]

The Illinois Department of Agriculture weighed in on the issue by advising farmers that it was better to "give half our fruit to birds than all to worms."[151] In 1878, it published an essay applauding barn swallows and chimney swifts for chasing gnats and mosquitoes. It likewise credited orioles, warblers, woodpeckers, and nuthatches with hunting insects, and it praised robins, flickers, and meadow-larks for "working harder and accomplishing more in the extermina-tion of insects in a single hour than we could do in a year." The only birds it found to be unworthy of protection were six types of hawk and the English sparrow.[152]

Agricultural experts touted birds as the frontline defenses against insect predations in part because of a lack of other options. To be sure, farmers did try chemical agents to reduce pests, as demon-strated by the case of the San José scale. This sap-sucking insect took its name from the scales that appeared on the fruit trees it in-fested. After discovering the pest in California in the 1880s, agrono-mists traced its origins to China, from whence they speculated it had come around 1870. Birds and wind spread the licelike young. Not only did the insect kill orchard trees within two to three years, but it also caused Canada and several European countries to quarantine U.S. plants and fruits.[153]

Stephen Forbes, the entomologist in charge of the Illinois State Laboratory of Natural History and a professor of zoology at the Uni-versity of Illinois, discovered the scale in Illinois in 1896. Following widespread practice, he used whale-oil soap as a remedial spray on his experimental orchard in Champaign. Coating Illinois apple trees with oceanic animal fluids had only limited effectiveness, however, so Forbes experimented with a Florida fungus, with cutting and burning, and with washes of lime, sulfur, and salt. He found the latter to be more effective than whale-oil soap and considerably cheaper. His discoveries helped propel him to the presidency of the Entomological Society of America, in which capacity he traveled to Oxford in 1912 as a delegate to the Second International Congress of Entomology, thereby extending his scientific agricultural connections.[154]

But the sulfur wash was just one defensive measure against the insect swarms. Until chemical warfare against insects took off during World War I—subsequently endangering birds as well as insects—birds remained major agents in pest control, as demonstrated by Forbes. Recognizing that the role of birds varied according to species, agricultural practice, place, and insect populations, Forbes embarked on a series of investigations to determine which birds ate what, and in what quantities, where.[155] It was his studies of bird craws that provided the numbers for Department of Agriculture reports on birds as insect controllers.[156]

Joining in the economic ornithology campaign, the *Courier* reported on devastating swarms of locusts that proliferated in the absence of birds.[157] Rather than chastise birds for poaching produce, it applauded them for policing "insect criminals."[158] After the United States entered World War I, the *Courier* shifted to more militaristic terms, depicting the Hessian fly and other destructive insects as "agents of the Kaiser busily at work in America" and birds as a well-organized "aerial arm of our forces."[159] Although the *Courier* did not use the term *food security*, its writings on birds addressed it. "Human life on this planet is one unending war with the insect world," it warned. "In this war the birds are our allies. Without their help the insects would win in a very few campaigns."[160]

The view through the lens of economic ornithology? Not just dinner or dearth, but the destiny of nations.

BATTLE FOR THE CROPS---FARMERS VS. INSECT PESTS

Following the U.S. entry into World War I, the battle against insect pests took on greater urgency. In reprinting this cartoon from *Country Gentleman*, the editor of *Bird-Lore* pointedly noted that the farmers on the front lines of farm defense were foolishly shooting their allies, the birds.

"Battle for the Crops," Bird-Lore *19 (Sept.–Oct. 1917), 296.*

DOMINION OF THE AIR

Concerns about the declining hunt and rising insect hordes helped push a number of Illinois farmers, including Grange members and Farmers' Institute speakers, into the movement for bird protection.[161] Having quantified the significance of birds for agricultural production, Forbes became a prominent advocate of bird preservation. Following a census of the summer bird population in Illinois in the summer of 1907, he concluded that the present bird population was less than it ought to be and less than it would be if birds were properly protected. He energetically advanced that point in public talks and writings.[162]

If Forbes came to preservation from agricultural science, Isaac Hess, a merchant in the town of Philo (about nine miles south of the Champaign County seat), came to it from hunting and gathering. Over the course of his life, Hess made it into the papers for two accomplishments, both connected to eggs. The first had to do with his wife's fertility: after delivering a set of triplets, three years later she had twins.[163] The second achievement, his "fine collection" of wild birds' eggs, won him even more acclaim.[164] Though an avid hunter as well as amateur oologist, Hess pressed for bird protection.[165] He gave illustrated talks on that issue in schools and to the Masons, the Illinois Corn Growers' Association, and audiences at the University of Illinois, the Illinois State Academy of Science, a Chautauqua gathering, and at least one farmers' institute. His wife, too, had a passion for birds, but Florence Hess made it into the paper on that matter only once, for a lecture on the topic to club women.[166]

The *Courier* publicized the legislative successes achieved by the bird protection movement in the early twentieth century: zones of protection, daily bag limits, restricted seasons, curbs on the sale of certain birds, and prohibitions on killing other types of birds, migratory songbirds chief among them.[167] Recognizing that state and federal laws were of limited utility in protecting birds that crossed jurisdictional lines, the *Courier* took favorable note of the bird protection treaty—justified in large part by hunting and agricultural concerns—that the U.S. secretary of agriculture negotiated with Canada in 1916.[168] Although it sometimes lamented the "veritable forest of regulations" that hedged in hunters, the *Courier* claimed that "the greater percentage of the fraternity regard the laws as beneficial."[169] Reminding readers that even seemingly good hunting years were outliers in a general pattern of long-term decline, that the ravages of insect pests could be traced to the destruction of native birds, the

Courier advanced the cause of the international treaty proponents and other protectionists.[170]

The multiple scales in which bird protection legislation advanced—from state to federal to international—raised the question: Who had what rights to mobile animals? The answer hinged on another question: Where did birds belong? Despite reports of robin sightings from U.S. servicemen stationed in Veracruz during the Mexican-American War, the *Illinois Farmer* placed the robin's southern limit in Georgia, well north of Veracruz. This might seem like an effort to nationalize the robin, but the *Illinois Farmer* noted that the bird's range extended to Hudson Bay and Nootka Sound. Its statement that "the Robin inhabits the whole of North America" thus used misleading claims about the range of robins to suggest that the United States and Canada formed a geographic unit that ended abruptly with Mexico.[171] According to the *Illinois Farmer*, the robin belonged not only to the United States and Canada, but also to a united dominion of the North.

The *Illinois Farmer* was by no means alone in such efforts to lump the United States and Canada together in opposition to points farther south. Upon its founding in 1883, the American Ornithologists' Union directed its attention to the United States and British America.[172] Giving a different name to the same geographical unit, U.S. Department of Agriculture ornithologists focused on "North America north of Mexico."[173] Following these approaches to bird study, writings on birds tended to treat the United States and Canada as a singular entity that emptied of migrating birds in the fall and refilled in the spring. Not only did this conception slight birds such as snow buntings, chickadees, and grosbeaks that wintered in the Midwest after summering farther north, it also warped geography by exaggerating east-west connections and shrinking ones that ran north and south. The unit "North America north of Mexico" wrongly implied that Illinois birds had closer connections to Newfoundland and Oregon than to Mexico and Panama.[174]

The more ornithologists mapped long-distance travels, the more they wondered where birds truly belonged. Rather than accept migratory birds as nomadic, they tried to domesticate them, to pin their citizenship down. Those who favored the North as the true home for most migrating birds pointed out that some were so eager to return in the spring that they froze or starved in ice and storms. Those who favored the South countered that birds flew there sooner than necessary, as soon as their fledglings could shift for themselves.[175] The most compelling argument had to do with birthplace. That nailed down the case for the North.[176] According to the birthright citizenship logic, birds from "North America north of Mexico" resembled the northern tourists who went to the Caribbean for seasonal diversion, on winter cruises advertised as "south with the birds."[177]

Beyond associating northernness, and only northernness, with mobility and access, the idea that migrating birds had "true homes" suggested that the different peoples these birds encountered had different claims on them, just as states had sovereignty over their own citizens and farmers had dominion over their own herds.

Having established northern claims to birds, protectionists placed a disproportionate amount of blame for their decline on outsiders. Along with blaming the "market hunters" who traveled long distances to shoot for profit, protectionists looked south for culprits—to Italians arriving from southern Europe, to "negroes" in the rural South, to the lax regulatory regimes of southern states.[178] Although *Bird-Lore* acknowledged the work of bird protection in Mexico, Mexican hunters also came under fire.[179] *Field and Stream* took Mexicans to task for harvesting migratory ducks, baiting them with barley and corn and then driving them to the place of slaughter. At one hacienda, hunters reportedly killed nearly a quarter of a million ducks in a winter, "and as there are hundreds of other haciendas doing the same business of weekly or twice a week shoots, the amount of slaughtered ducks is almost incalculable." Commented the author:

Cruise ads urging wealthy white tourists to head south in the winter with the birds resonated with claims that migrating birds merely visited warmer climes; that their true homes lay in the North.

"The Great White Fleet," Life, *Sept. 28, 1916, 556.*

"I think this statement will give Americans an idea of what becomes of the ducks which they protect by their prohibitory laws after they reach Mexico where they are 'harvested,' as they have been from time immemorial, in the manner here described."[180]

Readers of the hunting press would have known that there was plenty of bird-killing in Canada, too, and not only by inhabitants. British sportsmen saw Canada as they saw places like Kaffirland: as an imperial hunting ground.[181] But coverage of Canadian birdlife drew comparatively more attention to protective legislation and co-operation with the United States in conservation measures. Indeed, pamphlets on U.S. game laws typically included sections on Canadian regulations.[182] This gave the impression that the unit "North America north of Mexico" applied to humans in their relations with birds as well as to birds themselves, that the true tragedy of the commons was the southern destruction of a rightfully northern resource best left to northern custodial care.

The view from the ground was, in sum, filtered through politics. Mexicans did, indeed, kill ducks, though not in disproportionate excess. The U.S. Fish and Wildlife Service later estimated that in a given year, hunters in Mexico shot about as many ducks as U.S. hunters shot on the opening day of the season. And not all these Mexican hunters were Mexican. *Field and Stream*'s reference to "time immemorial" deflected blame from the likely culprits at the bait-and-kill hacienda: the U.S. sportsmen who relished this form of tourism, no doubt its own subscribers among them.[183]

THE MYSTERY OF MIGRATION

In addition to prompting questions of rightful dominion, investments in wild birds prompted questions of range. The more acute the concerns about decline, the more pressing the mystery of migration. Where did birds go in the fall? And where did they come from in the spring? For hunters and farmers, figuring out the mysteries of migration was more than just an intellectual pursuit, it had bearing on food security.

Writings on bird migration in the Illinois area can be dated back at least as far as John James Audubon's efforts, in the first decades of the nineteenth century, to settle the long-standing debates over whether swallows became torpid in the winter—perhaps hiding in the mud—or migrated. After some years of observation and reflection, Audubon concluded that birds such as swallows migrated, and, furthermore, that observers could estimate the distances by keeping track of arrivals and departures. Among all the species of migratory birds, he wrote, "those that remove furthest from us, depart sooner than those which retire only to the confines of the United States, and by a parity of reasoning, those that remain later, return earlier in the spring."[184]

As Audubon built a case against the hibernation theory and in favor of associating travel dates with distance traveled, his contemporary Alexander Wilson tackled another great mystery: Which direction did migrating birds travel? From their viewpoint in the Caribbean, European naturalists had claimed that ricebirds passed from Cuba north to Carolina for the winter. After consulting with informants from Maine to the Mississippi who told him that the birds were seen in their areas only in summer, Wilson determined that the migration went in the other direction, that regardless of which direction the birds took to the air, they ultimately headed south when the weather got cold.[185]

In the ensuing years, ornithologists continued the work of tracking migration. In 1856, the *Illinois Farmer* ran an article refuting the stubbornly persistent presupposition that swallows hibernated by explaining where they went: "He passes to the south; and is seen in Louisiana, Mexico, and even in Central America."[186] The *Illinois Farmer* provided similar details on the purple martin: "They are found in the far north, and in the south in Chili, and even in Terra Del Fuego."[187] That was a start. But so much remained unknown, even for large and common birds, such as the Canada goose. In an 1864 article, the *Prairie Farmer* admitted "how far north they travel is not well known and how far south their journey is taken is a like mystery."[188]

Solving this mystery was no easy task. Until ornithologists—including a pathbreaking team from the University of Illinois—began to use radar in the post–World War II period, it was nearly impossible to track nocturnal migrations.[189] Even the minority of birds that flew during daylight hours could not always be clearly observed. Lacking better methods, naturalists sometimes shot birds down to determine what they were.[190] But the luckiest of shots revealed only a dot, not the entire line of travel or general array. It was like predicting the weather based on the view from the porch.

From the start, mapping migrations relied on human communications networks and human mobility. To track migration, the American Ornithologists' Union called on meteorological networks for observational help.[191] The Audubon Society developed its own network of correspondents through appeals in its magazine, *Bird-Lore*. Observers from Alberta and British Columbia to the Isle of Pines off the southwestern coast of Cuba responded to such appeals.[192] Reports came in to the Smithsonian from agents of the Hudson's Bay Company and to *Ornithologist and Oölogist* from a Mexican observer named Juan Renadro.[193] In hopes of adding still more pieces to the puzzle, the U.S. Department of Agriculture also solicited the help of volunteers. Its Department on the Geographical Distribution and Migration of Birds cooperated with the American Ornithologists' Union to ascertain where migrating birds went in the winter and what routes they followed.[194] Over two thousand observers in North and South America and the West Indies responded to the call for cooperation. By 1918, the survey had more than five hundred thousand observations on file, some from Champaign.[195] The Ekblaw family sent in a notable number of reports. George E. Ekblaw and W. Elmer Ekblaw were early participants in the Audubon Society's Christmas bird count, and Eddie L. Ekblaw and Sidney E. Ekblaw later joined the work.[196]

Along with drawing avocational bird-watchers such as the Ekblaws into the migration-tracking effort, groups such as the Audubon Club, the American Ornithologists' Union, the Smithsonian Institution, and the National Geographic Society backed expeditions that gathered ornithological data.[197] Following from the importance placed on economic ornithology, the U.S. Department of Agriculture's Biological Survey group became the major government player in the migration-tracking game, sending field naturalists to study birds "from Panama to the Arctic Circle."[198] The findings from these studies appeared in the annual reports of the U.S. Department of Agriculture and in the many agricultural magazines that publicized the government's work.[199] Hunting magazines such as *Chicago Field*, *American Sportsman*, and *The American Field* also relayed information on migration, as did ornithological journals such as the *Auk*, *Bird-Lore*, and *Ornithologist and Oölogist*.[200] The *Courier*, too, like other daily newspapers, spread newfound ornithological knowledge to more general-interest audiences.[201]

Despite the diversion into latitudinal theories of western migration, most reports on bird mobility focused on seasonal migrations along longitudinal lines. The more precise these mappings became over time, the more incredible the stories of connection they told. "Everybody knows that birds when they migrate in the fall generally 'go south,' but knowledge is seldom more specific," claimed the *Courier* in 1915. Now more specific answers were at hand. The U.S. Department of Agriculture's new bulletin revealed "that while some birds go to Florida or the West Indies or Mexico, others go as far south as Paraguay and the southern part of Brazil."[202] A later article reported that a hundred northern U.S. and Canadian species traveled to Central and South America for the winter, among them the scarlet tanager (which migrated from Canada to Peru) and blackpoll warblers (which flew from Alaska to the southern coast of the Caribbean Sea). The most astounding discovery was the distance traveled by nighthawks, which flew all the way to Patagonia, eight thousand miles from their summer nesting grounds.[203] In addition to birds that departed from or passed through the Midwest, other birds relocated to the area in the fall from points farther north, including myriads from the Yukon.[204]

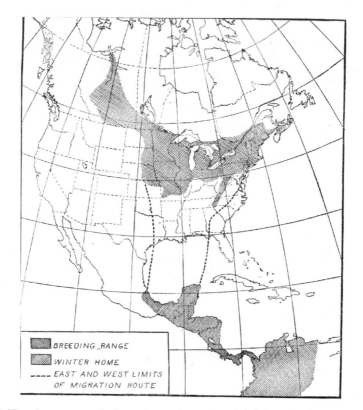

Thanks to networked watchers who reported sightings, ornithologists began to figure out the mysteries of migration, as this Department of Agriculture map depicting the distribution and migration of the rose-breasted grosbeak shows. The U.S. Department of Agriculture took the lead in governmental efforts to study and protect birds because of their significance for agriculture.

Wells W. Cooke, "Bird Migration," Bulletin of the U.S. Department of Agriculture *185 (April 17, 1915), 30.*

Such reports of migration made it clear that Illinois was not only a flyover state, but also a place where birds of the tropics met those from the Arctic.[205] It was a place in the middle, a place of encounter; a place both to land and to take off.

INSIDE THE ARCTIC CIRCLE

Elmer Ekblaw became a polar explorer because of migrating birds. As a boy, this member of the Ekblaw band of birders explored the fields and wetlands near his home in Rantoul (in northern Champaign County), with an eye on perches and the sky. After a stint teaching school, he enrolled in the University of Illinois, where he pursued his interest in the natural world.[206] Following his graduation in 1910, his alma mater hired him as an assistant instructor in geology.[207] By 1912, he had written several geographical articles and become a member of the Illinois State Academy of Science, the American Association for the Advancement of Science, the Wilson Ornithologists' Club, the American Ornithological Union, and the National Geographical Society.[208]

Thus when F. W. Pitman and F. N. Pitman, Jr., shot five ducks that they could not identify, they took the birds to Elmer Ekblaw, who identified them as "the rather rare species of American merganser, which is not typically found here, though its ordinary range is from New Brunswick to California and from the Gulf of Mexico to Hudson Bay." Lest there be any doubt of Ekblaw's expertise, the article reporting on this incident identified him as the head of ornithology on the Crocker Land expedition, "which leaves in July for a three years' stay in the Arctic regions."[209]

The Crocker Land expedition aimed to explore an area off the northwest coast of Greenland spotted from afar by the Peary Arctic expedition in 1906.[210] It was sponsored by the American Museum of Natural History and the American Geographical Society, with the co-operation of the University of Illinois, which supplied two members of the expedition team.[211] The second Illinois graduate was Dr. Maurice Cole Tanquary, a professor of entomology at Kansas State Agricultural College.[212] The prospect of two homegrown men exploring the Arctic caught the imaginations of many residents of Champaign. About a hundred people subscribed to an "Illinois Arctic Club," which helped the two men purchase personal equipment.[213] To explain Ekblaw's desire for a polar adventure, the *Courier* turned to his Swedish heritage, describing him as "descended from old Viking stock."[214] Subsequent stories covered trip preparations, the grand farewell party, and embarkation.[215]

The *Courier* also reported the embarrassing discovery that Crocker Land did not exist, at least not in the range that Peary had ascribed to it.[216] Rather than head immediately home, the expedition proceeded to explore what they could. Sometimes together, sometimes apart, always living in great intimacy with the indigenous Inuit people, the explorers surveyed the country.[217] Ekblaw kept himself in the news by leaving letters on a coastal rock, for pickup by occasional Danish schooners.[218] Despite the disruptions of World War I, some of these exciting letters, with stories of snow blindness, frozen feet, walrus hunts, and sleeping on ice at 50 degrees below zero, made it back to Champaign—covered in multiple postmarks—and from the recipients, they traveled to the offices of the *Courier* and onward to newspaper readers.[219]

Upon his return, thousands turned out to welcome the explorer home.[220] Ekblaw subsequently hit the speakers' circuit, giving illustrated lectures—some with motion pictures—on his Arctic trip to seemingly anybody who would listen: the men's class of the Methodist Sunday school, the High Twelve Club of the Masonic Temple, the University of Illinois, the Urbana Association of Commerce, the Elks, the Omicron Nu household science fraternity, and the University Republican Club.[221] Newspaper reports described packed auditoriums and Sunday school rooms.[222] Those who missed the talks or wanted still more could view some of the materials used in his travels, on display in the campus natural history building.[223] The readers of the *Courier* got a laugh at his expense in 1918, when Ekblaw froze his ears in an Illinois blizzard. The explorer reportedly enjoyed the irony of his predicament as much as anyone. Despite the injury, he praised the cold. Whereas heat was "oppressive," the northern atmosphere was "light, bracing, and invigorating."[224]

We can imagine the contents of his public talks based on his published writings. Many of Ekblaw's observations were ethnographic. In the *Annals of the Association of American Geographers*, he described the "Eskimo" as a "vanishing race," which was not to say that the group known as Eskimo would disappear from Greenland, but that their numbers had declined and those who remained were "losing their racial character, becoming alien in blood." That was the closest Ekblaw came to hinting at whatever intimacies he and other expedition members had with women during the four years they lived among the northernmost people of Greenland, eating their food, driving their dogs, and sharing their hunting grounds.[225]

Among the animals they killed and ate were birds. Ekblaw wrote about birds as both an epicure and an explorer, in so doing coming full circle back to his childhood passion. After years of hunting for birds in the marshes of Rantoul, he had followed them to their northern limits. Beyond the edge of the known world, he discovered people who had lived there all along. Together in the Arctic Circle, the traveling provincial and resident Danish colonial subjects had feasted on the very things that had brought them together in the first place: migratory birds. For Ekblaw, birds were an entrée into both scientific and cross-cultural webs.

AERIAL CIRCUITS

Bird-watchers were not the only ones drawn into larger ambits through a fascination with the flight paths overhead, as seen in the events of July 17, 1911. That evening, a "fiery meteor" sped across the "northwestern heavens" above Champaign, "throwing off a great light which gradually grew dim as the phenomenon passed to the southeast." Astronomy students at the University of Illinois ran to the observatory from their rooming houses and, finding the doors locked, they smashed the windows in their eagerness to reach the telescope. Some observers mistook the meteor for a comet. Others reported having seen an airship.[226] Unusual though this event was, it was not the only incidence of suspected airships in the night.

Headlines from the *Courier* reveal a pattern of sightings: "Mysterious Airship over Illinois," "Was It an Air Ship?," "Say They Saw Airship," "Thought They Saw Airship." These confounding sightings typically occurred at night and they involved searchlights and strange noises.[227] To understand why spectators mistook a meteor for a UFO, and why other flashes in the night suddenly brought airships to mind, we need to consider the larger context of aerial ascents.

The recorded history of aerial contraptions in Champaign began with kites, typically flown by children or for advertising purposes, or distributed by advertisers to children, but on occasion the features of public exhibitions. In 1910, a "scientific kite flyer from Boston" gave an exhibition in a park. A few years later, the ladies of the Grand Army of the Republic took umbrage when a contestant in a kite-flying contest cut up a flag for material. Winners of subsequent contests, held in the village of Philo and a military field by the armory, demonstrated a more appropriate spirit of patriotism, by flying American flags rather than snipping them apart.[228]

For all the patriotism, kite flying brought to mind distant places. After acknowledging a centuries-long tradition of kite flying in Europe, the *Courier* traced the birth of the sport to ancient China.[229] In explaining the rules of the game—to cut or entangle the opponent's string—it held up South and East Asian rules of sportsmanship, claiming that "it is regarded as very unsportsmanlike in Burma or

China to use ground glass and paste on the string." This recognition of Chinese expertise in kite flying helps explain why the organizers of a 1916 kite-flying contest with a fight component recruited Chinese students to serve as judges.[230]

Like kite flying, ballooning drew attention outward as well as up. The turn of the century was a great era of long-distance ballooning competitions, with prizes going to the farthest distance traveled and longest time aloft. Given the dangers of setting down in water or mountains, midwestern cities such as Kansas City, St. Louis, and Indianapolis became popular launching places. Thousands showed up for the ascents, and papers covered the international cast of competitors, race routes, and results, often in breathless tones: "St. Louis, Oct. 19—Heading straight for Ontario, across the great lakes, along the best balloon route in America, Captain Von Abereron, the famous German pilot, with his balloon Germania, is believed to be leading in the international race for the James Gordon Bennett cup, which started from this city late Monday."[231] Such coverage placed the rural heartland in the thick of the ballooning world, on the same circuits as the people downwind from Cologne and Berlin.[232]

Even as it reported on distances covered and time aloft, the *Courier* also captured some views from the ground. It ran reports of people being showered with sand and gravel as balloonists reduced their ballast. It noted sightings of balloons that had become entangled in telegraph wires or landed on farms.[233] It tracked down the mystery of a mammoth balloon that floated over the county one morning on a record-breaking trip.[234] It claimed that the entire town of Urbana looked up one afternoon when seven long-distance racing balloons passed overhead.[235] And it enabled readers to share in the surprise of a farmer named Charles Grein upon hearing a voice calling to him one day from the heavens.[236]

Grein had likely seen airborne balloons before that startling episode. Though long-distance competitors took off from only a few cities, balloon ascensionists, like circus performers, popped up in small towns and county fairs around the turn of the century. In Champaign, balloon entertainers appeared at a Modern Woodmen Association picnic, an interscholastic athletic carnival, a corn carnival, a Sunday school picnic, a horse show, a Commercial Club gathering, and multiple Fourth of July celebrations.[237] Announcements proclaiming that the Champaign County Fair would have balloon ascensions "and all the usual features of a great fair" reveal that this type of amusement was so common as to be expected at carnivalesque events. Their popularity can be deduced from advertisements promising special traincars for spectators and estimates of twenty-five-thousand-person crowds.[238]

To enhance the excitement, balloonists on the fair circuit would carry a parachutist who would leap from the balloon at about a thousand feet.[239] One carnival company that stopped in Champaign attached a monkey to the chute, but its screams of protest did not go over well with the audience.[240] On another occasion, a spectator persuaded the regular parachute jumper to let her make the leap. Mae DeWitt-Ratford, described as a petite divorcée who was "simply crazy" about aeronautics, got the thrill of her life on the first leap and would have gone again if her father and brother had not "put the 'kabosh' on it."[241]

By 1910, aeroplanes had joined balloons in the air over Champaign. Members of a university aeronautic club flew the first ones, attracting crowds estimated at nearly a thousand.[242] In 1911, several people from Champaign were among those who watched a monoplane ascent one county over.[243] By 1912, biplanes could be spotted at the state fair, leading the *Courier* to run headlines proclaiming: "Country Is Mad over Aviation."[244] In 1915, pedestrians spotted an aeroplane sailing just over the roofs of the business district of Urbana.[245] In 1916, the university appointed an assistant professor of aeronautics and enrolled a seasoned aerial exhibitor who went by the name Satan Day.[246]

Day was from the area, having grown up in Gibson City, a farm town one county to the north. According to the *Courier*, he had become the youngest licensed pilot in the country after studying flying at the Curtiss airplane school in New York. One of his classmates there, Charles F. Niles, went on to direct the aerial corps of the Carranza forces in the Mexican Revolution. The *Courier* claimed that General Villa had tried, via telegram, to recruit Day as head of *his* flying corps. Villa sweetened the offer by promising Day "charge of the aviation department of Mexico" following the "subjugation of the country." Though tempted, Day turned Villa down so that he could fulfill his stunt-flying contract. The decision to stick with exhibition flying avoided what would have been, as the *Courier* put it, "the unusual situation of two American airmen pitted against each other in the opposing forces of the armies of Mexico."[247]

Day was not the only exhibitionist to loop the loop in the Champaign skies as balloon entertainments gave way to planes. Some of the most famous aerial performance artists at the turn of the twentieth century were members of the Moisant family, from Kankakee (two counties to the north of Champaign). They ran Moisant International Aviators, a performance company that arranged for flights in a variety of public gatherings, including at the Champaign County Fair.[248] Though they were known by the seemingly rural appellation "barnstormers," part of the appeal of these aerial entertainers lay in their apparent cosmopolitanism.[249] John B. Moisant was the first in the family to win widespread fame, following a Paris-to-London flight and a victory over French and English champions. Another flying Moisant, Mathilde, "established a reputation as the most skillful aviatrix of the world" on a Mexican tour.[250]

Aerial performers did not have to work for the Cosmopolitan Amusement Company to bring a whiff of cosmopolitanism to the small towns where they performed.[251] The Moisants' roster included an "unemotional Irishman," "the French fool flyer," and a "Russian birdman [with] a big reputation in his native country."[252] The aviator Bud Mars told a *Courier* reporter that he had given exhibitions in sixteen different countries, including Japan, where he flew before nobility, with four hundred thousand paid admissions on the field.[253] Upon the conclusion of each fair, the entertainers headed on, to other U.S. towns, and to places such as Ottawa, Winnipeg, and Toronto.[254] At least once, the departing carnival company took a local boy with them as the latest recruit to the itinerant aerial performance life.[255] The crowds who gathered for aerial entertainments could count themselves part of a worldly circuit.

GROUNDED

As aerial ascents connected spectators to cosmopolitan worlds of flight, they also distanced them from more parochial people, such as the rubes to the south who reportedly fired on balloonists overhead.[256] These downstate clodhoppers were not the only backward troublemakers who surfaced in the *Courier*. Other sources of resistance from below included the Arab sharpshooters who fired on the Italian planes that had been dropping bombs in Tripoli and the Mexicans who fired on U.S. aviators along the Rio Grande. The latter led the *Courier* to call for firmer policies—the kind adopted by Italy and France in their campaigns in North Africa against "the hostile native tribes." The restive observers on the ground included the birds on the Illinois state game farm. When they saw their first biplane, great confusion broke out in the yard. It took the keepers several hours to calm the disturbed animals.[257] The people who had been to the fairgrounds could chuckle at such behavior, regarding flight as more a menace to the pilots than to spectators. As they applauded the cosmopolitan cast of aerial performance artists, they had good reason to agree with the predictions that human flight would bring the world together, that it would bridge continents, eliminate frontiers, and mix people and interests so as to "evolve a world-nation."[258] Every day would be a fair day in this wonderful new age, and none of the kite strings would have shards.

The possibility that human flight might have other meanings—such as fear, danger, and death for those on the ground—seemed very far away to these festive crowds. And yet, for readers of the *Courier*, that possibility surfaced in more than just reports of mysterious airships, downstaters, Mexicans, and panicked turkeys. It could be glimpsed in story after story coming through the wires, as seen in headlines such as these:

> *March 19, 1912:* "Airship Bombs Kill Arabs"[259]
> *Aug. 26, 1914:* "German Airship Drops Bombs on Antwerp Citizens"[260]
> *Feb. 15, 1915:* "Thousands See Fight in Air"[261]
> *July 13, 1918:* "Air Raids Terrorize Germans"[262]

And if not in headlines, then the view from the ground could be glimpsed in letters from the Champaign servicemen stationed in France. These reported bombs came down with an "awful hissing noise." Next time, wrote a soldier who watched the bombs falling on Paris, he would seek shelter in the cellar.[263] There were plenty of next times, if not for him, then for others. Another letter, by a different soldier: "We have witnessed aerial battles galore."[264]

No wonder that after lionizing aerial artists, the *Courier* so soon made celebrities of military aces. It was not just that they were thrilling to watch, but that their reports transcended the terrifying view from below. From the earliest days of aerial ascents, the people on the ground understood the power differentials between flyover and flownover perspectives.

AIRPOWER

Although the Midwest does not have as much of a military presence as the U.S. South and coastal states such as California and New York, military installations have long connected this region to the wider world. One such base sprang up near Flatville following the U.S. entry into the Great War.[265] That location may seem like a strange choice, given the human terrain. Known as the "German Flats," the area was composed almost entirely of ethnic Germans, whom others in the vicinity saw as a threat.[266] Although some accounts praised the German speakers of Flatville as thrifty and industrious, indeed, as model citizens, others worried about their colonizing tendencies. Having turned worthless swamps into prime farmland, they were "becoming expansionists." With all the land in their vicinity taken, they were "reaching out into other sections," picking up farms here and there. Once they acquired land, they kept it, assigning it to their heirs, turning it into hereditary estates.[267]

After the United States entered World War I, the preponderance of Germans in the area raised concerns about security risks. The anti-German sentiments that had been simmering along came to a full boil when news spread that a resident of Flatville had flown a German flag. Making things worse, he had refused to take it down and replace it with the Stars and Stripes. After violence broke out, residents vigorously denied the rumor, but concerns about loyalty did not go away.[268]

However concerning its populace, Rantoul had several things going in its favor. The first was its proximity to the University of

Illinois, which had established a professorship in aeronautics in 1916.[269] Student aviators could receive their theoretical training at the university and then join other servicemen at Chanute for flight instruction.[270] The price of land, and its flatness, added to Rantoul's attractiveness. It was cheaper to build from scratch downstate than to expand an existing aviation field near Chicago, due to real estate costs.[271] Though comparatively inexpensive, Rantoul still offered the necessary railroad connections. The grid, too, was a plus. In a time when pilots relied on landmarks such as railroad tracks and waterways to tell where they were, the roads that followed the section lines provided straight lines of flight and mile markers, as the military's flight manual noted.[272]

The crowning inducements were the flatness of the area and the massive investments in drainage. All pilots—and especially pilots in training—faced the possibility of "playing the field," that is, making an emergency landing on unfamiliar ground. The military's flight manual dwelt on this concern. It instructed pilots to "be constantly searching out available landing fields in case of engine failure." Yet those who trained in Illinois could exhale. Again, the military's guide: "In the State of Illinois the question of landing fields is almost nonexistent, because there are large, flat fields and pastures in almost every square mile of the farming district, and a cross-country flight from Rantoul to Chicago could have no terrors for the beginner as regards the choice of a landing ground."[273] The field was far easier to play when it was indeed a field, not a forest; a flat field, not a hilly one; and a solid field, not muck.[274] The wisdom of the choice seemed apparent when plane after plane went down, and pilot after pilot walked away.[275]

The quality of the air likewise enhanced the likelihood of survival. The "rarified air" of high altitudes threw engines out of tune, as revealed in the report of a military scout who had to walk back under the cover of darkness when his plane went down in the Sierra

The Chanute airfield extended beyond the parameters of the base to the surrounding fields of corn, as seen in this photograph of a plane that went down due to engine trouble in 1917. The plane and aviators apparently fared well, although some stalks of corn were totaled.

Chanute Collection, Champaign County Historical Archives, The Urbana Free Library, Box 13, Series 9: Aerial and Aircraft, Folder 3: Aircraft, 1917–1930s.

Madres in Mexico.[276] The "Mexican Campaign" against Pancho Villa had taught several other lessons besides: high temperatures took a toll on radiators; dry air made wooden propellers "go to pieces." The aviators stationed along the Mexican border also complained of fierce whirlwinds. "We appear to be dealing with an absolutely abnormal climate," wrote one.[277] Rantoul, in contrast, seemed normal and thus an appropriate place to prepare U.S. pilots for another presumably normative location: the war-torn skies over France. Military planners may have reconsidered their assumptions about midwestern air quality in January 1918, when paralyzing winter storms prevented a squadron from deploying overseas, but by then the base was well established and a slew of aviators trained.[278]

The military named the base after Octave Chanute, the Paris-born engineer who designed the Union Stock Yards in Chicago. Chanute had experimented with gliders and planes, founding the Aero Club of Illinois, which took up the cause of international aviation meets. Chanute saw the political implications of airplanes as far vaster than collaborative efforts and friendly competition. Before his death in 1910, Chanute had written that airplanes would "make war so terrible as to compel peace."[279]

The hope of compelling peace through deterrence may have motivated many of the two million men and women who lived, worked, and trained at Chanute over the next seventy-five years.[280] But in 1917, the goal was to compel peace through military victory. From its establishment in a time of war to the Treaty of Versailles, the military personnel at Chanute looked toward France. Aviation instructors arrived from France to offer instruction.[281] The *Rantoul Weekly News* reported on the popularity of French language classes.[282] Graduates served in the Third Provisional Aero Squadron in France.[283]

As they directed their own thoughts toward France, the aviators at Chanute helped make the war tangible to the surrounding communities. They did so when they socialized with the women of Rantoul, who greeted their arrival with cherry and custard pies, when they patronized nearby bars and other businesses, when they departed for Europe with great fanfare, and when they wrote of their experiences at the front. Whether they gained great celebrity as aces, won more modest acclaim for felling a plane or two, insisted on the need to withhold details, or were shot down by the enemy, Chanute airmen brought the war home through the papers as well as through their presence on the ground.[284]

But above all, they brought the war home when they flew.

MILITARIZED AIRSPACE

The airmen of Rantoul turned Chanute into the military equivalent of the county fairgrounds. According to the *Courier*, "scores of automobiles" lined the nearby roads as crowds as large as eight thousand to nine thousand people came to watch the pilots in training fly.[285]

Those well used to exhibition flights did not leave disappointed, for in the final stage of combat training, pilots practiced the acrobatic tricks—the loops, tailspins, spirals, and so forth—that typified aviation entertainment.[286] They also engaged in live combat: "An unknown hero created some excitement at Chanute Field Wednesday morning when at a height of about 100 feet he met the enemy and plunged headlong into them . . . What chance has a poor pigeon with a Curtis plane?"[287]

The show spilled well beyond Chanute Field, for its pilots militarized airspace for miles around. The people of Urbana, reported the *Courier*, had formed the habit of scanning the sky for planes, "as there is now no telling when one may appear."[288] The airmen circled around before landing for gas.[289] They took nearby bigwigs on trial flights.[290] They "bombed" towns in central Illinois with Liberty Loan circulars and colored flares.[291] They performed aerial circuses over Red Cross parades.[292] They were featured attractions at patriotic events and drew crowds to off-base exhibitions featuring "fancy flying" and "all kinds of aerial stunts."[293] The most moving display: a lone aeroplane dipping low over a military funeral, so as to drop flowers into the grave.[294]

And they went down, mostly landing in fields, but on one occasion on a coal car on a moving freight train.[295] Reports of the two pilots who died in the center of the business district in the village of Fisher provide a glimpse into the proximity of military aviation to civilian space. They had been flying "very low directly up the street" and their plane, no more than a story overhead, hit a flagpole.[296] Two other pilots from Chanute scared a farmer so badly that he jumped off his wagon to avoid being hit. According to witnesses, the pilots "arose almost perpendicularly" to clear the nearby telephone wires. The farmer lost a leg, above the knee, after his frightened mules turned course.[297]

Thousands of spectators flocked to Rantoul to watch World War I aviators train.
They lined the roads and walked onto the field itself, taking particular
pleasure in the stunt flying that prepared the pilots for combat.

Pilots in training navigated by the grid,
sometimes swooping below treetop height.

It was not just the aviators who blurred the line between civilian and military airspace—their messenger birds did as well. In 1917, Major General John J. Pershing, the commander of the American forces in France, asked for thousands of carrier pigeons "to assist the American aeroplane observers in sending their reports and maps of German positions back to headquarters."[298] Following through on that call, the airmen at Chanute built a pigeon loft on the base. The fliers in charge of the pigeons trained seventy-five young carriers. Every morning, they took a bunch out in a motorcycle and let them loose. Two deserted. A few went AWOL but eventually returned. Those that made it through "basic training" got to ascend in a plane. All that were released from the air made it home. The Rantoul papers warned "the amateur Nimrods in Champaign" to turn their heads if they saw any pigeons in the sky, because it was a crime to kill "one of Uncle Sam's trained Homers" as they prepared for service in France.[299]

BIRDMEN

The people of Champaign and the airmen themselves called the aviators "birdmen," and, like birds, they were migratory, for they decamped to Texas for the winter months, when the ground turned hard and snowy and the air became bitingly cold.[300] Lieutenant John M. Foote, who flew from Chanute Field to San Antonio, reported a flying time of ten hours and twenty minutes, despite a snowstorm so fierce that his propeller blades dulled.[301] Other men took the Illinois Central, on routes previously advertised to home seekers in search of land in the Southwest.[302] These routes provided such reliable connections to Texas that the U.S. military assigned Illinois Guard members—including over a hundred from Champaign County—to service on the Mexican border. On the long haul south, the Chanute birdmen may have mingled with Illinois guardsmen and with some of the prospective aviators from Champaign assigned to basic flight training in Texas.[303] Their fellow travelers may have taught them the lyrics to "We Came to Kill the Greasers," a song they sang upon detraining.[304] But it is likely that the Chanute airmen already knew the words.

According to ornithological standards, Texas was the true home for at least some of the Chanute aviators, because that is where they fledged as military pilots. Several of the first instructors at the base had served with General Pershing along the U.S.-Mexican border and in the "Mexican Punitive expedition" that chased after Pancho Villa.[305] Among the 159 members of the Tenth Aerial Squadron who arrived from San Antonio was Captain J. E. C. McDonnell, "one of the best known aviators in the United States service."[306] McDonnell came to attention in Champaign well before his arrival at Chanute, because, as the Rantoul paper reminded readers, he was one of two American aviators "lost in the desert at the time of the Mexican troubles."[307] McDonnell and the other pilots of the squadron had flown reconnaissance and communications missions, completing 540 flights during six months of military operations.[308] One reconnaissance flight was over 315 miles, round-trip. Another plane, headed for the city of Chihuahua, crashed into the side of a mountain, sparking a forest fire that burned for forty miles. The pilots' subsequent complaints about mountain and desert operations helped lead to the founding of the base in Champaign.[309] It was, claimed the *Courier*, the Mexican theater that had made American army fliers "the superior of any aerial force in the world."[310]

If the standard for true homes was not the first airborne mission, but the first tour of overseas duty, then the true homes of some birdmen lay even farther from Champaign. For some of the Chanute airmen, that true home was the Philippines, where they had served as part of U.S. occupation forces, amid the same winds that meteorologists of the time traced to the Midwest.[311] Looking up at the military planes overhead, or flying themselves, the people of Champaign could place themselves at a different kind of true home: at the birthplace of a rising power, at the heart of an ascendant nation with a military that could determine the destinies of millions, somewhere far beyond view.[312]

PROVINCIAL WORLDVIEWS

Flyover jokes arose from the presumption of heartland provinciality. But the last joke may be on the joker, for positioning the heartland as a place that can be both literally and figuratively looked down upon reveals another strain of provinciality: the inability to recognize the heartland as a vantage point. Tracing the view from the ground uncovers forms of geographic consciousness not visible from peripheral perspectives. It shows a sense of being in the middle of everything.

This sense of geographic connection unfolded both laterally and in 3-D. Flatter imaginings resonated with maps depicting set routes between different points and jurisdictional bounds. Aerial awareness, in contrast, lent itself to an understanding of place that was relatively more open, a vision of place that spilled into space. And yet, even as looking to the air opened up all kinds of vistas, it also prompted efforts to draw boundaries: to limit access, insist on distance, and privilege some forms of connection over others. The world as seen from Flatville was anything but flat, for it was stratified by power. Though disparaged by self-proclaimed sophisticates in the urban centers of culture and capital, the supposed bumpkins of the heartland did more than look up, they looked down. Though derided as being in the middle of nowhere, the heart of the nation coalesced smack in the middle of everywhere: between north and south, east and west, and flyover and flownover, too.

ARCHIVAL TRACES
America for Americans

History of Champaign County Illinois, 1878: "About 1832, a large body of Indians (believed to have been the Miamas), nine hundred in number, in removing from their reservation in Indiana to the Western Territories, passed through Champaign County. . . . These Indians were entirely friendly to the whites, and encamped two days at the Point for rest, where the settlers gathered around them for trade and to enjoy their sports."[1]

History of Champaign County Illinois, 1878: "In the winter of 1852–3 came a company of braves from the West, through Urbana, on their way to Washington to have a talk with the President. While stopping here one of their number sickened, died, and was buried in the old cemetery at Urbana. His comrades greatly mourned him, and planted at the head of his grave a board, upon which were divers cabalistic signs."[2]

Champaign Daily Gazette, 1899: "Mrs. W. T. Green will speak on 'My Work in Mexico' at the Christian church."[3]

Urbana Courier, 1914: "Dreaming that he was being chased by a crowd of Indians intent on scalping him, Barney Hyatt, the local restaurant man, plunged out of his bed Wednesday night and dislocated one of his knees."[4]

A Standard History of Champaign County, Illinois, 1918: "Her motto has always been America for Americans."—On Champaign resident Mary A. Taylor, born in Dundee, Scotland[5]

Urbana Courier, 1918: "This was the first day for registration of alien enemies but none put in an appearance at police headquarters where they are to have their finger prints taken, leave their photographs and submit to other requirements of the law."[6]

Urbana Courier, 1918: "One elderly German woman who appeared before the registrars [of alien enemies] yesterday afternoon became so nervous that she forgot what English she knew and had to depend on an interpreter. She has been in this country many years and under ordinary circumstances speaks the language well. There was no little sympathy for her for her family connections are of undoubted loyalty and her predicament was embarrassing to say the least."[7]

Rantoul Weekly Press, 1920: Sheriff Davis, his deputy, and a federal officer came to Rantoul, looking for Bernard Gardeman, who was charged with violating the immigration law. They found him at his uncle's home. The young man had left Germany several months earlier. When his ship neared the United States, he jumped overboard and swam to shore, thereby eluding the U.S. immigration bureau. Following Gardeman's arrest, State's Attorney L. A. Busch went to Chicago to intercede for him. "Mr. Busch says that if the public could have seen the mess of humanity the officials have to deal with at the Chicago office it would little wonder that no favors are shown. . . . He saw nearly 200 undesirable Russians, Roumanians and others who are radicals herded together for deportation." Immigration officials released Gardeman after some leading businessmen in Rantoul enlisted their congressman to plead his case.[8]

HOME, LAND, SECURITY

Exile, Dispossession, and Loss

THE ULTIMATE SAFE SPACE

The heartland of myth draws the nation together around a shared sense of vulnerability. As the quintessential home referenced by its lexical offshoot, the homeland, the heartland is the place that must be protected at all costs. It is the ultimate safe space, the national stronghold or keep. And as with other such citadels, its security appears to depend on its well-guarded walls, for the heartland myth starts from the assumption that danger arises from outside, not from injustice at home.

We might call the comforting promise of a national safe space in the midst of a fearsome and dangerous world a little white lie—a little white nationalist lie—except its politics are far from harmless and its magnitude is far too large. The heartland is not a microcosm of the nation as a whole nor is it just any old place. It is no coincidence that the innermost redoubt in fantasies of national security is generally considered to be especially white. The mythical heartland is more little house on the big prairie than wickiup or cotton fields; more the starched farmers of American Gothic than the sunburned workers of migrant camps. Despite its antislavery commitments and pivotal support for the Union in the Civil War, it is a place shaped by long histories of antiblack legislation, dotted with sundown towns that forbade people of color to loiter on the premises when the working day was done.[9] The whiter-than-average homes of the rural heartland built on earlier foundations, hacked out by settler colonialists in the heyday of Indian removal. In affixing security to this particular place, the heartland myth has attached it to particular people, at the cost of detaching it from others.

Along with hiding various forms of insecurity emanating from the homeland, the promise of a safe space at the heart of the nation hides the tremendous reach of U.S. power. Depictions of the heartland as a place of innocence at risk plaster over the reality of U.S. engagement in the world. The heartland myth fails to recognize that at its most self-aggrandizing, the nation's heart has added its muscle to empire, that the struggle to achieve security for some has created tremendous insecurities for others, among them the Kickapoo people, whose claims to the heartland precede the prairie's enshrinement in myth. While Chanute aviators, inspired by calls to make the world safe for democracy, were winging through the air in pursuit of openness, access, and influence, the Kickapoo people who had once hunted on the aviators' training grounds were confronting an ever more bordered world.

For the Kickapoos, the heartland of myth is less a safe space than ground zero for generations of exile, dispossession, and loss. For the members of the Kickapoo diaspora who sought refuge in Mexico, the wall-building impulses of the heartland myth were not the solution to existential angst but the all too palpable cause. The Mexican Kickapoos' unfolding history may seem out of place in a history of the heartland, but that is precisely the point. The white nationalist boundary drawing of the heartland myth has contributed to larger processes of erasure. Writing the Kickapoos back into the history of the heartland can help us understand some of the consequences of these politics as well as other, less bunkered, ways of being in the world.

DISPLACEMENT

Seemingly oblivious to policies that tore native peoples from their villages and forced them onto the road, U.S. officials insisted that they wished to turn Indians into settled farmers. As the head of the Kickapoo Indian School in Kansas told his students in 1914: "Farm your own land and as much of the other fellow's as you can get, do your own work, stay at home."[10] Disregarding Kickapoo women's historical roles as agriculturalists, the Bureau of Indian Affairs agents assigned to the Kickapoos strove mightily to tie Kickapoo *men* to plows. Objecting to the Kickapoos' heavy reliance on hunting, they also urged Kickapoo men to tend livestock, an endeavor that would keep them close to home.[11] As Kickapoo men replaced women in the fields, agents urged Kickapoo women to dedicate themselves to housekeeping.

Only some of the Kickapoos heeded these admonitions. The white agents charged with supervising them did not give up, believing that if admonishments wouldn't change behavior, then necessity would. In addition to restricting the Kickapoos' ability to leave their reservations to hunt, U.S. Indian policies continued to carve away the Kickapoos' lands, thereby preventing them from sustaining themselves by hunting on their own holdings. Promises of perpetual rights in their removal treaties notwithstanding, the Kickapoos continued to lose land as the nineteenth century unfolded. They lost it

Indian agents strove to tie Kickapoo women to settled households,
believing that their path to civilization lay in housekeeping. For these
and other indigenous women, domesticity meant spatial constriction.

*Photograph of Kickapoo women, 1906. The back of the photograph says: "Mrs. Anderson (Kickapoo),
Ubya daughter of Masheena, Kawkeas grand-daughter." Courtesy of the McLean County
Museum of History, Bloomington, Illinois.*

to the government, to railroad lines that claimed rights-of-way, and to
swindlers, including one of their government-appointed translators.[12]
As more white settlers occupied and traveled through their lands,
Kickapoo men were set to work on public roads, under the direction
of overseers.[13]

The allotment policies of the second half of the nineteenth century hit them particularly hard. Allotment had two significant implications. The first was to shift land from tribal control to individual
ownership, making it alienable to non-Indians. The second was to
reduce the amount of acreage in Indian hands, for once each tribal
member had been allotted his or her stipulated parcel, the remaining
land was sold to white settlers. According to the treaty that began the

allotment process among the Kansas Kickapoos in 1862, chiefs were entitled to 320 acres, other heads of family 160 acres, and everybody else a mere 40 acres. Those who "went south" would get nothing at all unless they returned within the year and pledged to "occupy, improve, and cultivate" their allotment. In a generous corporate giveaway, the treaty granted the Atchison and Pike's Peak Railroad Company the right to buy the remainder of the land at $1.25 per acre, without granting the Kickapoos any corresponding right to ride the rails.[14]

Several years after their land had been divided up, the Kansas Kickapoos still could not "point out with accuracy the boundary lines of these allotments." This troubled the superintendent of Indian affairs for Kansas, who thought it "very desirable that the Indians should know the exact boundaries of their several allotments." The point seems not so much that they should be able to protect their holdings from outsiders. Rather, the superintendent seemed concerned that if they did not know where the boundaries were, they would stray onto the lands recently occupied by white farmers. The purpose of clarifying the boundary lines was to keep the Kickapoos within them.[15]

The Kickapoos who left Kansas for Oklahoma did not escape the allotment process, they only delayed it. An 1891 treaty reduced the Kickapoo land in central Oklahoma to eighty acres for each member of the tribe, freeing up eighty thousand acres for "home seekers," a term understood to mean white settlers.[16] In anticipation of the impending land grab, the Atchison, Topeka, and Santa Fe Railroad Company printed pamphlets on how to reach the reservation from distant points such as Texas, California, and Chicago. Only at the end of the pamphlets, in the equivalent of small print, did the company remind those hopeful of overnight riches that ownership would require "actual residence on the land."[17]

When the Kickapoos heard about the 1891 allotment treaty for their Oklahoma lands, they sent members of the tribe to Washington to defend their claims to home.[18] Failing to achieve a change in the treaty, the Oklahoma Kickapoos refused to parcel out and open up their reservation.[19] Fed up with this resistance, their agent set aside eighty acres for each member of the tribe who would not make an allotment selection. If the Kickapoos wouldn't pick, he would do it for them.[20]

The Oklahoma Kickapoos continued to resist. About a hundred of the objectors built a village "on a section of fine school land" and declared they would not vacate. The governor threatened to ask the United States Army to eject them.[21] Unable to prevent the land seizure, the protesters set fire to their reservation, obscuring the sun with the smoke. "They have burned the whole reservation bare," claimed one newspaper account. "Flames swept over into the settled country and ruined scores of farmers. Hundreds of settlers awaiting on the line of the reservation have been burned out."[22] Yet even this last-ditch gesture of defiance did not stop the seizure of their land.

The process by which the would-be farmers who had rushed in from all directions claimed Kickapoo land showed that this generation of settlers, like the pioneers who preceded them, had little respect for the Kickapoos, much less their attachment to place. Accounts of the growing crowds who gathered on the outskirts of the reservation prior to the 1895 land rush spoke of each land rusher's eagerness to "outstrip the other and secure for himself a homestead settlement."[23] Their eagerness to strip the Kickapoos went without saying. The new arrivals divvied up the Kickapoos' land in a mad scramble lasting less than an hour.[24] When the dust had settled, the Kickapoos found their Oklahoma holdings reduced by about 168,000 acres.[25] Once again, colonial encroachments had forced both mobility—this time onto allotment parcels—and tighter spatial containment, from a net loss of land.

BECOMING UNDOCUMENTED

As onetime Indian lands were privatized by state-supported white proprietors, it became increasingly difficult for Kickapoos to move through them, because of fencing, hedgerows, and proscriptions against trespassing.[26] Some of these barriers had been erected with Indians specifically in mind: barbed wire advertisements in the nineteenth century touted the capacity of the product to keep marauding Indians out as well as to keep livestock in.[27] As the inrush of white settlers depleted game and other wild foodstuffs, and as settler colonists passed laws prohibiting hunting on private land without permission, it became more difficult for the Kickapoos to sustain themselves on their travels without running into trouble.[28] Even though their growing reliance on railroads offered more opportunities for speed and distance, it also had costs that went beyond the occasional accident. In 1911, a group of Oklahoma Kickapoos decided to travel to Washington to discuss their allotments. They secured the necessary permission from their agent, but they did not make the trip, because railroad tickets cost money, and they could not raise enough.[29]

Their increasing visibility in ever whiter ethnoscapes further altered the Kickapoos' relations to space. The mere appearance of Kickapoos "taking in the sights" in town sometimes made the papers. The scrutiny to which off-reservation Kickapoos were subjected can be gleaned from newspaper reports that they walked single file and that the women carried the loads. Crowds reportedly gathered to watch them "in open-mouthed wonder," intrigued by their "peculiar dress."[30] When ten Kickapoos attended the circus, they reportedly attracted as much attention as the show.[31] This kind of visibility made it more difficult for the Kickapoos to travel without altercations or assault. It helps explain why a Kickapoo man named Wa-pah-ka asked a U.S. Indian agent to notify distant military posts that he would be passing by. As the agent subsequently reported, Wa-pah-ka "did not wish to be punished, for he would be going peaceably on his way." The agent told Wa-pah-ka that even advance notice would not assure his safety if he went without a military escort.[32]

The Kickapoos' increasingly constrained spatial experience was a racialized experience, in keeping with the enslavement-enforcing pass laws that inhibited the movement of black people in the U.S. South. Northern states also limited the mobility of people of color through Black Laws that restricted residence and employment to proven freemen, facilitated the expulsion of poor African Americans, offered no sanctuary to runaway slaves, and enforced the 1850 Fugitive Slave Act.[33] Though the United States did not require passports for entry prior to World War I, Mah-Qua-Ta-Uathena and his band had to carry a "Pass Port" to travel across Texas to Kansas in 1875.[34]

However much their supporters touted reservations as preserves that would enable native peoples to maintain traditional ways apart from hostile settlers, their residents well knew that reservations kept inhabitants in as much as they kept would-be encroachers out. Reservations became particularly restrictive during the Reconstruction period, but their jail-like character can be seen as early as the Indian Intercourse Act of 1802, which gave U.S. courts the right to arrest and press criminal charges against Indians who left their reservations. Another section of the act made it an offense for Indians to use the roads that led to white settlements.[35] Such provisions led to policies requiring Indians who wanted to leave their reservations to first obtain passes from their agents.[36] Whether to go hunting, visit friends, pick berries, or find materials to construct the *wickiups* that sheltered them, off-reservation Kickapoos needed proper documentation.[37]

The necessary permission was not always granted. As one account put it: "Due to the fear inspired by these Indians in their recent conduct, i.e. raiding into Texas, it was deemed unwise to permit them to leave their reservation to follow the chase."[38] Another request to travel was denied on the grounds that the trip would be too expensive and that it would take the delegates away from their fields "at a time of the year when your agricultural interests demand your presence." In response to the petitioners' point that they would like to represent their own interests pertaining to a proposed treaty, the Interior Department official who denied their request told them that correspondence would suffice. The words written by their agents went to Washington; the Kickapoos did not.[39]

When U.S. officials did grant Kickapoos permission to travel off-reservation, they sometimes instructed the Kickapoos' agents to accompany their charges or delegated someone to tag along as an overseer.[40] After smallpox hit the Oklahoma Kickapoos in the late nineteenth century, a company of armed soldiers enforced the quarantine placed upon them. The military escorted Kickapoos to their reservations, and on more than one occasion it held Kickapoos prisoner to forestall potential trouble. When bands of Kickapoos slipped out of reservations without passes, or when they failed to return in a timely fashion, the War Department sent detachments to track them down.[41] The land of the free had become a policed state for the Kickapoos.

STRATEGIES OF CONTAINMENT

Reservations were not the only, nor the most extreme, forms of containment. Indian agents issued arrest warrants commanding Kickapoo children to attend boarding schools created for the express purpose of destroying Indian identities.[42] There they spent long hours seated inside at desks, learning their geography lessons from a textbook, rather than from firsthand experience, as their unconfined ancestors had.[43]

Of all the state efforts to restrict the Kickapoos, prisons squeezed

Kickapoo students sitting primly at their desks, under the watchful eye of
their American teacher. The colonial state sought to foster assimilation
through sedentarization, starting with schoolchildren.

*"A Class in the Kickapoo Indian School, Brown County, Kansas, 1905,"
courtesy of the McLean County Museum of History, Bloomington, Illinois.*

the tightest. The Kickapoos had no history of imprisoning each other
for offenses. Although they had a long history of taking and exchang-
ing captives and of being taken captive themselves, their experiences
of captivity meant time on the trail typically followed by death or
incorporation into the other group. Captivity did not imply incarceration. Early treaties had recognized that incarceration had no place in
the Kickapoos' legal practices by spelling out other forms of punishment, with one treaty from the 1820s stipulating that murders between Indian groups could be settled by a penalty of $1.00 for each
individual killed.[44] But the practice of payouts in place of prison did

not last. When a Kickapoo man killed another man in St. Louis some years later, his associates tried to atone for the offense by offering horses. White authorities decided that jail was more appropriate, and they stuck to that reasoning in later cases.[45]

In the absence of personal accounts from the time, we can only imagine what such confinement meant to people who experienced imprisonment not just as an individual punishment, but more generally, as a form of colonial domination. The incongruity of imprisoned Indians was not lost on white observers. In 1896, White Water, identified as "a full blooded Kickapoo Indian" by the *Atchison Daily Globe*, was arrested for drunkenness and sentenced to ten days of manual labor. "Think of it!" exclaimed the article in the *Globe*. "White Water's grandfather roamed the present townsite when this section was a wilderness. The vulgar whites not only destroyed the Kickapoo hunting grounds, but now they take one of the tribe's poor wronged braves, and actually put him on the rock pile!"[46] Rather than demand justice for this greater wrong, the *Globe* just marveled at how far white settlers had come, how diminished the people they had dislodged.

Not only did the Kickapoos have to leave homes and relinquish lands that were deeply meaningful to them, they also found their ability to go where they pleased increasingly constrained. Although many Kickapoos tenaciously defended their new homes and lands during the removal and allotment eras, they experienced localization as a form of oppression. Localization meant surveillance, control, material deprivation, and attenuated social ties. If the freedom of mobility made the Kickapoos more able to realize their identities as Kickapoos, localization threatened the Kickapoos' culture and existence as a people.

The Kickapoo poet Ekoneskaka said as much more than a century after the forced removal from Illinois. Rejecting the word *Kickapoo* as "some name the white people came up with because they didn't have the inclination to fit their mouths around Ki-ki-ka-pa-wa," Ekoneskaka explained that Ki-ki-ka-pa-wa meant to walk about, "like to walk from here over to there, and then maybe to walk back, or then maybe to keep going. But it means you go out on foot, maybe hunting, maybe just wandering free and easy, but always moving only on your own two feet; maybe you're looking for something, anything, and maybe you're not, but you're walking around, that's for sure, you're walking about here and there, usually searching and seeking, but always waiting for something to happen." Even after "walking about here and there" had come to imply driving around in four-wheel drive pickups, the point remained: the term for his people referred to free and easy movement, not claims to only one particular place.[47]

For a people who had begun referring to migratory birds as "Indian birds" because of their travels to distant reaches, to be spatially constrained meant to lose a fundamental part of what it meant to be Kickapoo.[48] The Kickapoos experienced spatial compression as a form of colonial violence. The existential importance of this issue to the Kickapoos can be seen in the lengths to which they went to resist.

EXODUS

One of the most astounding components of the Kickapoo resistance was the exodus of several groups to Mexico. The nineteenth-century Illinois Kickapoos who left the tallgrass prairie for cactus-studded ranges followed earlier footsteps. In 1763, when New France ceded the trans-Mississippi West to Spain, a Kickapoo band had accepted a Spanish invitation to build a village on the Missouri River near St. Louis. (This served Spanish interests by providing a buffer against the Osages.)[49] Building on that earlier relationship, the Spanish government persuaded some Kickapoos to move to its Mexican colony's northern province of Tejas in 1805, as a bulwark against Americans in Louisiana and Kiowas and Comanches on the plains. Another band of Kickapoos relocated to the Nacogdoches area (then part of the Lone Star Republic) in 1838. Yet another group, led by a man named Papicua (or Papequah), crossed the Rio Grande in 1850, in company with a band of Seminoles and their slaves.[50]

Like the Spanish before them, the Mexican government welcomed the newcomers as allies against the Comanches, Kiowas, and Apaches, who had been devastating their northern settlements. Although the leader of an 1828 boundary commission, General Mier y Terán, vilified the Kickapoos as nearly as savage as the Comanches, he recognized the value of immigrant Indian groups in a newer struggle: offsetting immigrant Anglos. When the Kickapoos and Seminoles sent delegates to Mexico City in the 1850s to ask for land, they received grants in Coahuila. This fostered further settlement, for in 1862, about six hundred Kickapoos led by a man named Machemanet went to Mexico from Kansas.[51] After the Seminoles and another immigrant group, the Muscogees, returned to the United States, the Kickapoos added some of their former holdings to their own.[52]

Wherever the destination, the choice to move came with considerable costs. Perhaps most painfully, it meant greater distances from other Kickapoos. The anguish of diaspora can be glimpsed in an 1855 appeal to the Office of Indian Affairs, which lamented how the tribe had been "broken up and scattered."[53] Rather than ending the violence that the Kickapoos had known in Illinois, dispersal produced new conflicts, including with other native nations that had reason to see groups such as the Kickapoos as encroachers who exacerbated the threat posed by Anglo pioneers.[54] White settlers were no more welcoming. Texas Rangers and Confederate Texans launched particularly brutal attacks—including on family groups en route to Mexico—that bred long-lasting bitterness among the Kickapoos.[55] A

A delegation of Kickapoo Indians in Mexico City around 1865. Kickapoos
met with the Austrian-born emperor Maximilian to secure their rights
to land and to discuss their security situation vis-à-vis other
Native American nations and U.S. raiders.

François Aubert, "Indios Kikapos," Getty Research Institute, Los Angeles (96.R.122).

delegation of Kickapoos that met with Emperor Maximilian at
Chapultepec Castle in Mexico City in 1865 complained of ongoing
raids on the part of American (presumably Confederate) deserters.
Maximilian's promise that the French army would protect them
came to naught.[56]

Moving did more than stretch group ties and embroil the Kickapoos in new cycles of violence—it distanced them from meaningful
places and the ecosystems that had sustained their ancestors in the
Great Lakes area. This was not completely new to the Kickapoos.
In 1827, a group that requested land in Nacogdoches, Texas, claimed,
through their interpreter, that the Americans had moved them
"from their own country" to a bad country, one in which women and

children were dying.[57] Yet Coahuila had even less in common with the lands that they had known. As one group of Kickapoos that decided not to relocate said of northern Mexico: "There was no grass and the land was no good, and the weather was too hot."[58]

An anthropological report on the Mexican Kickapoos from the 1970s reveals some of their struggles to adapt as well as their struggles to adhere to traditional ways. According to this report, there were no cattails within fifty miles of the El Nacimiento village. To build their *wickiups* in the traditional way, Kickapoo women had to travel by train to Cuatrociénegas, 150 miles to the southwest. There they hired a truck to take them another twenty-five miles or so to swamps where cattails grew.[59] That Kickapoo women went to such lengths to gather cattails generations after their ancestors had left the lakeshores and marshes of the Midwest hints at years of extraordinary perseverance in an unfamiliar clime.

The Kickapoos who chose to move did so in part to secure land, but the more they moved, the more tenuous their claims became. "All were intruders," said an 1841 history of Texas in reference to the Kickapoos and other native newcomers, "who took advantage of the weakness of the authorities, and the confusion which reigned in Mexico [in the 1820s], to 'squat' upon a fertile soil."[60]

Given the costs of moving, why did some Kickapoos choose to resettle far from other members of their nation, in the dry reaches of northern Mexico? Ironically, some of the things that might seem to have made Mexico unattractive—such as its aridity and history of intergroup violence—actually added to its appeal. The terrain might have been forbidding, but that meant a thinner, less settled population. The region might have been torn by violence, but that led Mexican officials to welcome the Kickapoos, in hopes of using them as buffers like the Spanish had. In sum, the wildness of northern Mexico offered the Kickapoos a chance to live their lives without as much meddling from Indian agents. The freedoms they found in Mexico

Six men standing in front of a winter lodge in the Kickapoo village
in Nacimiento, Mexico, in 1910. Dry and scrubby hills can be spotted
in the background. Unable to obtain birch bark as readily as their ancestors
had in the Great Lakes area, Kickapoo women relied more heavily
on cattail canes, obtained at some distance.

National Museum of the American Indian, Smithsonian Institution, Catalog Number PO1824.

explain why U.S. anthropologists in the 1950s held up the Mexican Kickapoos as the "best preserved" Algonquian group, and thus Coahuila as the optimal place to learn about the traditional cultural practices of northern woodlands peoples.[61]

Prominent among the freedoms found in Mexico was the freedom of mobility. The Mexican Kickapoos did not need passes to leave their communal lands, granted to them by the Mexican government. They could hunt more widely in the surrounding hills, and, indeed, hundreds of miles away in places like Durango and Tamaulipas.[62] And they could raid Texan ranches with less danger of pursuit.

A photograph of the Kickapoo village near Múzquiz, in the northern
Mexican state of Coahuila, taken by a member of a 1954 anthropological
expedition sponsored by the Milwaukee Public Museum.

*Kickapoo Village, Mexico, 1954, negative number #35 17–21, courtesy of the
Milwaukee Public Museum, Milwaukee, Wisconsin.*

BORDER LIBERTIES

Texans living along the border complained that the Kickapoos,
sometimes in association with Lipan Apaches, frequently crossed the
Rio Grande to "pounce upon the frontier." They would then drive
their booty of horses and cattle back to their refuge in Mexico.[63]
Even as the Kickapoos living in Kansas were winning praise for their
agricultural pursuits (seen as all the more remarkable by their agent
because they "were never known to labour before"), those in the
borderlands were carving out a more fearsome reputation.[64] According to an 1871 report, their raids were so frequent "that stock raisers

in many instances have been compelled to abandon their ranches and drive their cattle into the interior for safety."[65]

What particularly enraged the Texan ranchers was the Kickapoos' impunity. There was much truth to their critics' livid claims that the Kickapoos "care little for boundary lines."[66] But when it came to raiding, the Kickapoos cared a lot about boundary lines, because the international border protected them from retaliation. Rather than restraining them, the border opened up new spatial possibilities—until the U.S. Cavalry went after them, that is.

Sending in the cavalry was a last-ditch option that followed a number of other attempts to control the Mexican Kickapoos, starting with efforts to entice them to go to the Kickapoo reservation in Kansas. Prodded by threats that the "citizens of Texas" would take matters into their own hands, thereby sparking "serious difficulties" with Mexico, in 1868 the Committee on Indian Affairs commissioned an agent named Stephen S. Brown to meet with the Kickapoos living near Múzquiz, Mexico. Believing that the Mexican Kickapoos were principally Kansas Kickapoos who had gone south only three years earlier, the committee charged Brown with persuading them to "consent to their removal to some portion of the United States." Adding to their hopes that this consent would be forthcoming was the conviction that the Kansas Kickapoos who had accompanied No-ko-what to Mexico in 1865 had become so "dissatisfied with their condition and prospects" that half of them had attempted to return to Kansas in 1866. All but forty turned back when their ponies gave out, and of the forty, only fourteen arrived at the Kickapoo agency in 1867. The report did not note what had happened to the other twenty-six who did not turn around, nor did it comment on the prospects of removing the Kickapoos "who had been living in that country for some twenty years past, and who were the remnant of a large number who had some sort of a contract with the Mexican government to serve it against the Comanches."[67]

Brown arrived in Santa Rosa only to find that many of the Kickapoos were out "on the war path." Despite this inauspicious start, he finally managed to meet with some Mexican officials and Kickapoo men. In the course of these meetings, Brown discovered that the Kickapoos had divided up their camps, to avoid being "gobbled up" by invading U.S. forces or extradited to the United States by Mexican officials. These camps, Brown reported, were so isolated that their localities were "unknown." Brown castigated the Mexicans for having "neither the material means the physical nor the moral power to control—to civilize—to support and keep these people in subjection." Instead of tracking them down in their wilderness haunts, the Mexicans seemed to regard the Kickapoos with favor. To Brown's horror, when the warriors returned "flushed with triumph" from their raids, the townspeople of Múzquiz greeted them with "the ringing of Bells." (Such evidence of community support may explain why Texas vigilante groups hesitated to go after the Kickapoos themselves.)[68]

The gap between Brown's desire for subjection and the Kickapoos' desire to avoid being gobbled up did not augur well for the talks. Although the Kickapoos were, according to Brown, in a state of destitution, when he pressed them to relocate, they said they would rather "arrange and determine all questions between them and the U.S." with a delegation of their own people. Adding to Brown's frustrations, the Kickapoos "occupied the time . . . on questions about the country and the Indians at home." Given his conviction that the Mexican Kickapoos were Kansans, Brown could not understand why they had so many questions about Kansas. When pressed to go "back to your own lands," one old man told Brown that "god is my Captain, the world my camping ground, and I am at liberty to go where I choose."[69]

Brown returned to the United States. The Kickapoos continued to raid. Texan ranchers continued to insist that the Kickapoos be removed to Kansas, claiming that their foes were "very anxious to return to their old home" but were afraid to pass through Texas without protection.[70]

The U.S. government did not give up. In 1870 Congress appropriated $25,000 to remove the Mexican Kickapoos to Kansas.[71] The following year, John D. Miles, the Kickapoo agent in Kansas, traveled to Mexico with three Kickapoo men (Nokowhat, Parthe, and Keoquark) and an interpreter in hopes of persuading the Mexican Kickapoos to "return to their reservation in Kansas, and again become wards of our government."[72] Miles reported that a Mexican spy from Piedras Negras had alerted the Kickapoos to his impending arrival in Santa Rosa. He also noted that "several squads were out on the 'Chase,' including Wah-pah-kah [this is one of several spellings that occur in the records], one of the principal chiefs." Whether there was any relation between these two happenings, he did not say. The Kickapoos remaining in Santa Rosa seemed "delighted to meet their Kansas brothers," who slipped away from their escorts to visit the Kickapoo village in Nacimiento without any Indian agents or infantry members to monitor them. Miles hired messengers to inform the absent Kickapoos of his visit and his desire to meet with them in council. About a week later, Wah-pah-kah returned to Santa Rosa and acceded to Miles's desire to meet with "our Kickapoo brothers."[73]

Despite their delight in meeting with the Kansas Kickapoos, the Mexican Kickapoos had mixed feelings about returning to a place where some had never lived. According to Miles, "quite a number of them, particularly the squaws, expressed a positive determination to go back with us." Others did not want to leave. Miles blamed their obduracy on "local influences" who worked to "buy up Chiefs and head men," so as to keep the Kickapoos as their defense against "marauding bands of Indians."[74]

Wy-mo-sho-na, "the oldest chief in the Nation," emerged as the leader of those who would stay. The younger negotiator, Wah-pah-kah, expressed some interest in departing, but he said he would need assurances "that the land was good, and where it was to be located, and how much was to be given them, and who their neighbors were to be." He asked if he could take a delegation to see it. But no money had been allocated for scouting purposes, perhaps because U.S. officials stubbornly persisted in seeing the issue as a matter of repatriation "to their proper reservation in Kansas." Wah-pah-kah's proposal to select thirty of his leading men and secretly travel from Mexico to Kansas without an escort came to naught when Miles said he could give him no assurances of safety in his travels or government recognition upon arrival.[75]

In the final council meeting, all the Kickapoos declined Miles's proposition, "asking to be let alone where they are." Miles ended his report on the venture by blasting the Mexican government. It ought to be held responsible for all depredations committed on the frontier of Texas, he wrote, because he would have succeeded were it not for its "very tangible and substantial interference" with his efforts. Like Brown two years earlier, Miles returned to the United States with no Mexican Kickapoos in tow. The Mexican Kickapoos returned to the United States on their own, but not to Kansas, at least according to the reports that continued to implicate them in cross-border raids.[76]

THE LIMITS OF SOVEREIGNTY

When appeals to the Mexican minister of foreign affairs proved no more effective than appeals to the Kickapoos, the U.S. military took action, knowing that Mexican officials had refused to publicly authorize an anti-Kickapoo incursion but with some unofficial assurances that the Mexican government was unlikely to seriously complain.[77] Guided by Seminole Negro Indian Scouts, a cavalry company led by

Colonel Ranald S. Mackenzie marched eighty miles into Coahuila in May 1873, in search of Kickapoos, Lipans, Potawatomis, and Mescalero Apaches. After traveling all night, they reached the Kickapoo settlement near Santa Rosa at dawn.[78]

They burned it to the ground and then proceeded about a quarter of a mile to a Lipan village, which they also destroyed. Mackenzie reported killing nineteen people and wounding two more, but these were just the casualties his men were able to count before beating it hastily back to Texas. They brought with them their prisoners: a Lipan chief and forty-one women and children, mostly Kickapoos, some lashed with lariats to their ponies. Fearing that they would escape if kept close to the Rio Grande, Mackenzie sent them under "strong guard" to San Antonio, recommending that they "be kept in a corral" until they could be further removed.[79]

The U.S. agent charged with peaceably removing the Kickapoos from Mexico was in Saltillo, the capital of Coahuila, at the time, awaiting an audience with the governor. He was shocked to learn of this turn of events. Fearing that it would make the remaining Kickapoos even more resistant to removal, he relayed their desire to have the captives restored to them in Mexico. He also reported that the chiefs had said, "with much truth and justice," that they had ceased their raiding and had been "innocent of any depredation upon citizens of the United States."[80] Colonel Mackenzie regretted that the Kickapoos had suffered more than the Lipans, who he thought were the greater offenders in cross-border raids, but he insisted that they had to take the consequences for their unsavory associations.[81]

Having captured some Kickapoos, the U.S. government faced the problem of what to do with them. In authorizing the incursion, the commissioner of the Office of Indian Affairs had called for the Kickapoos' immediate removal to the Kickapoo reservation in Kansas.[82] But having been eaten away by white settlement, the Kansas reservation had become too small to absorb the Mexican

Kickapoos. That left Indian Territory.[83] Using the captives as hostages to force their family members to move to the United States, the U.S. prepared to relocate about five hundred Mexican Kickapoos to Oklahoma.[84]

The "main body" of the Kickapoos (led by Wahpesee and Thah-pequah) traveled separately from the U.S. agents and their captives, arriving "worn out and . . . in a suffering condition." After settling on the North Fork of the Canadian River (thereby "returning" to a place they had never lived before), they planted corn and vegetables. But their agent seems to have questioned their intention to stay, for when some asked to go out on the plains, he said no, a decision in keeping with his supervisor's views that the Kickapoos' grounds should be not only plowed and cultivated but also fenced.[85]

The Mackenzie raid showed that even an international border did not protect the Kickapoos' place and space claims from the U.S. government. Rather than follow an 1862 extradition treaty, the United States had taken matters into its own hands.[86] True, when Mackenzie went after the Mexican Kickapoos, he feared that he might face the gibbet for his cross-border incursion, having been issued only oral orders to do whatever was necessary to "clean up this situation." Knowing he was on dicey diplomatic ground, Mackenzie did not loiter. The raid was a quick in-and-out operation, with no U.S. forces sent to follow the Kickapoos who fled deeper into Mexico to escape and none assigned to pursue those Kickapoos who returned to the Santa Rosa area the following spring.[87]

Yet Mexican sovereignty had its limits. In contrast to subsequent—and still ongoing—border enforcement efforts aimed at keeping people out, U.S. forces had marched into Mexico to forcibly patriate people believed to "properly belong within the limits of the United States."[88] Mexican Indians were American Indians (in the narrower sense of the word *American*) if and when that suited U.S. interests. Mackenzie's commanding officer summed up the matter by saying:

"There can not be any valid boundary line when we pursue Indians who murder our people and carry away our property."[89]

Mexico protested the raid, but it did not become a full-blown diplomatic incident, in part because the Mexican troops had their own history of border crossings in pursuit of Indians.[90] The people of the Piedras Negras area who rallied upon hearing reports that six hundred gringos had violated their national territory quieted down upon hearing that the purpose of the raid had been to chastise Indians who depredated Texas.[91] The United States had made it very clear that peace between the two nations depended on the removal of the Kickapoos, and the Mexican government pledged, in response, to support that end.[92]

NATIONAL INSECURITIES

Following the Mackenzie raid, the Mexican government worked harder to monitor the Coahuila Kickapoos so as to avoid a repeat incident. Its reading of public sentiment led it to place more emphasis on preventing U.S. military incursions than on protecting its residents from the harassment of Indian agents. Concerned by U.S. claims that the next intervention would mean annexation, the Mexican central government instructed the new governor of Coahuila to cooperate with U.S. agents in their efforts to remove Kickapoos, Mescaleros, and Lipans. The governor followed through on these orders by appointing a commissioner to do the cooperating.[93] Yet cross-border raiding continued, with the blame falling on Kickapoos even in cases when they were not at fault.[94] Hoping to avoid another intrusion, the Mexican government allowed the United States to send a special commissioner to try to remove the Kickapoos who were not captured in the Mackenzie raid.[95] He reported that many Kickapoos were out of the state hunting, and others were "scattered in bands several hundred miles apart." He also reported that "the Mexicans in this section appear more determined than ever before to prevent the removal of the remaining Kickapoos, as they claim with some truth that it would leave them subject to constant depredations from the Mescaleros, Lipans, and Comanches."[96]

In his next dispatch, three months later, the agent reported that some Kickapoos who were away at the time of the Mackenzie raid still had not returned. He also accused the appointed Mexican commissioner of trying to covertly defeat his efforts to remove the Kickapoos. "Yesterday," he wrote in elaboration, "the Mexican Commissioner failed to be present at the Council with the Kickapoos, and when he did come to day, he told them he was instructed by his Government to say that they could go, or remain here, as they might elect, and upon my request that he tell them that it was the desire of his Government that they should go, he declined, claiming it was exceeding his instructions."[97] The U.S. agent returned to the United States in a huff by rail, with one Kickapoo man who had elected to return with him. Another 116 Kickapoos departed on their own on horseback, outfitted with provisions that the agent had purchased at "outrageous prices" from opportunistic Mexican merchants. Among those who welcomed this group to the United States was a group of white men who fired upon them, killing one. At least 140 Kickapoos (by the agent's count) remained in Mexico, most of them still taking cover hundreds of miles in the interior.[98]

The U.S. minister to Mexico followed up on the noncooperation complaint with a protest to the minister of foreign affairs. The ministry replied that it would do all it properly could to "facilitate the return of the Indians to the United States," but that it had "no power to require their extradition." It attributed whatever support the Kickapoos enjoyed among their neighbors to the U.S. "projects of invasion and acquisition of territory."[99]

Refusing to accept that logic, the U.S. minister in Mexico City penned another note to the Mexican minister of foreign affairs. "I am constrained to express the conviction that your Excellency's Government has erred in deciding that it could not require these Indians to return to their reservations. . . . They could only be considered as refugees from the authority of the Government of the United States, and in the spirit of international comity, should have again been returned to the territory of the United States."[100] The Mexican government caved. It issued instructions to the governors of the states where the Kickapoos were located to "remove any obstacle that may present itself whenever their removal is again attempted."[101] The next visit from a U.S. agent resulted in the departure of a "small band" of Kickapoos for Indian Territory, leaving an estimated eighty still in Mexico. At this point the United States changed tack: instead of demanding removal *from* Mexico, it shifted to removal *within* Mexico. As the agent who proposed the idea put it, if the Kickapoos were required to remove to the interior of Mexico, "they could not raid upon the Texas border, by reason of their remoteness from it." Not only would this approach stop the raids, it would also "relieve the Government of their care, which is no small consideration."[102]

Once again, Mexican officials yielded to U.S. demands, prodding the Kickapoos in the vicinity of Santa Rosa to move farther from the border. By 1876, however, there were enough Kickapoos back in Santa Rosa to merit another visit from a U.S. Indian agent. This one, too, failed to persuade the Kickapoos to move to the United States, but the visit did prompt about sixty families to move to Chihuahua, farther from the threat of U.S. forces. The group camped outside the city in "destitute condition" while their scouts investigated the resettlement prospects in the mountains to the north.[103] In

July of that year, a U.S. cavalry unit attacked a Lipan and Kickapoo camp near Zaragoza, in the state of Chihuahua. More raids across the border, in pursuit of other Indian groups, followed.[104]

Fearful that the United States would again go after the Santa Rosa Kickapoos, the Mexican government took action. It moved one group of Kickapoos to Mexico City, where they subsisted for a while as street beggars, and from there on to Querétaro (about a hundred miles to the north of the capital). It moved others to the Chihuahuan municipality of Guerrero, in hopes that the German colony there would transform them. It set others to work on the railroad line between Mexico City and Cuernavaca. Resisters went to prison.[105] The U.S. military stopped pursuing the Kickapoos, because it did not have to, the Mexican government having done the dirty work for it.

Yet as cross-border raids by other groups continued, U.S. Secretary of State William M. Evarts reaffirmed his nation's right to send forces into Mexico in pursuit of marauders: "Undoubtedly it would be preferable to enter Mexican territory for the purpose indicated with the consent or with the acquiescence of the government of that republic. If, however, these should be refused and the outrages persisted in, this government may deem itself warranted in punishing the wrong-doers wherever they may be found."[106] U.S. forces rode into Mexico about a dozen times in the late 1870s.[107] Mexican displeasure with these incursions contributed to the 1882 "Treaty on Reciprocal Consent to Pursue Savage Hostile Indian Marauders Across the Border" that allowed the Mexicans to respond in kind.[108] In authorizing cross-border raids against Indians, and Indians only, the two governments agreed that place claims meant different things to Indians than to other people. They also revealed that the Kickapoos were not the only ones who associated security with an ability to move unfettered through space.

AMERICANS ABROAD

Just as the Mexican Kickapoos could not escape the long arm and influence of the U.S. government, neither could they escape the reach of border-crossing U.S. citizens and capital. By the 1880s, the Coahuila Kickapoos had to compete for game with wealthy U.S. hunters who went down to the Sierra Carmen Mountains to bag deer, antelope, and bear.[109] Soon the competition for resources came to involve land. During the regime of Porfirio Díaz (1876–1911), the Mexican government gave collectively owned Indian lands to railroad builders and hacienda owners. Among the expropriated were the Kickapoos, who lost about sixty thousand acres in Nacimiento to some Texas cattlemen in 1883.[110] When the Kickapoos refused to vacate the property, the Mexican government removed them, in hopes of assuring investors "that property rights of strangers will meet with full protection."[111]

Things got worse in 1898, when three U.S. investors purchased the first chunk of what eventually became a 1.237-million-acre hacienda, Piedra Blanca. The Kickapoos charged them with "usurpation," to no avail. Although the Kickapoos had been living in Mexico for years, U.S. *hacenderos* who ended up with parcels of their land benefited from closer ties to the Mexican political elite and a greater ability to negotiate the Mexican court system. In pressing their claims, the investors dismissed the Mexican Kickapoos as Oklahomans, the implication being they had no rights to place in Mexico. Some Kickapoos cut down the ranchers' pecan trees in protest, but they could not recover the disputed land titles.[112] The ranchers proceeded to string up fences that impaired the Kickapoos' ability to hunt.[113] By 1903, papers in Mexico City reported that the "Kickapoo Indian Chieftain" Wapichi Cucha had been seen wandering the streets of the capital as he sought a government grant of land.[114]

The Rosita smelter may have brought clean water to its workers,
but not to the nearby Kickapoos. Even Mexico offered little
refuge from the long reach of U.S. power.

*Rosita, 1946, Serie Oblicua, Número de Control FAO 01 003795,
Fondo Aerofotográfico Acervo Histórico Fundación ICA, A.C.*

In addition to reducing the Kickapoos' access to land and game,
U.S. border crossers threatened another resource fundamental to the
Kickapoos' survival: their water. In 1919, a U.S. company controlled
by the Guggenheim family purchased a coal operation in Rosita. By
1925, the American Smelting and Refining Company (ASARCO)
had broadened its Rosita operation to include the smelting of zinc. Its
smokestack was the highest in Mexico, its plant the largest of its kind
in the world.

A corporate history of the 1940s described it as being "like a
cross-section of Pittsburgh transplanted to the Coahuila plain." The
history went on to praise ASARCO for providing water to its workers
and their families, and not just any water, either, but water "treated

in a modern treatment plant, which includes chlorination, filtration, and sedimentation." What this account did not say was that the company polluted the Kickapoos' water supply and, making matters worse, further drained their depleted water table in a time of drought.[115] Already suffering from restricted hunting possibilities, the Kickapoos had to contend with withered fields and decimated herds.[116] They were not the only ones, it seemed, who could be accused of cross-border depredations.

Rather than being a refuge, by the turn of the twentieth century, Mexico had become like the United States, with its forced removals and land grabs. Instead of standing up for the Kickapoos, Mexican officials collaborated with U.S. opportunists, including those who sought Kickapoo holdings north of the border. In the spring of 1907, a partnership of U.S. deed seekers—referred to in the subsequent hearings as "the Chapman, Grimes and Conine people" but known more widely as the "Shawnee wolves"—traveled to Coahuila to defraud some visiting Kickapoos of their increasingly valuable lands in Oklahoma. The conspirators paid the Múzquiz police to have all the leading members of the tribe arrested and thrown into jail. Having intimidated their intended victims, they then took "a large number of Indians by force and under guard of policemen" to the house of the "jefe politico of that district." There they urged the Kickapoos to sell their lands in the United States. The captive men declined.

Undeterred, the conspirators faked the papers, putting down the names of men who were not in the area at the time. They also claimed to have a deed executed at the *jefe politico*'s house by a Kickapoo woman named Pah-na-tho, who had died more than five years earlier. Another deed bore the name of Paw-kaw-kah, "a known imbecile, who could not utter a word or make a sound and to whom no member of the tribe could talk nor make himself understood." Minors, too, supposedly signed their names to deeds. From Múzquiz, the schemers headed north, to the border town of Eagle Pass. After plying the Kickapoos there with liberal amounts of whiskey and mescal, they "herded" them into a wagon yard where they kept them interned until they signed away Oklahoma land. Resisters were arrested and sent across the border to Múzquiz, to work on the streets in chains.[117]

Fortunately for the defrauded Kickapoos—or at least it seemed at the time—their agent from Oklahoma, Martin Bentley, took the conspirators to court. But Bentley had his own ambitions involving Kickapoo land, ones that can be traced back at least as far as 1901, when he traveled with Pan O Wa and Pah Ko Tah to Mexico City, where they stayed in the Grand Hotel while seeking meetings with government officials who might grant them land. Bentley's scheme was to buy deeds from the Kickapoos near Shawnee, Oklahoma, and resell them for much higher amounts. He planned to pocket most of the difference himself but use some of the proceeds to buy cheaper land in Mexico. After one of his victims, Thapathethea, complained that she had never meant to sell her land, investigators found Bentley guilty of fraud. But Congress ignored their findings, leaving Bentley free to machinate.[118]

Promising his followers that in Mexico they would once more find "room to roam once more limitless prairie, vast forests and inaccessible mountains," Bentley persuaded over a hundred Oklahoma Kickapoos to go from Coahuila to Sonora with him in the latter part of 1907. Cashing in some of the titles that had been signed over to him in trust, Bentley bought an abandoned ranch. It was a disappointment, a tract of "mountain breaks and crags, through which is the channel of an intermittent stream, at times so violent with the water rush from the mountains as to tear out the surface of the only little valley they have." If this were not bad enough, the title to all this was of doubtful legitimacy. Left in straitened circumstances, the Sonoran Kickapoos were taken in by the Yaquis, an indigenous nation that had been largely dispossessed by the Mexican

A group of displaced Kickapoos heading toward Sonora, Mexico, in 1907. Like refugees in other places and times, they had to adjust to wildly different social and ecological conditions.

Natives Migrating to Mexico in Wagons, Feb. 1907, BAE GN 00741A 06177300, National Anthropological Archives, Smithsonian Institution.

government, with survivors fleeing to the mountains and across the border into the United States to avoid enslavement on the plantations of the Yucatán, or, even worse, extermination.[119] Upon realizing that Mexico was not the answer to their dreams, some of Bentley's former followers sued him for defrauding them of their land in Oklahoma.

The brief filed on their behalf by their new agent suggested that Bentley's motives had been more sinister than his followers had realized. As long as the Kickapoos lived in the United States, they could not alienate their land without consent of the U.S. government. But if they became "resident citizens of some foreign country," such consent was no longer necessary. From Bentley's perspective, expatriation was not so much the pathway to self-determination as the pathway to expropriation. The court sided with the Kickapoo plaintiffs. When their allotments were restored, some of the emigrants traveled straightaway to Oklahoma.[120] Others did not. In 1912, the secretary of the interior authorized the First National Bank of Douglas, Arizona, to cut checks payable to fifty-two Mexican Kickapoo Indians, ranging in age from about seventy-one (Ah che che), to a ten-year-old youth (Thy ka toke). More than half the recipients were women, among them Inez Hale, Ke o si ah quah (also known as Rachel Kirk), Kcah quah quah, and Nah me pesh qua.[121] Some of these so-called Mexican Kickapoos circled for years between Sonora, Coahuila, and Oklahoma, preferring a life on the move, however hard, to fixed residence in one of three scattered places.[122]

The era of great exoduses came to an end with the Bentley fiasco. Realizing that pulling up roots and relocating to Mexico meant losing place without gaining unlimited space, that not even an international border offered protection from Yankee incursions, that crooked schemers could manipulate the border as strategically as livestock raiders, most Kickapoos united behind the strategy of holding tight to place, with visits across the diaspora. The Kickapoos might return to places their people had once frequented, but in a larger sense, there was no going back.

FROM PAROLEES TO CITIZENS

About a hundred and fifty years after their ancestors had been expelled from the fledgling state of Illinois, some members of the Kickapoo nation gathered in a congressional committee room in

Kickapoo *wickiups* under the International Bridge connecting
Eagle Pass, Texas, to Piedras Negras, Coahuila.

"Confirming the Citizenship Status of the Texas Band of Kickapoo Indians," Hearings
Before the Committee on Interior and Insular Affairs, *97th Congress, House of Representatives*
(Washington, D.C.: Government Printing Office, 1983), 82.

Washington, D.C., to make a case for U.S. citizenship. This band had
lived for many years next to the northern side of the International
Bridge that connected Eagle Pass, Texas, to Piedras Negras, Mexico,
on opposite banks of the Rio Grande. After their camp had been
bulldozed, fenced, and turned into a parking lot, the Eagle Pass
Kickapoos rebuilt their homes *under* the bridge, literally on the U.S.-
Mexican border.

Life in this marginal spot was marked by daily tribulations. Com-
muters tossed their garbage down upon the cane and cardboard
houses. The area was too small to perform important ceremonies.
Given their uncertain citizenship status—some having been born in
Mexico, some in the United States, with no documentation as to one
case or the other—the Eagle Pass Kickapoos did not qualify for U.S.

public health services and could not enroll their children in public schools.[123]

Things had only gotten worse. Eagle Pass officials had recently forced them to relocate to city land. As Wipecuinacudita (also known as Jose Naco Jiminez) put it: "We have no outhouses and sometimes no water. We have many mosquitoes. We have no stoves and we must use an open fire. My biggest fear is that we could be thrown out at any moment." In introducing the citizenship bill, Texas congressman Abraham Kazen played up this theme of dispossession, claiming: "They just want a place they can call home."[124] Kickapoo representative Makateonenodua (also known as Raul Garza) agreed in his plea for "a permanent land base where we can worship in peace and privacy."[125] This logic seemed compelling to the committee, and later to Congress and the president. In 1983 the Eagle Pass Kickapoos obtained U.S. citizenship and tribal recognition.[126]

But the Eagle Pass Kickapoos wanted more than a home. Those who spoke at the hearing also made it clear that they wanted the right to cross the border—into the United States and back to Mexico again. They did not want to be fenced in any more than they wanted to be displaced. They wanted what their people had been struggling for since their first encounters with the pioneers—rights to the kinds of belonging associated with place and to the freedoms associated with movement through space. The officials in the hearing room construed this desire as wanting dual citizenship—U.S. and Mexican. But the Kickapoos who testified spoke of their desire to be Kickapoos. And that implied the right to a home and a way of being in the world that had preceded both the United States and Mexico. In a time of tightening border enforcement, the Eagle Pass Kickapoos testified that they had been Americans—Kickapoo Americans—first. Long before the United States and Mexico began drawing lines between insiders and outsiders, Kickapoos had belonged in the heart of the land. As in the cases of other indigenous people and their descendants (some of them coming to identify as Mexican), border-patrolling efforts to produce national safe spaces had led to insecurity, suffering, and pain.

So how did this group of Eagle Pass Kickapoos end up in a congressional hearing room in 1982? As their water dried up, their hunting options shrank, and their land began to suffer from overgrazing, the Mexican Kickapoos had begun to seek work as migrant laborers in the United States. Starting in the drought years of the 1940s, they sought seasonal agricultural work in Texas, Arizona, Oklahoma, Colorado, Idaho, Montana, Nebraska, Wisconsin, Michigan, Illinois, Ohio, California, and New York. With the end of the Mexican *bracero* (guestworker) program in 1964, the demand for Kickapoo workers increased.[127] Unlike most Mexican farmworkers, Kickapoos could still enter the United States, thanks to notarized photocopies of a pass written for them by a U.S. Army major at Fort Dearborn, Michigan, in 1832. This document certified that the Kickapoos were "to be protected by all persons from any injury whatever, as they are under the protection of the U.S. and any person so violating shall be punished accordingly."[128] Although intended to allow the Kickapoos of Michigan to move around the Detroit area without injury, over a century later this document enabled their Mexican descendants to visit friends and relatives in the United States and, increasingly, to work.

As border enforcement grew tighter in the late 1950s, the photocopies no longer sufficed, except among some Eagle Pass agents. By the 1970s, the Mexican Kickapoos had to obtain "parole papers" from the immigration officers at Eagle Pass. These papers identified the bearers as: "Parolee, Kickapoo Indian, pending clarification of status by Congress."[129] The federal officers insisted that "it's not a criminal thing," but the affected Kickapoos objected to the language of "parolee," understanding this all too keenly as the status of being outside of a penitentiary on condition. Officials considered them to be U.S.

citizens when in the United States and Mexican citizens when in Mexico, pending a determination of their status by Congress.[130]

Countering the local histories from the Midwest that declared the Kickapoos long gone, in the aftermath of the bracero program they traveled to Michigan and Wisconsin to work in the cucumber fields and to Illinois to pick tomatoes.[131] In a reversal of traditional seasonal patterns, summer mobility enabled settled winters in the Nacimiento village. Yet in the 1980s all this was imperiled by even tighter border controls, which made it ever more difficult for Chicapoos (a term some Kickapoos adopted in jest to mean Chicano and Kickapoo mixed together) to circulate between the United States and Mexico.[132] It was in this context that the Eagle Pass Kickapoos made their claims.

The Eagle Pass Kickapoos made it clear that they did not want to have to choose between the United States and Mexico—they wanted to be able to move back and forth across the border. Like their ancestors before them, they sought both place (a home) and space (the ability to move freely). The great irony of the hearings—one that went unremarked at the time—was that one of the Kickapoos' witnesses cited the Mackenzie raid on behalf of their claims. The violent incursion that had devastated Kickapoos in the nineteenth century had become proof in the twentieth that the Eagle Pass Kickapoo did indeed hail from the United States and should be able to claim the rights that followed from that if they pleased.[133]

It may seem that in claiming U.S. citizenship, the Eagle Pass Kickapoos had come to accept the idea of territorially based identities and rights. After all, the hearings were called by the representative of the Texas district in which they lived. The executive director of the Texas Indian Commission testified on their behalf.[134] A Michigan representative also took the stand, to speak of their ancestral ties to his state. All these speakers connected the Kickapoos' citizenship claims to place—or rather, several places.

But these were not the only parties involved in the matter. Congressman Kazen worked with the Department of the Interior and the Bureau of Indian Affairs to perfect the bill. These agencies helped broaden the issue from district and state jurisdiction to the federal level. Kazen also consulted with the Department of Immigration and Naturalization—which had purview over border crossing—and the U.S. State Department, the agency in charge of international relations.[135] In the course of the hearings, Dr. Oscar Arze Quintanilla, a Bolivian anthropologist, lawyer, and indigenous rights activist then serving as the executive director of the Inter-American Indian Institute, brought his hemispheric stature to bear on the Kickapoos' case. Placing the Kickapoos' struggle in a wider context, he argued that they should be able to cross the border in the same way that Indians along the border with Canada could, under the 1794 Jay Treaty. Representatives from several First Nations located within the United States also spoke on behalf of the Kickapoos, recognizing that modern border enforcement regimes curtailed the rights of all people of Native American ancestry.[136]

The participation of so many different parties in the citizenship hearings reveal that in the 1980s, the Eagle Pass Kickapoos placed themselves in a series of nesting political units that scaled up from the municipal level to district, state, federal, and hemispheric bodies; from tribal to indigenous affiliations, from members of particular Kickapoo groups to members of a larger Kickapoo diaspora and nation. Yet they also understood themselves in terms of lateral identities that overlapped along the edges: U.S. and Mexican; indigenous and citizens of federal nation states; Kickapoos in relation to other indigenous peoples. They were First Americans first, before being forced to choose between the United States and Mexico. Through their efforts to preserve their identity as a people—the very struggle that had brought many of their ancestors to the U.S.-Mexican borderlands in the first place—the Eagle Pass Kickapoos argued against the fixed conceptions of security that the heartland myth propounds.

In opposition to those who would pin security solely to place, they insisted that boundaries could cage people and sunder communities as readily as they could guard them. In arguing for the right to return—and to leave, and to come back again—they insisted that rights should adhere to people, even if they moved about. Arguing that place and space are always, inevitably, relational, they insisted that true security does not emerge from walling people in and out, but from extending human rights and justice. As seen by the heartlanders-in-exile under the International Bridge, the tribalists who had inherited their earth were far from securing both.

ARCHIVAL TRACES

The world is a pretty small place after all

Urbana Courier, 1906: A report on the Thirteenth Annual Meeting of the Woman's Foreign Missionary Society of the Champaign district of the M. E. Church, featuring an address by Mrs. Stephens of Poona, India. Participants from the town of St. Joseph came "in costume representing women of India, China and Japan."[1]

Urbana Courier, 1908: Mrs. Ira N. Reed, "who has a warm spot in her heart for all Celestials because her daughter is a missionary in China, entertained a party of Chinese university students on Friday at her home." Two of the guests were personally acquainted with Reed's daughter.[2]

Urbana Courier, 1909: The eighteen-year-old son of Mr. and Mrs. John Casdorf of Urbana who ran away to sea nearly four years ago "arrived home early this morning . . . Young Casdorf's story is familiar to nearly everyone in Urbana. Since leaving his home he has had adventures in nine countries, having stopped in Australia, Japan, China, Egypt, Holland, Germany, England, Scotland, and Ireland." Casdorf "tried the life of a sailor until he fell out of the rigging during a storm and fractured his arm. Then he tried other pursuits, finally enlisting in the Irish army. Becoming homesick he deserted twice, but was captured and imprisoned each time. Finally securing a discharge through the efforts of the American consul, young Casdorf hastened home, but says he doesn't expect to stay."[3]

David Kinley Papers, 1910: University of Illinois President David Kinley, once a professor of economics, served as a U.S. delegate to the fourth Pan-American Congress at Buenos Aires.[4]

Urbana Courier, **1911**: Jessie Mae Keffer of Champaign married Miguel Espinosa, a Mexican student in mining engineering at the University of Illinois. Espinosa's father, of Mexico City, is a millionaire mine owner. They left after the ceremony for Mexico City, so Miguel could help his father cope with the effect of "revolutionary troubles" on his business. "The groom is a handsome young fellow, due probably to the fact that his parents are Spaniards."[5]

A Standard History of Champaign County, Illinois, **1918**: Samuel H. Patton, the son of a Champaign farmer, worked as a civil engineer before taking up farming in the county. During his stint as an engineer, the U.S. government sent him to Haiti to build railroads. He subsequently worked for three years in El Salvador and Guatemala, "locating railways."[6]

Urbana Courier, **1919**: Captain Chester A. Morehouse of Mahomet (on the western edge of Champaign County), now in France, sent a letter to Champaign County Clerk Fred Hess, enclosing a copy of the Paris edition of the *New York Herald* that had Champaign news in it. "These familiar local items appearing in a foreign country bring realization that the world is a pretty small place after all, especially since the war."[7]

THE NATION, AT HEART

The heartland myth insists that there is a stone-solid core at the center of the nation. Local, insulated, exceptional, isolationist, and provincial; the America of America First, the home of homeland security, the defining essence at the center of the land. This core may be threatened by outside forces, but stronghold that it is, it can be secured if locked down tight enough. By retreating back to a time of well-fenced fields and narrow paths, the nation can hold a fearsome and turbulent world at bay.

Though powerful as myth, the idea of the heartland as a kind of national safekeeping vault does not stand up well as history. It does not take much digging to discover the mesh of relationships, many not domestic in nature, lying at the center of the nation. Delving deep into this core reveals a heart alive with pumping valves in the center of a vast network of pulsing arteries and veins; a last local place thoroughly riddled with histories of foreign relations. The American heartland is as much a global heartland as a national one—not in the sense of being in the eye of the world but in the sense that it took an entire world to form it. National consolidation did not precede global integration; both proceeded simultaneously, along paths blazed in an age of empire. Rather than conceiving of the heartland as a fixed place—the kind of place that can be shored up by walls—we would do better to conceive of it as a more open place that has, from the start, been ensnared in a vast circulatory system. It would take an entire atlas of maps layered on top of one another, transparency style, to convey the far-flung relationships that formed it.

Despite the assumption that the heartland myth can tell us something about who Americans are, fundamentally, as a people, the answers it provides are more the glib commonplaces of valentine silhouettes than the real, bloody, beating thing. The heartland myth does not tell us how we came to be who we are. It does not help us understand our founding in settler colonialism, our history of national development, the ecological systems that underlie our land, the full range of our political commitments, the variegated scope of our worldviews, or the epic extent of our struggles for justice and freedom. It hides wellsprings of empire and mighty torrents of global power. It offers the pabulum of nostalgia instead of the kaleidoscopic banquet of the past.

However badly it stands up as history, the heartland myth does tell us something about who we are as a nation, as do all stories that people tell about themselves. As an assortment of hundreds of millions of people, fractured along all kinds of lines, the United States has relied on national narratives to hold itself together and to advance common interests in the vortex of an unruly world. The heartland myth reveals that the struggle to define the nation has been conceived as a contest between insiders and people on the margins. Whether the mythical heartland is celebrated or reviled, it fosters the perception that there is a gulf between the center and the edge, between the heart and the national body. By affixing political differences to a specific place, the heartland myth makes the figurative idea of national insiderdom literal, locating it squarely on the map. Love it or hate it, it is the baseline from which to measure the distance traveled or gone astray; the point of reference to brandish before the wayward or to define oneself against. The mythical heartland, in other words, emerged as a political tool, its capacity to bind balanced by its ability to divide.

And here's the irony. No matter which competing purpose it has served, it has achieved the same result: exacerbating the fundamental challenge of comprehending the world by insisting on fixity instead of flux, insularity instead of interdependence. For people looking to understand their place in the larger scheme of things, mythology is easy. As a figment of our imaginations, it tells us what we want to believe, offering us certainty where there is none. Geography and history are more difficult because they rely on evidence, which can be pigheaded and confounding. Just as it can be hard to see the prairie for the tallgrass, it can be difficult to dig up buried sources and track down elusive leads, harder still to grasp what they mean.

Whether we look back in time or out in space, we cannot easily see that which lies outside our own narrow horizons. Take some of the most observant and curious people who have figured in this history: bird-watchers. Try as they did to understand connections across space, knowledge came in hard-earned increments. Even as ornithologists gained the ability to pinpoint seasonal homes on maps and to draw lines indicating paths of flight, they still could not grasp the full implications of what was happening on the ground, in real time: the mining, the smelting, the stock raising, the coffee growing, the refining, the burning, the planting, the plowing, the ditching, the harvesting of mahogany for the chiffoniers sold in town.[8] If anybody noticed that all those ecological disturbances were somehow connected to the fate of the insectivorous birds of the tallgrass prairie, they did not say.

Their inability to comprehend the on-the-ground changes of their own day emerged from a flattened sense of the past. Before

environmental history began to flourish in the 1980s,
did not have the conceptual frameworks to understa
term ecological change, going back to the indigenous
altered their environments well before Columbus, had
they saw as a God-given natural world. They could not grasp the
ecological implications of the post-1492 demographic implosion, in
which an estimated 90 percent of Native Americans died from the
diseases introduced by Europeans, or the subsequent wilding of once
densely populated places. Nor could they comprehend what happened after that: the centuries of lumber harvesting across the Americas; the clearing of forests for agricultural purposes; the impact of
new crops and animals and farming methods to supply markets both
near and unprecedentedly far.[9] It could be tricky enough to spot a
bird. To understand where it came from and where it was heading lay
at the outer limits of available knowledge. As they began to put together their maps, dot by dot, the ornithologists of the late nineteenth century laid the groundwork for a broader understanding of
causal connections. But the sense of distance between here and away
remained too vast to truly see the world through the eyes of a bird:
under the water, in the brush, at the edge of the canopy, above the
once wet prairie, with hedges and fences merely faint little lines on
the ground.

Not even such an avid ornithologist as the Arctic explorer Elmer
Ekblaw grasped the long-distance relations between sky and ground.
Upon his return to Illinois from the northern reaches of Greenland,
Ekblaw spoke widely on the struggle to survive near the pole. Although other members of his expedition team recalled being offered
trade goods such as tea, coffee, sugar, milk, and biscuits, Ekblaw
claimed that his Inuit hosts subsisted on animal meat and bird eggs.
The Eskimos ate every bird they could, he claimed, "from the little
snow-bunting to the great northern raven." Their hungriest times
came in the early spring, before the birds returned. "Starvation would

many more times have overtaken them," wrote Ekblaw, "except for the timely arrival of the first birds."[10]

After four years observing—and depending upon—migratory birds and the people they sustained, it might seem that Ekblaw would have grasped the connections between here and away. If anybody, surely him. But for all his professed sympathy with the Inuit, and all his identification with the North, Ekblaw still treated the polar region as a place apart. In his mind, geography was all about identifying and comparing discrete regions, not mapping the connections between them. In an essay titled "The Attributes of Place," written well after his days eating bird eggs preserved in seal intestines, Ekblaw described geography as a field centered on the attributes that made each particular place unique. He found the study of matters such as the "routes of trade and travel" to be a distraction from the geographer's core concern with specificity.[11] The point was not to map paths of influence but to identify people's inner essences and inherent selves—to figure out who they really were at heart.

For all his fascination with migrating birds and all his wandering with binoculars in hand, Ekblaw never managed to look out and in at the same time. For all his dependence on birds for survival, he could not really see the full scope of their true homes. Though the evidence was all around him, he did not note the ways that the draining of midwestern wetlands may have affected wild birds—and the people so intimately connected to them—millions of wingbeats away. Though a widely acclaimed geographer, he still could not see the relations between place and space, because he did not think to look. If not Ekblaw, then who before our more globally self-aware age could have comprehended the intersecting contrails of connection? To do so would have been a feat akin to recognizing the Mexican Kickapoos' claims on the heartland, the imperial power relationships behind assertions of exceptionalism, or the extent to which the Midwest's fortunes depended on distant strangers. No wonder the heartland myth came to seem so commonsensical: its scaled-up localness was far easier to grasp than the vast complexity of the real world.

If not Ekblaw, then who now? Having the capacity is not enough: there must also be a desire to comprehend, to peer not only toward the horizons of space but also those of time. Though sustained by ongoing politics, the heartland myth derives its power from references to history. Depending on perspective, the heartland of myth enshrines tradition or stands for attributes better left behind. This national touchstone is less the future than the past, mapped onto place. But the heartland of myth can never be recuperated, much less preserved, because it never existed in the first place. The further we travel back toward the wellsprings of this heart, the closer we come to the past that binds us all: the global production of the modern world. Disavowal does not make this world any less real or pressing, it just walls us into a mythical land of once upon a place.

Delve deep into the heart of the heartland and you will find a place with a history that makes national mythologies look small.

ACKNOWLEDGMENTS

Having stared obsessively at a small, gray-tinged laptop screen long enough to exhaust several pairs of glasses, it is a tremendous pleasure to finally stand up, stretch, and recall that this book did, indeed, take me beyond the fluorescent confines of my office, into the ambits of many knowing, generous, and otherwise wonderful people. It is an even greater pleasure to acknowledge them here.

As a newcomer to Native American and U.S.-Mexican borderlands histories, I owe huge debts to those who shared their expertise in these fields: Lara Aase, Ned Blackhawk, Chris Boyer, Brian DeLay, Dave Edmunds, Andy Fisher, Amy Greenberg, Peter Guardino, José Angel Hernández, Joseph Herring, Benjamin Johnson, Bill Kemp, Greg Koos, Andrae Marak, Karen Marrero, J. Gabriel Martínez-Serna, George F. Perkins, Cynthia Radding, Andrés Reséndez, Michael J. Sherfy, Pamela Voekel, Elliot Young, Ernesto Isunza Vera, and participants in the 2006 Tepoztlán Institute. Howard Allen, a Kickapoo language teacher at the Kickapoo Nation School, deserves particular thanks for his correspondence and comments on my work. Fred Hoxie gave me key leads at the start, read a huge hunk of text in the middle, and kept me grounded near the end.

Generous colleagues continued to light the way as I ventured ever deeper into midwestern, rural, and agricultural history, so here's to Benjamin R. Cohen, Nick Cullather, Chris Endy, Sterling Evans,

Kory Gallagher, Prakash Kumar, Jon Lauck, Jeffrey Pilcher, Debra Ann Reid, Steven Topik, Jenifer Van Vleck, and Elliott West.

Nicole Phelps stands in a category by herself for her unparalleled expertise in the history of the U.S. consular service and her generous briefings.

Jeff Brawn, Marlis Douglas, Mike Douglas, Ed Heske, Tony Endress, Greg McIsaac, Kenneth R. Robertson, and Mike Ward kindly shared their knowledge of ecological change and natural history. Kurk Dorsey, Jerome Hoganson, and Tom Johnson also tutored me on birding basics.

Hosts and audiences for a number of talks provided crucial feedback. Special thanks are due to Jon Crane, Ramón A. Gutiérrez, and Geraldo Cadava, who weighed in at the Newberry Library borderlands workshop; Chainy Folsom, Kory Gallagher, and Dennis Merrill at the University of Missouri, Kansas City; Dan Bender, Elspeth Brown, Russell Kazal, and Susan Nance at the Centre for the Study of the United States at the University of Toronto; Brian DeLay, Daniel Immerwahr, Lynsay Skiba, and Erica Lee at the University of California, Berkeley; Gabriele Link at the University of Rostock; Christine Gerhardt at the University of Bamberg; Volker Depkat and Udo Hebel at the German Association for American Studies meeting held in Regensburg, Germany; Katharina Vester at the meeting of the Chesapeake chapter of the American Studies Association held at American University; Chandra Manning, Adam Rothman, and Zackary Gardner at Georgetown University; Brian Alberts and Will Gray at Purdue University; Anne Paulet at Humboldt State University; Dianne Harris at the Illinois Program for Research in the Humanities; Tyler Miller and Alison Orton at the University of Illinois, Chicago Circle; Leslie Butler and Jeff Friedman at Dartmouth College; Alex Goodall at the Institute of Historical Research, University of London; Jacqueline Fear-Segal and Thomas Smith at the University of East Anglia; Sarah Miller Davenport and Phil Withington at Sheffield

University; Bevan Sewell and Zoe Trodd at the University of Nottingham; Marc Palen at Exeter University; Halbert Jones and Alan Knight at the North American Studies Center at St. Anthony's College, Oxford; Andrew Preston and Gary Gerstle at Cambridge University; Marina Moskowitz at the University of Glasgow; Shaul Mitelpunkt at York University; attendees at the Americans Overseas Conference organized by Steve Tuffnell at Oxford University; Amanda Waterhouse, Natasha Lueres, and Ruthann Miller at Indiana University; and Klaus Weinhauer, Stefan Rinke, and Angelika Epple at Bielefeld University.

And then there are the generous people who sent me cites and leads out of the blue and in response to queries: Nicolas Barreyre, Duncan Bell, Thomas Bottelier, Nancy Brown, Catherine Cocks, Max Paul Friedman, Christina Heatherton, Kelly J. Sisson Lessens, John Plotz, Donald Worster, Judy Wu, and Michelle Zacks. Mapmakers Jenny Marie Johnson and Tracy Smith helped me visualize my data.

For big-picture and game-changing help, inspiration, and encouragement, I owe profound debts to Frank Costigliola, Ann Hoganson, Edward Hoganson, Mary Renda, Daniel Rodgers, Emily Rosenberg, Claudia Tavera, and my hosts and colleagues at the Ludwig-Maximilians Universität: Britta Waldschmidt-Nelson, Anke Ortlepp, and Christof Mauch.

For what will forever stand out as a year of wonder at Oxford, I would like to thank Provost Anthony Madden and the governing body of the Queen's College, IT specialist and aerial descent informant David Olds, and Elaine Evers. At the Rothermere American Institute, Jay Sexton, Gareth Davies, Pekka Hämäläinen, Mara Keire, Michèle Mendelssohn, Lisa Miller, Stephen Tuck, and Stephen Tuffnell honed my thoughts. Vyvyan and Alexandra Harmsworth shared, among other things, their expertise in country life and Berkshire pigs.

ACKNOWLEDGMENTS

Among the librarians and archivists to whom I am deeply indebted are Sara Rachel Benson, Susan Braxton, Erik Chapman, Adam Doskey, Kirk Hess, John Hoffman, Jenny Marie Johnson, Angela Jordan, Philippa Levine, Mary Mallory, Geoffrey Thomas Ross, Celestina Savonius-Wroth, Antonio Sotomayor, Mary Stuart, and Elizabeth Wohlgemuth of the University of Illinois library system and Prairie Research Institute; Anke Voss of the Champaign County Historical Archives at the Urbana Free Library; Karen Downing and Gabriella Hoskin of the Institute for Advanced Study Library; Bill Kemp, Greg Koos, and George F. Perkins of the McLean County Museum of History and its associated archives; Liz Allsopp of the Rothamsted Research Library; Isabel D. Holowaty at the Bodleian Library; Jane Rawson of the Vere Harmsworth Library; and the hardworked staff of the U.S. National Archives in Washington, D.C., and College Park, Maryland.

All of the students I have had the privilege of working with have shaped this book in some way, but I would like to note in particular those whose research interests have been closest: David Lehman, Zach Poppel, and Andrew Siebert. Michael Hughes sent back leads from London, Sandra Henderson did valiant legwork during an effort to go digital, Ethan Johnson located newspaper articles on Rantoul, and Megan White pursued some cold leads and permissions.

I am grateful to the University of Illinois for providing me with an academic home and nurturing my scholarship since my days as a fledgling professor. Space permitting, I would list every colleague I've had there over the years, but for brevity I'll note particular debts to Ikuko Asaka, Jim Barrett, Tom Bedwell, Antoinette Burton, Julie Cidell, Jerry Dávila, Dianne Harris, Fred Hoxie, John A. Lynn, Gigi MacIntosh, Erik McDuffie, Bob Morrissey, Kevin Mumford, Elizabeth Pleck, and Roberta Price. The late Don Crummey helped launch this book in an expedition to Paxton and Loda to look at pioneer graveyards. Leslie Reagan deserves particular thanks for years of listening, critical analysis, and understanding.

I am also profoundly grateful for financial support from the University of Illinois Campus Research Board and Scholars' Travel Fund, the American Council of Learned Societies, the Richard and Margaret Romano Professorial Scholarship, and the University of Illinois sabbatical leave program. In the protoplasmic stages of this book, I benefited tremendously from the Illinois Faculty Study in a Second Discipline initiative and a Fulbright fellowship.

Jill Lepore made this book what it is by issuing an invitation, permit, and title. One of the greatest immodesties of my professional life is the pride I take in making *her* list of worthwhile authors.

At Penguin Press, Kiara Barrow and Mia Council worked marvels as editors. Beena Kamlani, Laurie McGee, and Will Palmer deserve eagle eye awards for their careful readings. Scott Moyers, there at the start, stuck with me to the end.

Finally, I'd like to thank those closest to home: my mom for encouraging me to write what I wanted; my dad for encouraging me to do what I wanted; Charles, for helping me realize what both these things were; and my three heartland seedlings, now tall as full-grown compass plants, for taking me to places I never would have discovered on my own.

NOTES

Some of the publications cited in these notes were located via digital collections, as follows:

America's Historical Newspapers, Readex
  Dallas Morning News, Yankton Press

British Periodicals, ProQuest
  Blackwood's Edinburgh Magazine, Chamber's Journal, Manchester Guardian, The Gentleman's Magazine, The English Illustrated Magazine

Illinois Digital Newspaper Collections, University of Illinois, Urbana-Champaign
  Berkshire World and Cornbelt Stockman, Bureau County Tribune, Chicago Livestock World, Daily Illini, Illinois Farmer, Prairie Farmer, Rock Island Argus, Urbana Daily Courier

Nineteenth Century U.K. Periodicals, Gale Cengage Learning
  The Academy, The Age, The Australasian, Bell's Life in London and Sporting Chronicle, The Country Gentleman, The Illustrated Household Journal and Englishwoman's Domestic Magazine, John Bull

Nineteenth Century U.S. Newspapers, Gale Cengage Learning
  Arizona Miner, Arkansas State Democrat, Atchison Daily Globe, Atchison Champion, Bismarck Daily Tribune, Boston Courier, Boston Daily Advertiser, Boston Daily Atlas, Cleveland Herald, Daily Evening Bulletin, Emporia Gazette, Freedom's Champion, Galveston Daily News, Hawaiian Gazette, Inter Ocean, Kansas Herald of Freedom, Louisville Public Advertiser, Milwaukee Journal, Milwaukee Sentinel, New-York Spectator, North American and United States Gazette, Ohio Statesman, Oregonian, Rocky Mountain News, St. Louis Enquirer, St. Louis Globe-Democrat, United States' Telegraph

ProQuest Historical Newspapers
  Chicago Tribune

U.K. Parliamentary Papers Online, ProQuest.

World Newspaper Archive, Readex
   El Siglo Diez y Nueve, Franklin Herald, Mexican Herald

Introduction: What Is the Nation, at Heart?

1. Emily Badger and Kevin Quealy, "Where Is America's Heartland? Pick Your Map," *New York Times*, Jan. 3, 2017.
2. On midwesterners as uniquely isolated, see Richard C. Longworth, *Caught in the Middle: America's Heartland in the Age of Globalism* (New York: Bloomsbury, 2008), 23.
3. Longworth, *Caught in the Middle*; Anthony Harkins, "The Midwest and the Evolution of 'Flyover Country,'" *Middle West Review* 3 (Fall 2016): 97–121.
4. This can be seen in claims that Donald Trump had a 7.5-million-vote margin in the heartland—a claim made by excluding every county, including those in states such as Indiana and Kansas, that voted against him. Philip Bump, "Thanks to a Bad Map and Bizarre Math, Breitbart Can Report That Trump Won the REAL Popular Vote," *Washington Post*, Nov. 15, 2016.
5. W. H. Parker, *Mackinder: Geography as an Aid to Statecraft* (Oxford: Clarendon Press, 1982), 34, 54; Gerry Kearns, *Geopolitics and Empire: The Legacy of Halford Mackinder* (New York: Oxford University Press, 2009), 4–5, 16.
6. "Fleet of 'Forts' Pound Germans Thru 48th Hour," *Chicago Daily Tribune*, June 24, 1943.
7. "Traces Outline Regarding Russian Post-War Grab," *Chicago Tribune*, May 10, 1949; Frank Tobias Higbie, "Heartland: The Politics of a Regional Signifier," *Middle West Review* (Fall 2014): 81–90.
8. On "middlewest," see Will Davidson, "Mark Twain's Real Stature," *Chicago Tribune*, July 21, 1946; on "midlands," see Frederic Babcock, "Among the Authors," *Chicago Tribune*, April 13, 1947.
9. Lloyd Norman, "President Off to Woo Labor Aid in the Midwest," *Chicago Tribune*, Sept. 6, 1948.
10. Frederic Babcock, "Among the Authors," *Chicago Tribune*, April 13, 1947; John Abbot Clark, "Fine History of Midwest's Political Wars," *Chicago Tribune*, June 10, 1951; Clayton Kirkpatrick, "Tribune's Flying Office Spans Pulsing Heart of U.S.," *Chicago Tribune*, Nov. 2, 1954.
11. James Bryce, *Social Institutions of the United States* (New York: Chautauqua Press, 1891), 248; Andrew R. L. Cayton and Susan E. Gray, "The Story of the Midwest: An Introduction," in *The American Midwest: Essays on Regional History*, ed. Andrew R. L. Cayton and Susan E. Gray (Bloomington: Indiana University Press, 2001), 1–26; Andrew R. L. Cayton and Peter S. Onuf, *The Midwest and the Nation: Rethinking the History of an American Region* (Bloomington: Indiana University Press, 1990), 122.
12. For examples of more analytical local histories, see John Demos, *A Little Commonwealth: Family Life in Plymouth Colony* (New York: Oxford University Press, 1970); Kenneth A. Lockridge, *A New England Town: The First Hundred Years*, expanded ed. (1970; New York: W. W. Norton: 1985); Paul Boyer and Stephen Nissenbaum, *Salem Possessed: The Social Origins of Witchcraft* (Cambridge: Harvard University Press, 1974); Mary P. Ryan, *Cradle of the Middle Class: The*

Family in Oneida County, New York, 1790–1865, (Cambridge: Cambridge University Press, 1983); Darrett B. Rutman and Anita H. Rutman, *A Place in Time: Middlesex County, Virginia, 1650–1750* (New York: W. W. Norton, 1984); Robert Anthony Orsi, *The Madonna of 115th Street: Faith and Community in Italian Harlem, 1880–1950* (New Haven: Yale University Press, 1985); John Mack Faragher, *Sugar Creek: Life on the Illinois Prairie* (New Haven: Yale University Press, 1986).

13. Jean M. O'Brien, *Firsting and Lasting: Writing Indians Out of Existence in New England* (Minneapolis: University of Minnesota Press, 2010).

14. Joseph A. Amato, "Introduction: The Concept and the Practitioners of Local History," in *Rethinking Home: A Case for Writing Local History*, ed. Joseph A. Amato (Berkeley: University of California Press, 2002), 1–16.

15. Arjun Appadurai, *Modernity at Large: Cultural Dimensions of Globalization* (Minneapolis: University of Minnesota Press, 1996), 181. On parochialism, Amato, "Introduction: The Concept and the Practitioners of Local History," 5. On xenophobia, see Karen Ordahl Kupperman, "International at the Creation: Early Modern American History," in *Rethinking American History in a Global Age*, ed. Thomas Bender (Berkeley: University of California Press, 2002), 109. On faulting local history as anecdotal, inoffensive, and dull, see Geoffrey Elan, "How to Write a *Dull* Town History," in *The Pursuit of Local History: Readings on Theory and Practice*, ed. Carol Kammen (Walnut Creek, CA: Altamira Press, 1996), 209–11.

16. For some exemplary histories that break ground by looking outward, see Donald R. Wright, *The World and a Very Small Place in Africa: A History of Globalization in Niumi, the Gambia*, 2nd ed. (Armonk, NY: M.E. Sharpe, 2004); Catherine Lutz, *Homefront: A Military City and the American 20th Century* (Boston: Beacon Press, 2001); Leon Fink, *The Maya of Morganton: Work and Community in the Nuevo New South* (Chapel Hill: University of North Carolina Press, 2003); James L. Peacock, Harry L. Watson, and Carrie R. Matthews, eds., *The American South in a Global World* (Chapel Hill: University of North Carolina Press, 2005); Andrew Friedman, *Covert Capital: Landscapes of Denial and the Making of U.S. Empire in the Suburbs of Northern Virginia* (Berkeley: University of California Press, 2013); Catherine Cangany, *Frontier Seaport: Detroit's Transformation into an Atlantic Entrepôt* (Chicago: University of Chicago Press, 2014); Emma Rothschild, "Isolation and Economic Life in Eighteenth-Century France," *American Historical Review* 119 (Oct. 2014): 1055–82.

17. Doreen Massey, "'A Global Sense of Place,'" *Exploring Human Geography: A Reader*, ed. Stephen Daniels and Roger Lee (London: Arnold, 1996), 237–45.

18. Thomas Bender, "Introduction: Historians, the Nation and the Plenitude of Narratives," in *Rethinking American History in a Global Age*, ed. Thomas Bender (Berkeley: University of California Press, 2002), 1–22.

19. See, for example, Faranak Miraftab, *Global Heartland: Displaced Labor, Transnational Lives and Local Placemaking* (Bloomington: Indiana University Press, 2016).

20. John Gjerde, *The Minds of the West: Ethnocultural Evolution in the Rural Middle West, 1830–1917* (Chapel Hill: University of North Carolina Press, 1997); Dana Elizabeth Weiner, *Race and Rights: Fighting Slavery and Prejudice in the Old Northwest, 1830–1870* (Dekalb: Northern Illinois University Press, 2013), 41.

21. On toenails, Milton W. Mathews and Lewis A. McLean, *Early History and Pioneers of Champaign County* (Urbana: Champaign County Herald, 1886), 60.

J. L. Anderson, "Uneasy Dependency: Rural and Farm Policy and the Midwest since 1945," in *The Rural Midwest since World War II*, ed. J. L. Anderson (DeKalb: Northern Illinois University Press, 2014), 126–59.

22. E. Davenport, "What Shall He Do?," *The Illinois Agriculturist* 1 (1897): 61–68, 65. Timothy R. Mahoney, *Provincial Lives: Middle-Class Experience in the Antebellum Middle West* (New York: Cambridge University Press, 1999).

23. Faragher, *Sugar Creek*, 89; Robert Mazrim, *The Sangamo Frontier: History and Archaeology in the Shadow of Lincoln* (Chicago: University of Chicago Press, 2007), 28, 224. On the desire for market connections, David Blanke, *Sowing the American Dream: How Consumer Culture Took Root in the Rural Midwest* (Athens: Ohio University Press, 2000), 21.

24. James E. Davis, *Frontier Illinois* (Bloomington: Indiana University Press, 1998), 105; Faragher, *Sugar Creek*, 101; Jane Adams, *The Transformation of Rural Life: Southern Illinois, 1890–1990* (Chapel Hill: University of North Carolina Press, 1994), 90–96.

25. J. D. Vance, *Hillbilly Elegy: A Memoir of a Family and Culture in Crisis* (New York: HarperCollins, 2016).

26. Longworth, *Caught in the Middle*, 23, 98; on population loss, J. L. Anderson, introduction to *The Rural Midwest Since World War II*, ed. J. L. Anderson (DeKalb: Northern Illinois University Press, 2014), 3–11; on the farm crisis that swept across the Great Plains in the 1980s, sparked by a grain embargo against Russia, see Paula vW. Dáil, *Hard Living in America's Heartland: Rural Poverty in the 21st Century Midwest* (Jefferson, NC: MacFarland and Company, 2015), 3.

27. Cayton and Gray, "The Story of the Midwest: An Introduction," 1–26.

28. Illinois Department of Public Health, "West Nile Virus," http://www.dph.illinois.gov/topics-services/diseases-and-conditions/west-nile-virus, accessed Nov. 8, 2016.

29. "Rantoul," *Urbana Union*, May 20, 1858.

30. Champaign County Regional Planning Commission website, https://ccrpc.org/data/poverty-rate/, accessed March 22, 2018.

31. For the backstory, see Robert Michael Morrissey, "The Power of the Ecotone: Bison, Slavery, and the Rise and Fall of the Grand Village of the Kaskaskia," *Journal of American History* 102 (Dec. 2015): 667–92.

Chapter 1: Between Place and Space: The Pioneering Politics of Locality

1. "Muster Roll of a Company of Kickapoo Indians who have Emigrated West . . . ," Records Relating to Indian Removal—Other Removal Records, Miscellaneous Muster Roll ca. 1832–46, Record Group 75, Bureau of Indian Affairs, National Archives, Washington, DC.

2. "Spanish Avarice," *Urbana Union*, Aug. 11, 1853.

3. "Sufferings of Prussian Family," *Urbana Union*, July 13, 1854.

4. "New Homes," *Urbana Union*, May 19, 1855.

5. Na she nan et al. to Col. Cumming, Supt. of Indian Affairs, St. Louis, Nov. 21, 1855, Folder: Kickapoo 1855–56, *Letters Received by the Office of Indian Affairs, 1824–81, Kickapoo Agency, 1855–1876* (Washington, DC: National Archives Microfilm Publications, 1958), Roll 371.

6. "The Gazette," *Champaign Daily Gazette*, Dec. 26, 1899.

7. Kristin Hoganson, *Consumers' Imperium: The Global Production of American Domesticity, 1865–1920* (Chapel Hill: University of North Carolina Press, 2007).

8. On modernist denigration of the local, see Arif Dirlik, "The Global and the Local," in *Global/Local: Cultural Production and the Transnational Imaginary*, ed. Rob Wilson and Wimal Dissanayake (Durham: Duke University Press, 1996), 21–45. On the local as a site of resistance to the global, see Michael Geyer and Charles Bright, "World History in a Global Age," *American Historical Review* 100 (Oct. 1995): 1034–60. On local transformation as a part of globalization, see Anthony Giddens, "The Globalizing of Modernity," in *The Global Transformations Reader: An Introduction to the Globalization Debate*, ed. David Held and Anthony McGrew (Cambridge, MA: Polity Press, 2000), 92–98. On the production of locality, see Arjun Appadurai, *Modernity at Large: Cultural Dimensions of Globalization* (Minneapolis: University of Minnesota Press, 1996), 178–99.

9. Joseph B. Herring, *Kenekuk: The Kickapoo Prophet* (Lawrence: University of Kansas Press, 1988).

10. George R. Nielsen, *The Kickapoo People* (Phoenix: Indian Tribal Series, 1975), 2.

11. Nielsen, *The Kickapoo People*, 12. On Kickapoo migrations from Wisconsin to Illinois and Indiana by 1700, see R. David Edmunds, "A History of the Kickapoo Indians in Illinois from 1750–1834" (master's thesis, Illinois State University, 1966).

12. Margaret Carlock Harris, "Along the Salt Fork River," *Journal of the Illinois State Historical Society* 39 (Dec. 1946): 475.

13. William B. Brigham, "The Grand Kickapoo Village and Associated Fort in the Illinois Wilderness," in *Indian Mounds and Villages in Illinois*, (1960; reprint, Urbana: University of Illinois, 1982), 91–100.

14. On the Vermillion Kickapoos' connections to the Potawatomis, see Herring, *Kenekuk*, 111; James A. Clifton, "Potawatomi," *Northeast*, vol. 15, *Handbook of North American Indians*, ed. Bruce G. Trigger (Washington, DC: Smithsonian Institution, 1978), 725–42; Ives Goddard, "Mascouten," *Northeast*, vol. 15, *Handbook of North American Indians*, ed. Bruce G. Trigger (Washington, DC: Smithsonian Institution, 1978), 668–72. On ties to Potawatomis, see James A. Clifton, *The Prairie People: Continuity and Change in Potawatomi Indian Culture, 1665–1965* (Lawrence: The Regents Press of Kansas, 1977).

15. On marriages between Mexican men and Kickapoo women, see Robert E. Ritzenthaler and Frederick A. Peterson, *The Mexican Kickapoo Indians* (Milwaukee: Milwaukee Public Museum, 1956), 15. On a white woman and her children living among Kickapoos in 1823, see John Dunn Hunter, *Manners and Customs of Several Indian Tribes Located West of the Mississippi* (Philadelphia: J. Maxwell, 1823), 21.

16. The War Department registered 2,000 Kickapoos in Missouri; Stephen Aron, *American Confluence: The Missouri Frontier from Borderland to Border State* (Bloomington: Indiana University Press, 2006), 204.

17. Nielsen, *The Kickapoo People*, 10–11.

18. Herring, *Kenekuk*, 1–11, 40–42.

19. Edmunds, "A History of the Kickapoo Indians in Illinois," 50. On Lewis and Clark's encounters with Kickapoos in Missouri, see Meriwether Lewis, *History*

of the Expedition under the Command of Captains Lewis and Clarke, vol. 1 (New York: Allerton Book Co., 1922).

20. "Kickapoo Braves," *Atchison Daily Globe* (Atchison, Kansas), July 11, 1887.

21. Louise Green Hoad, *Kickapoo Indian Trails* (Caldwell, ID: Caxton Printers, 1946), 86.

22. On visits between the Potawatomi and Kickapoos, see "An Indian Pow-wow," *Inter Ocean* (Chicago), Aug. 30, 1874.

23. *An Affecting Narrative of the Captivity and Sufferings of Mrs. Mary Smith* (Williamsburgh: Ephraim Whitman, 1818), 7.

24. *An Affecting Narrative of the Captivity and Sufferings of Mrs. Mary Smith*, 3.

25. On Fort Towson, see Alexander Cummings to the Adjutant General, Fort Towson, Jan. 18, 1826, 184–85; on Texas, see Benjamin W. Edwards to George Gray, Natchitoches, May 28, 1827, 482–83; on Arkansas, see Peter B. Porter to Governor George Izard, June 11, 1828, 697, all in *The Territorial Papers of the United States*, vol. 20, *The Territory of Arkansas, 1825–1829*, ed. Clarence Edward Carter (Washington, DC: Government Printing Office, 1954).

26. Joshua A. Piker, "'White & Clean' and Contested: Creek Towns and Trading Paths in the Aftermath of the Seven Years' War," in *American Encounters: Natives and Newcomers from European Contact to Indian Removal, 1500–1850*, ed. Peter C. Mancall and James H. Merrell, 2nd ed. (New York: Routledge, 2007), 337–60.

27. William Biggs, *Narrative of the Captivity of William Biggs among the Kickapoo Indians in Illinois in 1788*, reprint, 1922, Heartman's Historical Series no. 37, Princeton University Firestone Library, Rare Books Collection.

28. Hiram A. Hunter, *A Narrative of the Captivity and Sufferings of Isaac Knight from Indian Barbarity* (Evansville: Printed at the Journal Office, 1839), 11.

29. On horses, Nielsen, *The Kickapoo People;* Paul H. Voorhis, *Kickapoo Vocabulary* (Winnipeg: Algonquian and Iroquoian Linguistics, 1988), 4, 109.

30. George Croghan, "Croghan's Journal, 1765," in *Early Western Travels, 1748–1846*, ed. Reuben Gold Thwaites, vol. 1 (Cleveland: The Arthur H. Clark Co., 1904), 126–73.

31. Hunter, *A Narrative of the Captivity and Sufferings of Isaac Knight*, 9–10. See also Biggs, *Narrative of the Captivity of William Biggs*, 8, 12, 15, 18, 21, 24.

32. *An Affecting Narrative of the Captivity and Sufferings of Mrs. Mary Smith*, 7–9.

33. Henry Trumbull, *History of the Discovery of America, of the Landing of Our Forefathers, at Plymouth, and of Their Most Remarkable Engagements with the Indians, in New-England . . . To Which Is Annexed, the Defeat of Generals Braddock, Harmer & St. Clair, by the Indians at the Westward* (Norwich: James Springer, 1812), 133.

34. Trumbull, *History of the Discovery of America*, 135; Mark J. Wagner, *The Rhoads Site: A Historic Kickapoo Village on the Illinois Prairie* (Urbana: University of Illinois Press, 2011), 24.

35. Trumbull, *History of the Discovery of America*, 140, 144–45.

36. "San Antonio," *Galveston Daily News*, July 23, 1878.

37. "Indian Credulity," *North American and United States Gazette* (Philadelphia), April 29, 1853.

38. "Will Migrate to Mexico," *Dallas Morning News*, May 12, 1904.

39. "Train Kills Indian," *Dallas Morning News*, Dec. 8, 1904. See also "Aged Kickapoo Killed by Train," *Dallas Morning News*, Jan. 16, 1914.

40. On feats of horsemanship, see Nicholas Haby, "Early Texas Pioneers," *Dallas Morning News*, Dec. 29, 1897.

41. James Joseph Buss, *Winning the West with Words: Language and Conquest in the Lower Great Lakes* (Norman: University of Oklahoma Press, 2011), 171.

42. Milton W. Mathews and Lewis A. McLean, *Early History and Pioneers of Champaign County* (Urbana: Champaign Country Herald), 112, 149.

43. Mathews and McLean, *Early History and Pioneers of Champaign County*, 4.

44. On turkeys, see Judge Ristine quoted in "From Fountain County, Indiana," *Inter Ocean* (Chicago), Nov. 28, 1874; on roving, see Hunter, *Manners and Customs of Several Indian Tribes Located West of the Mississippi*, 22–23; on roaming and wandering at will, see Mathews and McLean, *Early History and Pioneers of Champaign County*, 149, 160.

45. Harris, "Along the Salt Fork River," 471–75.

46. John Treat Irving, Jr., *Indian Sketches Taken During an Expedition to the Pawnee and Other Tribes of American Indians*, vol. 1 (London: John Murray, 1835), 71.

47. Henry Rowe Schoolcraft, *The American Indians, Their History, Condition and Prospects* (Buffalo: George H. Derby, 1851), 386.

48. "The Journal of Elijah Hicks," *The Chronicles of Oklahoma* 13 (March 1935): 68–99.

49. Michael Adas, *Dominance by Design: Technological Imperatives and America's Civilizing Mission* (Cambridge, MA: The Belknap Press, 2006), 48, 49, 61.

50. Joanne Barker, "For Whom Sovereignty Matters," in *Sovereignty Matters: Locations of Contestation and Possibility in Indigenous Struggles for Self-Determination*, ed. Joanne Barker (Lincoln: University of Nebraska Press, 2005), 1–32.

51. Isaac McCoy, *Remarks on the Practicability of Indian Reform, Embracing Their Colonization* (Boston: Lincoln & Edmands, 1827), 37.

52. Todd Depastino, *Citizen Hobo: How a Century of Homelessness Shaped America* (Chicago: University of Chicago Press, 2003), 5, 7, 26.

53. On "doomed to extinction," see A. V. Pierson, "Indians," in Folder: Pierson, A. V., "Livingston and McLean County Indians," 1913, McLean County Historical Society, Bloomington, Illinois. "It Is Announced That on Thursday of This Week the Kickapoo Indian Reservation . . . ," *Atchison Daily Globe*, May 21, 1895.

54. On Kickapoo Creek, see "Illinois," *United States' Telegraph* (Washington, DC), May 14, 1827; on Kickapoo Prairie, "Missouri and White River Railroad," *Arkansas State Democrat*, May 4, 1849. On Kickapoo River, "Weather Crop Bulletin," *Milwaukee Sentinel*, Sept. 27, 1893; on Kickapoo City, *Kansas Herald of Freedom*, Feb. 10, 1855; on Kickapoo Cave, "Kickapoo Cave," *Dallas Morning News*, Feb. 28, 1920; on Kickapoo Hills, see "The Galenian . . . ," *Boston Courier*, Dec. 24, 1832; on coal mines, see "Believed to be en Route for Europe," *Milwaukee Sentinel*, Feb. 15, 1891; on Kickapoo Falls, *Louisville Public Advertiser*, June 11, 1823; on the Kickapoo road, "Gossip of the State," *Milwaukee Journal*, Aug. 17, 1894; on eight states, see A. M. Gibson, *The Kickapoos: Lords of the Middle Border* (Norman: University of Oklahoma Press, 1963), ix. On the fourteen states, see United States Board on Geographic Names (GNIS) database, geonames.usgs.gov, accessed Feb. 20, 2014.

55. Holly M. Barker, "Confronting a Trinity of Institutional Barriers: Denial, Cover-Up, and Secrecy," *Oceania* 85 (Nov. 2015): 376–89.

56. Milo Custer to John Masquequa, Aug. 11, 1906, Folder 4, Kickapoo Correspondence; Milo Custer to John Mas-que-quah, June 26, 1906, Folder 5; both in Box 6: Kickapoo, McLean County Historical Society.

57. Milo Custer to E. M. Prince, Oct. 5, 1906, Folder 4: Kickapoo Correspondence, Box 6: Kickapoo, Milo Custer Collection, McLean County Historical Society.

58. "Heinrich Heine," *Milwaukee Sentinel*, Feb. 12, 1888. On the Kickapoos' presence in the eastern part of the Wisconsin Territory, see Samuel R. Brown, *The Western Gazetteer; or Emigrant's Directory* (Auburn, NY: H.C. Southwick, 1817), 265.

59. On T. B. Nolen's cure, see "From the Jaws of Death!," *Bismarck Daily Tribune*, May 17, 1897.

60. "Texas Quidnunc in Gotham," *Galveston Daily News*, Dec. 14, 1886. On kidney diseases and sagwa, see "From the Jaws of Death!," *Bismarck Daily Tribune*, May 17, 1897. On Hawai'ian show, see "Notes from Kau," *Hawaiian Gazette*, April 28, 1899. (Note: References in the present text to the state of Hawaii use the official spelling; references to the kingdom and the territory use the traditional spelling, Hawai'i.) On rescue, see "Woman's Hope," *Bismarck Daily Tribune*, April 23, 1897. This ad includes an endorsement by T. B. Nolen, of Urbana, Champaign Co., IL. On printed materials and hunting, see Everett W. Doane, *Life and Scenes Among the Kickapoo Indians* (New Haven: Messrs. Healy and Bigelow, nd), 78, 141.

61. On elopement, see "Fell in Love with an Indian," *Milwaukee Sentinel*, July 27, 1889; on lodge, see "Traveling Men's Union," *Galveston News*, May 23, 1884.

62. "Kickapoo Joy Juice," Bevnet website, http:/www.bevnet.com/reviews/Kickapoo, accessed Oct. 16, 2006.

63. See Charles Augustus Murray, *Travels in North America during the Years 1834, 1835, and 1836*, vol. 2 (London: Samuel Bentley, 1839), 82; on a missionary, "Father De Smet," *The Yankton Press* (Yankton, South Dakota), June 4, 1873; "The Germans in Texas," *Daily Evening Bulletin* (San Francisco), May 17, 1869; Elvid Hunt, *History of Fort Leavenworth, 1827–1927* (Fort Leavenworth, KS: The General Service Schools Press, 1926), 45.

64. F. G. Adams to W. P. Dole, July 18, 1865, *Letters Received by the Office of Indian Affairs, 1824–81, Kickapoo Agency, 1855–1876*, Roll 372, 1864–1866 (Washington, DC: National Archives, 1958).

65. Mathews and McLean, *Early History and Pioneers of Champaign County*, on New Hampshire, 129; Massachusetts, 46; Maryland, 86; New Jersey, 18; New York, 25; Pennsylvania, 21; Indiana and Ohio, 19; Michigan, 46; North Carolina, 41; Virginia and Kentucky, 23; Tennessee, 74; Ontario, 46; England, 16; Scotland, 21; Ireland, 93; Switzerland, 156; Hannover and Bavaria, 40; Württemberg, 155. *Biographical Record of Champaign County, Illinois* (Chicago: The S. J. Clarke Publishing Co., 1900), on Scotch, 350, 103.

66. Mathews and McLean, *Early History and Pioneers of Champaign County*; on slave traders, 78; military recruits, 79; drover, 26; salesman, 25; seamen, 146; Stevenson, 14. Erna Moehl, *A Century of God's Presence: A Centennial Tribute, Immanuel Lutheran Church, Flatville, Illinois* (Flatville, IL: The Immanuel Lutheran Church, 1974), 7. *History of Champaign County, Illinois* (Philadelphia: Brink, McDonough and Co., 1878), on Sadorus, 122; Shanly, 123; Roberts, 136; Rogerson, 172.

67. Mathews and McLean, *Early History and Pioneers of Champaign County*, 7.

68. Mathews and McLean, *Early History and Pioneers of Champaign County*; on Chicago, 27, 29; New Orleans, 24, 98; driving, 31; packing, 24; California, 17, 21, 106, 130, 150, 151; conductor, 34; Arkansas, 84; Pike's Peak, 146; education, 36, 100; livestock, 93, 105; "look around," 152. *History of Champaign County, Illinois;* on exhibiting, 73; Nicaragua, 142.

69. Allan G. Bogue, *From Prairie to Corn Belt: Farming on the Illinois and Iowa Prairies in the Nineteenth Century,* 1963 (Ames: Iowa State University Press, 1994), 40.

70. Mathews and McLean, *Early History and Pioneers of Champaign County*; on Blackhawk War, 65; Mormon War, 35; Mexican War, 69. On the Civil War, see, for example, 11, 16, 33, 71, 74, 75; on Kansas, 152; Andersonville, 73; family visits, 22, 98, 105; Sadorus, 162–63; Florida, 26; Europe, 36, 130; wedding, 12.

71. Mathews and McLean, *Early History and Pioneers of Champaign County*, 21, 66, 115.

72. Mathews and McLean, *Early History and Pioneers of Champaign County*, on Michigan, 42; Minnesota, 153; North Dakota, 68; Montana, 153; Nebraska, 27; Missouri, 59; Kansas, 36; Texas, 136; British Columbia, 85; Mexico, 34; Las Vegas, 14; San Diego, 44; Leadville, 151.

73. "The People's Domain," *Prairie Farmer* (Chicago), Feb. 4, 1871.

74. "Alberta," *Urbana Daily Courier,* July 15, 1913.

75. "Markets," *Prairie Farmer,* Dec. 20, 1890, 813.

76. On the Kingdom of Württemberg, see Mathews and McLean, *Early History and Pioneers of Champaign County,* 155.

77. *Portrait and Biographical Album of Champaign County, Ill.* (Chicago: Chapman Brothers, 1887), 961; Ireland, 235; Sweden, 252; Prussia, 271; England, 283; Alsace, 309, 336; Mecklenburg, 383.

78. *The Biographical Record of Champaign County,* 85, 130.

79. On remittances, Mathews and McLean, *Early History and Pioneers of Champaign County,* 94. J. R. Stewart, ed., *A Standard History of Champaign County, Illinois,* vol. 2 (Chicago: The Lewis Publishing Co., 1918), 684, 720, 863.

80. Felipe A. Latorre and Dolores L. Latorre, *The Mexican Kickapoo Indians* (Austin: University of Texas Press, 1976), 37.

81. Ritzenthaler and Peterson, *The Mexican Kickapoo Indians,* 81–88.

82. On homes as places where a fire is kept, see Voorhis, *Kickapoo Vocabulary,* 58.

83. Testimony of Ekoneskaka (Aurelio Valdez Garcia) as reported by Jim Salvator, in "An Oral History," *Parnassus: Poetry in Review* 17, no. 1 (1992): 170–83.

84. J. Joseph Bauxar, "History of the Illinois Area," *Northeast,* vol. 15 of *Handbook of North American Indians,* ed. Bruce G. Trigger (Washington, DC: Smithsonian Institution, 1978), 594–601. For the treaty language, see Edmunds, "A History of the Kickapoo Indians in Illinois," 65; for a discussion of "making property" through labor among the Creeks, see David A. Chang, *The Color of the Land: Race, Nation, and the Politics of Landownership in Oklahoma, 1832–1929* (Chapel Hill: University of North Carolina Press, 2010), 31.

85. Wayne C. Temple, "Indian Villages of the Illinois Country," *Illinois State Museum, Scientific Papers,* vol. 2, part 2, Springfield, Illinois, 1958, 163. On wartime alliances, see Donald D. Stull, *Kiikaapoa: The Kansas Kickapoo* (Horton, KS: Kickapoo Tribal Press, 1984), 30.

86. Edmunds, "A History of the Kickapoo Indians in Illinois," 57.

87. Paul David Nelson, "General Charles Scott, the Kentucky Mounted Volunteers, and the Northwest Indian Wars, 1784–1794," *Journal of the Early Republic* 6 (Fall 1986): 219–51; Edmunds, "A History of the Kickapoo Indians in Illinois," 59.

88. Trumbull, *History of the Discovery of America*, 146–47.

89. Edmunds, "A History of the Kickapoo Indians in Illinois," 85.

90. On alliance with Tecumseh, see David Agee Horr, ed., *Indians of Illinois and Northwestern Indiana* (New York: Garland Publishing, 1974), 30.

91. "Indians Defeated," *Franklin Herald* (Massachusetts), Dec. 29, 1812.

92. Gillum Ferguson, *Illinois in the War of 1812* (Urbana: University of Illinois Press, 2012), 82–83; on Edwards's attack, see Edmunds, "A History of the Kickapoo Indians in Illinois," 108–109; William D. Walters, Jr., *The Heart of the Cornbelt: An Illustrated History of Corn Farming in McLean County* (Bloomington: McLean County Historical Society, 1997), 6; on the Sauk, see Temple, "Indian Villages of the Illinois Country," 165; on Barbour's attack, see John Lewis Thomson, *Historical Sketches of the Late War, between the United States and Great Britain* (Philadelphia: John Bioren Printer, 1816), 57; Wagner, *The Rhoads Site*, 30, 32. The attacked encampment was at the upper end of Peoria Lake (to the northwest).

93. Temple, "Indian Villages of the Illinois Country," 168.

94. On the brutalities of midwestern Indian removal, see Susan Sleeper-Smith, "Resistance to Removal: The 'White Indian,' Frances Slocum," in *Enduring Nations: Native Americans in the Midwest*, ed. R. David Edmunds (Urbana: University of Illinois Press, 2008), 109–23; on 1803 as the critical removal year for Shawnees and Delawares, see John P. Bowes, *Exiles and Pioneers: Eastern Indians in the Trans-Mississippi West* (New York: Cambridge University Press, 2007), 17; on removal as ethnic cleansing, see Gary Clayton Anderson, *Ethnic Cleansing and the Indian: The Crime That Should Haunt America* (Norman: University of Oklahoma Press, 2014).

95. There were two treaties in 1809, signed at Fort Wayne and Vincennes. *Message from the President of the United States Transmitting a Copy of a Treaty, Concluded with the Kickapoo Tribe of Indians* (Washington, DC: A. and G. Wat, Printers, 1810).

96. "Illinois Lands," *The Illinois Emigrant* (Shawneetown, IL), Aug. 21, 1819; Herring, *Kenekuk*, 21.

97. "Treaty with the Kickapoo Indians," *St. Louis Enquirer*, Dec. 8, 1819.

98. Aron, *American Confluence*, 204.

99. Edmunds, "A History of the Kickapoo Indians in Illinois," 129.

100. George Vashon to Secretary of War John A. Eaton, Oct. 27, 1829, *Letters Received by the Office of Indian Affairs, 1824–81, St. Louis Superintendency, 1824–1851*, Roll 749 (Washington, DC: National Archives and Records Service, 1956).

101. The Vermillion band surrendered their Indiana-Illinois land at Fort Harrison on Aug. 30, 1819. Because they were on friendly terms with their white neighbors, "the treaty failed to specify immediate removal to the west." But Secretary of War Calhoun said the Kickapoos and other Indians should be removed beyond the Mississippi, "where a more extensive scope is afforded for the indulgence of the barbarous propensities and habits." Mecina (or Elk Horn), the leader of a

Prairie band, said he did not have to leave because he'd never signed the treaty; Herring, *Kenekuk*, 22. On settling to the east and the Castor Hill treaty, see Nielsen, *The Kickapoo People*, 34–35. On the location of the Prairie and Vermillion bands, see Stull, *Kiikaapoa*, 194–96.

102. "More Indian Treaties," *New-York Spectator*, April 22, 1833.

103. On seizure, see Charles Callender, Richard K. Pope, and Susan M. Pope, "Kickapoo," in Bruce G. Trigger, vol. ed., *Northeast*, vol. 15 of *Handbook of North American Indians*, ed. William C. Sturtevant (Washington, DC: Smithsonian Institution, 1978), 656–67.

104. William Clark to the Secretary of War, Aug. 12, 1831, *Letters Received by the Office of Indian Affairs, 1824–81, St. Louis Superintendency, 1824–1851*, Roll 749 (Washington, DC: National Archives and Records Service, 1956).

105. Stewart, *A Standard History of Champaign County*, 93.

106. G. S. Hubbard to Gov. Clark, Dec. 9, 1833, *Letters Received by the Office of Indian Affairs, 1824–81, St. Louis Superintendency, 1824–1851*, Roll 750 (Washington, DC: National Archives and Records Service, 1956).

107. Edmunds, "A History of the Kickapoo Indians in Illinois," 130, 134–35, 141, 146.

108. On traveling to the spirit world, see Latorre and Latorre, *The Mexican Kickapoo Indians*, 197; on burial practices and spirits, Hoad, *Kickapoo Indian Trails*, 31, 101.

109. Thomas Forsyth, "An Account of the Manners and Customs of the Sauk and Fox Nations of Indians Tradition," in *The Indian Tribes of the Upper Mississippi Valley and Region to the Great Lakes*, ed. Emma Helen Blair, vol. 2 (1911; New York: Kraus Reprint, 1969), 183–245.

110. Mathews and McLean, *Early History and Pioneers of Champaign County*, 54.

111. "Witnessed End of Urbana's Indian," *Urbana Daily Courier*, March 9, 1916.

112. A. V. Pierson, "Livingston and McLean County Indians," 1913, document held by the McLean County Historical Society, Bloomington, Illinois.

113. *The Biographical Record of Champaign County, Illinois*, 182.

114. "Story of a Buried Treasure," *St. Louis Globe-Democrat*, March 16, 1887.

115. "The Glorious Fourth," *St. Louis Globe-Democrat*, July 5, 1887.

116. Tim Mitchell, "Kickapoo Powwow Draws Thousands," *Champaign News-Gazette*, May 23, 1999; Jacqueline C. Vermaat, "History of the Grand Village of the Kickapoo Park" (A with Honors Projects, paper 27, Parkland College, 2011), http://spark.parkland.edu/ah/27, accessed Sept. 11, 2018.

117. Scott Richardson, "Tribal Reunion Returns to Kickapoo Park near LeRoy," pantagraph.com, June 6, 2007; Tim Mitchell, "Kickapoo Powwow Draws Thousands," *Champaign News-Gazette*, Oct. 12, 2006.

118. "Illinois, Welcome the Kickapoo Home," http://www.geocities.com/soawing/kicklong.html, accessed July 20, 2007. For more on Salazar, see Melissa Merli, "Kickapoo Powwow Showcases Traditions," *Champaign News-Gazette*, Oct. 12, 2006.

Chapter 2: Meat in the Middle: Converging Borderlands in the U.S. Midwest

1. *Urbana Clarion*, Aug. 4, 1860.

2. "Cirsium arvense—Canada Thistle," *Illinois Farmer*, June 9, 1864, 169.

3. *History of Champaign County, Illinois*, 120.

4. *History of Champaign County, Illinois*, 855.
5. "Mexicans Are Coming," *Urbana Daily Courier*, May 13, 1909.
6. "Twin City Amusements," *Urbana Courier*, Dec. 9, 1909.
7. "Urbana Woman Flees Mexico," *Urbana Courier*, March 16, 1912.
8. Richard White, *The Middle Ground: Indians, Empires, and Republics in the Great Lakes Region, 1650–1815* (New York: Cambridge University Press, 1991); Robert Michael Morrissey, *Empire by Collaboration: Indians, Colonists, and Governments in Colonial Illinois Country* (Philadelphia: University of Pennsylvania Press, 2015).
9. On the Midwest as a place in the middle of a horizontal map, see François Furstenberg, "The Significance of the Trans-Appalachian Frontier in Atlantic History," *American Historical Review* 113 (June 2008): 647–77; Clarence Walworth Alvord, *The Illinois County, 1673–1818*, 1922 (Chicago: Loyola University Press, 1965), 326; Andrew R. L. Cayton and Susan E. Gray, "The Story of the Midwest: An Introduction," in *The American Midwest: Essays on Regional History*, ed. Andrew R. L. Cayton and Susan E. Gray (Bloomington: Indiana University Press, 2001), 1–26; Stephen Aron, *American Confluence: The Missouri Frontier from Borderland to Border State* (Bloomington: Indiana University Press, 2006).
10. On the history of the borderlands idea and later developments in this scholarship—including efforts to expand its geographies—see Ramón A. Gutiérrez and Elliott Young, "Transnationalizing Borderlands History," *The Western Historical Quarterly* 41 (Spring 2010): 27–53. On U.S.-Canada borderlands, see, for example, Beth LaDow, *The Medicine Line: Life and Death on a North American Borderland* (New York: Routledge, 2001); Sheila McManus, *The Line Which Separates: Race, Gender, and the Making of the Alberta-Montana Borderlands* (Lincoln: University of Nebraska Press, 2005); John J. Bukowczyk, Nora Faires, David R. Smith, and Randy William Widdis, *Permeable Border: The Great Lakes Basin as Transnational Region, 1650–1990* (Pittsburgh: University of Pittsburgh Press, 2005). One notable effort to consider the relations between the northern plains and, to a lesser extent, the U.S. Midwest to Mexico is Sterling Evans, *Bound in Twine: The History and Ecology of the Henequen-Wheat Complex for Mexico and the American and Canadian Plains, 1880–1950* (College Station: Texas A&M University Press, 2007). On northern and southern border patrolling, see Patrick Ettinger, *Imaginary Lines: Border Enforcement and the Origins of Undocumented Immigration, 1882–1930* (Austin: University of Texas Press, 2009). For a comparative study, see Benjamin H. Johnson and Andrew R. Graybill, eds., *Bridging National Borders in North America: Transnational and Comparative Histories* (Durham: Duke University Press, 2010). My conception of borderlands is borrowed loosely from Elliott Young, *Catarino Garza's Revolution on the Texas-Mexico Border* (Durham: Duke University Press, 2004), 7. This definition is based on the premise that the establishment of national borders in North America did not lead to rigidly bordered states in the nineteenth century.
11. Paul Wallace Gates, "Cattle Kings in the Prairies," *Mississippi Valley Historical Review* 35 (Dec. 1948): 379–412.
12. Dannel McCollum, *Essays on the Historical Geography of Champaign County from the Distant Past to 2005* (Champaign: Champaign County Historical Museum, 2005), 20, 51.

13. Paul Wallace Gates, "The Promotion of Agriculture by the Illinois Central Railroad, 1855–1870," *Agricultural History* 5 (April 1931): 57–76.

14. On population, see Gates, "The Promotion of Agriculture by the Illinois Central Railroad," 67; Paul Wallace Gates, "Large-Scale Farming in Illinois, 1850 to 1870," *Agricultural History* 6 (Jan. 1932): 14–25.

15. Milton W. Mathews and Lewis A. McLean, *Early History and Pioneers of Champaign County* (Urbana: Champaign County Herald, 1886), passim; J. O. Cunningham, *History of Champaign County* (1905; reprint, Champaign: Champaign County Historical Archives, 1984), passim; *The Biographical Record of Champaign County, Illinois* (Chicago: The S. J. Clarke Publishing Co., 1900), passim.

16. On drives, see Mary Vose Harris, "The Autobiography of Benjamin Franklin Harris," *Transactions of the Illinois State Historical Society* (Springfield: Illinois State Historical Library, 1923), 72–101; on farm purchase, Gates, "Large-Scale Farming," 22; on sales, Gates, "Cattle Kings," 381–82.

17. Gates, "Cattle Kings," 381–82; on European sales, see Harris, "The Autobiography of Benjamin Franklin Harris," 89, 92. On the heaviest herd, see "Died Full of Years," *Champaign County Gazette*, May 19, 1905, B. F. Harris and Family Vertical File, Urbana Free Library Archives, Urbana, Illinois. On Harris, see also Gates, "Large-Scale Farming," 14–25.

18. Gates, "Large-Scale Farming," 24–25. In 1890, there were 1,968,654 beef cattle in the state. By 1900, the number had fallen to 1,373,024, Allan G. Bogue, *From Prairie to Corn Belt: Farming on the Illinois and Iowa Prairies in the Nineteenth Century*, 1963 (Ames: Iowa State University Press, 1994), 86.

19. On corn fattening, see James W. Whitaker, *Feedlot Empire: Beef Cattle Feeding in Illinois and Iowa, 1840–1900* (Ames: Iowa State University Press, 1975), 33, 63, 73, 133–38; J. R. Dodge, "Report of the Statistician," *Report of the Commissioner of Agriculture, 1888* (Washington, DC: Government Printing Office, 1889), 405–76; on British consumer preferences, see "The Short-Horns of Aberdeenshire, Scotland," *The Breeder's Gazette*, Aug. 31, 1882, 288. On selling steers at two years, rather than three or four years, see Edward Everett Dale, *The Range Cattle Industry* (Norman: University of Oklahoma Press, 1930), 162; Wilson J. Warren, *Tied to the Great Packing Machine: The Midwest and Meatpacking* (Iowa City: University of Iowa Press, 2007). On marbling, see Lewis F. Allen, "Short-Horn Cattle," *Harper's New Monthly Magazine* 73 (Sept. 1886): 537–50.

20. Paul Wallace Gates, *Frontier Landlords and Pioneer Tenants* (Ithaca: Cornell University Press, 1945), 23; clippings in Sullivant Family Vertical File, Urbana Free Library Archives, Urbana Illinois; on Alexander, see Gates, "Cattle Kings," 402–03; Whitaker, *Feedlot Empire*, 58.

21. Gates, *Frontier Landlords*, 23; on Alexander, see Gates, "Cattle Kings," 402–03; *History of Champaign County, Illinois*, 149.

22. Whitaker, *Feedlot Empire*, 124.

23. Samuel Plimsoll, *Cattle Ships: Being the Fifth Chapter of Mr. Plimsoll's Second Appeal for Our Seamen* (London: Kegan Paul, French, Trübner, and Co., 1890). On the shift from pork, see Roger Horowitz, *Putting Meat on the American Table: Taste, Technology, Transformation* (Baltimore: Johns Hopkins University Press, 2006), 32.

24. Robert Leslie Jones, *History of Agriculture in Ontario, 1613–1880* (Toronto: University of Toronto Press, 1946), 142, 148, 155; Dodge, "Report of the Statistician," 453.

25. John C. Hudson, *Making the Corn Belt: A Geographical History of Middle-Western Agriculture* (Bloomington: Indiana University Press, 1994), 145; Margaret E. Derry, *Bred for Perfection: Shorthorn Cattle, Collies, and Arabian Horses since 1800* (Baltimore: Johns Hopkins University Press, 2003), 24; on buyers, see Christabel S. Orwin and Edith H. Whetham, *History of British Agriculture, 1846–1914* (London: Archon Books, 1964), 269.

26. "Illinois Stock Importing Association," *Illinois Farmer*, Feb. 1857, 36–37, 45, 47; "The Imported Stock," *Illinois Farmer*, June 1857, 143.

27. Bogue, *From Prairie to Corn Belt*, 88; Clarence H. Danhof, *Change in Agriculture: The Northern United States, 1820–1870* (Cambridge: Harvard University Press, 1969), 171–72. Shorthorns were popular through the 1880s; Herefords and Angus cattle gained favor thereafter; Warren, *Tied to the Great Packing Machine*, 185.

28. *History of Champaign County, Illinois*, 41, 125.

29. Mathews and McLean, *Early History and Pioneers of Champaign County*, 10, 29.

30. *Prairie Farmer's Reliable Directory of Farmers and Breeders, Champaign County* (Chicago: Prairie Farmer, [1917]), 139–41.

31. "The Avondale Herd of Galloway Cattle," *Champaign Daily Gazette*, July 24,1900.

32. W. C. Flagg, "The Agriculture of Illinois, 1683–1876," in *Transactions of the Department of Agriculture of the State of Illinois*, ed. S. D. Fisher vol. 5 (Springfield: State Journal, 1876), 286–346.

33. Jones, *History of Agriculture in Ontario*, on 1830s, 127; on duties, 182–83.

34. Michael Hart, *A Trading Nation: Canadian Trade Policy from Colonialism to Globalization* (Vancouver: UBC Press, 2002), 51; Jones, *History of Agriculture in Ontario*, 190–91, 193, 225. On speculators, see "Cattle Trade in Canada," *Prairie Farmer*, Sept. 16, 1865, 205.

35. Jones, *History of Agriculture in Ontario*, 279. On 100,000 cattle, see Derry, *Bred for Perfection*, 25.

36. "Stock Sales and Purchases," *Prairie Farmer*, Nov. 5, 1870, 348; "A Trip to Canada," *Prairie Farmer*, Aug. 26, 1865, 143; Derry, *Bred for Perfection*, 25, 45. On the U.S. demand, see also Margaret Derry, *Ontario's Cattle Kingdom: Purebred Breeders and Their World, 1870–1920* (Toronto: University of Toronto Press, 2001), 47.

37. James Mills, *The First Principles of Agriculture* (Toronto: The J. E. Bryant Company, 1890), 188.

38. "State Agricultural Associations," *Transactions of the Illinois State Agricultural Society*, vol. 1, 1853–1854 (Springfield: Lanphier & Walker, 1855), 10–33.

39. *An Official Handbook of Information Relating to the Dominion of Canada* (Ottawa: Government Printing Bureau, 1897), 7.

40. Derry, *Bred for Perfection*, 20, 25, 28–30.

41. Jones, *History of Agriculture in Ontario*, 150; "Items for Breeders and Buyers," *Prairie Farmer*, Sept. 2, 1876, 285.

42. *United States Consular Reports: Cattle and Dairy Farming, part II* (Washington, DC: Government Printing Office, 1888), 541.

43. On Miller, see Derry, *Ontario's Cattle Kingdom*, 20–21; Derry, *Bred for Perfection*, 28–30.

44. Joanna R. Nicholls, "The United States Revenue Cutter Service," *Frank Leslie's Popular Monthly* 42 (Oct. 1896): 25. On minimum border control and smuggling, see Reginald C. Stuart, *Dispersed Relations: Americans and Canadians in Upper North America* (Baltimore: Johns Hopkins University Press, 2007), 171, 247; Reginald C. Stuart, *United States Expansionism and British North America, 1775–1871* (Chapel Hill: University of North Carolina Press, 1988), 106–07; Ettinger, *Imaginary Lines*, 53, 65.

45. On "animals" as the operative category, see *Statistics of the Foreign and Domestic Commerce of the United States* (Washington, DC: Government Printing Office, 1864), 99; on dollar values, *Commerce and Navigation of the United States* (Washington, DC: Government Printing Office, 1880), 46; *Commerce and Navigation of the United States* (Washington, DC: Government Printing Office, 1883), 47.

46. "Our Trade with Canada," *Bradstreet's*, Sept. 13, 1890, 586.

47. *The Statistical Year-Book of Canada for 1890* (Ottawa: Department of Agriculture, 1891), 225.

48. *Canada: Statistical Abstract and Record for the Year 1888* (Ottawa: Department of Agriculture, 1889), 264; *The Statistical Year-Book of Canada* (Ottawa: Government Printing Bureau), 1901, 99. These reports provide multiyear tables. *American Commerce: Commerce of South America, Central America, and Mexico* (Washington, DC: Government Printing Office, 1899), 3351–52. In 1880, about 66 percent of the value of enumerated animals that crossed Canadian borders into the United States was entered in customs houses from New York to Wisconsin; about 33 percent from Maine to New Hampshire, and less than 1 percent from Minnesota to Alaska. See *Commerce and Navigation of the United States*, 1880, 98; see also *Commerce and Navigation* (Washington, DC: Government Printing Office, 1883), xxxiv–xxxv.

49. "The West Liberty Sales," *Prairie Farmer*, May 26, 1877, 164; "Was a Great Sale of Shorthorns," *Champaign Daily Gazette*, Aug. 9, 1900; "Live Stock Department," *Prairie Farmer*, Oct. 14, 1876, 333.

50. On a Canadian buyer in Illinois, see "Great Sale of Short Horns," *Prairie Farmer*, Nov. 30, 1867, 344. "Official List of Awards," *Prairie Farmer*, Oct. 19, 1867, 242; "Official List of Awards," *Transactions of the Department of Agriculture of the State of Illinois*, ed. A. M. Garland, vol. 1 (Springfield: Illinois Journal Printing Office, 1872), 25–60; *Transactions of the Department of Agriculture of the States of Illinois*, ed. S. D. Fisher, vol. 6 (Springfield: D. W. Lusk, 1878), 45; John P. Reynolds, "State Fair Prospects," *Prairie Farmer*, Sept. 5, 1868, 73; Derry, *Bred for Perfection*, 30.

51. "Western Cattle at the United States Fair, Chicago," *Prairie Farmer*, Jan. 5, 1860, 2.

52. "A Serious Outbreak," *Canadian Farm*, Nov. 13, 1914, 1.

53. "Short-Horns and Swine for Illinois," *Prairie Farmer*, April 23, 1870, 124; "The Canada Sales," *Prairie Farmer*, Jan. 24, 1876, 205. On Canadian ancestry, "Items about Ford County, Ill.," *Prairie Farmer*, June 4, 1870, 172; "Vermilion County," *Prairie Farmer*, Oct. 15, 1870, 322.

54. On economic integration in the Great Lakes region, see Stuart, *Dispersed Relations*, 5, 10, 143, 288; "Canada and the Illinois," *The Journal of Agriculture*, 1836, 628.

55. James Caird, *Letter on the Lands of the Illinois Central Railway Company* (London: np, 1859); *Caird's Slanders on Canada Answered and Refuted!* (Toronto: Lovell and Gibson, 1859), 4, 7, 19.

56. "International Railroad Excursion," *Prairie Farmer*, July 26, 1860, 56; "Our Canadian Visitors," *Illinois Farmer*, Aug. 1860, 128–29.

57. C. D. B., "The Canadian Excursion," *Prairie Farmer*, Aug. 2, 1860, 65. On Sullivant's farm, see "An Illinois Farm," *The Canadian Agriculturalist* 9 (Nov. 1857): 301.

58. "Our Canadian Visitors," *Illinois Farmer*, Aug. 1860, 128–29.

59. Paul Wallace Gates, *The Illinois Central Railroad and Its Colonization Work* (Cambridge: Harvard University Press, 1934), 234. On Canadian migration to the Mississippi Valley in the 1840s, see Marcus Lee Hansen, *The Mingling of the Canadian and American Peoples*, vol. 1, compiled and prepared for publication by John Bartlet Brebner (New Haven: Yale University Press, 1940), 90, 115, 128; John J. Bukowczyk, "Migration, Transportation, Capital, and the State in the Great Lakes Basin, 1815–1890" (29–77), and Nora Faires, "Leaving the 'Land of the Second Chance': Migration from Ontario to the Upper Midwest in the Nineteenth and Early Twentieth Centuries" (78–119), both in *Permeable Border*.

60. On adult immigrants, see *Champaign County, Illinois Naturalization Record*, vol. B, *1878–1902*, np; on immigrant minors, see *A Naturalization Record (Minors)* (Chicago: Culver, Page and Hoyne, nd); both in the Urbana Free Library Archives.

61. Frances E. Roehm, "Champaign County, Illinois 1850, A Historical Overview," 1986; *1860 U.S. Federal Census of Champaign County, Illinois* (Urbana: Champaign County Genealogical Society, 1988), both held in the Urbana Free Library Archives; federal census records in AncestryLibrary.com.

62. On the Tuckers, see *1860 U.S. Federal Census of Champaign County*, 86. Census records list 869 residents born in the British Isles in 1860 and 1,891 in 1870.

63. *History of Champaign County, Illinois*, 105, 139, 172. On Richards, O'Brien, McIntyre, and Crawford, *The Biographical Record of Champaign County, Illinois*, 86, 160, 410, 532. On Lock, "A Day in the Country," *Illinois Farmer*, June 1863, 182–83.

64. *Annual Report of the Illinois Farmers' Institute* (Springfield: Phillips Brothers, 1901), 155–56; "New Professors at the University of Illinois," *Farmer and Breeder for the Farm Home*, vol. 11, Aug. 1899, 1.

65. *1860 U.S. Federal Census of Champaign County*, 182.

66. J. S. Lothrop, *J. S. Lothrop's Champaign County Directory, 1870–71* (Chicago: Rand, McNally and Co., 1871), 118.

67. Mathews and McLean, *Early History and Pioneers of Champaign County*, 129.

68. On Vancouver, Mathews and McLean, *Early History and Pioneers of Champaign County*, 85; on Toronto, "Urbana Locals," *Champaign Daily Gazette*, Dec. 9, 1889; on railroad, Gretchen S. Rauschenberg, *Chicago's 'Mr. Rural': The Life of Matthias Lane Dunlap* (Baltimore: Gateway Press, 2007), 101.

69. David D. Harvey, *Americans in Canada: Migration and Settlement since 1840* (Lewiston, NY: The Edwin Mellen Press, 1991), iv–v, 246. "Big Four," *Champaign Daily Gazette*, Dec. 8, 1899.

70. "The American Rush into Canada," *The Economist*, Aug. 17, 1912, 312–13. Karel Denis Bicha, *The American Farmer and the Canadian West, 1896–1914* (Lawrence, KS: Coronado Press, 1968), 63, 96. Bicha notes that many emigrants returned to the United States, 138. He estimates 600,000 emigrants for this period, 117.

71. "Freed Lee Rice Goes to Canada," *Champaign Daily Gazette*, July 13, 1900.

72. "The American Rush into Canada," 312; "Canadian Annexation," *Bradstreet's*, May 12, 1883, 291.

73. *The Statistical Year-Book of Canada for 1900* (Ottawa: Government Printing Bureau, 1901), 404.

74. "News of the Week," *Prairie Farmer*, Jan. 24, 1876, 206. On importations via Canada, see *Annual Report of the Secretary of the Treasury on the State of the Finances for the Year 1882* (Washington, DC: Government Printing Office, 1882), xxxvii.

75. Henry Tyler, "The Grand Trunk's Relations with American Roads," *Railroad Gazette*, Nov. 12, 1880, 596. On the line to Chicago, see Mary Yeager, *Competition and Regulation: The Development of Oligopoly in the Meat Packing Industry* (Greenwich, CT: Jai Press, 1981), 90.

76. G. R. Stevens, *Canadian National Railways*, vol. 1, *Sixty Years of Trial and Error (1836–1896)* (Toronto: Clarke, Irwin and Co., 1960), 339, 363.

77. "The Market Systems of the Country," *Report of the Commissioner of Agriculture for the Year 1870* (Washington, DC: Government Printing Office, 1871), 241–54.

78. Plimsoll, *Cattle Ships*, 40–41, 48–58.

79. Plimsoll, *Cattle Ships*, 42, 56.

80. On pleuropneumonia, see "Canadian Regulations Concerning the Importation and Transit of Live Stock," *Railroad Gazette*, May 7, 1880, 249; on the Grand Trunk, see Whitaker, *Feedlot Empire*, 48.

81. "Canadian Regulations Concerning the Importation and Transit of Live Stock," *Railroad Gazette*, May 7, 1880, 249.

82. Stevens, *Canadian National Railways*, 363; William Cronon, *Nature's Metropolis: Chicago and the Great West* (New York: W. W. Norton, 1991), 239; on 59 percent, see Warren, *Tied to the Great Packing Machine*, 13. Canadian harvesters exported ice to U.S. meat shippers; "Markets," *Prairie Farmer*, March 8, 1890, 157.

83. Whitaker, *Feedlot Empire*, 48; "The Grand Trunk Railway," *Bradstreet's*, Dec. 5, 1885, 355; Yeager, *Competition*, 92, 102–04.

84. "On to the Seaboard," *Prairie Farmer*, Nov. 21, 1874, 369. See also "Extortionate Stock Yards," *Prairie Farmer*, Feb. 24, 1877, 60.

85. "The Farmer's Favorite," *Prairie Farmer*, Dec. 15, 1877, 396. "Publishers' Notices," *Prairie Farmer*, Sept. 23, 1871, 300.

86. "Foreign," *Prairie Farmer*, Jan. 5, 1860, 9; "To Measure Hay and Wheat," *Prairie Farmer*, July 16, 1864, 34.

87. "Agricultural Items," *Prairie Farmer*, Jan. 20, 1872, 18.

88. L. H. Bailey, ed., *Cyclopedia of American Agriculture*, vol. 1, 4th ed. (New York: The Macmillan Co., 1912), 1–6.

89. "Short-Horn History," *The Breeder's Gazette*, Dec. 1, 1881, 4–5.

90. Donald F. Warner, "The Farmers' Alliance and the Farmers' Union: An American-Canadian Parallelism," *Agricultural History* 23 (Jan. 1949): 9–19.

91. "Notes from the Granges," *Prairie Farmer*, July 1, 1876, 211.

92. "Keeping Up an Interest in the Grange," *Prairie Farmer*, April 28, 1877, 131.

93. "Convention of Short-Horn Breeders of the United States and Canada," *Prairie Farmer*, July 20, 1872, 229.

94. "To the Breeders of Short-Horns in the United States and Canada," *Prairie Farmer*, Feb. 20, 1875, 61. On Canadian attendance, see "National Short-Horn Cattle Breeders' Association," *Prairie Farmer*, Dec. 20, 1873, 405.

95. "The Short-Horn Breeders," *Prairie Farmer*, Dec. 11, 1875, 397.

96. Derry, *Bred for Perfection*, 36–42.

97. "The Short-Horn Herd Book," *The Breeder's Gazette*, Dec. 29, 1881, 99.

98. "Convention of Short-Horn Breeders," 229.

99. "The Short-Horn Breeders," *Prairie Farmer*, Dec. 11, 1875, 397.

100. "Discovery of Illinois," *Prairie Farmer*, Aug. 19, 1858, 119.

101. "The Canadian Excursion," *Prairie Farmer*, Aug. 16, 1860, 97.

102. Colonel Blair, "Remarks," *Annual Report of the Illinois Farmers' Institute* (Springfield: Phillips Bros., State Printers, 1901), 155–56.

103. "Stock Bred . . . ," *Prairie Farmer*, March 2, 1872, 69. On family feelings, see Edward P. Kohn, *This Kindred People: Canadian-American Relations and the Anglo-Saxon Idea, 1895–1903* (Montreal: McGill-Queen's University Press, 2004), 4.

104. James J. Hill, *Highways of Progress* (New York: Doubleday, Page, and Co., 1912), 86; "Our Relations with Canada," *Bradstreet's*, March 3, 1880, 4.

105. G. Mercer Adam, ed., *Handbook of Commercial Union* (Toronto: Hunter, Rose & Company, 1888), xiv, 55.

106. Alexander Monro, *The United States and the Dominion of Canada: Their Future* (Saint John, NB: Barnes and Co., 1879), vi.

107. Hill, *Highways of Progress*, 86.

108. Stuart, *United States Expansionism*, 193, 218, 237.

109. William Renick, *Memoirs, Correspondence and Reminiscences* (Circleville, OH: Union-Herald Book and Job Printing House, 1880), 24–25.

110. On service in Texas, see, for example, *History of Champaign County, Illinois*, 141. Dale, *The Range Cattle Industry*, 33–34.

111. John Gamgee, "Report of Professor Gamgee on the Splenic or Periodic Fever of Cattle," *Report of the Commissioner of Agriculture on the Diseases of Cattle in the United States* (Washington, DC: Government Printing Office, 1871), 82–132.

112. J. R. Dodge, "Report of Statistical and Historical Investigations of the Progress and Results of the Texas Cattle Disease," *Report of the Commissioner of Agriculture on the Diseases of Cattle in the United States* (Washington, DC: Government Printing Office, 1871), 175–202.

113. On Highthorn, see "Stock Sales and Purchases," *Prairie Farmer*, Feb. 25, 1871, 60; on Duke, see "Items Gathered at Springfield," *Prairie Farmer*, July 1, 1871, 201.

114. "Chicago Live Stock Market," *Prairie Farmer*, June 1, 1872, 176. On Chicago pricing, see James MacDonald, *Food from the Far West* (London: William P.

Nimmo, 1878), 183; Jimmy M. Skaggs, *Prime Cut: Livestock Raising and Meat-packing in the United States, 1607–1983* (College Station: Texas A&M Press, 1986), 72; on Texas pricing, see Joseph Nimmo, Jr., *Report in Regard to the Range and Ranch Cattle Business of the United States* (1885; reprint, New York: Arno Press, 1972), 4.

115. L. F. Allen, "The Short-Horn Breed of Cattle," *Report of the Commissioner of Agriculture for the Year 1875* (Washington, DC: Government Printing Office, 1876), 416–26. On the suitability of Texan cattle for stocking ranches in western states like Colorado and Montana, see Joshua Specht, "The Rise, Fall, and Re-birth of the Texas Longhorn: An Evolutionary History" *Environmental History* 21 (April 2016): 348–63.

116. Allen, "The Short-Horn Breed of Cattle," 417. On degeneracy, see *United States Consular Reports: Cattle and Dairy Farming, Part I* (Washington, DC: Government Printing Office, 1888), 51.

117. On domestication and color, see Wm. Le Baron, "Natural History of the Domes-ticated Animals," *Prairie Farmer*, Dec. 26, 1868, 201; on Moorish ancestry, see Dale, *The Range Cattle Industry*, 3.

118. MacDonald, *Food from the Far West*, 269.

119. On human crossings of the U.S.-Mexico border, see Ettinger, *Imaginary Lines*, 38; on U.S. duties and Mexican taxes as high as $2.50 a head (instituted in the 1880s), *United States Consular Reports: Cattle and Dairy Farming, Part II*, 580; on Mexican duties, "Foreign and Colonial," *Mark Lane Express*, Nov. 11, 1889, 658.

120. George A. Wallis, *Cattle Kings of the Staked Plains* (Dallas: American Guild Press, 1957), 119–20.

121. *United States Consular Reports: Cattle and Dairy Farming, Part II*, 585–86.

122. Alan L. Olmstead and Paul W. Rhode, *Creating Abundance: Biological Innovation and American Agricultural Development* (New York: Cambridge University Press, 2008), 292; Harriet Ritvo, *The Animal Estate: The English and Other Creatures of the Victorian Age* (Cambridge: Harvard University Press, 1987), 55, 60, 74–76. On pro-jecting identities onto animals, see Ann Norton Greene, *Horses at Work: Harnessing Power in Industrial America* (Cambridge: Harvard University Press, 2008), 12.

123. C. L. Sonnichsen, *Colonel Greene and the Copper Skyrocket* (Tucson: University of Arizona Press, 1974), 23–26, on markets, 238; Rachel St. John, "Divided Ranges: Trans-border Ranches and the Creation of National Space along the Western Mexico-U.S. Border," in *Bridging National Borders in North America*, ed. Johnson and Graybill, 116–40. On *hacendados*, see Juan Mora-Torres, *The Making of the Mexican Border* (Austin: University of Texas Press, 2001), 115. Mora-Torres notes that Nuevo León was a net importer of Texan cattle prior to 1872, 63. Mark Was-serman, *Capitalists, Caciques, and Revolution: The Native Elite and Foreign Enter-prise in Chihuahua, Mexico, 1854–1911* (Chapel Hill: University of North Carolina Press, 1984), 48, 75, 82.

124. Julius Morton to T. M. Paschal, June 20, 1895, Letterbook v. 353 (June 1, 1895, to Nov. 6, 1895), Record Group 16, Animal Industry, National Archives, College Park.

125. Mora-Torres, *The Making of the Mexican Border*, 129; Arnoldo De León, *The Te-jano Community, 1836–1900* (Albuquerque: University of New Mexico Press, 1982), 17.

126. *Foreign Commerce and Navigation of the United States* (Washington, DC: Government Printing Office, 1896), 954. These districts were: Brazos de Santiago, Corpus Christi, Galveston, Paseo del Norte, and Saluria. On number of employees, see *Annual Report of the Secretary of the Treasury on the State of the Finances for the Year 1883* (Washington, DC: Government Printing Office, 1883), 72–101.

127. *Annual Report of the Secretary of the Treasury on the State of the Finances* (Washington, DC: Government Printing Office, 1901), 32.

128. *Datos Mercantiles* (México: Oficina Tip. de la Secretaría de Fomento, Colonización, é Industria, 1892), 3–4.

129. M. Romero, "The Free Zone in Mexico," *North American Review* 154 (April 1892): 459–71; *American Commerce: Commerce of South America, Central America, Mexico, and West Indies* (Washington, DC: Government Printing Office, 1899), 3182–84; "Topics of the Day," *Prairie Farmer*, Jan. 3, 1874, 4.

130. *American Commerce: Commerce of South America, Central America, Mexico, and West Indies*, 3371–72. Of these, 1,786,261 were entered as duty-free; 928,175 as dutiable. As in the Canadian case, there are discrepancies between U.S. import and Mexican export figures, again apparently undercounting exports; *Comercio Exterior, Año Fiscal de 1897–1898* (Mexico: Oficina Impresora del Timbre, 1901), 204.

131. *United States Consular Reports: Cattle and Dairy Farming, Part II*, 580, 582, 588.

132. "Mexican Cattle Imports," *The National Provisioner*, Nov. 30, 1895, 15; "Mexican Cattle," *The National Provisioner*, April 16, 1898, 22.

133. D. E. Salmon, *Mexico as a Market for Purebred Beef Cattle from the United States* (Washington, DC: Government Printing Office, 1902), 6.

134. "Cattle Transportation," *Railroad Gazette*, Feb. 13, 1875.

135. E. E. Chester, "Cattle in Central Illinois," *Annual Report of the Illinois Farmers' Institute* (Springfield, Illinois, 1898), 261–64.

136. James E. Poole, "Future Meat Supply of North America," *The National Provisioner*, Sept. 27, 1913, 99. The byline identifies him as a *Chicago Live Stock World* reporter.

137. "Memorandum Regarding Importation of Ticky Cattle from Mexico into Texas," Feb. 14, 1914, Folder: Animals–Cattle; Box 115: Alcohol-Animals-Cattle, 1914; RG 16, General Correspondence of the Office of the Secretary, Records of the Office of the Secretary of Agriculture, National Archives, College Park.

138. "Cattle Stealing on the Mexican Border," *Prairie Farmer*, Oct. 26, 1872, 341. On transborder production on the far western stretch of the U.S.-Mexico border, see St. John, "Divided Ranges," 116–40.

139. "News of the Week," *Prairie Farmer*, Nov. 30, 1872, 384.

140. "A New Cause of Trouble with Mexico," *Daily Evening Bulletin* (San Francisco), Aug. 23, 1871.

141. "News of the Week," *Prairie Farmer*, July 14, 1877, 224. On recognizing that stealing went both ways, see "Topics of the Day," *Prairie Farmer*, May 31, 1873, 172; "News of the Week," *Prairie Farmer*, Jan. 13, 1874, 192. *Reports of the Committee of Investigation Sent in 1873 by the Mexican Government to the Frontier of Texas* (New York: Baker and Godwin, 1875), iii, 55, 65.

142. McManus, *The Line Which Separates*, 80; David H. Breen, *The Canadian Prairie West and the Ranching Frontier, 1874–1924* (Toronto: University of Toronto Press, 1983), 85; Joseph Nimmo, Jr., "The American Cow-Boy," *Harper's New Monthly Magazine* 73 (Nov. 1886): 880–84. On complaints that Canadian Indians killed U.S. cattle, see Hana Samek, *The Blackfoot Confederacy 1880–1920: A Comparative Study of Canadian and U.S. Indian Policy* (Albuquerque: University of New Mexico Press, 1987), 154.

143. "The Mexican Question," *Prairie Farmer*, Dec. 15, 1877, 396.

144. Marian C. McKenna, "Above the Blue Line: Policing the Frontier in the Canadian and American West, 1870–1900," in *The Borderlands of the American and Canadian Wests: Essays on Regional History of the Forty-ninth Parallel*, ed. Sterling Evans (Lincoln: University of Nebraska Press, 2006), 81–106; "Cattle Stealing on the Mexican Border," *Prairie Farmer*, Oct. 26, 1872, 341.

145. Pedro Saucedo Montemayor, *Historia de la Ganadería en México*, vol. 1 (Mexico City: Universidad Nacional Autónoma de México, 1984), 44–53. Mathews and McLean, *Early History and Pioneers of Champaign County*, 34, 69. On last heard, *The Biographical Record of Champaign County, Illinois*, 152. On Mexican war veterans, see "Decoration Day," *Prairie Farmer*, May 29, 1875, 172; *History of Champaign County, Illinois*, 36, 138; on Acapulco, 143.

146. *A Naturalization Record (Minors)*, vol. A (Chicago: Culver, Page and Hoyne, nd), Urbana Free Library Archives.

147. *1860 U.S. Federal Census of Champaign County*, 217. AncestryLibrary.com lists her as Dorena Swett, but the original census records do appear to spell her name Donena Sweet, which is the spelling used in the typescript noted above. Sweet is her married name.

148. Arthur C. Davenport, *The American Live Stock Market: How It Functions* (Chicago: Drovers Journal Print [1922]), 23.

149. Richard W. Slatta, *Cowboys of the Americas* (New Haven: Yale University Press, 1990); Terry G. Jordan, *North American Cattle-Ranching Frontiers: Origins, Diffusion, and Differentiation* (Albuquerque: University of New Mexico Press, 1993), 157, 207, 267.

150. "The Texas Cattle Trade," *Report of the Commissioner of Agriculture for the Year 1870* (Washington, DC: Government Printing Office, 1871), 347. For a rare reference to Mexican herders, see "Advance in Texas Beeves," *Prairie Farmer*, Nov. 26, 1870, 369. Jacqueline M. Moore, *Cow Boys and Cattle Men: Class and Masculinities on the Texas Frontier, 1865–1900* (New York: New York University Press, 2010), 136.

151. H. W. Mumford, "Beef Production in the Argentine," *The Breeder's Gazette*, Dec. 16, 1908, 1221–22.

152. Jeffrey M. Pilcher, "Empire of the 'Jungle': The Rise of an Atlantic Refrigerated Beef Industry, 1880–1920," *Food, Culture and Society* 7 (Fall 2004): 63–78.

153. "The English Market, by Way of Canada," *Prairie Farmer*, June 1843, 135. As a Treasury Department report put it, "Canada is nearer to and in more constant steamship communication with the European countries than is Mexico"; *American Commerce: Commerce of South America, Central America, Mexico, and West Indies*, 3165.

154. On Mexican policies to attract immigrants, see "Topics of the Day," *Prairie Farmer*, Oct. 31, 1874, 348; on land sales, see "Agricultural Items," *Prairie Farmer*, May 23, 1874, 162. On annexation to end cross-border rustling, see "The friends of the project . . . ," *Prairie Farmer*, Feb. 17, 1872, 53.

155. "Foreign and Colonial," *Mark Lane Express*, Dec. 16, 1889, 826. On Mexican Shorthorn imports starting in 1889, see "Chronology of the Trade for 25 Years," *The Breeder's Gazette*, Nov. 28, 1906, 1155–59. Salmon, *Mexico as a Market*, 5.

156. *History of Champaign County, Illinois*, 126. On "half-breed," see John Mason Hart, *Empire and Revolution: The Americans in Mexico since the Civil War* (Berkeley: University of California Press, 2002), 367. This is not to say that racism emerged from livestock breeding, but that the principles behind livestock production contributed to racist thinking. On assessments of Mexican Americans, see De León, *The Tejano Community*, 11; Laura E. Gómez, *Manifest Destinies: The Making of the Mexican American Race* (New York: New York University Press, 2007).

157. Mathews and McLean, *Early History and Pioneers of Champaign County*, 71.

158. On beef suppliers, see Dale, *The Range Cattle Industry*, 45–46, 56–57, 100–01. J. Diane Pearson, "Building Reservation Economies: Cattle, American Indians and the American West," *International Journal of Business and Globalisation* 1, no. 3 (2007): 404–48.

159. Norman Arthur Graebner, "History of Cattle Ranching in Eastern Oklahoma," *Chronicles of Oklahoma* 21 (Sept. 1943): 300–311.

160. "A. J. Smith . . . ," *Atchinson Daily Globe*, June 26, 1886.

161. Ernest S. Osgood, *The Day of the Cattleman* (Chicago: University of Chicago Press, 1929); see also Graebner, "History of Cattle Ranching," 301, 304; on grazing herds on Cheyenne and Arapaho lands, Donald J. Berthrong, "Cattlemen on the Cheyenne-Arapaho Reservation, 1883–1885," *Arizona and the West* 13 (Spring 1971): 5–32.

162. Graebner, "History of Cattle Ranching," 304–05, leasing, 310–11; Pearson, "Building Reservation Economies," 417; Robert M. Burrill, "The Establishment of Ranching on the Osage Indian Reservation," *Geographical Review* 62 (Oct. 1972): 524–43. Northwestern groups such as the Blackfoot Confederacy began to take up stock raising in the 1880s as well, but it took time for cattle raising to gain acceptance among native peoples and Bureau of Indian Affairs agents alike; Samek, *The Blackfoot Confederacy*, 80–82; Russel L. Barsh, "The Substitution of Cattle for Bison on the Great Plains," in *The Struggle for the Land: Indigenous Insight and Industrial Empire in the Semiarid World*, ed. Paul A. Olson (Lincoln: University of Nebraska Press, 1990), 103–26; on grazing leases, see Nimmo, *Report in Regard to the Range and Ranch Cattle Business*, 15.

163. "Desire the Earth," *Champaign Daily Gazette*, Feb. 10, 1890.

164. *The Biographical Record of Champaign County, Illinois*, western lands, 124, children, 36, 92, 129, 229, 344; Dale, *The Range Cattle Industry*, 37, 45.

165. On cattle production as women's work among the Choctaw, see James Taylor Carson, *Searching for the Bright Path: The Mississippi Choctaws from Prehistory to Removal* (Lincoln: University of Nebraska Press, 1999), 77–78.

166. Graebner, "History of Cattle Ranching," 307.

167. "The Cattle Disease," *Prairie Farmer*, Aug. 22, 1868, 60.

168. "The Cattle Disease," *Prairie Farmer*, Sept. 12, 1868, 81.

169. Ibid.; "The Spanish Fever," *Prairie Farmer*, Sept. 26, 1868, 98; "The Cattle Disease," *Prairie Farmer*, Oct. 3, 1874, 313.

170. Gamgee, "Report of Professor Gamgee," 85, 102, 110–11. On eyeballs, stiffness, and windpipes, see H. S. Ozburn, "Texas Cattle and Texas Fever," *Prairie Farmer*, Feb. 23, 1867, 114.

171. On fifty, see Dale, *The Range Cattle Industry*, 37; on 15,000, see Whitaker, *Feedlot Empire*, 58. On "poverty," see Joseph G. McCoy, *Historic Sketches of the Cattle Trade of the West and Southwest* (1874; reprint, Washington, DC: The Rare Book Shop, 1932), 148.

172. On market rush, see McCoy, *Historic Sketches of the Cattle Trade*, 148; Gamgee, "Report of Professor Gamgee," 110–11.

173. Gates, *Frontier Landlords*, 23; Gates, "Cattle Kings," 402–03; Whitaker, *Feedlot Empire*, 58; on finding a buyer, see McCoy, *Historic Sketches of the Cattle Trade*, 175.

174. "Cattle Disease," *The American Farmer*, September 1868, 3. On the 5,000 figure, see Dodge, "Report of Statistical and Historical Investigations," 202.

175. H. J. Detmers, "Investigation of Texas Cattle Fever," *Annual Report of the Commissioner of Agriculture for the Year 1880* (Washington, DC: Government Printing Office, 1881), 595–601.

176. The role of ticks was discovered in 1890 by Bureau of Animal Industry scientists; R. Douglas Hurt, *American Agriculture: A Brief History*, revised ed. (West Lafayette: Purdue University Press, 2002), 203.

177. On the mixing of Cherokee and Texas cattle in Abilene, see "The Cattle Disease," *Prairie Farmer*, Sept. 12, 1868, 81.

178. "American Convention of Cattle Commissioners," *Prairie Farmer*, Dec. 12, 1868, 185. On "foreign," see "The Cattle Plague," *Prairie Farmer*, Oct. 13, 1877, 325.

179. "State Reports of Agriculture," *Report of the Commissioner of Agriculture for the Year 1870* (Washington, DC: Government Printing Office, 1871), 487–517; on Champaign participant, see "American Convention of Cattle Commissioners," *Prairie Farmer*, Dec. 12, 1868, 185; on ticks, "American Convention of Cattle Commissioners," *Prairie Farmer*, Dec. 5, 1868, 180.

180. Whitaker, *Feedlot Empire*, 62.

181. J. Stanley Clark, "Texas Fever in Oklahoma," *Chronicles of Oklahoma* 29 (Winter 1951–52): 429–43, 429–30. "Texas Cattle Disease," *Prairie Farmer*, Aug. 8, 1868, 44; Claire Strom, *Making Catfish Bait Out of Government Boys: The Fight Against Cattle Ticks and the Transformation of the Yeoman South* (Athens: University of Georgia Press, 2009), 21, 23, 30; Cecil Kirk Hutson, "Texas Fever in Kansas," *Agricultural History* 68 (Winter 1994): 74–104.

182. "Jas. N. Brown's Report on the Cattle Disease," *Prairie Farmer*, Aug. 23, 1860, 116.

183. Derry, *Ontario's Cattle Kingdom*, 62.

184. "The American Association of Breeders of Short-horns," *Prairie Farmer*, Dec. 16, 1876, 404.

185. Julius Morton to James J. Hill, August 17, 1895, Letterbook v. 353 (June 1, 1895, to Nov. 6, 1895), Record Group 16, Animal Industry, National Archives, College Park.

186. *General Regulations under the Customs and Navigation Laws of the United States* (Washington, DC: Government Printing Office, 1884), 175. Natalia Molina, *Fit to Be Citizens? Public Health and Race in Los Angeles, 1879–1939* (Berkeley: University of California Press, 2006), 13, 63. Alexandra Minna Stern, *Eugenic Nation: Faults and Frontiers of Better Breeding in Modern America* (Berkeley: University of California Press, 2005), 57–81; Ettinger, *Imaginary Lines*, 68.

Chapter 3: Hog-Tied: The Roots of the Modern American Empire

1. "Illinois as a Grain Growing State," *Urbana Union*, Sept. 6, 1855.
2. "The First National Bank of Champaign, Illinois," *Champaign Daily Gazette*, Dec. 11, 1899.
3. A. D. Shamel, "History of Indian Corn," *Illinois Agriculturist* 6 (1902): 22–28.
4. "International Stock Food," *Urbana Courier*, March 13, 1905.
5. "Interesting Trade Gossip on Change," *Chicago Daily Tribune*, Nov. 18, 1909.
6. J. Ogden Armour, "The Supremacy of the American Hog," *The Breeder's Gazette*, Dec. 20, 1911, 1333.
7. "Must Increase Food Exports," *Urbana Courier*, Dec. 2, 1918.
8. Robert James McFall, *The World's Meat* (New York: D. Appleton and Co., 1927), 3–4, 33, 65.
9. William Earl Weeks, *The New Cambridge History of American Foreign Relations: Dimensions of the Early American Empire, 1754–1865*, vol. 1 (New York: Cambridge University Press, 2013), xvii–xviii, 41.
10. "The Breeds of Pigs and Their Utilisations," *American Swine and Poultry Journal* 3 (July, 1875): 17.
11. C. F. Boshart, "First Prize Essay," *Berkshire Year Book, 1895* (Springfield: American Berkshire Association, 1895), 15–19.
12. W. F. M. Arny, "Essay on the Best Breeds of Swine," *Transactions of the Illinois State Agricultural Society (1853–1854)* (Springfield: Lanphier & Walker, Printers, 1855), 554–58.
13. Sam White, "From Globalized Pig Breeds to Capitalist Pigs: A Study in Animal Cultures and Evolutionary History," *Environmental History* 16 (Jan. 2011): 94–120.
14. White, "From Globalized Pig Breeds," 96; Benj. F. Johnson, "More about the Hog, and Its History," *Illinois Farmer* 5 (Jan. 1860): 2–3.
15. Arny, "Essay on the Best Breeds of Swine," 555.
16. W. J. Fraser, "History of the Berkshire Swine," *Berkshire Year Book* (Springfield: American Berkshire Association, 1896), 49–50.
17. On heavy hams and unexcelled bacon, see Boshart, "First Prize Essay," *Berkshire Year Book, 1895*, 17.
18. *Year Book American Berkshire Association, 1894* (Springfield: American Berkshire Association, 1894), 74; Boshart, "First Prize Essay," *Berkshire Year Book, 1895*, 15–19.
19. A. B. Allen, "On the Origin, Breeding, and Management of Berkshire Swine," *Transactions of the Department of Agriculture of the State of Illinois (for the Year 1876)* (Springfield: D. W. Lusk, 1878), 208–20.
20. William Oliver, *Eight Months in Illinois, with Information to Immigrants*, 1843 (Chicago: Walter M. Hill, 1924), 80–81.

21. *Year Book American Berkshire Association, 1894*, 74. On woods hogs, see Allan G. Bogue, *From Prairie to Corn Belt: Farming on the Illinois and Iowa Prairies in the Nineteenth Century* (1963; Chicago: University of Chicago, reprint ed., 1994), 109.

22. Dewitt C. Wing, "Fighting the Battle for Live Stock Improvement," *Breeder's Gazette*, Dec. 16, 1908, 1210.

23. Clarence H. Danhof, *Change in Agriculture: The Northern United States, 1820–1870* (Cambridge: Harvard University Press, 1969), 176–77.

24. Arny, "Essay on the Best Breeds of Swine," 554–55.

25. Allen, "On the Origin, Breeding, and Management of Berkshire Swine," 212–13. Another account dates the Albany farmer first; see George W. Curtis, *Horses, Cattle, Sheep and Swine*, 2nd ed. (New York: The Rural Publishing Co., 1893), 294.

26. *Year Book American Berkshire Association, 1894*, 6–7.

27. "Death of a Profitable Berkshire," *Prairie Farmer*, Jan. 10, 1885, 20; E. J. Barker, "We Are Advertised by Our Loving Friends," *The Berkshire World and Cornbelt Stockman* 6 (July 1914): 9. For inflation calculation, http://www.in2013dollars.com, accessed May 23, 2017.

28. Arny, "Essay on the Best Breeds of Swine," 555–57.

29. M. T. Stookey, "Class D, Swine," *Transactions of the Department of Agriculture of the State of Illinois (for the Year 1876)* (Springfield: D. W. Lusk, 1878), 18–19.

30. W. C. Flagg, "The Agriculture of Illinois, 1683–1876," *Transactions of the Department of Agriculture of the State of Illinois (for the Year 1875)* (Springfield: State Journal Book, 1876), 286–346.

31. Bogue, *From Prairie to Corn Belt*, 103.

32. Frances E. Roehm, *Champaign County, Illinois 1850, A Historical Overview*, Urbana Free Library Archives, 1986, 95.

33. "Hogs, Fleas, &c.," *Urbana Union*, April 12, 1855.

34. William D. Walters, Jr., *The Heart of the Cornbelt: An Illustrated History of Corn Farming in McLean County* (Bloomington: McLean County Historical Society, 1997), 40.

35. "Large Farms in Illinois," *Friends' Review: A Religious, Literary and Miscellaneous Journal*, Sept. 26, 1863, 60.

36. "The Champaign Stock Shipment," *Champaign Daily Gazette*, Nov. 27, 1889.

37. "Honor to Whom Honor Is Due," *Urbana Union*, July 5, 1855.

38. W. C. Flagg, "Indian Corn—Its Varieties, Preparation of Soil, and Most Profitable Uses," *Transactions of the Department of Agriculture of the State of Illinois (1872)* (Springfield: State Journal Steam Print, 1873), 72–81.

39. "Corn," *Transactions of the Department of Agriculture of the State of Illinois (for the Year 1876)* (Springfield: D. W. Lusk, 1878), 331.

40. *History of Champaign County, Illinois, With Illustrations Descriptive of its Scenery and Biographical Sketches of Some of Its Prominent Men and Pioneers* (Philadelphia: Brink, McDonough & Co., 1878), 41.

41. On rank, Fred H. Rankin, "Points on Pork," *Illinois Agriculturist* 3 (1899): 68–74. D. S. Dalbey, "Pork Production in Illinois," *Illinois Agriculturist* 6 (1902): 74–80.

42. Johnson, "More about the Hog, and Its History," 3.

43. *History of Champaign County, Illinois*, 41.

44. "Official List of Awards at the Eighteenth Annual Exhibition (1870)," *Transactions of the Illinois State Agricultural Society* 8 (1869–70), 113; "Official List of Awards," *Transactions of the Department of Agriculture of the State of Illinois (for the Year 1871)* (Springfield: Journal Printing Office, 1872), 25–60.

45. A. M. Fanley, "Swine Breeding," in *J. S. Lothrop's Champaign County Directory, 1870–71*, by J. S. Lothrop (Chicago: Rand, McNally and Co., 1871), 150–52.

46. Johnson, "More about the Hog, and Its History," 2–3.

47. "Origin of Berkshires," *Prairie Farmer*, Feb. 8, 1890, 89.

48. H. P. Allen, cited in Phil Thrifton, "Large and Small Berkshires," *Prairie Farmer*, Aug. 9, 1890, 500.

49. Fraser, "History of the Berkshire Swine," 49–50.

50. Allen, "On the Origin, Breeding, and Management of Berkshire Swine," 210.

51. "Things in America, Social and Agricultural," *Prairie Farmer*, Dec. 8, 1866, 18, 23.

52. British Berkshire Society, *British Berkshire Herd Book*, vol. 1 (Salisbury: Edward Roe and Co., 1885), front matter. Harriet Ritvo, *The Animal Estate: The English and Other Creatures of the Victorian Age* (Cambridge: Harvard University Press, 1987), 53.

53. J. W. Jaquith, "Urbana Drug Store," *Urbana Union*, July 28, 1853; on silks, satins, and hats, see "For the Gentlemen," ad for Gessie and Sherfy, *Urbana Union*, Aug. 18, 1853.

54. Natalia Maree Belting, "Early History of Urbana-Champaign to 1871" (master's thesis, University of Illinois, 1937), 71–72.

55. "Berkshire Breeders," *Prairie Farmer*, Jan. 24, 1885, 52.

56. *Year Book American Berkshire Association, 1894*, 6.

57. Allen, "On the Origin, Breeding, and Management of Berkshire Swine," 211.

58. Allen, "On the Origin, Breeding, and Management of Berkshire Swine," 208–20.

59. Allen, "On the Origin, Breeding and Management of Berkshire Swine," 212.

60. W. Jos Grand, *Illustrated History of the Union Stockyards: Sketch-Book of Familiar Faces and Places at the Yards* (Chicago: W. Jos Grand, 1901), 132–33.

61. "The Status of Berkshires," *The Berkshire World and Cornbelt Stockman* 6 (Jan. 1914): 8.

62. Boshart, "First Prize Essay," *Berkshire Year Book, 1895*, 15–19.

63. D. Z. Evans, Jr., "Items on Breeding Stock," *American Swine and Poultry Journal* 3 (Dec. 1875): 116.

64. Arny, "Essay on the Best Breeds of Swine," 558. O. S. [Orson Squire] Fowler, and L. N. Fowler, *Phrenology Proved, Illustrated, and Applied*, 4th ed. (Philadelphia, Fowler and Brevoort, 1839), 20–24.

65. Arny, "Essay on the Best Breeds of Swine," 554–58.

66. Allen, "On the Origin, Breeding, and Management of Berkshire Swine," 211.

67. *Year Book American Berkshire Association, 1894*, 7.

68. Allen, "On the Origin, Breeding, and Management of Berkshire Swine," 213.

69. Boshart, "First Prize Essay," *Berkshire Year Book, 1895*, 15–19; Johnson, "More about the Hog, and Its History," 2–3.

70. Thomas Shaw, "The Berkshire Hog," *Berkshire Year Book, 1896* (Springfield: American Berkshire Association, 1896), 30–42.

71. D. W. May, "History of the Berkshire," *Berkshire Year Book, 1896* (Springfield: American Berkshire Association, 1896), 43–44. On the role of pigs in colonization more generally, see Mark Essig, *Lesser Beasts: A Snout-to-Tail History of the Humble Pig* (New York: Basic Books, 2015), 151.

72. Allen, "On the Origin, Breeding, and Management of Berkshire Swine," 208–11.

73. *Year Book American Berkshire Association, 1894*, 7.

74. Shaw, "The Berkshire Hog," 30.

75. Shaw, "The Berkshire Hog," 30–31.

76. British Berkshire Society, *British Berkshire Herd Book*, vol. 1, viii.

77. Wing, "Fighting the Battle for Live Stock Improvement," 1210.

78. D. W. May, *Annual Report of the Porto Rico Agricultural Experiment Station for 1911* (Washington, DC: U.S. Department of Agriulture, 1912), 12.

79. "Swine," *National Stockman and Farmer*, Nov. 1, 1913, 780.

80. Alan L. Olmstead and Paul W. Rhode, *Creating Abundance: Biological Innovation and American Agricultural Development* (New York: Cambridge University Press, 2008), 307–08; on the Berkshire ancestry of Duroc-Jerseys, see Curtis, *Horses, Cattle, Sheep and Swine*, 301; on the Berkshire ancestry of the Poland China breed, "Raising and Packing Hogs," *The National Provisioner* 15 (July 11, 1896): 15.

81. John G. Clark, *The Grain Trade in the Old Northwest*, 1966 (Westport: Greenwood Press, 1980), 181, 233–34.

82. "American Bacon and Pork," *The Illustrated Household Journal and Englishwoman's Domestic Magazine*, May 22, 1880, 326.

83. *First Report from the Select Committee of the House of Lords Appointed to Inquire into the Policy and Operation of The Navigation Laws; And to Report Thereon to the House; Together with Minutes of Evidence* (London: 1848), 85, Parliamentary Papers Online.

84. *Preliminary Report from Her Majesty's Commissioners on Agriculture* (London: 1881), 817, Parliamentary Papers Online.

85. *Report from the Select Committee on Preserved Meats (Navy), Together with the Minutes of Evidence* (London: 1852), 74, Parliamentary Papers Online.

86. On fine quality, see "Working on the New Tariff," *John Bull*, Nov. 19, 1842, 556.

87. On rattlesnakes, see "Royal Visit to Strathfieldsaye," *Bell's Life in London and Sporting Chronicle*, Dec. 29, 1844. On cow manure, *Report from the Select Committee on Merchandise Marks; Together with the Proceedings of the Committee, Minutes of Evidence, Appendix and Index* (London: 1897), 7, Parliamentary Papers Online.

88. Rankin, "Points on Pork," 68.

89. Fred H. Rankin, "Our Swine Interests," *Annual Report of the Illinois Farmers' Institute* (Springfield: 1898), 84–88.

90. *Year Book American Berkshire Association, 1894*, 6.

91. Phil Thrifton, "A Berkshire Claimant," *Prairie Farmer*, Dec. 26, 1885, 840.

92. Allen, "On the Origin, Breeding, and Management of Berkshire Swine," 220. On purebred animals as markers of distinction, see Ritvo, *The Animal Estate*, 61, 81.

93. Kelly J. Sisson Lessens, "Master of Millions: King Corn in American Culture" (PhD diss., University of Michigan, 2011), 7.

94. On leaner meat, *Preliminary Report from Her Majesty's Commissioners on Agriculture*, 817. On better breeding and market opportunities, see Allen, "On the Origin, Breeding, and Management of Berkshire Swine," 220.

95. James E. Davis, *Frontier Illinois* (Bloomington: Indiana University Press, 1998), 180.

96. Milton W. Mathews and Lewis A. McLean, *Early History and Pioneers of Champaign County* (Urbana: Champaign County Herald, 1886), 24, 31; on driving and plants, see Bogue, *From Prairie to Corn Belt*, 111.

97. W. J. Edwards, "Roads and Road Making in Illinois," *Transactions of the Department of Agriculture of the State of Illinois (1874)* (Springfield: State Journal Steam Print, 1875), 140–63.

98. *Documents Relating to the Organization of the Illinois Central Rail-Road Company*, 2nd ed. (New York: Geo. Scott Roe, 1852), 5, 8; C. H. Markham, *The Development, Strategy, and Traffic of the Illinois Central System*, reprint from *Economic Geography* 2 (Jan. 1926), 1; "Rail Road Meeting," *Urbana Union*, June 22, 1854.

99. Lance E. Davis and Robert J. Cull, *International Capital Markets and American Economic Growth, 1820–1914* (New York: Cambridge University Press, 1994), 111.

100. Howard Gray Brownson, "History of the Illinois Central Railroad to 1870" (Ph.D. diss., University of Illinois, 1909), 121–22.

101. Paul Wallace Gates, *The Illinois Central Railroad and Its Colonization Work* (Cambridge: Harvard University Press, 1934), 89.

102. Brownson, "History of the Illinois Central Railroad to 1870," 123–29. On the $5 million, see *Illinois Central Railroad Company, Report to the Shareholders, 1858*, Documents and Pamphlets Relating to American Railroads in the Late Nineteenth Century, University of Illinois Urbana-Champaign (hereafter UIUC) Rare Books and Manuscript Library, 1.

103. *Illinois Central Railroad Company, Report to the Shareholders, 1857*, Documents and Pamphlets Relating to American Railroads in the Late Nineteenth Century, UIUC Rare Books and Manuscript Library, 1, 9; Brownson, "History of the Illinois Central Railroad to 1870," 137.

104. *Illinois Central Railroad Company, Report to the Shareholders, 1858*, 1–2. Brownson, "History of the Illinois Central Railroad to 1870," 137.

105. Gates, *The Illinois Central Railroad and Its Colonization Work*, 80; on the books, *Illinois Central Railroad Company, Report to the Shareholders, 1858*, 2.

106. *The Ten Best States of America for Agriculture, Horticulture, and General Industries, Traversed by the Illinois Central Railroad* (Cedar Rapids: Republican Printing Company, 1893), 14.

107. James Caird, *Letter on the Lands of the Illinois Central Railway Company* (London: Jan. 1859), 3–9; Gates, *The Illinois Central Railroad and Its Colonization Work*, 215.

108. Gates, *The Illinois Central Railroad and Its Colonization Work*, 218.

109. Homer E. Socolofsky, "William Scully: His Early Years in Illinois, 1850–1865," *Journal of the West* 4 (Jan. 1965): 41–55. Although he had land in Illinois, Scully did not own any in what became Champaign County, 41–44; on protest, 52.

110. "The Scully Estate—Lords of 211,000 Acres," *Prairie Farmer*, March 22, 1919, 8.

111. Caird, *Letter on the Lands of the Illinois Central Railway Company*, 3–9.

112. Gates, *The Illinois Central Railroad and Its Colonization Work*, 218.

113. Gates, *The Illinois Central Railroad and Its Colonization Work*, 89–90, 172.

114. *Portrait and Biographical Album of Champaign County, Ill.* (Chicago: Chapman Brothers, 1887), 546.

115. "Literary Society," *Urbana Union*, June 1, 1854.

116. Census figures accessed via Ancestry.com, June 8, 2010. In 1850, 14 percent of immigrants to the United States as a whole came from England, Scotland and Wales; 45 percent from Ireland. By 1870, the former sent 27 percent of immigrants and Ireland only 15 percent. Kathleen Burk, *Old World, New World: Great Britain and America from the Beginning* (New York: Atlantic Monthly Press, 2007), 312.

117. Duncan Bell, *The Idea of Greater Britain: Empire and the Future of World Order, 1860–1900* (Princeton: Princeton University Press, 2007), 54.

118. *A Guide to the Illinois Central Railroad Lands* (Chicago: Illinois Central Railroad Office, 1859), 52.

119. Harry Fornari, *Bread upon the Waters: A History of United States Grain Exports* (Nashville: Aurora Publishers, 1973), 28–29.

120. "British Agriculture and Foreign Competition," *Blackwood's Edinburgh Magazine*, Jan. 1850, 94–136.

121. Christabel S. Orwin and Edith H. Whetham, *History of British Agriculture 1846–1914* (London: Archon Books, 1964), 40, 261; on Canadian pigs' diets, see C. G. Hopkins, "Breeding Corn for Improvement in Composition," *Illinois Agriculturist* 6 (1902): 1–12.

122. Fornari, *Bread upon the Waters*, 32.

123. Russell Howard Anderson, "Agriculture in Illinois During the Civil War Period, 1850–1870: An Abstract of a Thesis" (PhD diss., abstract, University of Illinois, 1929), 3–4.

124. *Documents Relating to the Organization of the Illinois Central Rail-Road Company*, 84.

125. Clipping: Democratic Press, "The Farm and Garden," no. 83, Rural, West Urbana, April 2, 1857, Dunlap, volume 3, Letterbooks, Matthias L. Dunlap, Matthias L. Dunlap Papers, Box 1, UIUC Archives, Urbana, Illinois.

126. Richard Perren, *The Meat Trade in Britain, 1840–1914* (London: Routledge and Kegan Paul, 1978), 71. Some pork went to Europe: starting in the 1840s, Cincinnati packers began to put up pork expressly for northern European markets; Rudolf Alexander Clemen, *The American Livestock and Meat Industry* (New York: The Ronald Press Company, 1923), 98.

127. Roger Horowitz, *Putting Meat on the American Table: Taste, Technology, Transformation* (Baltimore: Johns Hopkins University Press, 2006), 50.

128. "New Records for U.S. Pork Export Volume," *National Hog Farmer*, Feb. 7, 2018.

129. Grand, *Illustrated History of the Union Stockyards*, 19, 22.

130. "The Export Commerce of To-Day," *Bradstreet's*, July 10, 1880, 4.

131. On Liverpool, see Perren, *The Meat Trade in Britain*, 171. On 8 percent and the Liverpool trade, see Alexander Maclure, "America as a Power," *The Nineteenth Century: A Monthly Review*, June 1896, 809, 906–13.

132. Rankin, "Our Swine Interests," 86.

133. Rankin, "Points on Pork," 71.

134. Rankin, "Our Swine Interests," 86.

135. Clark, *The Grain Trade in the Old Northwest*, 181, 233–34.

136. J. R. Dodge, "Report of the Statistician," *Report of the Commissioner of Agriculture, 1885* (Washington, DC: Government Printing Office, 1885), 344–430.

137. "Foreign Restrictions," *Prairie Farmer*, Nov. 28, 1885, 774; Paul W. Gates, *Agriculture and the Civil War* (New York: Alfred A. Knopf, 1965), 184.

138. Rankin, "Our Swine Interests," 85.

139. John L. Gignilliat, "Pigs, Politics, and Protection: The European Boycott of American Pork, 1879–1891," *Agricultural History* 35 (Jan. 1961): 3–12.

140. Gignilliat, "Pigs, Politics, and Protection," 3, 10–11.

141. *Annual Report of the Veterinary Department of the Privy Council Office for the Year 1879, With an Appendix* (London: 1880), 10, Parliamentary Papers Online.

142. "It is not without a touch of humour . . . ," *The Country Gentleman*, April 23, 1881, 433. On 60 percent, see Gignilliat, "Pigs, Politics, and Protection," 4.

143. Rankin, "Our Swine Interests," 86.

144. *The Foreign Commerce and Navigation of the United States for the Year Ending June 30, 1895*, part 1, vol. 2 (Washington, DC: Government Printing Office, 1896), 966.

145. The company was run under the name Fowler Brothers Limited from 1869 to 1885; John F. Hobbs, "Our Great Meat Kingdom in the West," *The National Provisioner* 23 (Dec. 22, 1900): 13.

146. Michael D'Antonio, *A Full Cup: Sir Thomas Lipton's Extraordinary Life and His Quest for the America's Cup* (New York: Riverhead Books, 2010), 38, 90–91, 124.

147. "William Simpson (Liverpool), Ltd.," *The National Provisioner* 51 (Feb. 11, 1911): 49.

148. "Rural Topics and Events," *The Australasian*, May 31, 1879.

149. *Annual Report of the Veterinary Department of the Privy Council Office for the Year 1879*, 10.

150. "The Inquiry Which the Local Government Board Has Ordered," *The Country Gentleman*, July 10, 1880, 693.

151. "American Pork," *Bell's Life in London and Sporting Chronicle*, Nov. 6, 1842.

152. "The English Market, by Way of Canada," *Prairie Farmer*, June 1843, 3, 6.

153. Orwin and Whetham, *History of British Agriculture 1846–1914*, 40, 261; on Canadian pigs' diets, see C. G. Hopkins, "Breeding Corn for Improvement in Composition," *Illinois Agriculturist* 6 (1902): 1–12.

154. Perren, *The Meat Trade in Britain*, 171.

155. Rankin, "Our Swine Interests," 85.

156. The *Echo*, cited in "Rural Topics and Events," *The Australasian*, May 31, 1879.

157. "American Bacon and Pork," *The Illustrated Household Journal and Englishwoman's Domestic Magazine*, May 22, 1880, 326.

158. *Report from the Select Committee on Marking of Foreign Meat, &c.* (London: 1893), x, Parliamentary Papers Online.

159. "Alleged Dishonesty in the Provision Trade," *The Manchester Guardian*, Dec. 16, 1897.

160. W. T. Crandall, "Report," *Report of the Commissioner of Agriculture and Dairying for the Dominion of Canada, 1897* (Ottawa: S. E. Dawson, 1898), part 15, 6.

161. *Report from the Select Committee on British Shipping* (London: 1844), 100–01, Parliamentary Papers Online. Until the 1880s many houses relied on all-round butchers but thereafter they relied more on unskilled workers laboring in

assembly-line conditions; James R Barrett, *Work and Community in the Jungle: Chicago's Packinghouse Workers, 1894–1922* (Urbana: University of Illinois Press, 1987), 25.

162. Perren, *The Meat Trade in Britain*, 71, 171.

163. Charles Randolph, *Twentieth Annual Report of the Trade and Commerce of Chicago for the Year Ending December 31, 1877, Compiled for the Board of Trade* (Chicago: Knight and Leonard Printers, 1878), lxxv-lxxvi.

164. "Spices," *The National Provisioner* 15 (July 4, 1896): 41.

165. "Guide to the B. Heller & Co. Collection, 1896–2003," University of Chicago Library, 2010.

166. "American Bacon and Pork," *The Illustrated Household Journal and Englishwoman's Domestic Magazine*, May 22, 1880, 326.

167. On packing methods and their changes over time, Perren, *The Meat Trade in Britain*, 71; Horowitz, *Putting Meat on the American Table*, 45. "American Bacon and Pork," 326. Mark Kurlansky, *Salt: A World History* (New York: Walker and Company, 2002), 249, 318.

168. "Wholesale and Retail Provision Trade," *The Age*, Oct. 30, 1842, 3.

169. W. H. Simmonds, *The Practical Grocer*, vol. 3 (London: The Gresham Publishing Company, 1906), 241.

170. *Report of the Departmental Committee Appointed to Inquire into the Use of Preservatives and Colouring Matters in the Preservation and Colouring of Food* (London, 1901), 1–2, 15, 203–05, Parliamentary Papers Online.

171. *Report of the Departmental Committee Appointed to Inquire into the Use of Preservatives and Colouring Matters*, 1–2, 15, 203–05. On color enhancement, see "Restriction of American Meats in Switzerland," *The National Provisioner* 16 (Feb. 27, 1897): 29.

172. "Markets for American Products," *Bradstreet's* 23 (Sept. 7, 1895): 573.

173. W. H. Thomas, "A Missouri Farmer Argues," *Prairie Farmer*, Dec. 6, 1890, 769, 777.

174. J. R. Dodge, "Report of the Statistician," *Report of the Commissioner of Agriculture, 1886* (Washington, DC: Government Printing Office, 1887), 359–458; Wm. G. Le Duc, "Report," *Annual Report of the Commissioner of Agriculture for the Year 1880* (Washington, DC: Government Printing Office, 1881), 32–35.

175. W. H. Thomas, "A Missouri Farmer Argues," *Prairie Farmer*, Dec. 6, 1890, 769; William Elder, *The American Farmer's Markets at Home and Abroad* (Philadelphia: Ringwalt and Brown, 1870), 3.

176. John Darwin, *The Empire Project: The Rise and Fall of the British World-System, 1830–1970* (Cambridge: Cambridge University Press, 2009), 182.

177. "Commercial Results of a War with the United States," *Mark Lane Express and Agricultural Journal* 73 (Dec. 30, 1895): 906; on fears of dependency among Populists, flour millers, and cattlemen, see Morton Rothstein, "The American West and Foreign Markets, 1850–1900," in *The Frontier in American Development: Essays in Honor of Paul Wallace Gates*, ed. David M. Ellis, (Ithaca: Cornell University Press, 1969), 381–406.

178. James T. Dwyer, "Manufactures in Illinois," *Transactions of the Department of Agriculture of the State of Illinois (for the Year 1871)* (Springfield: Journal Printing Office, 1872), 87–108. On frequency of Indian famines, James Vernon, *Hunger: A*

Modern History (Cambridge: The Belknap Press of Harvard University Press, 2007), 51. On Indian grain exports, see also Mike Davis: *Late Victorian Holocausts: El Niño Famines and the Making of the Third World* (London: Verso, 2001), 26.

179. Markham, *The Development, Strategy, and Traffic of the Illinois Central System*, 8, 12, 14, 17; *Sixty-Fourth Annual Report of the Illinois Central Railroad Company for the Year Ended June 30, 1914*, np. On bananas and coconuts, see *The Ten Best States of America for Agriculture, Horticulture, and General Industries*, 18.

180. Orwin and Whetham, *History of British Agriculture 1846–1914*, 240–41, 257.

181. W. J. Gordon, "The Way of the World at Sea," *The Leisure Hour*, July 1893, 604–08.

182. *Report from the Select Committee on Preserved Meats (Navy)*, 70.

183. Testimony of George Hart, *Report of the Committee Appointed by the Board of Trade to Inquire into Certain Questions Affecting the Mercantile Marine, II—Minutes of Evidence* (London: House of Commons, 1903), 650, Parliamentary Papers Online.

184. Clements R. Markham, "Report of the Scurvy Committee," *The Academy*, June 2, 1877, 485–86. *Armour and Company: Containing Facts About the Business and Organization* (Np: Armour and Company, 1917), 34.

185. Jimmy M. Skaggs, *Prime Cut: Livestock Raising and Meatpacking in the United States, 1607–1983* (College Station: Texas A&M Press, 1986), 40.

186. John Regan, *The Emigrant's Guide to the Western States of America* (Edinburgh: Oliver and Boyd, [1852]), 337.

187. "Must Have More Hogs," *The National Provisioner* 57 (Nov. 17, 1917): 19.

188. *Report of a Committee Appointed by the Secretary of State for War to Enquire into the Administration of the Transport and Supply Departments of the Army* (London: 1867), 365, Parliamentary Papers Online.

189. *Report from the Select Committee on the Abyssinian Expedition* (London: 1870), 94, Parliamentary Papers Online.

190. *Army Medical Department. Statistical, Sanitary, and Medical Reports, Volume VII, for the Year 1865* (London: 1867), 291, Parliamentary Papers Online.

191. "We May Feed British Army," *The National Provisioner* 21 (Oct. 7, 1899): 12.

192. "Canned Meat for China," *The National Provisioner* 23 (July 28, 1900): 12.

193. J. Ogden Armour, "The Supremacy of the American Hog," *The Breeder's Gazette*, Dec. 20, 1911, 1290, 1333, 1336, 1338, 1340, 1342.

194. "Sea-Fare," *Chamber's Journal*, September 20, 1882, 623–26.

195. *Report of the Committee Appointed to Inquire into the Question of Navy Rations, Meal Hours, The Prices Paid for "Savings," and the Management of Canteens* (London: 1901), 16, Parliamentary Papers Online.

196. On depots, see *Report of the Committee Appointed by the Lords Commissioners of the Admiralty to Inquire into the System of Purchase and Contract in the Navy* (London: 1887), 68–70, Parliamentary Papers Online; on salt junk, see Frederick Dolman, "How the Navy Is Fed," *The English Illustrated Magazine*, Oct. 1900, 8–17.

197. *Report from the Select Committee on Preserved Meats (Navy)*, 68, 398.

198. "British Agriculture and Foreign Competition," *Blackwood's Edinburgh Magazine*, Jan. 1850, 94–136.

199. *Report from the Select Committee on Preserved Meats (Navy)*, 68, 398, on superior quality, 401.

200. *Report from the Select Committee on Preserved Meats (Navy)*, 115, 127, 401.

201. *Navy (Health). Return to an Order of the Honourable The House of Commons, dated 29 April 1870;—for, A Copy of the Statistical Abstract of the Health of the Navy, for the Year 1869–70* (London: 1870), 22, Parliamentary Papers Online.

202. *Report from the Select Committee on Public Departments (Purchases, &c.)* (London: 1873), 449, Parliamentary Papers Online.

203. *Report of the Committee Appointed by the Lords Commissioners of the Admiralty to Inquire into the System of Purchase and Contract in the Navy*, 48.

204. *Report of the Committee Appointed to Inquire into the Question of Navy Rations*, 13.

205. "Sea-Fare," *Chamber's Journal*, September 20, 1882, 623–26, 625.

206. *Report from the Select Committee on Preserved Meats (Navy)*, 114.

207. *Annual Report of the Chief of the Bureau of Statistics on the Commerce and Navigation of the United States for the Fiscal Year Ended June 30, 1870* (Washington, DC: Government Printing Office, 1871), 184.

208. Treasury Department, *Annual Report and Statements of the Chief of the Bureau of Statistics on the Commerce and Navigation of the United States for the Fiscal Year Ended June 30, 1883* (Washington, DC: Government Printing Office, 1883), 194.

209. "Imports into South Africa," *The National Provisioner* 19 (August 13, 1898): 14.

210. Treasury Department, *Annual Report and Statements of the Chief of the Bureau of Statistics on the Foreign Commerce and Navigation, Immigration, and Tonnage of the United States for the Fiscal Year Ending June 30, 1888* (Washington, DC: Government Printing Office, 1888), 298–99.

211. Nathaniel Edward Yorke-Davies, "The Feeding of the Soldier: The Lesson of the Great Boer War," *The Gentleman's Magazine*, Dec. 1902, 601–17.

212. "Live-Stock and Kindred Markets," *Breeder's Gazette* 2 (July 13, 1882): 93.

213. *The Illinois Agriculturist* 8 (March 1904): 114.

214. Frank M. Surface, *American Pork Production in the World War* (Chicago: A. W. Shaw Company, 1926), 5.

215. Robert James McFall, *The World's Meat* (New York: D. Appleton and Co., 1927), 135, 514.

216. Avner Offer, *The First World War: An Agrarian Interpretation* (Oxford: Oxford University Press, 1989), 1, 51, 354, 376.

217. John W. Coogan, *The End of Neutrality: The United States, Britain, and Maritime Rights, 1899–1915* (Ithaca: Cornell University Press, 1981), 162–63, 199–201.

218. Offer, *The First World War: An Agrarian Interpretation*, 354, 366.

219. Clemen, *The American Livestock and Meat Industry*, 292–93.

220. Frank M. Surface, *The Grain Trade During the World War* (New York: The Macmillan Company, 1928), 17.

221. Offer, *The First World War: An Agrarian Interpretation*, 1, 354, 376.

222. W. H. Thomas, "A Missouri Farmer Argues," *Prairie Farmer*, Dec. 6, 1890, 769, 777.

223. *Minutes of the Proceedings of the Navy League Conference to Consider the Position of the Country If Involved in War* (London: Spottiswoode and Co., 1898), 93.

224. Loudon M. Douglas, "Bacon-Curing," *Journal of the Royal Agricultural Society of England* 9 (March 31, 1898), 68–103.

225. "War and the Importation of Provisions," *The National Provisioner* 18 (May 7, 1898): 23.

226. Thomas G. Read, "Our Food Supplies in Time of War," *Mark Lane Express and Agricultural Journal* 81 (Nov. 20, 1899): 593.

227. "War with Great Britain," *Illinois Farmer* 1 (March 1856): 58–59.

228. Edward P. Crapol, *America for Americans: Economic Nationalism and Anglophobia in the Late Nineteenth Century* (Westport, CT: Greenwood Press, 1973), 14–17. John Darwin discusses "semi-colonial" investments in the British Empire in *Unfinished Empire: The Global Expansion of Britain* (London: Penguin Books, 2012), 395.

229. Chicago's rising ability to stand alongside centers of capital likewise resulted from regional ties to Britain; James Belich, *Replenishing the Earth: The Settler Revolution and the Rise of the Anglo-World, 1783–1939* (New York: Oxford University Press, 2009), 495.

230. "Britain, Peace and War," *The National Provisioner* 22 (Feb. 24, 1900): 11. The United States shipped on average half of its total exports to the UK from 1837 to 1873, getting 40 percent of its imports from the UK in return; Jay Sexton, *Debtor Diplomacy: Finance and American Foreign Relations in the Civil War Era, 1837–1873* (Oxford: Oxford University Press, 2005), 3.

231. Gordon Robert Lyall, "From Imbroglio to Pig War: The San Juan Island Dispute, 1853–71, in History and Memory," *BC Studies*, no. 186 (Summer 2015): 73–93; Stuart Anderson, *Race and Rapprochement: Anglo-Saxonism and Anglo-American Relations, 1895–1904* (East Brunswick, NJ: Associated University Presses, 1981), 11.

Chapter 4: The Isolationist Capital of America: Hotbed of Alliance Politics

1. J. M. Peck, *New Guide for Emigrants to the West, Containing Sketches of Ohio, Indiana, Illinois, Missouri, Michigan, with the Territories of Wisconsin and Arkansas, and the Adjacent Parts* (Boston: Gould, Kendall & Lincoln, 1836), 259.

2. H. J. D., "Chat from Abroad," 28, Scrapbook of H. J. Dunlap, Furth, Baker-Busey-Dunlap Family Papers, Box 14, Illinois Historical Survey, UIUC.

3. J. O. Cunningham, *History of Champaign County* (1905; reprint, Champaign: Champaign County Historical Archives, 1984), 884.

4. "Geo. Busey Tells of Southern Trip," *Urbana Courier*, March 12, 1912.

5. "Andrew Rutherford Is Dead," *Urbana Courier*, May 4, 1915.

6. "Chinese Girl to Be Missionary," *Urbana Courier*, May 4, 1915.

7. "Miss Kyle Will Not Leave U. of I.," *Urbana Courier*, July 26, 1916.

8. On "isolation" as the result of ethnic groups' disinclination to fight the Central powers, see Ray Allen Billington, "The Origins of Middle Western Isolationism," *Political Science Quarterly* 60 (March 1945): 44–64. On isolationism as "an attitude of opposition to binding commitments," see Leroy N. Rieselbach, *The Roots of Isolationism: Congressional Voting and Presidential Leadership in Foreign Policy* (New York: Bobbs-Merrill Company, 1966), 7. On isolationism as opposition to committing U.S. forces outside the hemisphere, see John Milton Cooper, Jr., *The Vanity of Power: American Isolationism and the First World War, 1914–1917* (Westport: Greenwood Publishing Corporation, 1969), 2.

9. "Isolationism" owes a debt to references to diplomatic "isolation" in cases when European powers pursued their interests independently. See "The News This Morning," *New York Tribune*, Feb. 28, 1896.

10. William A. Williams, "The Legend of Isolationism in the 1920's," in *Essays in American Diplomacy*, ed. Armin Rappaport (New York: The Macmillan Company, 1967), 215–28.

11. On so-called isolationists as nationalists and imperialists, see William G. Carleton, "Isolationism and the Middle West," *The Mississippi Valley Historical Review* 33 (Dec. 1946): 377–90, 386. On claims that if isolationism means "total abstention from international affairs" then it should "have no place in accounts of American history," see Thomas N. Guinsburg, *The Pursuit of Isolationism in the United States Senate from Versailles to Pearl Harbor* (New York: Garland Publishing, 1982). On wanting to keep the United States out of war, not out of the world, see Brooke L. Blower, "From Isolationism to Neutrality: A New Framework for Understanding American Political Culture, 1919–1941," *Diplomatic History* 38 (April 2014): 345–76.

12. On the rural roots of isolationism, see Robert P. Wilkins, "The Nonpartisan League and Upper Midwest Isolationism," *Agricultural History* 39 (April 1965): 102–09. On associating the Midwest with noninterventionist policies, even though midwesterners were never the only or even the majority of voters who backed them, see Joseph A. Fry, "Place Matters: Domestic Regionalism and the Formation of American Foreign Policy," *Diplomatic History* 36 (June 2012): 451–82. On isolationist capital, Ricselbach, *The Roots of Isolationism*, 110.

13. On idealized vision, see Cooper, *The Vanity of Power*, 140. On isolationists as agriculturalists who had suffered after World War I, see Guinsburg, *The Pursuit of Isolationism*, 266–67.

14. Wayne S. Cole, "Gerald P. Nye and Agrarian Bases for the Rise and Fall of American Isolationism," in *Three Faces of Midwestern Isolationism: Gerald P. Nye, Robert E. Wood, and John L. Lewis*, ed. John N. Schacht (Iowa City: The Center for the Study of the Recent History of the United States, 1981), 1–10. Warren F. Kuehl debunks the idea of midwestern isolationism in "Midwestern Newspapers and Isolationist Sentiment," *Diplomatic History* 3 (July 1979): 283–306.

15. Based on keyword searching "isolationism" and "isolationist" in the *Prairie Farmer* and *Urbana Daily Courier* through 1945, Illinois Digital Newspaper Collection.

16. "Dysentery in Calves and Other Young Animals," *Prairie Farmer*, April 29, 1899; "Isolation in Arctics," *Urbana Daily Courier*, May 29, 1917; "Ever Hear of the Island of Mahe?" *Urbana Daily Courier*, Dec. 20, 1918. Similarly, the *New York Tribune* ran stories alluding to the isolation of islands like Labrador and Guam, the Kentucky mountains, Nevada deserts, and sheep stations in New South Wales. See "Women of Labrador," *New York Tribune*, May 21, 1904; "Army and Navy Notes," *New York Tribune*, July 25, 1909; "An Eccentric Kentuckian Dead," *New York Tribune*, Dec. 25, 1897; "New Mines in Nevada," *New York Tribune*, Nov. 13, 1869; "Australian Housekeeping," *New York Tribune*, Feb. 23, 1903.

17. "The Farmer's Automobile," *Prairie Farmer*, Oct. 9, 1915; "Practical Talk about Rural Telephones," *Prairie Farmer*, Dec. 15, 1909; "A Granger Interviewed,"

Prairie Farmer, Sept. 15, 1877; "How Rural Delivery Pays," *Prairie Farmer*, April 6, 1905; "A Word to the Wise," *Prairie Farmer*, Jan. 21, 1904; on newspapers and telegrams, "Co-operation of Farmers," *Prairie Farmer*, June 14, 1873.

18. "Hermits Abnormal," *Urbana Daily Courier*, Sept. 24, 1906.

19. Anne Effland, "International Programs of the USDA: Cross-Purposes or a Delicate Balance?," *Agricultural History* 87 (Summer 2013): 349–58.

20. Eugene V. Davenport, "The Relation of Agricultural Organizations to Agricultural Development," 1–2, speech of 1902; Folder: Agricultural Organizations, Box 5, Eugene V. Davenport Papers, University of Illinois Urbana-Champaign (hereafter UIUC) Archives.

21. "Champaign County," *Prairie Farmer*, Jan. 20, 1877.

22. John Agnew, *The United States in the World-Economy: A Regional Geography* (Cambridge: Cambridge University Press, 1987), 53.

23. J. R. Dodge, "Report of the Statistician," *Report of the Commissioner of Agriculture, 1886* (Washington, DC: Government Printing Office, 1887), 359–458.

24. "Corn," *The Illinois Agriculturist* 2 (1898), 81.

25. "Illinois Traction System Monument to Genius of Hon. William B. McKinley," *Urbana Courier*, Dec. 13, 1909.

26. "M'Kinley for Senator," *Chicago Daily Tribune*, Aug. 16, 1920.

27. "Made Right Selection," *Urbana Courier*, Dec. 13, 1905.

28. *William B. McKinley: Memorial Addresses Delivered in the Senate and House of Representatives of the United States in Memory of William B. McKinley* (Washington, DC: U.S. Government Printing Office, 1927), 6. On reciprocity tariff positions, see "What T.R. Asks Has Become Law," *Urbana Courier*, Oct. 4, 1912.

29. On protection, see "Facts! To Think About," *Urbana Courier*, Oct. 29, 1914. On trade, see "McKinley's Prestige a Factor," *Urbana Courier*, Oct. 24, 1912.

30. "Knox Praises W.B. M'Kinley," *Urbana Courier*, Aug. 21, 1912.

31. On shipping rights, "End of Peace Conference," *Urbana Courier*, July 26, 1906; "War Airships under Ban," *Urbana Courier*, Sept. 21, 1912. Fredrik Sterzel, *The Inter-Parliamentary Union* (Stockholm: P. A. Norsted and Söner, 1968), 9, 26–27. The members in 1912: Australia, Belgium, Britain, Bulgaria, Canada, Denmark, France, Germany, Greece, Hungary, Italy, Japan, Liberia, Netherlands, Norway, Portugal, Rumania, Russia, Serbia, Spain, Sweden, Switzerland, Turkey, and the United States; Inter-Parliamentary Bureau, *The Inter-Parliamentary Union: Its Work and Its Organisation* (Geneva: Inter-Parliamentary Bureau, 1948), 18–19.

32. "The News Boiled Down," *Urbana Courier*, Jan. 15, 1904.

33. *William B. McKinley: Memorial Addresses*, 8, 35.

34. "M'Kinley to Visit Rome," *Urbana Courier*, Aug. 29, 1911.

35. "M'Kinley Says Reduce War Cost," *Urbana Courier*, Oct. 24, 1912.

36. On Italian war, "M'Kinley Comes Home 'Broke,'" *Urbana Courier*, Oct. 31, 1911; on "foremost," "M'Kinley Says Reduce War Cost," *Urbana Courier*, Oct. 24, 1912; "Eminent Divine Out for M'Kinley," *Urbana Courier*, Sept. 24, 1912.

37. Jack R. Harlan, "Gene Centers and Gene Utilization in American Agriculture," *Environmental Review* 1, no. 3 (1976): 26–42.

38. Philip J. Pauly, *Fruits and Plains: The Horticultural Transformation of America* (Cambridge: Harvard University Press, 2007).

39. John C. Van Tramp, *Prairie and Rocky Mountain Adventures or Life in the West* (Baltimore: H. Miller, 1859), 565–66. On biological innovation, see Alan L. Olmstead and Paul W. Rhode, *Creating Abundance: Biological Innovation and American Agricultural Development* (New York: Cambridge University Press, 2008), 390.

40. "Origins of Various Trees, Plants, and Shrubs," *Urbana Union*, Sept. 22, 1853.

41. J. S. Budd, "History of the Duchess Apple," *Prairie Farmer*, March 29, 1890, 198.

42. "Red Astrachan," *Illinois Farmer* 5 (Sept. 1860): 151.

43. "What Is Imphee," *Illinois Farmer* 2 (Nov. 1857): 263.

44. "Aurora. Second Day of the Northern Illinois Horticultural Society," vol. Dunlap 2, Box 3, Matthias L. Dunlap Papers, UIUC Archives.

45. Alfred W. Crosby, Jr., *The Columbian Exchange: Biological and Cultural Consequences of 1492* (Westport, CT: Greenwood Press, 1972). On "neo-ecological imperialism," see Gregory T. Cushman, *Guano and the Opening of the Pacific World: A Global Ecological History* (Cambridge: Cambridge University Press, 2013), 19, 77.

46. "Hall Hardware Co.," *Urbana Courier*, July 1, 1913.

47. *Prairie Farmer's Reliable Directory of Farmers and Breeders, Champaign County* (Chicago: Prairie Farmer [1917]), 13, 260.

48. C. R. Overman, "On the Germination, Cultivation, Use and Value to the State of Illinois, of the 'Maclura' or Osage Orange Hedge," *Transactions of the Illinois State Agricultural Society* 1 (1853–1854): 412–23. On hedges and civilization, see William D. Walters, Jr., *The Heart of the Cornbelt: An Illustrated History of Corn Farming in McLean County* (Bloomington: McLean County Historical Society, 1997), 15.

49. Samuel Edwards, "On the Cultivation of Timber on the Prairies for Shelter," *Transactions of the Illinois State Agricultural Society* 1 (1853–1854): 478–79.

50. "Fruit Trees for Ornamental Purposes," *Illinois Farmer* 5 (Jan. 1860): 12.

51. National Forest Foundation, "Restoring a Lost Landscape at Midewin National Tallgrass Prairie," https://www.nationalforests.org/who-we-are/our-impact/midewin, accessed Sept. 2015.

52. Pauly, *Fruits and Plains*, 104–05. On seeds, Sarah T. Phillips, "Antebellum Agricultural Reform, Republican Ideology, and Sectional Tension," *Agricultural History* 74 (Autumn, 2000): 799–822.

53. Knowles A. Ryerson, "History and Significance of the Foreign Plant Introduction Work of the United States Department of Agriculture," *Agricultural History* 7 (July 1933): 110–28. On imports, "President M'Kinley," *Farmer and Breeder for the Farm Home* 12 (Dec. 1899): 1. Courtney Fullilove, *The Profit of the Earth: The Global Seeds of American Agriculture* (Chicago: University of Chicago Press, 2017), 28–66.

54. Charles M. Gardner, *The Grange—Friend of the Farmer* (Washington, DC: National Grange, 1949), 163. This practice ended in 1923, 165.

55. Harlan, "Gene Centers and Gene Utilization in American Agriculture," 28.

56. "Substitutes and Adulterations of Coffee," *Illinois Farmer* 7 (April 1862): 115–16.

57. Charles T. Leavitt, "Attempts to Improve Cattle Breeds in the United States, 1790–1860," *Agricultural History* 7 (April 1933): 51–67.

58. "Japan Oranges," *Prairie Farmer*, Jan. 11, 1890, 22. On the earlier circulation of agricultural information, see Joyce E. Chaplin, *An Anxious Pursuit: Agricultural Innovation and Modernity in the Lower South, 1730–1815* (Chapel Hill: University of North Carolina Press, 1993), 136, 142.

59. "The Illinois Farmer," *Illinois Farmer* 5 (Aug. 1860): 130.

60. "Illinois Department of Agriculture," *Prairie Farmer*, Jan. 13, 1877.

61. Rural, "Our Country Correspondence," *The Farm and Garden*, July 10, 1856, vol. Dunlap 3, Box 3, Matthias L. Dunlap Papers, UIUC Archives.

62. "The Farm and Garden. An Unexpected Present," vol. Dunlap 3, Box 3, Matthias L. Dunlap Papers, UIUC Archives.

63. [M. L. Dunlap], "The Farm and Garden," *Illinois Farmer*, May 1858, 74–75.

64. Marina Moskowitz, "Broadcasting Seeds on the American Landscape," in *Cultures of Commerce: Representation and American Business Culture, 1877–1960*, ed. Elspeth H. Brown, Catherine Gudis, and Marina Moskowitz (New York: Palgrave Macmillan, 2006), 9–26.

65. *Briggs and Bros. Quarterly Illustrated Floral Work* (Chicago: Briggs and Bros., 1876), 67, 68, 69.

66. *Bull's Catalogue of Seeds*, 1901, inside cover.

67. *General Trade Catalogue of Vegetable, Agricultural, Flower, Tree, and Other Seeds Offered by Ernst Benary Seed Merchant and Grower Erfurt (Germany), 1898–99* (Erfurt: G.A. Koenig, [1898]).

68. Alan I. Marcus, *Agricultural Science and the Quest for Legitimacy: Farmers, Agricultural Colleges, and Experiment Stations, 1870–1890* (Ames: Iowa State University Press, 1985).

69. Anne Norton Greene, *Horses at Work: Harnessing Power in Industrial America* (Cambridge: Harvard University Press, 2008), 103–09. Allan G. Bogue, *From Prairie to Corn Belt: Farming on the Illinois and Iowa Prairies in the Nineteenth Century*, 1963 (Ames: Iowa State University Press, 1994), 121. One Champaign horse breeder made five purchasing journeys to the "old world" (meaning northwest Europe) prior to 1900; *Biographical Record of Champaign County, Illinois* (Chicago: The S. J. Clarke Publishing Co., 1900), 565.

70. "List of Awards at the Illinois State Fair for 1875," *Transactions of the Department of Agriculture of the State of Illinois with Reports from County Agricultural Boards, for the Year 1875*, 5 (Springfield: State Journal Book, 1875), 36, 41–43.

71. "Wanted, for Sale and Exchange," *Prairie Farmer*, Dec. 26, 1907, 18.

72. "Breeders' Directory," *American Swine and Poultry Journal* 3 (Sept. 1875): 80.

73. L. C. Francis, "The Successful Bee-Keeper," *Transactions of the Department of Agriculture of the State of Illinois, with Reports from County Agricultural Boards, for the Year 1872*, 2 (1873), 205–07.

74. "Italian Bees," *The American Bee Journal* 10 (March 1874): 68; on fecundity, P. J. Colburn, "Italians vs. Black Bees," *The American Bee Journal* 10 (Oct. 1874): 227–28.

75. Eugene Secor, "New Races of Bees—Are They an Improvement?" *The American Bee Journal* 30 (Oct. 20, 1892): 531; Wm. S. Barclay, "The Races of Bees—Italians Are the Best," *The American Bee Journal* 30 (Oct. 27, 1892): 567.

76. C. G. Hopkins to A. D. McNair, March 17, 1903, Letterbook 6, Box 2, Agricultural Experimental Station Letterbooks, UIUC Archives. On German cultures,

see E. Davenport to A.S. Draper, May 5, 1897, Folder: Eugene Davenport, Box 3, President Andrew S. Draper, Faculty Correspondence, UIUC Archives.

77. Erin K. Cameron, Kyle M. Knysh, Heather C. Proctor, and Erin M. Bayne, "Influence of Two Exotic Earthworm Species with Different Foraging Strategies on Abundance and Composition of Boreal Microarthropods," *Soil Biology and Biochemistry* 57 (2013): 334–40. Nico Eisenhauer, Stephan Partsch, Dennis Parkinson, and Stefan Scheu, "Invasion of a Deciduous Forest by Earthworms: Changes in Soil Chemistry, Microflora, Microarthropods and Vegetation," *Soil Biology and Biochemistry* 39 (2007): 1099–1110. K. E. Lee, *Earthworms: Their Ecology and Relationships with Soils and Land Use* (New York: Academic Press, 1985), chaps. 10–13.

78. C. G. Hopkins to E. D. Coons, Feb. 13, 1903, Letterbook 6, Box 2, Agricultural Experimental Station Letterbooks, UIUC Archives; C. G. Hopkins to A. D. McNair, March 17, 1903, Letterbook 6, Box 2, Agricultural Experimental Station Letterbooks, UIUC Archives. On German cultures, see E. Davenport to A. S. Draper, May 5, 1897, Folder: Eugene Davenport, Box 3, President Andrew S. Draper, Faculty Correspondence, UIUC Archives.

79. Marina Moskowitz, "The Limits of Globalization? The Horticultural Trades in Postbellum America," *Food and Globalization: Consumption, Markets and Politics in the Modern World*, ed. Alexander Nützenadel and Frank Trentmann (New York: Berg, 2008), 57–74.

80. On prices, Charles Postel, *The Populist Vision* (New York: Oxford University Press, 2007), 108. William Appleman Williams, *The Roots of the Modern American Empire: A Study of the Growth and Shaping of Social Consciousness in a Marketplace Society* (New York: Random House, 1969), 177, 182. J. W. McHarry, [Report of the Mason County Pomona Grange], *Journal of Proceedings. Nineteenth Session of the Illinois State Grange, Patrons of Husbandry (1889)* (Old Harmony: Grange News Publishing Co., 1890), 61–62.

81. Oscar S. Straus, "Reform in the Consular Service" (Washington, DC: National Civil-Service Reform League, 1894), 5, 9.

82. Dodge, "Report of the Statistician," *Report of the Commissioner of Agriculture, 1886*, 359–458; *Regulations Prescribed for the Use of the Consular Service of the United States* (Washington, DC: Government Printing Office, 1870), 37–39, 68–70.

83. Thomas G. Paterson, "American Businessmen and Consular Service Reform, 1890's to 1906," *The Business History Review* 40 (Spring 1966): 77–97; Elmer Plischke, *U.S. Department of State: A Reference History* (Westport, CT: Greenwood Press, 1999), 223.

84. "The Illinois Press Association," *Inter Ocean*, June 24, 1879.

85. "Local and Near-By," *Urbana Daily Courier*, June 16, 1903. On mayor, see "Is Critically Ill," *Urbana Daily Courier*, Aug. 3, 1910.

86. "W. R. Grant Enthused by Canadian Opportunities," *Urbana Courier*, Feb. 23, 1910.

87. "Ten Months of Travel and Study in Europe," Folder: Travel in Europe, Box 3, President John M. Gregory Papers, UIUC Archives.

88. Gretchen S. Rauschenberg, *Chicago's "Mr. Rural": The Life of Matthias Lane Dunlap* (Baltimore: Gateway Press, 2007), 132, 146.

89. "The Late Mrs. Dunlap," Scrapbook of H. J. Dunlap, Box 14, Baker-Busey-Dunlap Family Papers, Illinois History and Lincoln Collections, UIUC.

90. "H. J. Dunlap Is Taken by Death," *Urbana Daily Courier*, Oct. 27, 1919.

91. "Inter-Ocean," clipping, Scrapbook of H. J. Dunlap, Box 14, Baker-Busey-Dunlap Family Papers, Illinois History and Lincoln Collections, UIUC. "Hiram J. Dunlap," Department Register, Oct. 15, 1912, Folder: Hiram Dunlap, Applications and Recommendations for Appointment to the Consular and Diplomatic Services, 1901–24, Box 68, RG 59, General Records of the Department of State, National Archives, College Park.

92. "Training for Consular Service," *Urbana Courier*, March 31, 1911.

93. Third Assistant Secretary, Department of State, to Hiram J. Dunlap, Dec. 6, 1905, Consular Posts, Cologne Germany, vol. 46, RG 84 Records of Foreign Service Posts, National Archives, College Park.

94. Rauschenberg, *Chicago's "Mr. Rural,"* 56, 249.

95. "Off for Germany," *Champaign Daily Gazette*, Jan. 3, 1890, 1.

96. "Local Brevities," *Champaign Daily Gazette*, Jan. 14, 1890, 1.

97. "A Week in Washington," *Champaign Daily Gazette*, Jan. 16, 1890, 1.

98. "Landed Safely," *Champaign Daily Gazette*, Feb. 19, 1890, 1. On Phelps, see H. J. D., "From Germany," June 14, 1890, Scrapbook of H. J. Dunlap, Box 14, Baker-Busey-Dunlap Family Papers, Illinois History and Lincoln Collections, UIUC.

99. H. J .D., "Poland in Germany," Feb. 25, 1890, Scrapbook of H. J. Dunlap, Box 14, Baker-Busey-Dunlap Family Papers, Illinois History and Lincoln Collections, UIUC. On Nellie as clerk, Hiram J. Dunlap, Feb. 14, 1890 entry, Log book, vol. 57, Breslau, Germany, Consular Posts, Records of Foreign Service Posts, RG 84, National Archives, College Park.

100. "Local Brevities," *Champaign Daily Gazette*, Nov. 30, 1889, 1.

101. H. J. Dunlap to Assistant Secretary of State W. F. Wharton, April 19, 1890, Despatches from United States Consuls in Breslau, 1878–1906, reel 2, The National Archives. On crop reports, Alvey A. Adee to the Consular Officers of the United States, Nov. 21, 1889; Consular Posts, Cologne Germany, v. 44; RG 84, Records of Foreign Service Posts, National Archives, College Park.

102. H. J. Dunlap to Assistant Secretary of State W. F. Wharton, May 13, 1890, Despatches from United States Consuls in Breslau, 1878–1906, Reel 2, National Archives.

103. H. J. D., "H. J. Dunlap's Experiences on the Ocean—Germany, As He Sees It," clipping dated Feb. 10, 1890, Scrapbook of H. J. Dunlap, Box 14, Baker-Busey-Dunlap Family Papers, Illinois History and Lincoln Collections, UIUC.

104. H. J. D., "From Germany," June 9, 1890, Scrapbook of H. J. Dunlap, Box 14, Baker-Busey-Dunlap Family Papers, Illinois History and Lincoln Collections, UIUC.

105. Clipping, "H. J. Dunlap Resigned His Position . . ." Scrapbook of H. J. Dunlap, Box 14, Baker-Busey-Dunlap Family Papers, Illinois History and Lincoln Collections, UIUC.

106. H. J. D., "Chat from Abroad," 28, Scrapbook of H. J. Dunlap, Furth, Baker-Busey-Dunlap Family Papers, Box 14, Illinois History and Lincoln Collections, UIUC.

107. H. J. D., "German Methods," April 30, [1890], Scrapbook of H. J. Dunlap, Box 14, Baker-Busey-Dunlap Family Papers, Illinois History and Lincoln Collections, UIUC.

108. "The Late Mrs. Dunlap," Scrapbook of H. J. Dunlap, Box 14, Baker-Busey-Dunlap Family Papers, Illinois History and Lincoln Collections, UIUC.

109. Rauschenberg, *Chicago's "Mr. Rural,"* 251.

110. "Great Crowd on Illinois Day," *Urbana Courier*, April 5, 1904.

111. "H. J. Dunlap Is Taken by Death," *Urbana Daily Courier*, Oct. 27, 1919.

112. "Impecuneous [*sic*] Americans in Europe," report, Nov. 29, 1907, vol. 53, Letters and Reports from Consul to State Department, 1907, Consular Posts, Cologne Germany, RG 84 Records of Foreign Service Posts, National Archives, College Park.

113. H. J. Dunlap, "American Apple Trade in Germany," July 23, 1908, v. 53, Letters and Reports from Consul to State Department, 1907, Consular Posts, Cologne Germany, RG 84 Records of Foreign Service Posts, National Archives, College Park.

114. "Farming Methods in Germany," *Urbana Courier*, Sept. 13, 1906.

115. H. J. D., "Our Germany Letter," April 14, 1890, Scrapbook of H. J. Dunlap, Box 14, Baker-Busey-Dunlap Family Papers, Illinois History and Lincoln Collections, UIUC.

116. H. J. D., "Our Germany Letter," Aug. 6, 1890, Scrapbook of H. J. Dunlap, Box 14, Baker-Busey-Dunlap Family Papers, Illinois History and Lincoln Collections, UIUC.

117. H. J. D., "Threshing Grain," Scrapbook of H. J. Dunlap, Box 14, Baker-Busey-Dunlap Family Papers, Illinois History and Lincoln Collections, UIUC.

118. Alexander Nützenadel, "A Green International? Food Markets and Transnational Politics, c. 1850–1914," in *Food and Globalization: Consumption, Markets and Politics in the Modern World*, ed. Alexander Nützenadel and Frank Trentmann (New York: Berg, 2008), 153 71.

119. Gardner, *The Grange—Friend of the Farmer*, 292–95.

120. R. Douglas Hurt, *American Agriculture: A Brief History*, revised ed. (West Lafayette: Purdue University Press, 2002), 204. Daniel T. Rodgers, *Atlantic Crossings: Social Politics in a Progressive Age* (Cambridge: The Belknap Press, 1998), 326.

121. Gardner, *The Grange—Friend of the Farmer*, 334–35.

122. Rodgers, *Atlantic Crossings*, 336.

123. Asher Hobson, *The International Institute of Agriculture: An Historical and Critical Analysis of Its Organization, Activities, and Policies of Administration* (Berkeley: University of California Press, 1931), 5–9, 13, 33, 87, 151.

124. "Plan Worldwide Crop News," *Urbana Courier*, April 4, 1911.

125. Hobson, *The International Institute of Agriculture;* vision, 25; charter, 52; publications 105, 110, 131, 133; contributors, 333. International Institute of Agriculture, *Bulletin of Agricultural Statistics* 1 (Nov. 1910): 130.

126. Wilford M. Wilson, "Weather Service and Weather Knowledge," *Cyclopedia of American Agriculture*, vol. 1, 4th ed., ed. L. H. Bailey (New York: The Macmillan Co., 1912), 534–50; Jamie L. Pietruska, "Hurricanes, Crops, and Capital: The

Meteorological Infrastructure of American Empire in the West Indies," *The Journal of the Gilded Age and Progressive Era* 15 (Oct. 2016): 418–45, 422.

127. M. F. Maury, "Science—Its Applicability to Agriculture," *Transactions of the Department of Agriculture of the State of Illinois (1872)* (Springfield: State Journal Steam Print, 1873), 182–95. On demands for appropriations to the Signal-office and for an international conference, see the *Proceedings of the Illinois Farmers' State Convention Held at Bloomington, Ills., January 15 and 16, 1873* (Chicago: Inter-Ocean, 1873), 5; on Champaign delegates, 14.

128. *Report of the Chief of the Weather Bureau, 1895–96* (Washington, DC: Government Printing Office, 1896), x, xi; Donald Whitnah, *A History of the United States Weather Bureau* (Urbana: University of Illinois Press, 1961); 94, 108, 113.

129. Whitnah, *A History of the United States Weather Bureau*, 36, 73, 113; "Wireless to Give Weather Reports," *Urbana Courier*, May 25, 1909.

130. H. J. Dunlap to J. G. Cannon, Dec. 4, 1910, and H. J. Dunlap to Mr. Speaker, Dec. 22, 1910, both in Folder: Hiram Dunlap, Applications and Recommendations for Appointment to the Consular and Diplomatic Services, 1901–24, Box 68, RG 59 General Records of the Department of State, National Archives, College Park.

131. Jeremy Sarkin, *Germany's Genocide of the Herero: Kaiser Wilhelm II, His General, His Settlers, His Soldiers* (Cape Town: UCT Press, 2011), 5, 13, 28, 243.

132. Andrew Zimmerman, *Alabama in Africa: Booker T. Washington, the German Empire, and the Globalization of the New South* (Princeton: Princeton University Press, 2010), 81.

133. U.S. Department of Agriculture, Division of Botany, *Foreign Seeds and Plants Imported by the Section of Seed and Plant Introduction* (Inventory No. 1, [1898]). "New Trees and Plants for U.S.," *Urbana Courier*, Feb. 21, 1917.

134. E. Davenport to A. S. Draper, April 12, 1897, Folder: Eugene Davenport (Agriculture), Box 3, 1896–1897, President Andrew S. Draper, Faculty Correspondence, 1894–1904, UIUC Archives; on alfalfa, C. G. Hopkins to J. C. Whetsel, Nov. 9, 1903, Letterbook 10, Box 3, Agricultural Experimental Station Letterbooks, UIUC Archives. On arboretum, *Catalogue and Circular of the University of Illinois*, 1890–91, published by the University, UIUC Archives, 29.

135. O. F. Cook, *Inventory No. 1, Foreign Seeds and Plants Imported by the Section of Seed and Plant Introduction, Numbers 1–1000* (Washington, DC: Department of Agriculture, nd), 10, 17; O. F. Cook, *Inventory No. 2 of Foreign Seeds and Plants Imported by the Section of Seed and Plant Introduction, Numbers 1001–1900* (Washington, DC: Department of Agriculture, 1899), 5, 7, 8, 11, 37, 44; U.S. Department of Agriculture. Division of Botany, *Inventory No. 7, Foreign Seeds and Plants Imported by the Department of Agriculture, through the Section of Seed and Plant Introduction, for Distribution in Cooperation with the State Agricultural Experiment Stations, Numbers 2701–3400* (Washington, DC, Department of Agriculture, 1900), 7, 9. U.S. Department of Agriculture, Section of Seed and Plant Introduction, *Inventory No. 8, Seeds and Plants, Imported for Distribution in Cooperation with the Agricultural Experiment Stations, Numbers 3401–4350* (Washington, DC: Department of Agriculture, 1901), 61.

136. David Fairchild, assisted by Elizabeth and Alfred Kay, *The World Was My Garden: Travels of a Plant Explorer* (New York: Scribner's, 1938), 136, 157, 243.

137. Frank N. Meyer to Mr. Fairchild, Jan. 15, 1907, Folder 2, Box 1, Letters, Records of Frank N. Meyer, Plant Explorer, 1902–18, RG 54 Records of the Bureau of Plant Industry, Soils and Agricultural Engineering, Division of Plant Exploration and Introduction, National Archives, College Park.

138. Frank N. Meyer to Mr. Fairchild, Feb. 16, 1906, Folder 1, Box 1, Letters, Records of Frank N. Meyer, Plant Explorer, 1902–18, RG 54 Records of the Bureau of Plant Industry, Soils and Agricultural Engineering, Division of Plant Exploration and Introduction, National Archives, College Park.

139. Frank N. Meyer to Mr. Fairchild, Jan. 15, 1907, Folder 2, Box 1, Letters, Records of Frank N. Meyer, Plant Explorer, 1902–18, RG 54 Records of the Bureau of Plant Industry, Soils and Agricultural Engineering, Division of Plant Exploration and Introduction, National Archives, College Park.

140. Frank Meyer to Mr. Fairchild, Habarowsk, Nov. 9, 1906, Folder 1, Box 1, Letters, Records of Frank N. Meyer, Plant Explorer, 1902–18, RG 54 Records of the Bureau of Plant Industry, Soils and Agricultural Engineering, Division of Plant Exploration and Introduction, National Archives, College Park.

141. Fairchild, *The World Was My Garden*, 225, 227.

142. Richard Drayton, *Nature's Government: Science, Imperial Britain, and the "Improvement" of the World* (New Haven: Yale University Press, 2000), 75–76. 108, 172; on gardens as experimental stations, see Londa Schiebinger, *Plants and Empire: Colonial Bioprospecting in the Atlantic World* (Cambridge: Harvard University Press, 2004), 11.

143. Harlan, "Gene Centers and Gene Utilization in American Agriculture," 34–35.

144. Cook, *Foreign Seeds and Plants Imported by the Section of Seed and Plant Introduction, Numbers 1–1000*, 7–8, 10.

145. David Fairchild, "How to Send Living Plant Material to America" (Washington, DC: United States Department of Agriculture, [1913]), 3. Frank Meyer to Mr. Fairchild, Nov. 9, 1906, Folder 1, Box 1, Letters, Records of Frank N. Meyer, Plant Explorer, 1902–18, RG 54 Records of the Bureau of Plant Industry, Soils and Agricultural Engineering, Division of Plant Exploration and Introduction, National Archives, College Park.

146. Fairchild, *The World Was My Garden*, 166, 220.

147. Stuart McCook, *States of Nature: Science, Agriculture, and Environment in the Spanish Caribbean, 1760–1940* (Austin: University of Texas Press, 2002), 19, 26.

148. E. D. Merrill, *A Descriptive Catalogue of the Plants Cultivated in the City Nursery at the Cementerio del Norte Manila* (Manila: Bureau of Science, 1912).

149. Jim Endersby, *Imperial Nature: Joseph Hooker and the Practices of Victorian Science* (Chicago: University of Chicago Press, 2008), 3.

150. Fairchild, *The World Was My Garden*, 64.

151. Frank N. Meyer, typescript manuscript, 14, Folder 1, Box 3, Records of Frank N. Meyer, Plant Explorer, 1902–18, RG 54 Records of the Bureau of Plant Industry, Soils and Agricultural Engineering, Division of Plant Exploration and Introduction, National Archives, College Park.

152. Frank Meyer to Mr. Fairchild, Nov. 9, 1906, Folder 1, Box 1, Letters, Records of Frank N. Meyer, Plant Explorer, 1902–18, RG 54 Records of the Bureau of Plant Industry, Soils and Agricultural Engineering, Division of Plant Exploration and Introduction, National Archives, College Park.

153. Frank Meyer to Mr. Fairchild, Jan. 21, 1907, Folder 2, Box 1, Letters, Records of Frank N. Meyer, Plant Explorer, 1902–18, RG 54 Records of the Bureau of Plant Industry, Soils and Agricultural Engineering, Division of Plant Exploration and Introduction, National Archives, College Park.

154. *Prairie Farmer's Reliable Directory of Farmers and Breeders, Champaign County*, 13, 260. On the origins of the newly introduced "Soja Bean," see L. S. Robertson, "The Importance of Leguminous Crops to Agriculture," *The Illinois Agriculturist* 3 (1899): 25–33. D. S. Dalbey, "Pork Production in Illinois," *The Illinois Agriculturist* 6 (1902): 74–80. Sonya Salamon, *Prairie Patrimony: Family, Farming, and Community in the Midwest* (Chapel Hill: University of North Carolina Press, 1992), 24.

155. On unscientific, see H. Han, "Farmers of Forty Centuries," *Chinese Students' Monthly* 7 (March 10, 1912): 474–75; on self-maintaining, see "Agriculture of China and Japan," *Urbana Courier*, March 16, 1910.

156. "Agricultural Institute at the Illinois Industrial University," Folder: Institutes and Short Courses, 1879–1910, Box 1, Dean's Office, Agriculture, Conference lecture and Short Course Publications, UIUC Archives; "University College Institute," *Western Rural*, Feb. 24, 1883.

157. "M'Kinley Interviewed," *Urbana Courier*, Dec. 27, 1913.

158. H. S. Grindley, "The Science of Agriculture," *Illinois Agriculturist* 2 (1898): 50–53.

159. Phillips, "Antebellum Agricultural Reform," 803.

160. On planting, see "Foreign Correspondence," *Illinois Farmer* 9 (Sept. 1864): 261.

161. "Abortion in Cows Produced by Smut on Corn," *Illinois Farmer* 9 (April 1864): 152.

162. H. S. Grindley, "The Science of Agriculture," *Illinois Agriculturist* 2 (1898): 50–53, 51.

163. Rural [Matthias L. Dunlap], "The Farm and Garden," clipping of March 17, 1869, Dunlap 2, vol. of clippings, Box 3, Matthias L. Dunlap Papers, UIUC Archives.

164. On study in Germany in general, Charles Franklin Thwing, *The American and the German University: One Hundred Years of History* (New York: The Macmillan Company, 1928); Clara Eve Schieber, *The Transformation of American Sentiment toward Germany, 1870–1914* (1923; reprint, New York: Russell and Russell, 1973), 256–58.

165. "Landwirtschaft," Folder 1863–67, Box 1, Willard C. Flagg Papers, UIUC Archives.

166. "State Agricultural Associations," *Transactions of the Illinois State Agricultural Society; With the Proceedings of the County Societies and Kindred Associations* 1 (1853–1854), 1–5, 23–24, 28.

167. "Report of the Executive Committee for 1853–54," *Transactions of the Illinois State Agricultural Society* (Springfield: Lanphier & Walker, 1855), 1–5.

168. "Education of Farmers," *Illinois Farmer* 2 (June 1857): 125–26.

169. Lyman Carter, "The United States Agricultural Society, 1852–1860: Its Relation to the Origin of the United States Department of Agriculture and the Land Grant Colleges," *Agricultural History* 11 (Oct. 1937): 278–88.

170. Phillips, "Antebellum Agricultural Reform," *Agricultural History*, 799.

171. "Illinois Industrial University," Folder: 1877; Box 1: President John M. Gregory, Publications Scrapbooks, 1868, 1873–1890; Series 2/1/11; UIUC Archives.

172. "Biennial Report of the Illinois Industrial University to the State," Folder: University Discourses 1882–1886; Box 1: President John M. Gregory, Publications Scrapbooks, 1868, 1873–1890; Series 2/1/11; UIUC Archives.

173. Marcus, *Agricultural Science and the Quest for Legitimacy*, ix, 8; Mark R. Finlay, "The German Agricultural Experiment Stations and the Beginnings of American Agricultural Research," *Agricultural History* 62 (Spring, 1988): 41–50. On researches, H. S. Grindley, "The Science of Agriculture," *Illinois Agriculturist* 2 (1898): 50–53.

174. Winton U. Solberg, *The University of Illinois 1894–1904: The Shaping of the University* (Urbana: University of Illinois Press, 2000), 125.

175. E. Davenport to President Draper, Dec. 7, 1903, Folder: Eugene Davenport, Box 10, President Andrew S. Draper, Faculty Correspondence, UIUC Archives.

176. Cyril G. Hopkins to Sir J. Henry Gilbert, August 14, 1901, Letterbook 1, Agricultural Experimental Station Letterbooks, UIUC Archives.

177. C. G. Hopkins to O. O. Churchill, April 2, 1900, Letterbook April 22, 1909, to Nov. 7, 1910, Box 4, Agricultural Experimental Station Letterbooks, UIUC Archives.

178. C. G. Hopkins to K. L. Sharp, June 19, 1902, Letterbook 3, Box 1, Agricultural Experimental Station Letterbooks, UIUC Archives.

179. C. G. Hopkins to H. W. Mumford, June 11, 1902, Letterbook 3, Box 1, and C. G. Hopkins to William Rennie, March 20, 1903, Letterbook 6, Box 2, both in Agricultural Experimental Station Letterbooks, UIUC Archives.

180. C. G. Hopkins to Farmers Seed Company, March 20, 1903, Letterbook 6, Box 2, Agricultural Experimental Station, Letterbooks, UIUC Archives. On poor land corn, C. G. Hopkins to George Oldendorph, April 18, 1903, Letterbook 6, Box 2, Agriculture Experimental Station Letterbooks, UIUC Archives.

181. C. G. Hopkins to W. Atlee Burpee & Co., Jan. 14, 1904, Letterbook 10, Box 3, Agriculture Experimental Station Letterbooks, UIUC Archives.

182. Cyril G. Hopkins to Meyer and Raapke, Jan. 21, 1902, Letterbook 2, Box 1, Agricultural Experimental Station Letterbooks, UIUC Archives.

183. C. G. Hopkins to T. L. Lyon, April 16, 1903, Letterbook 6, Box 2, Agricultural Experimental Station Letterbooks, UIUC Archives.

184. C. G. Hopkins to Professor C. Fruwirth, May 30, 1902, Letterbook 3, Box 1; C. G. Hopkins to W. H. Fairfield, Aug. 17, 1903, Letterbook 8, Box 3, both in Agriculture Experimental Station, UIUC Archives.

185. C. G. Hopkins to Professor F. Wohltmann, March 17, 1902, Letterbook 2, Box 1, Agricultural Experimental Station Letterbooks, UIUC Archives.

186. Thomas F. Hunt, "George Espy Morrow," *The Illinois Agriculturist* 4 (1900): 3–15, UIUC Archives.

187. *The Biographical Record of Champaign County, Illinois*, 350.

188. C. G. Hopkins to Port Huron Co., July 3, 1903, Letterbook 8, Box 3, Agricultural Experiment Station Letterbooks, UIUC Archives.

189. On travel with colleague, Cyril G. Hopkins to J. A. Widtsoe, June 11, 1901, Letterbook 1, Box 1, Agricultural Experimental Station Letterbooks, UIUC Archives. I owe the term *agronaut* to Zachary Poppel's dissertation, "Sierra Leone

and the Rural University in the Wake of Empire" (PhD diss., University of Illinois, Urbana-Champaign, 2014).

190. Cyril G. Hopkins to Professor S. A. Hoover, July 13, 1901, Letterbook 1, Box 1, Agricultural Experimental Station Letterbooks, UIUC Archives.

191. L. H. Smith to Prof. A. T. Wiancko, May 7, 1910, Letterbook April 22, 1909–Nov. 7, 1910, Box 4, Agricultural Experimental Station Letterbooks, UIUC Archives.

192. "New Professors at University of Illinois," *Farmer and Breeder for the Farm Home* 11 (August 1899): 1. On Detmers and McIntosh, Winton U. Solberg, *The University of Illinois, 1867–1894* (Urbana: University of Illinois Press, 1968), 106, 239.

193. "Draft University Man into Kaiser's Army," *Urbana Courier*, Aug. 5, 1914.

194. "University," *Urbana Courier*, May 7, 1909; "University," *Urbana Courier*, May 11, 1909.

195. Remarks by Colonel Blair of Nova Scotia, *Annual Report of the Illinois Farmers' Institute (1901)* (Springfield: Phillips Bros., 1901), 155–56.

196. "Mexicans Are Coming," *Urbana Courier*, May 13, 1909.

197. "Escapes from Mexican Prison," *Urbana Courier*, January 19, 1917.

198. Richard Yates, "Address of Welcome," *Sixth Annual Meeting of the Illinois Farmers' Institute* (Springfield: Phillips Bros., 1901), 55–57.

199. S. F. Null, "Education for the Farmer," *The Illinois Agriculturist* 7 (Oct. 1902), np.

200. "The Spirit of Human Progress . . . ," *Breeder's Gazette*, Dec. 19, 1900, 945.

201. [Remarks by Colonel Blair of Nova Scotia—untitled], *Annual Report of the Illinois Farmers' Institute*, 155–56.

202. "Knowledge as Applied to Agriculture," *Prairie Farmer*, Jan. 1, 1850.

203. J. R. Dodge, "Report of the Statistician," *Report of the Commissioner of Agriculture, 1885* (Washington: Government Printing Office, 1885), 344–430.

204. "Farming in India," *Farmers Advance* (Chicago: McCormick Harvesting Machine Co., 1884), 2.

205. C. G. Hopkins to Dr. D. Morris, April 15, 1903, Letterbook 6, Box 2; C. G. Hopkins to John R. Clisby, Feb. 24, 1903, Letterbook 6, Box 2, both in Agricultural Experimental Station Letterbooks, UIUC Archives.

206. Volume: Notable People I Have Known or Seen, [np], Box 4, Eugene V. Davenport Papers, UIUC Archives.

207. Cyril G. Hopkins to German Kali Works, Dec. 5, 1901, Letterbook 2, Box 1, Experimental Station Letterbooks, UIUC Archives.

208. [Eugene V. Davenport], "Subdivision of Agriculture for Purposes of Instruction," speech of 1901, Folder: Subdivision of Agriculture for Purposes of Instruction, Box 5, Eugene V. Davenport Papers, UIUC Archives.

209. [Eugene V. Davenport], "The Relation of Agricultural Organizations to Agricultural Development," speech of 1902, 1–2; Folder: Agricultural Organizations, Box 5, Eugene V. Davenport Papers, UIUC Archives.

210. E. Davenport, "Rural Improvement in America," speech of 1908; Folder: Address—Rural Improvement, Nov. 19, 1908; Box 5, Eugene V. Davenport Papers, UIUC Archives.

211. E. Davenport, *The Development of American Agriculture: What It Is and What It Means* (Urbana: np, 1909), 5.

212. Davenport, "Rural Improvement in America."
213. Ibid.
214. Davenport, *The Development of American Agriculture*, 10.
215. Davenport, "Rural Improvement in America."
216. On new worlds, Davenport, *The Development of American Agriculture*, 10. On moving, E. Davenport, "The Development of American Agriculture," speech delivered 1909; Folder: Publications 1909; Box 20; Eugene V. Davenport Papers, UIUC Archives.
217. "Dean Illinois College of Agriculture," *Farmer and Breeder for the Farm Home* 11 (August 1899): 1. Solberg, *The University of Illinois 1894–1904*, 121–22.
218. Eugene V. Davenport, "What One Life Has Seen," Binder 2, Box 4, Eugene V. Davenport Papers, UIUC Archives, 8.
219. On socializing, see Emma E. Davenport, Brazil Diary, Jan. 1, 1892, Box 1, Eugene V. Davenport Papers, UIUC Archives. Davenport, "What One Life Has Seen," 19, 24, 43–44.
220. Eugene Davenport to Dr. H. H. Gilbert, May 18, 1892, Gil 6: Letters from USA, Box 552 Sir Henry Gilbert, Rothamsted.
221. Davenport, "What One Life Has Seen," 49, 51, 58.
222. Eugene Davenport to Joseph E. Gilbert, Dec. 28, 1898, Gil 6: Letters from USA, Box 552 Sir Henry Gilbert, Rothamsted.
223. "University," *Urbana Courier*, May 5, 1909.
224. "College News," *The Illinois Agriculturist* 7 (Dec. 1902): 43.
225. E. Davenport, "Agriculture at the University of Illinois," *University of Illinois Bulletin* 14 (March 19, 1917): 1–2; Folder: Publications 1917; Box 20, Eugene V. Davenport Papers, UIUC Archives.
226. Camili R. Lopez, "Coffee Growing in Mexico," *The Illinois Agriculturist* 19 (June 1915): 767–68; Box 20, Eugene V. Davenport Papers, UIUC Archives.
227. "Congress of Nations at Local Commercial Session," *Urbana Courier*, Dec. 2, 1913.
228. "Foreigners Show How U.S. Misses Its Opportunities," *Urbana Courier*, May 26, 1920.
229. C. G. Hopkins to Bausch & Lomb Optical Company, April 26, 1902, in Letterbook 3, Box 1, Agricultural Experiment Station Letterbooks, UIUC Archives.
230. Louie H. Smith to "Whom It May Concern," July 29, 1911, Letterbook Nov. 19, 1910–Aug. 6, 1912, Box 4, Agriculture Experimental Station Letterbooks, UIUC Archives.
231. Dean C. Worcester, *The Philippines Past and Present*, vol. 1 (New York: The Macmillan Co., 1914), frontispiece.
232. Antonio Bautista, "Agriculture in the Philippines," *The Illinois Agriculturist* 8 (Feb. 1904): 113–15.
233. *Notable People I Have Known or Seen*, [np], Box 4, Eugene V. Davenport Papers, UIUC Archives.
234. Ibid.
235. *William B. McKinley: Memorial Addresses*, 8.
236. "Five Hunder [*sic*] People Hear Address by McKinley," *Urbana Courier*, June 24, 1914.

237. "Hon. W. B. M'Kinley Is at 'Home, Sweet Home,'" *Urbana Courier*, Oct. 3, 1905.

238. "M'Kinley in Urbana," *Urbana Courier*, Nov. 22, 1905.

239. "Speaker Cannon Back from His Holiday Trip," *Urbana Courier*, April 9, 1907.

240. Rathindranath Tagore, *On the Edges of Time*, 1958 (Westport: Greenwood Press, 1978), 23, 85.

241. Tagore, *On the Edges of Time*, 75.

242. Tagore, *On the Edges of Time*, 75–81.

243. Tagore, *On the Edges of Time*, 79, 81, 123–24; Harold M. Hurwitz, "Tagore in Urbana, Illinois," *Indian Literature* 4 (1961): 27–36.

244. Tagore, *On the Edges of Time*, 80–81.

245. Tagore, *On the Edges of Time*, 80.

246. Mayce F. Seymour, "The Golden Time," *Visvabharati Quarterly* 25 (Summer 1959): 1–15.

247. "Ten Nations Included," *Urbana Courier*, May 15, 1907.

248. "University," *Urbana Courier*, May 15, 1909.

249. "Cosmopolitan Club Meeting," *Daily Illini*, Dec. 13, 1906.

250. On slides, "Cosmopolitan Club Meeting," *Daily Illini*, April 24, 1907; on Hindu life, "Cosmopolitan Club," *Daily Illini*, Jan. 30, 1907.

251. "Cosmopolitan Club Meeting," *Daily Illini*, Dec. 17, 1907.

252. "Mr. W. Y. Hu," *Daily Illini*, March 10, 1909.

253. On slides, "Cosmopolitan Club Meeting," *Daily Illini*, April 24, 1907; on Hindu life, "Cosmopolitan Club," *Daily Illini*, Jan. 30, 1907; on reforms in China, "Cosmopolitan Club," *Daily Illini*, Dec. 11, 1907.

254. On Bose as Secretary, "Foreign Students Form Club," *Daily Illini*, Oct. 29, 1906; "Foreign Student's Career," *Daily Illini*, May 24, 1907.

255. "Cosmopolitan Club," *Daily Illini*, Feb. 26, 1907.

256. "Filipinos Entertain with Program of Native Stunts," *Daily Illini*, April 6, 1909.

257. "Convention of Cosmopolitan Clubs," *Daily Illini*, Dec. 15, 1907.

258. "The Cosmopolitan Club at Michigan," *Daily Illini*, Dec. 18, 1908.

259. "Cosmopolitan Club [*sic*] Have Laudable Aims," *Daily Illini*, Feb. 22, 1910.

260. Tagore, *On the Edges of Time*, 82–84.

261. Tagore, *On the Edges of Time*, 86–88.

262. On flags, "Cosmopolitan Club Holds Dance," *Daily Illini*, May 6, 1911.

263. "Cosmopolitan Clubs Favor World Peace," *Daily Illini*, Jan. 7, 1909.

264. "Cosmopolitan Club Holds Third Annual Banquet," *Daily Illini*, May 15, 1910.

265. "Cosmopolitan Club [*sic*] Have Laudable Aims," *Daily Illini*, Feb. 22, 1910.

266. "Cosmopolitan Club to Plead for Rudowitz," *Daily Illini*, Dec. 15, 1908; "Cosmopolitan Club Calls Mass Meeting," *Daily Illini*, Dec. 18, 1908.

267. Tagore, *On the Edges of Time*, 113; "Urbana Is Named as an International Capital," *Urbana Courier*, Jan. 7, 1911; "World's Peace Burlesque True Cosmopolitan Success," *Daily Illini*, Jan. 7, 1911.

268. Tagore, *On the Edges of Time*, 123–24.

269. Tagore, *On the Edges of Time*, 75–81; on narrowness, 81, 123–24. Hurwitz, "Tagore in Urbana, Illinois," 27–36. "Illinois News," *Urbana Courier*, Nov. 20, 1913.

270. "Dr. Tagore Will Deliver Third Talk Saturday," *Urbana Courier*, Dec. 29, 1916; "Nationalism Is Tagore's Theme," *Urbana Courier*, Dec. 30, 1916.

271. "America Daring and Crude Says Tagore," *Urbana Courier*, Jan. 18, 1917.

Chapter 5: Flownover States: The View from the Middle of Everything

1. "Champaign," *Urbana Courier*, July 19, 1911.

2. "Ringling Parade All New," *Urbana Courier*, Aug. 21, 1912.

3. Ad for F. K. Robeson, *Urbana Courier*, Oct. 30, 1915.

4. "Homer Does Full Share in War," *Urbana Courier*, July 13, 1917.

5. "Santiago Is After Passport," *Urbana Courier*, Dec. 24, 1917.

6. "Greatest Authority on Poultry to Lecture," *Urbana Courier*, April 4, 1918.

7. "Letters from Our Boys in France," *Urbana Courier*, Aug. 10, 1918.

8. "Shower of Butterflies," *Urbana Courier*, Aug. 5, 1918.

9. "May Study Bird Life at Renner's," *Urbana Courier*, June 19, 1920.

10. Margaret Whitewater quoted in Randy Eli Grothe, "The Kickapoo: Strangers in Their Own Land," *Dallas Morning News*, May 8, 1977.

11. Peter Adey, *Aerial Life: Spaces, Mobilities, Affects* (Malden, MA: Wiley-Blackwell, 2010), 88. On panoptic depictions of the Midwest, see Jason Weems, *Barnstorming the Prairies: How Aerial Vision Shaped the Midwest* (Minneapolis: University of Minnesota Press, 2015), xiv, xix, 18.

12. Digitized issues of the *Urbana Daily Courier* run from 1903 to 1905. From 1906 to 1915, the masthead read *Urbana Courier-Herald*. Starting in 1916, the newspaper resumed publication as the *Urbana Daily Courier*. I cite this paper as the *Urbana Courier* for brevity and continuity and because that is how it is identified in the Illinois Digital Newspaper Collection.

13. Robert Michael Morrissey, "The Power of the Ecotone: Bison, Slavery, and the Rise and Fall of the Grand Village of the Kaskaskia," *Journal of American History* 102 (Dec. 2015): 667–92; on population density, Allan G. Bogue, *From Prairie to Corn Belt: Farming on the Illinois and Iowa Prairies in the Nineteenth Century*, 1963 (Ames: Iowa State University Press, 1994), 8.

14. "War to the Death on the Illinois Mosquito," *Urbana Courier*, Jan. 29, 1917; Ann Vileisis, *Discovering the Unknown Landscape: A History of America's Wetlands* (Washington, DC: Island Press, 1997), 82.

15. J. O. Cunningham, *History of Champaign County* (1905; reprint, Champaign: Champaign County Historical Archives, 1984), 650–51. John T. Cumbler, *Northeast and Midwest United States: An Environmental History* (Santa Barbara: ABC Clio, 2005); glacier, 2, 133; beavers, 13, 39.

16. Margaret Beattie Bogue, "The Swamp Land Act and Wet Land Utilization in Illinois, 1850–1890," *Agricultural History* 25 (Oct. 1951): 169–80.

17. J. M. Peck, *New Guide for Emigrants to the West, Containing Sketches of Ohio, Indiana, Illinois, Missouri, Michigan, with the Territories of Wisconsin and Arkansas, and the Adjacent Parts* (Boston: Gould, Kendall & Lincoln, 1836), 254.

18. Cited in Roger A. Winsor, "Environmental Imagery of the Wet Prairie of East Central Illinois, 1820–1920," *Journal of Historical Geography* 13 (Oct. 1987): 375–97.

19. Charles Gleason Elliott, *Engineering for Land Drainage*, 2nd ed. (New York: John Wiley and Sons, 1912), 11.

20. Marion M. Weaver, *History of Tile Drainage (in America Prior to 1900)* (Waterloo, NY: M. M. Weaver, 1964), 227.
21. Bogue, "The Swamp Land Act and Wet Land Utilization in Illinois," 178–79; Roger Andrew Winsor, *Artificial Drainage of East Central Illinois, 1820–1920* (PhD diss., University of Illinois, Urbana-Champaign, 1975), 175.
22. "Draining," *Illinois Farmer* 6 (June 1861): 170–73.
23. H. D. Woodruff, "Draining and Subsoiling," *Illinois Farmer* 5 (July 1860): 107–09; Weaver, *History of Tile Drainage*, 26, 222–27; on English patterns, 58. Quotation and country list from Elliott, *Engineering for Land Drainage*, 15.
24. Robert W. Frizzell, "Reticent Germans: The East Frisians of Illinois," *Illinois Historical Journal* 85 (Autumn 1992): 161–74.
25. Erna Moehl, *"A Century of God's Presence": A Centennial Tribute, Immanuel Lutheran Church, Flatville, Illinois* (Flatville, IL: Immanuel Lutheran Church, 1974), 6–7. On school, J. R. Stewart, ed., *A Standard History of Champaign County, Illinois*, vol. 2 (Chicago: The Lewis Publishing Co., 1918), 695.
26. "Land Near German Flats Moving Fast," *Urbana Courier*, February 2, 1917.
27. Frizzell, "Reticent Germans," 161–74; on land value, "Good Talk by T. B. Thornburn," *Urbana Courier*, Feb. 8, 1917. Faye Emma Corner, "Culture Change in a Low-German Rural Community in Champaign County, Illinois" (master's thesis, University of Illinois, 1930); Dale Joseph Flinders, "Flatville, Illinois—Area and Community" (master's thesis, University of Illinois, 1952).
28. Frizzell, "Reticent Germans," 171.
29. H. W. S. Cleveland, "An Essay on Farm Drainage," in *Transactions of the Department of Agriculture of the State of Illinois*, ed. S. D. Fisher, vol. 6 (Springfield: D. W. Lusk, 1878): 221–31.
30. Walter Havighurst, *The Heartland: Ohio, Indiana, Illinois* (1956; revised, New York: Harper and Row Publishers, 1974). See also Bogue, "The Swamp Land Act and Wet Land Utilization in Illinois," 169.
31. "Reclaimed Lands of Louisiana," *Urbana Courier*, Oct. 19, 1909.
32. The farm was in Aurora, Illinois. "Entire Field of Corn Disappears," *Urbana Courier*, February 21, 1912. L. O. Howard, *Biographical Memoir of Stephen Alfred Forbes, 1844–1930* (Washington, DC: National Academy of Sciences, 1932), 3.
33. Henry Trumbull, *History of the Discovery of America, of the Landing of our Forefathers, at Plymouth, and of their Most Remarkable Engagements with the Indians, In New-England . . . To Which is Annexed, the Defeat of Generals Braddock, Harmer, & St. Clair, By the Indians at the Westward* (Norwich: James Springer, 1812), 140, 144.
34. W. T. Stackpole, "Inland Transportation," in *Transactions of the Department of Agriculture of the State of Illinois with Reports from County Agricultural Boards, for the Year 1873*, ed. A. M. Garland, vol. iii (Springfield: State Journal Steam Print, 1874), 155–68.
35. Gretchen Heefner, *The Missile Next Door: The Minuteman in the American Heartland* (Cambridge: Harvard University Press, 2012).
36. Robert Luther Thompson, *Wiring a Continent: The History of the Telegraph Industry in the United States, 1831–1866* (New York: Arno Press, 1972), 263; Cunningham, *History of Champaign County*, 856–57.
37. Jonathan Silberstein-Loeb, *The International Distribution of News: The Associated Press, Press Association, and Reuters, 1848–1947* (New York: Cambridge University

Press, 2014), 12–13; Menahem Blondheim, *News Over the Wires: The Telegraph and the Flow of Public Information in America, 1844–1897* (Cambridge: Harvard University Press, 1994), 172, 195.

38. "Wire Report of Day's Best News," *Urbana Courier*, March 18, 1912; "Big British Army in Egypt," *Urbana Courier*, Dec. 7, 1914; "Two-Day Battle Is Won by Rebels," *Urbana Courier*, Oct. 21, 1911.

39. Robert MacDougall, *The People's Network: The Political Economy of the Telephone in the Gilded Age* (Philadelphia: University of Pennsylvania Press, 2014), 29.

40. Cunningham, *History of Champaign County*, 857.

41. "Poles Are Unsightly," *Urbana Courier*, July 13, 1906.

42. "Those Poles Again," *Urbana Courier*, Feb. 5, 1908.

43. "Friends and Foes of the Farmer," *Urbana Courier*, Jan. 29, 1914.

44. "Colored People Leave Danville," *Urbana Courier*, July 28, 1903.

45. "Tree Felled by Wind Set Afire by Wires," *Urbana Courier*, May 15, 1916; "Is Nearly Electrocuted," *Urbana Courier*, June 5, 1905; "Lineman Meets Instant Death," *Urbana Courier*, June 27, 1910; "Storm Brings Death to Two," *Urbana Courier*, July 12, 1911; "Fatal Shock for Cow," *Urbana Courier*, June 12, 1907; "Risks of Feathered Tribe," *Urbana Courier*, Jan. 6, 1904.

46. "May Remove Phones at Tolono," *Urbana Courier*, April 21, 1914.

47. "Saved by Wireless," *Urbana Courier*, May 28, 1909; "Wireless Meet Opens," *Urbana Courier*, June 4, 1912.

48. "Urbana Now Has Wireless Plant," *Urbana Courier*, March 9, 1911.

49. "Wireless Telegraph at St. Joseph," *Urbana Courier*, Oct. 5, 1911.

50. "Frank Scroggins Has Thrilling Adventure," *Urbana Courier*, Sept. 7, 1910.

51. "Falls from Cherry Tree," *Urbana Courier*, June 28, 1911.

52. "Radio Club Chosen Officers," *Urbana Courier*, May 12, 1915.

53. "Wireless Club Is Organized," *Urbana Courier*, June 1, 1916.

54. On inspector, "Amateur Aerial Stations to Be Closed Shortly," *Urbana Courier*, April 7, 1917. "Will Wreck Wireless," *Urbana Courier*, April 13, 1917. "Scouts Spied Hun Wireless," *Urbana Courier*, March 25, 1919.

55. "U.S. Lifts Ban against Amateur Wireless Men," *Urbana Courier*, June 27, 1919; "Urbana to Have Wireless Class," *Urbana Courier*, Nov. 29, 1919; "Champaign County Radio Association to Reorganize," *Urbana Courier*, Oct. 13, 1919.

56. "Via Wireless!" *Urbana Courier*, March 18, 1914.

57. "Wireless Amateurs Notice!" *Urbana Courier*, April 16, 1920.

58. "Local Wireless Men Have Chance," *Urbana Courier*, March 24, 1917.

59. "University of Illinois," *Urbana Courier*, Oct. 20, 1919.

60. "Will Forecast by Wireless," *Urbana Courier*, June 23, 1915.

61. "To Have Wireless Exhibit in Floral Hall during Fair," *Urbana Courier*, Aug. 12, 1920.

62. "Freaks of Wireless," *Urbana Courier*, March 1, 1911; "Astronomical Department Has New Receiving Outfit," *Urbana Courier*, Aug. 1, 1914; "Wireless in U.S. and Mexico," *Urbana Courier*, Dec. 1, 1916.

63. "Hints for the Radio Operator," *Urbana Courier*, Sept. 27, 1917.

64. "Wireless Crosses Pacific," *Urbana Courier*, Oct. 6, 1911; "Pick Up Wireless at 11,500 Miles," *Urbana Courier*, Jan. 18, 1917.

65. "Urbana Now Has Wireless Plant," *Urbana Courier*, March 9, 1911.

66. "University of Illinois Receives Government Time Signals by Wireless," *Urbana Courier*, Aug. 10, 1914.

67. "Radio Club Chosen Officers," *Urbana Courier*, May 12, 1915.

68. "Mumford Wins Kite Contest," *Urbana Courier*, Nov. 27, 1916.

69. "Settlers Assemble at Park," *Urbana Courier*, Oct. 2, 1908.

70. James P. Caird, *Prairie Farming in America* (London: Longman, Brown, Green, Longmans, & Roberts, 1859); Britain, 2; ague, 5; extremes, 79, 92. On U.S. meteorological collaboration and the assumption that the British climate was normative, see Jan Golinski, *British Weather and the Climate of Enlightenment* (Chicago: University of Chicago Press, 2007), 195.

71. Gretchen S. Rauschenberg, *Chicago's "Mr. Rural": The Life of Matthias Lane Dunlap* (Baltimore: Gateway Press, 2007), 39.

72. M. L. Dunlap, "Air Currents," *Transactions of the Illinois State Agricultural Society; With the Proceedings of the County Societies, and Kindred Associations*, vol. 1, 1853–1854 (Springfield: Lanphier & Walker, 1855), 524–527. Alfred W. Crosby, *Ecological Imperialism: The Biological Expansion of Europe, 900–1900* (Cambridge: Cambridge University Press, 1986), 127.

73. Dunlap, "Air Currents," 524–27.

74. "Weather Pointers," *Urbana Courier*, April 28, 1905.

75. "Signs that Foretell Weather," *Urbana Courier*, Jan. 25, 1912.

76. "Birds as Weather Guides," *Urbana Courier*, July 29, 1910.

77. "Birds Foretell Weather Change," *Urbana Courier*, Oct. 24, 1919.

78. "Weather Pointers," *Urbana Courier*, April 28, 1905; "Signs That Foretell Weather," *Urbana Courier*, Jan. 25, 1912.

79. "Hits at Popular Illusions," *Chicago Livestock World*, March 7, 1905. Katherine Anderson, *Predicting the Weather: Victorians and the Science of Meteorology* (Chicago: University of Chicago Press, 2005), 42.

80. Irl R. Hicks, cited in "Bad September Storm," *Urbana Courier*, Sept. 7, 1907.

81. "Warning Against Fake Forecasters," *Urbana Courier*, May 25, 1904.

82. "How to Use a Barometer," *Urbana Courier*, Aug. 11, 1909.

83. On deducing weather from laws of physics, see H. Helm Clayton, "Recent Efforts toward the Improvement of Daily Weather Forecasts," *The American Meteorological Journal* 9 (July 1892): 128–34. "Hits at Popular Illusions," *Chicago Livestock World*, March 7, 1905; "A Weather Scheme," *The Rock Island Argus*, April 6, 1906. Anderson, *Predicting the Weather*, 2, 130.

84. "Wireless to Give Weather Reports," *Urbana Courier*, May 25, 1909.

85. "Cold Wave Envelops West," *Urbana Courier*, Jan. 7, 1909; "Work of Weather Man Explained," *Urbana Courier*, Nov. 20, 1915.

86. "The Northern Illinois Horticulture Society," *Prairie Farmer*, Feb. 6, 1875.

87. "A Weather Scheme," *The Rock Island Argus*, April 6, 1906.

88. "Foretell Coming Weather," *Bureau County Tribune*, July 11, 1913.

89. "Meteorology," *Western Rural*, Jan. 21, 1869; "Cold Wave Coming," *Urbana Courier*, Jan. 28, 1916.

90. On maps with Canada, see "Weather Forecast," *Chicago Livestock World*, May 22, 1915.

91. "Work of Weather Man Explained," *Urbana Courier*, Nov. 20, 1915.

92. "Tornado Sweeps Champaign County," *Urbana Courier*, July 14, 1917.

93. "Nearly 2,000 Go from Twin Cities," *Urbana Courier*, May 28, 1917.

94. "Wind Brings Storm Relic," *Urbana Courier*, May 28, 1917; "Nearly 2,000 Go from Twin Cities," *Urbana Courier*, May 28, 1917. On tornadoes in Champaign County, see "Storm Works Ruin," *Urbana Courier*, July 21, 1907; "Tornado Passes West of Town," *Urbana Courier*, May 11, 1914; "Tornado Sweeps Champaign County," *Urbana Courier*, July 14, 1917; "Nearby Briefs," *Urbana Courier*, June 8, 1904; "Gifford Folks See Tornado," *Urbana Courier*, June 6, 1917.

95. "Count 238 Dead and 1,220 Injured," *Urbana Courier*, May 28, 1917.

96. "Deadly Tornado in Mauritius," *Urbana Courier*, March 27, 1904; "Deadly Russian Tornado," *Urbana Courier*, July 1, 1904; on Arizona, "Loss of Life Feared," *Urbana Courier*, July 25, 1903; on Manitoba, "Hen's Egg Size Hail Kills," *Urbana Courier*, July 6, 1909; on New Jersey, "Deaths in a Tornado," *Urbana Courier*, July 25, 1903; "Ohio Swept by Tornado," *Urbana Courier*, July 8, 1915; "Struck by Tornado," *Urbana Courier*, Aug. 13, 1907. The *Urbana Courier* ran over 1,600 stories on tornadoes from 1903 through 1920, with this region, extending to Wisconsin in the north and Arkansas to the south, figuring largely.

97. "300 Are Dead in Twin Equinoctial Storms in West," *Urbana Courier*, March 25, 1913. On the Mississippi Valley as their "region of greatest frequency," see "Defines a Tornado," *Urbana Courier*, April 20, 1918. For a British view of the prairies as particularly tornado prone, see H. N. Dickson, *Meteorology: The Elements of Weather and Climate* (London: Methuen & Co., 1893), 89–91.

98. On Northwest Territory, "As to Unseasonable Weather," *Chicago Livestock World*, March 28, 1904; on possessions, "Temperature of the Air," *Monthly Weather Review* 18 (March 1890): 65–66; on wave, J. B. Turner, "Climate and Weather," *Prairie Farmer*, July 19, 1873.

99. "Dissect Heat Wave," *Urbana Courier*, July 29, 1916.

100. "Reason Spring Is Cold," *Urbana Courier*, March 6, 1903.

101. "Storm over South," *Urbana Courier*, Sept. 28, 1906; "Cold Wave over Mid West Is Breaking," *Urbana Courier*, Dec. 10, 1919; "Blizzard Hits Middle West," *Urbana Courier*, Dec. 15, 1914; "Blizzard Raging in Northwest," *Urbana Courier*, Jan. 26, 1904. On "Bermuda High," see "Dissect Heat Wave," *Urbana Courier*, July 29, 1916.

102. "London Weather," *Urbana Courier*, Sept. 21, 1906. On "titanic," "Storms Cause Disturbances," *Chicago Livestock World*, Oct. 23, 1906. On "invasions," "Heat Toll Big, Many Prostrated," *Urbana Courier*, June 28, 1913. On Goths, "The Blizzard," *Urbana Courier*, Jan. 13, 1904. On convergence, see "Dissect Heat Wave," *Urbana Courier*, July 29, 1916.

103. "Island Is Swept by a Hurricane," *Urbana Courier*, Aug. 12, 1903. The article also calls the storm a cyclone.

104. "Hurricane Does Severe Damage," *Urbana Courier*, April 26, 1912.

105. "Tornado Plucks Geese," *Urbana Courier*, May 26, 1909.

106. "Death List Is Large," *Urbana Courier*, Oct. 20, 1906; "Three Towns in Iowa Struck by Cyclones," *Urbana Courier*, Aug. 8, 1907.

107. "Hurricane Does Severe Damage," *Urbana Courier*, April 26, 1912.

108. "Deaths in Storm," *Urbana Courier*, Sept. 22, 1909; "Hurricane in Cuba," *Urbana Courier*, Oct. 19, 1906; "Hundreds Die in Hurricane," *Urbana Courier*, Sept. 1, 1903; "Town Partly Ruined by Severe Hurricane," *Urbana Courier*, Oct. 16, 1906; "Hurricane in Cuba," *Urbana Courier*, Oct. 19, 1906; "Hurricane in Philippines," *Urbana Courier*, June 6, 1903.

109. "Strange Bird Is Captured," *Urbana Courier*, Nov. 18, 1911.

110. "Are We to Miss Cyclone?" *Urbana Courier*, May 27, 1903.

111. "The Ellison Calamity," *Urbana Union*, June 10, 1888.

112. H. P. Curtis, "The Terms Cyclone and Tornado," *American Meteorological Journal* 11 (March 1895): 425–26; Gustavus Hinrichs, "Tornadoes and Derechos," *American Meteorological Journal* 5 (Oct. 1888): 306–17.

113. "Tornado Differs from Cyclone," *Urbana Courier*, June 5, 1917.

114. "Defines a Tornado," *Urbana Courier*, April 20, 1918.

115. "Tornado Differs from Cyclone," *Urbana Courier*, June 5, 1917.

116. "Defines a Tornado," *Urbana Courier*, April 20, 1918; "Tornado Sweeps Champaign County," *Urbana Courier*, July 14, 1917.

117. [S. A. Mitchell], *Illinois in 1837* (Philadelphia: S. A. Mitchell, 1837): 41.

118. Paul W. Parmalee and Walter E. Klippel, "The Role of Native Animals in the Food Economy of the Historic Kickapoo in Central Illinois," in *Lulu Linear Punctuated: Essays in Honor of George Irving Quimby*, ed. Robert C. Dunnell and Donald K. Grayson (Ann Arbor: Museum of Anthropology, University of Michigan, 1983), 253–324.

119. Robert Ridgway, "Bird Life in Southern Illinois," *Bird-Lore* 17 (May–June, 1915): 191–98.

120. Calamink, "The Oldest Club in America—The Audubon Club," *Chicago Field*, Sept. 20, 1879, 88–89.

121. T. S. Palmer, *Legislation for the Protection of Birds Other than Game Birds* (Washington, DC: U.S. Department of Agriculture, 1902), 88.

122. Geo. H. Brown, "Duck Shooting Along the Mississippi in 1881," *American Field*, Aug. 2, 1890, 100.

123. On nearby ponds, see "Duck Hunting Popular," *Urbana Courier*, March 12, 1913.

124. "Duck Shooting Is Good This Year," *Urbana Courier*, April 2, 1913.

125. On Illinois River, "Friends Feast on Fowls," *Urbana Courier*, April 1, 1904; on Mississippi, "One Wholesale Killing," *Urbana Courier*, Nov. 16, 1907; on Effingham County, "Late News from Big Four Shops," *Urbana Courier*, Oct. 16, 1910; on Indiana, "Big Four Shop News," *Urbana Courier*, March 16, 1910; on northwest, "Hunting Season Is Now Open," *Urbana Courier*, Sept. 4, 1903; on an Urbana resident's shoot in the Everglades, see Athos, "Five Weeks' Shooting in Florida," *American Field*, Feb. 8, 1902, 117–18.

126. "Game and Insectivorous Birds," *Prairie Farmer*, Oct. 22, 1864, 263; "Duck Shooting Is Good This Year," *Urbana Courier*, April 2, 1913.

127. "Birds That Need Special Protection," *American Field*, July 5, 1902, 4–5.

128. V. N. R., "Old Shanties Along the Kankakee," *American Field*, Feb. 22, 1902, 167–68.

129. Cyrus Thompson, "Passenger Pigeons," *American Field*, March 29, 1902, 287.

130. On sparrows, C. Hart Merriam, "Report of Ornithologist and Mammalogist," *Report of the Commissioner of Agriculture, 1886* (Washington, DC: Government

Printing Office, 1887), 236. "No Protection for Starling," *Urbana Courier*, Feb. 1, 1915.

131. "Swat the Sparrow Too," *Urbana Courier*, July 19, 1913.

132. On course, A. E. S., "The Cause of the Dimunition of Game," *Chicago Field*, July 31, 1880, 39; on haunts, Charles Linden, "Preservation of Woodcock," *The Rod and Gun*, 6 (May 1, 1875): 67.

133. On pigs, Maurice Thompson, "Our Vanishing Birds," *The Drainage Journal* 20 (October 1898): 290–91; on cats, Rolla Warren Kimsey, "Why the Birds Are Decreasing," *Bird-Lore* 16 (July–August 1914): 265–66. For a case study on agriculture's effects on birds, see Michael Shrubb, *Birds, Scythes and Combines: A History of Birds and Agricultural Change* (Cambridge: Cambridge University Press, 2003). On mowing, G. G., Princeton, Illinois, "The Enemies of Our Game Birds," *Chicago Field*, Aug. 7, 1880, 413; plowing, Robert W. Hegner, "The Prairie Horned Lark," *Bird-Lore* 1 (Oct. 1899): 152–154; brush, "Children to Aid the Birds," *Urbana Courier*, July 21, 1913; on thorough cultivation, see Frank Elmer Wood, "A Study of the Mammals of Champaign County, Illinois," *Bulletin of the Illinois State Laboratory of Natural History* 8 (1908–1910): 504–05.

134. Robert Ridgway, *The Ornithology of Illinois, Part I. A Descriptive Catalogue of the Birds of Illinois* (Springfield: H. W. Rokker, 1889), 16.

135. Stephen A. Forbes, *The Native Animal Resources of the State*, reprint from *Transactions of the Illinois Academy of Science*, 5th annual meeting (Bloomington, IL, Feb. 23–24, 1912), 10. The mid-twentieth-century turn to monoculture, more pesticide use, and roadside-to-roadside cultivation further affected habitat; Vernon M. Kleen, Liane Cordle, and Robert A. Montgomery, *The Illinois Breeding Bird Atlas*, Illinois Natural History Survey Special Publication No. 26, 2004.

136. W. L. Johnston, Evansville, Ind., "The Dimunition of Game," *The American Field*, Oct. 24, 1885, 388. See also Edward Howe Forbush, "The Sora Rail," *Bird-Lore* 16 (July–Aug. 1914): 303–06; nesting, 304; draining, 306. On more recent efforts to figure out the long-term effects of settlement farming on prairie avifauna, see Richard E. Warner, "Agricultural Land Use and Grassland Habitat in Illinois: Future Shock for Midwestern Birds?," *Conservation Biology* 8 (March 1994): 147–56.

137. Cunningham, *History of Champaign County*, 701; "Was Extremely Wet at Broadlands," *Urbana Courier*, April 1, 1913.

138. Maurice Thompson, "Our Vanishing Birds," *Drainage Journal* 20 (October 1898): 290–91. A recent study estimates that by 1900, only 2% of the prairies of 1820 remained; Jeffery W. Walk, Michael P. Ward, et al., *Illinois Birds: A Century of Change* (Champaign: Illinois Natural History Survey, Institute of Natural Resource Sustainability, Special Publication 31, 2011), 14. T. E. Musselman, "A History of the Birds of Illinois," *Journal of the Illinois State Historical Society* 1–2 (April–July 1921): 1–73.

139. On reservations, "How Illinois Protects Game," *Urbana Courier*, Sept. 13, 1915; see also "Buffalo Herds on Increase," *Urbana Courier*, Dec. 28, 1916. On narrow sanctuaries near waterways, Market Hunter, "Abolish Spring Shooting," *American Field*, Oct. 24, 1885, 387–88.

140. "Game and Insectivorous Birds," *Prairie Farmer*, Oct. 22, 1864, 263.

141. Merriam, "Report of Ornithologist and Mammalogist," 227–58.

142. His fields were in Ford and Livingston Counties, Havighurst, *The Heartland*, 146–47.

143. Merriam, "Report of Ornithologist and Mammalogist," 244–45.

144. "The English Sparrow," *Urbana Courier*, May 1, 1904.

145. T. Gilbert Pearson, "The English Sparrow," *Bird-Lore* 19 (Jan.–Feb. 1917): 60–63. On bounties, Illinois State Archives, Record Descriptions, County Board of Supervisors/Board of County Commissioners, https://www.cyberdriveillinois .com/departments/archives/IRAD/rd_countyboard.html, accessed Jan. 20, 2016.

146. "Twelve-Year-Old Kills Brother," *Urbana Courier*, April 6, 1920.

147. Norman J. Colman, "Report of the Commissioner of Agriculture," *Report of the Commissioner of Agriculture, 1886* (Washington, DC: Government Printing Office, 1887), 7–45. On economic ornithology, see Matthew D. Evenden, "The Laborers of Nature: Economic Ornithology and the Role of Birds as Agents of Biological Pest Control in North American Agriculture, ca. 1880–1930," *Forest & Conservation History* 39 (Oct. 1995): 172–83; on the creation of an office of Economic Ornithology within the Division of Entomology of the Department of Agriculture in 1885, see Keir B. Sterling, "Builders of the U.S. Biological Survey, 1885–1930," *Journal of Forest History* 33 (Oct. 1989): 180–87. In 1895 the agency was retitled the Division of Biological Survey, 181.

148. William Le Baron, "Observations upon Some of the Birds of Illinois Most Interesting to the Agriculturist," *Transactions of the Illinois State Agricultural Society; With the Proceedings of the County Societies, and Kindred Associations*, vol. 1, 1853–1854 (Springfield: Lanphier & Walker, 1855), 559.

149. "The Feed and Growth of the American Robin," *Illinois Farmer* 6 (Nov. 1861): 328–29.

150. "Birds and Insects," *Illinois Farmer* 9 (Oct. 1864): 293–94.

151. "Game and Insectivorous Birds," *Prairie Farmer*, Oct. 22, 1864, 263.

152. Mrs. John V. Farwell, Jr., "The Study of Birds," in *Transactions of the Department of Agriculture of the State of Illinois*, vol. 6, ed. S. D. Fisher (Springfield: D. W. Lusk, 1878): 422–26.

153. The quarantine took effect in 1898. Robert A. Croker, *Stephen Forbes and the Rise of American Ecology* (Washington, DC: Smithsonian Institution Press, 2001); lice-like young, 112–13; scale, 114.

154. Forbes moved the state entomologist's office and the state laboratory onto the Champaign campus. Croker, *Stephen Forbes and the Rise of American Ecology*, on Forbes as state entomologist, 92; congress, 122.

155. Edmund Russell, *War and Nature: Fighting Humans and Insects with Chemicals from World War I to Silent Spring* (New York: Cambridge University Press, 2001), 7. Evenden, "The Laborers of Nature: Economic Ornithology and the Role of Birds as Agents of Biological Pest Control," 175, 180.

156. On the practice of economic ornithology in the Agriculture Department's Division of Entomology, see Merriam, "Report of Ornithologist and Mammalogist"; on economic ornithology division, 227; on research methods, 233.

157. "W. L. Finley Gives Paper on Wild Birds," *Urbana Courier*, Sept. 28 1909. See also "Bob White Helps the Farmer," *Urbana Daily Courier*, June 2, 1904. On stomach studies, see "What the Government is Doing for Birds," *Urbana Daily*

Courier, May 7, 1910; "Celebrated Work by Forbes," *Urbana Daily Courier*, April 27, 1904.

158. "Campaign against Insect Criminals," *Urbana Courier*, June 19, 1918.

159. "Big Campaign on Farm Pests," *Urbana Courier*, Aug. 20, 1917.

160. "Why Birds Should Be Protected," *Urbana Courier*, July 20, 1920.

161. On Grange support for bird protection, see Maude E. Young, "Pomona's Report," in *Thirty-Sixth Annual Session of the State Grange of Illinois* (pamphlet), 1907, 20–22; Charles M. Gardner, *The Grange—Friend of the Farmer* (Washington, DC: National Grange, 1949), 175. On an Illinois Farmers' Institute bird protection resolution, see Mary Drummond, "Reports of State Societies. Illinois," *Annual Report of the National Association of Audubon Societies for 1907*, 335–36.

162. S. A. Forbes, "The Mid-summer Bird Life of Illinois: A Statistical Study," *American Naturalist* 42 (August 1908): 505–19. On a talk, "Deep Study of Our Bird Friends," *Urbana Courier*, July 11, 1908.

163. "Triplets Three Years Ago; Now Come Twins," *Urbana Courier*, April 6, 1912.

164. "Philo Man has Fine Collection of Bird's Eggs," *Urbana Courier*, March 30, 1910.

165. "Will Legislature Protect Prairie Chicken?" *Urbana Courier*, April 4, 1911.

166. "Has Many Engagements," *Urbana Courier*, Dec. 23, 1914; "Masons Give Banquet," *Urbana Courier*, Feb. 12, 1915; on corn growers' association, "Will Address Convention," *Urbana Courier*, Jan. 15, 1915; on talk, "Philo," *Urbana Courier*, Feb. 26, 1910; on Chautauqua, "Philo," *Urbana Courier*, Aug. 25, 1916; on academy, "Annual Meeting at University This Week," *Urbana Courier*, Feb. 14, 1910. "Local and Personal," *Urbana Courier*, April 26, 1918.

167. "Rules for Bird Protection Fathered by Government," *Urbana Courier*, Aug. 11, 1913; "Illinois Arbor Day and Bird Day," *Urbana Courier*, Feb. 19, 1908; Charles B. Reynolds, *The Game Laws in Brief* (New York: Forest and Stream Publishing Co., 1911), 4, 19. See also Mary Drummond, "State Audubon Reports—Illinois," *Bird-Lore* 12 (Nov.–Dec. 1910): 288–90; Palmer, *Legislation for the Protection of Birds Other Than Game Birds*, 13.

168. "Birds Show Increase," *Urbana Courier*, Feb. 6, 1920; Kurkpatrick Dorsey, *The Dawn of Conservation Diplomacy: U.S.-Canadian Wildlife Protection Treaties in the Progressive Era* (Seattle: University of Washington Press, 1998): 213. See also "The Treaty Wins," *Bird-Lore* 18 (Sept.–Oct. 1916): 346–48; "Migratory Bird Treaty Act," *Bird-Lore* 20 (Sept.–Oct. 1918): 387–88; "Bird Treaties with Other Countries," *Bird-Lore* 22 (May–June 1920): 195.

169. "Hunting Season Will Open Soon," *Urbana Courier*, Aug. 20, 1912.

170. "Protect 'Bob White,'" *Urbana Courier*, Sept. 6, 1904.

171. "The Robin," *Illinois Farmer* 1 (May 1856): 109.

172. Wells W. Cooke, *Report on Bird Migration in the Mississippi Valley in the Years 1884 and 1885*, ed. and revised by C. Hart Merriam, Bulletin of the U.S. Department of Agriculture, No. 2 (Washington, DC: Government Printing Office, 1888), 9–10.

173. Palmer, *Legislation for the Protection of Birds Other Than Game Birds*, 20; see also Merriam, "Report of Ornithologist and Mammalogist," 250.

174. "Winter Bird Neighbors," *Urbana Courier*, Dec. 15, 1905.

175. Wells W. Cooke, Assistant Biologist, *Bird Migration*, Bulletin of the U.S. Department of Agriculture, No. 185 (Washington, DC: Government Printing Office, 1915), 1–47.

176. "Why Do Birds Migrate?" *Canadian Farm* 11 (Oct. 2, 1914): 12. On true homes, see also "Winter Bird Neighbors," *Urbana Courier*, Dec. 15, 1905.

177. "The Great White Fleet," *Life* 68 (Sept. 28, 1916): 556.

178. B. S. Bowdish, "Alien License Law," *Bird-Lore* 10 (March–April 1908): 97; Edward Howe Forbush, "The Sora Rail," *Bird-Lore* 16 (July–Aug. 1914): 303–06; "Local Sportsmen Are Asked Opinions," *Urbana Courier*, Feb. 7, 1916. On southern Europeans, see J. R. Stewart, ed., *A Standard History of Champaign County Illinois*, vol. 1 (Chicago: The Lewis Publication Co., 1918), 15.

179. "Report of the National Committee for 1904," *Bird-Lore* 7 (Jan.–Feb. 1905): 58–74, 67. It reports that "the work of bird protection is being carried on admirably in Mexico through the Comision de Parasitologia Agricola." The commission had been proposing laws to protect birds useful to agriculture, studying useful birds, distributing circulars among farmers, forming ornithology leagues, and promulgating laws to restrict hunting.

180. H. W. Howe, "How Ducks Are Slaughtered in Mexico," *Field and Stream* 7 (July 1902): 378–80.

181. Captain R. G. A. Levinge, *Echoes from the Backwoods; or Sketches of Transatlantic Life*, in two vols., vol. 1 (London: Henry Colburn, Publisher, 1846), chap. 5; W. Ross King, *The Sportsman and Naturalist in Canada* (London: Hurst and Blackett, 1866); *The Canadian Sportsman and Naturalist* 1 (June 15, 1881).

182. Reynolds, *The Game Laws in Brief*, 93–100; "Game Laws Digest in U.S.–Canada," *Urbana Courier*, Aug. 2, 1917. On Canadian game laws see also Palmer, *Legislation for the Protection of Birds Other than Game Birds*, 20; "Federal Game Wardens Are on the Alert," *Urbana Courier*, March 26, 1917.

183. Mark Cioc, *The Game of Conservation: International Treaties to Protect the World's Migratory Animals* (Athens: Ohio University Press, 2009), 93.

184. John L. Audubon, "Facts and Observations Connected with the Permanent Residence of Swallows in the United States," *Annals of the Lyceum of Natural History of New-York* 1 (New York: J. Seymour, 1877): 166–68.

185. George Ord, *Sketch of the Life of Alexander Wilson: Author of the American Ornithology* (Philadelphia: H. Hall, 1828), c–ci.

186. "The Blue Bird," *Illinois Farmer* 1 (April 1856): 86–87.

187. "The Purple Martin," *Illinois Farmer* 1 (June 1856): 136.

188. "Game and Insectivorous Birds," *Prairie Farmer*, Oct. 22, 1864, 263.

189. Richard R. Graber and Sylvia Sue Hassler, "The Effectiveness of Aircraft-Type (APS) Radar in Detecting Birds," *The Wilson Bulletin* 74 (Dec. 1962): 367–80.

190. William Hosea Ballou, "Natural History," *American Field* 16 (Dec. 10, 1881): 380.

191. "Migration of Birds," *American Meteorological Journal* 1 (April 1885): 511–12.

192. "Bird-Lore's Eleventh Bird Census," *Bird-Lore* 13 (Jan.–Feb. 1911): 18–44; Illinois, 39; foreign, 43–44.

193. On Hudson's Bay Co., Robert Ridgway, "The Sparrow Hawk or American Kestril," *The Rod and Gun* 6 (June 26, 1875): 20; Juan Renadro, "Notes on Some Birds

of the United States Which Occur in the Mexican Fauna," translated by F. H. Carpenter, *Ornithologist and Oölogist* 11 (Sept. 1886): 132–33.

194. Merriam, "Report of Ornithologist and Mammalogist," 250. On the American Ornithologists' Union's Committee on the Migration of Birds circa 1883 and its network of observers in the United States and Canada, see Sterling, "Builders of the U.S. Biological Survey, 1885–1930," 180. On U.S. natural history museum efforts to build collections of Latin American birds through relationships with U.S. and European expats, see Camilo Quintero Toro, *Birds of Empire, Birds of Nation: A History of Science, Economy, and Conservation in United States-Colombia Relations* (Bogotá: Universidad de los Andes, 2012), 68, 76.

195. "Bird Migration and Its Secrets," *Urbana Courier*, Feb. 19, 1918; on Urbana bird-watcher Frank Smith and his associates, see "A Coöperative Study of Bird Migration," *Bird-Lore* 16 (July–Aug. 1914): 270–73.

196. A report also came in from aptly named Newton L. Partridge of White Heath, in Piatt County. See "Bird-Lore's Eleventh Bird Census," *Bird-Lore* 13 (Jan.–Feb. 1911): 18–44; on Illinois, 39; George, Eddie and Census, "Bird Lore's Sixteenth Christmas Census," *Bird-Lore* 18 (Jan.–Feb. 1916): 19–42; on Sidney, "A Record of the Bald Eagle from Champaign County, Ill.," *Bird-Lore* 20 (Nov.–Dec. 1918): 421.

197. Calamink, "The Oldest Club in America—The Audubon Club," *Chicago Field*, Sept. 20, 1879, 88–89. On Smithsonian sponsorship of expedition to study the birds of Antigua and Barbuda, see Stuart T. Danforth, "The Birds of Antigua," *The Auk* 51 (July 1934): 350–64. On the AOU, see Cooke, *Report on Bird Migration in the Mississippi Valley in the Years 1884 and 1885*, 9–10.

198. Cooke, *Bird Migration*, 1–47. On Mexican agents, Sterling, "Builders of the U.S. Biological Survey, 1885–1930," 185.

199. Merriam, "Report of Ornithologist and Mammalogist," 252.

200. On the AOU, see Cooke, *Report on Bird Migration in the Mississippi Valley in the Years 1884 and 1885*, 9–10. A regular contributor to *American Field* was Urbana resident A. J. Miller; "Strange Was the Sight," *Urbana Courier*, April 11, 1906.

201. "Beats Record of Best Aeroplane," *Urbana Courier*, June 29, 1915.

202. "Beats Record of Best Acroplane," *Urbana Courier*, June 29, 1915.

203. "Bird Migration and Its Secrets," *Urbana Courier*, Feb. 19, 1918. The ornithological press reported on many more discoveries than the *Courier*. See, for example, W. W. Cooke, "The Migration of Warblers," *Bird-Lore* 6 (Jan.–Feb. 1904): 21–24; Frank M. Chapman, "The Bobolink," *Bird-Lore* 11 (May–June 1909): 137–40; Harry C. Oberholser, "The Migration of North American Birds III, The Summer and Hepatic Tanagers, Martins, and Barn Swallows," *Bird-Lore* 20 (March–April 1918): 145–52.

204. "Where Wild Fowl Breed," *Urbana Courier*, March 6, 1918.

205. "The Game Birds and Mammals of the Chicago Market," *Chicago Field*, April 10, 1880, 136.

206. "Teachers Are Engaged," *Urbana Courier*, Aug. 12, 1905.

207. "University Alumni Meet to Organize," *Urbana Courier*, Jan. 22, 1912.

208. "Rantoul Man to Visit Arctics," *Urbana Courier*, Dec. 12, 1912.

209. "Urbana Men Kill Five Rare Birds," *Urbana Courier*, March 25, 1913.

210. Donald B. MacMillan, *Four Years in the White North* (Boston: The Medici Society, 1925).

211. "Receive News from Crockerland," *Urbana Courier*, May 23, 1914.

212. "Local Explorers Start Wednesday," *Urbana Courier*, July 1, 1913. On Tanquary, "Illinois Arctic Club Organized," *Urbana Courier*, May 22, 1913; MacMillan, *Four Years in the White North*, 4.

213. "Illinois Arctic Club Organized," *Urbana Courier*, May 22, 1913.

214. "Rantoul Man to Visit Arctics," *Urbana Courier*, Dec. 12, 1912.

215. "Miss James Entertains in Ekblaw's Honor," *Urbana Courier*, Feb. 20, 1913; "Local Explorers to Leave July 2," *Urbana Courier*, June 28, 1913.

216. "Crockerland Is Proven a Myth," *Urbana Courier*, Nov. 25, 1914.

217. "Receives Letter from W. Elmer Ekblaw," *Urbana Courier*, June 21, 1915. MacMillan, *Four Years in the White North*, 281.

218. "Local Explorers Start Wednesday," *Urbana Courier*, July 1, 1913.

219. "Is Elmer Ekblaw Dead or Alive?" *Urbana Courier*, April 18, 1917; "Mrs. Slawson Hears from Elmer Ekblaw," *Urbana Courier*, June 28, 1915. On hunts, see "Crockerland is Proven a Myth," *Urbana Courier*, Nov. 25, 1914.

220. "Rantoul Folk Honor Ekblaw," *Urbana Courier*, Sept. 11, 1917.

221. "Ekblaw to Show Pictures," *Urbana Courier*, Aug. 8, 1919; on illustrations, "University of Illinois Weekly Calendar," *Urbana Courier*, Dec. 15, 1917; "Ekblaw to Speak at Rantoul," *Urbana Courier*, Dec. 1, 1917; "Ekblaw Will Deliver Address at Danville," *Urbana Courier*, Sept. 27, 1917; on Masonic, "University of Illinois Weekly Calendar," *Urbana Courier*, Dec. 15, 1917; "Ekblaw Is Next Luncheon Speaker," *Urbana Courier*, Sept. 11, 1920; "Curier U. P. Wire at Elks," *Urbana Courier*, Oct. 30, 1920; "Elmer Ekblaw to Address Omicron NU," *Urbana Courier*, Jan. 30, 1919; "University Republican Club Meets Friday," *Urbana Courier*, Oct. 1, 1919.

222. "Ekblaw's Lecture Was Well Attended," *Urbana Courier*, March 1, 1919.

223. "Ekblaw's Relics Exhibited," *Urbana Courier*, Nov. 22, 1918.

224. "Laugh Is on Ekblaw; He Froze His Ears," *Urbana Courier*, Jan. 16, 1918.

225. W. Elmer Ekblaw, "The Material Response of the Polar Eskimo to Their Far Arctic Environment," *Annals of the Association of American Geographers* 17 (Dec. 1927): 148–98.

226. "Meteor Creates Much Excitement," *Urbana Courier*, July 17, 1911.

227. "Mysterious Airship over Illinois," *Urbana Courier*, Aug. 13, 1909; "Was It an Air Ship?" *Urbana Courier*, July 21, 1909; "Say They Saw Airship," *Urbana Courier*, Jan. 12, 1910; "Thought They Saw Airship," *Urbana Courier*, May 15, 1912; "Air Ship Had Searchlight," *Urbana Courier*, Sept. 30, 1911; "Thought They Saw Airship," *Urbana Courier*, Oct. 8, 1910; "Lady Saw Queer Light," *Urbana Courier*, Dec. 3, 1907.

228. "Merchant Distributes 500 Kites among Children," *Urbana Courier*, April 6, 1912; "Attraction at Park," *Urbana Courier*, May 31, 1910; "Opinions of Our Reader," *Urbana Courier*, Dec. 30, 1915; "Name Those in Final Contest," *Urbana Courier*, Nov. 24, 1916; "Philo Boys Fly Flag from Kite," *Urbana Courier*, April 19, 1917; "Mumford Wins Kite Contest," *Urbana Courier*, Nov. 27, 1916.

229. "Children's Games," *Urbana Courier*, July 6, 1906.

230. "Kite Battle to Be Introduced," *Urbana Courier*, Nov. 16, 1916; "Twenty-five Qualify in Preliminaries," *Urbana Courier*, Nov. 20, 1916.

231. On crowds, Dateline Quincy, "Balloon Tries Record Flight," *Urbana Courier*, May 12, 1910. On a Kansas City to South Bend flight, "St. Louis IV Wins Air Race," *Urbana Courier*, July 13, 1911; "Men Are Lost in Forest," *Urbana Courier*, Oct. 9, 1911; "Centennial Fetes Open in St. Louis," *Urbana Courier*, Oct. 4, 1909; "Balloons Sail Across Lake," *Urbana Courier*, Oct. 20, 1910. On French, British, and German competitors in a St. Louis race, see "Lakes Are Their Peril," *Urbana Courier*, Oct. 13, 1907.

232. Cologne, "Big Storm Wrecks Balloon," *Urbana Courier*, Dec. 22, 1909; Berlin, "Seventeen Balloons Contest for Trophy," *Urbana Courier*, Oct. 15, 1906.

233. "Balloon Causes Storm," *Urbana Courier*, July 3, 1909; "Aeronauts Hurt When Balloon Falls," *Urbana Courier*, Oct. 6, 1911; "Aeronauts in Long Fall," *Urbana Courier*, May 12, 1910.

234. "Balloon Mystery Is Solved; Record Is Made," *Urbana Courier*, April 28, 1911.

235. "Balloons Pass Over Urbana," *Urbana Courier*, Oct. 25, 1920.

236. "Balloon Sails Over Urbana," *Urbana Courier*, April 27, 1911.

237. "The Modern Woodmen," *Urbana Courier*, June 9, 1905; athletic carnival, "What Time Does Balloon Go Up?," *Urbana Courier*, May 23, 1909; corn carnival, "Will Have Balloon Ascensions," *Urbana Courier*, Sept. 27, 1910; Sunday school, "Rev. Walden Is Captain," *Urbana Courier*, July 17, 1907; horse show, "Balloon Ascension by Local Talent," *Urbana Courier*, Sept. 24, 1915; Commercial Club, "Will Be a Double Header," *Urbana Courier*, July 17, 1914; Fourth of July, "Sam M'Williams, Aeronaut," *Urbana Courier*, May 13, 1903.

238. "University Exhibit at Fair," *Urbana Courier*, Aug. 14, 1910; on usual features, "Business Men Punch Eagle in the Ribs," *Urbana Courier*, May 28, 1903; "Special Cars to Balloon Ascension at Homer Park," *Urbana Courier*, July 25, 1907; on crowd size, "Bud Mars Makes Daring Flights," *Urbana Courier*, Aug. 29, 1912.

239. Dolly Shepherd with Peter Hearn, in collaboration with Molly Sedgwick, *When the 'Chute Went Up . . . The Adventures of an Edwardian Lady Parachutist* (London: Robert Hale, 1984), 44, 46.

240. "Humane Officer Told Showmen to Play Monk," *Urbana Courier*, Aug. 22, 1907; "Repeated Performance," *Urbana Courier*, July 15, 1907.

241. "Balloon Ascension by Local Talent," *Urbana Courier*, Sept. 24, 1915.

242. "Aeronautic Club Is Organized," *Urbana Courier*, May 19, 1910; "Bi-Plane Wrecked in Trial Ascension," *Urbana Courier*, May 21, 1910.

243. "Villa Grove Boy Will Fly Within Two Weeks," *Urbana Courier*, Sept. 8, 1911; "Villa Grove Boy Will Fly Next Monday," *Urbana Courier*, Sept. 15, 1911.

244. "Woman Aviator Falls to Death," *Urbana Courier*, June 18, 1912; "Country Is Mad Over Aviation," *Urbana Courier*, Sept. 24, 1912.

245. "Aeroplane Seen Passing O'er City," *Urbana Courier*, April 15, 1915.

246. "Aeronautical Course at the University of Illinois," *Aerial Age Weekly* 3 (Aug. 28, 1916): 721; "Satan Day to Fly at University of Illinois," *Aerial Age Weekly* 2 (Jan. 17, 1916): 424.

247. His real name was also unusual: Curtis La Q. Day. "Villa Would Make Local Boy Chief," *Urbana Courier*, April 19, 1915.

248. "Moisant Is Native of Kankakee," *Urbana Courier*, Sept 7, 1911. "Moisant Here to Plan for Flight," *Urbana Courier*, Aug. 19, 1911. On European and South American travels, see "Moisant Flyers again at Kankakee," *Urbana Courier*, Aug. 21, 1912.

249. Peter Simons, "Aviation's Heartland: The Flying Farmers and Postwar Flight," *Agricultural History* 89 (Spring 2015): 225–46.

250. "British Aviator Wins Bennett Cup," *Urbana Courier*, Oct. 31, 1910; "Moisant Flyers Again at Kankakee," *Urbana Courier*, Aug. 21, 1912.

251. "This Week at West End Park," *Urbana Courier*, July 12, 1903.

252. Irishman, "Close Contract with Moisant," *Urbana Courier*, Aug. 21, 1911; fool flyer, "Simon Feared Dangerous Wind," *Urbana Courier*, Sept 5, 1911; Russian, "Bud Mars Will Fly during Fair," *Urbana Courier*, Aug. 21, 1912.

253. "Bud Mars Makes Daring Flights," *Urbana Courier*, Aug. 29, 1912.

254. "Hutchinson Is No Novice," *Urbana Courier*, Aug. 27, 1915.

255. "John Russell—Aeronaut!," *Urbana Courier*, Nov. 12, 1908.

256. "Balloon Indiana Wins," *Urbana Courier*, June 9, 1909; "Balloonists Are Fired Upon," *Urbana Daily Courier*, Jan. 10, 1911.

257. "Airman Spy Is Shot," *Urbana Courier*, Feb. 2, 1912; "U.S. Aviators Fired On," *Aerial Age Weekly* 1 (Sept. 13, 1915): 613–14; "Biplane Fooled Game Birds," *Urbana Courier*, Oct. 16, 1910.

258. Henry Woodhouse, "What the Aircraft Will Do for Humanity after the War," *Flying* 3 (Oct. 1914): 261.

259. "Airship Bombs Kill Arabs," *Urbana Courier*, March 19, 1912.

260. "German Airship Drops Bombs on Antwerp Citizens," *Urbana Courier*, Aug. 26, 1914.

261. "Thousands See Fight in Air," *Urbana Courier*, Feb. 15, 1915.

262. "Air Raids Terrorize Germans," *Urbana Courier*, July 13, 1918.

263. "Letters from Soldiers at Home and Abroad," *Urbana Courier*, Aug. 1, 1918.

264. "Sees Plenty of Excitement," *Urbana Courier*, Aug. 10, 1918.

265. Thomas S. Snyder, *Chanute Field: The Hum of the Motor Replaced the Song of the Reaper, 1917–1921* (Chanute Technical Training Center: History Office, 1975), 32.

266. "Will Build Fine Flatville Church," *Urbana Courier*, Jan. 13, 1914; "English in October," *Urbana Courier*, Sept. 11, 1907.

267. "Something about the Dutch 'Flats,'" *Urbana Courier*, July 1, 1911.

268. On suspicions of spies, see Snyder, *Chanute Field*, 13; "Flatville Minister Denies Incident," *Urbana Daily Courier*, April 7, 1917.

269. "Professorship in Aeronautics in the University of Illinois," *Flying* 5 (Sept. 1916): 329.

270. "School Grows Rapidly," *Aerial Age Weekly* 5 (July 16, 1917): 599.

271. "Air Squadron in Long Flight to New Field," *Aerial Age Weekly* 5 (July 23, 1917): 629.

272. E. N. Fales, *Learning to Fly in the U.S. Army: A Manual of Aviation Practice* (New York: McGraw-Hill, 1917), 89–94.

273. Fales, *Learning to Fly in the U.S. Army*, 89–94.

274. J. G. Gilpatric, "Flying From Small Fields," *Aerial Age Weekly* 4 (Dec. 25, 1916): 386.

275. "Company Leaves Very Soon," *Rantoul Weekly News*, Oct. 24, 1917; "Captain O. E. Carlstrom Ordered to Camp Logan," *Rantoul Weekly News*, Sept. 26, 1917; "Rantoul Flyers Drop 300 Feet," *Urbana Courier*, Dec. 3, 1917; "Novices Hard on Aeroplanes," *Urbana Courier*, Sept. 17, 1917.

276. "Government's Aeros Not Suitable for Mexico," *Aerial Age Weekly* 3 (April 3, 1916): 86. In 1918, the U.S. Army Signal Corps had twenty-nine flying fields. Seven were north of Tennessee: two in Illinois, two in Ohio, and one each in Michigan, New York, and Pennsylvania, "Where Flying Fields of U.S. Aviation Service Are Located," *Urbana Courier*, Sept. 12, 1918.

277. "Difficulties of the Mexican Campaign," *Aerial Age Weekly* 3 (July 3, 1916): 470. Roger G. Miller, *A Preliminary to War: The 1st Aero Squadron and the Mexican Punitive Expedition of 1916* (Washington, DC: Air Force History and Museums Program, 2003).

278. Snyder, *Chanute Field*, 28.

279. W. H. Williamson, *Octave Chanute: Aviation Pioneer* ([Rantoul]: Chanute Field [Air Base], 1940), 1, 7, 11.

280. Donald O. Weckhorst, *75 Year Pictorial History of Chanute Air Force Base, Rantoul, Illinois* (Nappanee, IN: Evangel Press, 1992), 21.

281. "Officers Moved," *Rantoul Weekly News*, July 18, 1917.

282. "Air Men Who Have Passed Their H. M. A. Tests Leave Today," *Rantoul Weekly News*, Sept. 12, 1917.

283. Weckhorst, *75 Year Pictorial History of Chanute Air Force Base*, 48.

284. On pies, Snyder, *Chanute Field*, 14. "Large Crowd Bid God-Speed," *Rantoul Weekly News*, Feb. 13, 1918. "Former Illinois Man is American 'Ace,'" *Urbana Courier*, Jan. 21, 1919; "Champaign Boy 'Got Hun or Two,'" *Urbana Courier*, Feb. 11, 1919; "Lieut. W. W. Spain Writes from France," *Rantoul Weekly Press*, April 17, 1918. On brought down, see "Campus Brevities," *Daily Illini*, Nov. 13, 1918.

285. "Novices Hard on Aeroplanes," *Urbana Courier*, Sept. 17, 1917.

286. "Celebration Was Double Header," *Rantoul Weekly Press*, July 10, 1918; "Thousands Again Flock to Rantoul," *Rantoul Weekly News*, Sept. 26, 1917; "Chanute Fliers Thrill Crowd at Exposition," *Air Puffs*, Dec. 7, 1918. Weckhorst, *75 Year Pictorial History of Chanute Air Force Base*, 44.

287. "Lone American Brings Down Seven Flyers," *Air Puffs*, June 28, 1918, 8.

288. "Every Day like County Fair in Twin Cities," *Urbana Courier*, July 18, 1917.

289. "Plane Alights near Homer," *Urbana Courier*, June 6, 1918.

290. "Chanute Field News," *Aerial Age Weekly* 6 (Dec. 24, 1917): 645.

291. "Chanute Field News," *Aerial Age Weekly* 7 (May 13, 1918): 439. On flares, "Illinois Day at Chanute," *Rantoul Weekly Press*, May 14, 1919.

292. "Thousands Will Pour into City," *Urbana Courier*, May 16, 1918.

293. "Was Big Day for Champaign," *Urbana Courier*, May 18, 1918; on fancy flying, "High Twelve Club Goes on Visit to Chanute Field," *Urbana Courier*, July 18, 1918; "Twin City Residents Given Exhibition by Chanute Fliers," *Urbana Courier*, Nov. 11, 1918.

294. "Body Arrives from Overseas," *Urbana Courier*, July 29, 1920.

295. "Airplane Crashes onto Moving Train," *Urbana Courier*, April 30, 1918.

296. "Lieut. Wm. Slade Died of His Injuries This Morning," *Rantoul Weekly Press*, July 23, 1919.

297. J. N. Smith to Newton B. Baker, Nov. 16, 1918, file 153, Papers Pertaining to Chanute Field Damage Claims, Box 1449, Chanute Field, RG 18 Army Air Forces, Central Decimal Files, 1917–38, Project Files-Airfields, National Archives, College Park.

298. "Carrier Pigeons Wanted at Front," *Aerial Age Weekly* 6 (Sept. 17, 1917): 13.

299. "Field Has Excellent Record," *Rantoul Weekly Press*, June 26, 1918.

300. Weckhorst, *75 Year Pictorial History of Chanute Air Force Base*, 48.

301. "Chanute Field News," *Aerial Age Weekly* 6 (Dec. 24, 1917): 645.

302. "Illinois Central," *Urbana Courier*, April 10, 1905.

303. "Homer Does Full Share in War," *Urbana Courier*, July 13, 1917; "G .O. Saddler Injured," *Urbana Courier*, Jan. 18, 1918; "Former U. of I. Man Is Killed at Kelley Field," *Urbana Courier*, April 10, 1918.

304. Walter Shea Wood, "The 130th Infantry, Illinois National Guard: A Military History, 1778–1919," *Journal of the Illinois State Historical Society (1908–1984)* 30 (July 1937): 193–255. On Champaign guardsmen, *Roster of the Illinois Guard on the Mexican Border, 1916–1917* (Springfield, IL: np, 1928). "Member of Co. M Comes Home on Furlough," *Urbana Courier*, Dec. 21, 1916. On song, "First Cavalry Faces Mexico," *Urbana Courier*, July 5, 1915.

305. Maxwell Kirby, the commanding officer from Sept. 22–30, 1917, was part of the First Aero Squadron in the 1916 Punitive Expedition into Mexico; Snyder, *Chanute Field*, 14, 49; on further training in San Antonio, 25. "Field Loses Popular Officer," *Air Puffs*, Oct. 11, 1918, 1; "Personals," *Urbana Courier*, Dec. 4, 1917.

306. "Tenth Aerial Squadron Arrives Saturday," *Rantoul Weekly News*, July 11, 1917.

307. "Was Lost in Desert," *Rantoul Weekly News*, July 11, 1917.

308. "Aeroplanes in Mexican Manoeuvers," *Aerial Age Weekly* 4 (Jan. 8, 1917): 432, 452–53.

309. William C. Pool, "Military Aviation Texas, 1913–1917," *The Southwestern Historical Quarterly* 59 (April 1956): 429–54.

310. "U.S. Troops Win First Battle," *Urbana Courier*, March 31, 1916.

311. Major Arthur E. Wilburn came to Champaign from the "Villa campaign into Mexico" and, several years before that, the Philippines; "Major Arthur E. Wilburn," *Rantoul Weekly Press*, July 31, 1918. On Charles Way's Philippine service, see "Squadron D," *Air Puffs*, Nov. 30, 1918, 1; on Ira Longanecker's service in the Philippines, Hawai'i, and the border outpost of Douglas, Arizona, see Snyder, *Chanute Field*, 57. On U.S. aviation detachments in Hawai'i and the Philippines, see "Aircraft as a Military Asset," *Flying* 3 (June 1914): 133.

312. On aviation after World War II, Simons, "Aviation's Heartland," 240.

Chapter 6: Home, Land, Security: Exile, Dispossession, and Loss

1. *History of Champaign County, Illinois* (Philadelphia: Brink, McDonough and Co., 1878), 14.

2. Ibid.

3. "The City and Vicinity," *Champaign Daily Gazette*, Dec. 16, 1899.

4. "Pesotum," *Urbana Courier*, March 16, 1914.

5. J. R. Stewart, ed., *A Standard History of Champaign County, Illinois*, vol. 2 (Chicago: The Lewis Publishing Co., 1918), 1057–58.

6. "No Alien Enemies Report on First Day," *Urbana Courier*, Feb. 4, 1918.

7. "Well Known Woman Registers as an Alien," *Urbana Courier*, June 20, 1918.

8. "Immigration Officer Arrests German Boy," *Rantoul Weekly Press*, April 7, 1920; "German Boy Was Deported," *Rantoul Weekly Press*, April 14, 1920; "German Boy Was Not Deported," *Rantoul Weekly Press*, April 28, 1920.

9. Mark Wyman and John W. Muirhead, "Jim Crow Comes to Central Illinois: Racial Segregation in Twentieth-Century Bloomington-Normal," *Journal of the Illinois State Historical Society* 110 (Summer 2017): 154–82; James W. Loewen, *Sundown Towns: A Hidden Dimension of American Racism* (New York: Simon and Schuster, 2006).

10. Edwin Minor, "Annual Report Kickapoo Indian School, 1914," Superintendents' Annual Narrative and Statistical Reports from Field Jurisdictions of the Bureau of Indian Affairs, 1907–1938, Roll 70 (Washington, DC: National Archives Microfilm Publications, 1975).

11. Joseph B. Herring, *Kenekuk, The Kickapoo Prophet* (Lawrence: University of Kansas Press, 1988), 14.

12. On railroad rights, *Treaty between the United States and the Kickapoo Indians*, 1854, Princeton University Rare Books Library, 5; on the Atchison and Pike's Peak Railroad Company's rights, see "Kickapoo Treaty," *Freedom's Champion* (Atchison, KS), June 20, 1863. On a swindling agent, see "There Were a Large Number of Indians," *Atchison Daily Globe*, Oct. 14, 1889.

13. Edwin Minor, "Kickapoo School and Agency Report, 1912," Kickapoo School Records, 1910–1920, Record Group 75, Superintendents' Annual Narrative and Statistical Reports from the Field, Jurisdictions of the Bureau of Indian Affairs, 1907–1938, Roll 70 (Washington, DC: National Archives Microfilm Publications, 1975).

14. Donald D. Stull, *Kiikaapoa: The Kansas Kickapoo* (Horton, KS: Kickapoo Tribal Press, 1984), 105; for a text of the 1862 treaty, 199–200.

15. Thomas Murphy, Superintendent Indian Affairs, to Hon. H. G. Taylor, Commissioner, April 8, 1869, Letters Received by the Office of Indian Affairs, 1824–81, Kickapoo Agency, 1855–1876, Roll 373, 1867–1871 (Washington, DC: National Archives Microfilm Publications, 1958).

16. "The Red Man Gets There," *Galveston Daily News*, Sept. 11, 1891; on homeseekers, see Atchison, Topeka, and Santa Fe Railroad Company, *Cherokee Strip and Oklahoma. Opening of Cherokee Strip; Kickapoo, Pawnee and Tonkawa Reservations* (Chicago: Poole Bros., 1893), 9.

17. Atchison, Topeka, and Santa Fe Railroad Company, *Cherokee Strip and Oklahoma*, 13, 15; on residence, 20.

18. "The Story of a 'Treaty,'" *Boston Daily Advertiser*, May 21, 1895.

19. "Kickapoo Craft," *Atchison Daily Globe*, June 23, 1891.

20. "Allotments Almost Made," *Emporia Gazette*, April 19, 1894.

21. "Refuse to Vacate," *Atchison Daily Globe*, Aug. 15, 1895.

22. "Havoc of Flames," *Dallas Morning News*, Aug. 24, 1894.

23. "The Story of a 'Treaty,'" *Boston Daily Advertiser*, May 21, 1895.

24. "The Race for a Claim," *Morning Oregonian*, May 24, 1895.

25. "Kickapoos Will Agree," *Galveston Daily News*, Nov. 13, 1893.
26. Felipe A. Latorre and Dolores L. Latorre, *The Mexican Kickapoo Indians* (Austin: University of Texas Press, 1976), 52–54.
27. Lyn Ellen Bennett and Scott Abbott, "Barbed and Dangerous: Constructing the Meaning of Barbed Wire in Late Nineteenth-Century America," *Agricultural History* 88 (Fall 2014): 566–90.
28. T. S. Palmer, *Legislation for the Protection of Birds Other Than Game Birds*, U.S. Department of Agriculture (Washington, DC: Government Printing Office, 1902).
29. "Proceedings of a Kickapoo Council . . . July 16, 1912," Folder 1, Box 1, Records Concerning Affairs of the Mexican Kickapoo, 1895–1914, Finance Division, RG 75 Records of the Bureau of Indian Affairs, National Archives, 11.
30. On sights, "Street Gossip," *Atchison Champion*, June 22, 1890; on single file, "The Populist Mania for Office Has Broken Out among the Kickapoo Indians . . . ," *Atchison Daily Globe*, Oct. 13, 1894; on dress, "Will Migrate to Mexico," *Dallas Morning News*, May 12, 1904.
31. "W. W. Letson . . ." *Atchison Daily Globe*, May 6, 1891.
32. John D. Miles to General J. J. Reynolds, June 6–21, 1871, *Letters Received by the Office of Indian Affairs, 1824–81, Kickapoo Agency, 1855–1876*, Roll 373, 1867–1871 (Washington, DC: The National Archives, 1958).
33. Dana Elizabeth Weiner, *Race and Rights: Fighting Slavery and Prejudice in the Old Northwest, 1830–1870* (Dekalb: NIU Press, 2013), 43, 53, 203.
34. Wm. M. Edgar to Hon. E. P. Smith, Oct. 27, 1875, *Letters Received by the Office of Indian Affairs, 1824–81, Kickapoo Agency, 1855–1876*, Roll 374, 1872–1876 (Washington, DC: National Archives, 1958); on passports, see Mae M. Ngai, *Impossible Subjects: Illegal Aliens and the Making of Modern America* (Princeton: Princeton University Press, 2004), 19; Craig Robertson, *The Passport in America: The History of a Document* (New York: Oxford University Press, 2010), 16.
35. These provisions were affirmed by the Act of 1834; Martha Menchaca, *Recovering History, Constructing Race: The Indian, Black, and White Roots of Mexican Americans* (Austin: University of Texas Press, 2001). On removal as protective, see Edward Everett, "Speech of Mr. Everett, of Massachusetts, on the Bill for Removing the Indians from the East to the West Side of the Mississippi" (Washington: Gales & Seaton, 1830), 9–10.
36. Louis S. Warren, *Buffalo Bill's America: William Cody and the Wild West Show* (New York: Alfred A. Knopf, 2005), 361.
37. "Lost—One Hundred and Fifty Kickapoos," *Atchison Daily Globe*, Jan. 2, 1897.
38. "The Mexican Kickapoos," part II, *Chronicles of Oklahoma* 11 (June 1933): 823–37.
39. Wm. P. Dole to So-Ko-watt, Pe-shaw-gen, Pah-kah-kah, and Ke-o-quawk, May 5, 1862, *Letters Received by the Office of Indian Affairs, 1824–81, Kickapoo Agency, 1855–1876*, Roll 371, 1855–1863 (Washington, DC: National Archives, 1958).
40. "Street Fair Notes," *Emporia Weekly Gazette*, Oct. 5, 1899.
41. "All Have Smallpox," *Milwaukee Journal*, Jan. 19, 1899; on guard, "The Indian Troubles in Wisconsin," *Cleveland Herald*, March 5, 1846; on hostages, "More Indian Treaties," *New-York Spectator*, April 22, 1833; on military confinement, "Great Salt Plain," *Ohio Statesman*, Dec. 5, 1843; on imprisonment at Fort

Gibson, "The Mexican Kickapoos," *Atchison Daily Globe,* Jan. 2, 1897; on detachments, "Kickapoo Trouble," *Dallas Morning News,* April 29, 1896; "Lost—One Hundred and Fifty Kickapoos," *Atchison Daily Globe,* Jan. 2, 1897.

42. J. A. Scott to Dan Kan-ke-ka and Jno. Mas-que-qua, Policemen, Oct. 20 1892, in Folder 6: Arrest Warrant, Box 6, Kickapoo, Milo Custer Collection, McLean County Historical Society.

43. On geography lessons, see David Kinnear to Major R. W. Cummins, Sept. 30, 1838, *Letters Received by the Office of Indian Affairs, 1824–81, Fort Leavenworth Agency, 1824–1851,* Roll 301, 1837–1842, microcopy no. 234 (Washington, DC: National Archives Microfilm Publications, 1959).

44. On the $1.00 fine, see Brig. Genl. Henry Atkinson to Edmund P. Gaines, St. Louis, Oct. 7, 1826, in *The Territorial Papers of the United States,* vol. 20, *The Territory of Arkansas, 1825–1829,* ed. Clarence Edwin Carter (Washington, DC: Government Printing Office, 1954), 294.

45. On jail, see John W. Spencer, *Reminiscences of Pioneer Life in the Mississippi Valley* (Davenport: Griggs, Watson & Day, 1872), 31; "Conviction," *Louisville Public Advertiser,* April 20, 1841; "Kickapoos Shot," *Daily Evening Bulletin* (San Francisco), July 11, 1887.

46. "White Water," *Atchison Daily Globe,* June 10, 1896, 31.

47. Testimony of Ekoneskaka (Aurelio Valdez Garcia) as reported by Jim Salvator, in "An Oral History," *Parnassus: Poetry in Review* 17, no. 1 (1992): 170–83.

48. Latorre and Latorre, *The Mexican Kickapoo Indians,* 1976.

49. George R. Nielsen, *The Kickapoo People* (Phoenix: Indian Tribal Series, 1975), 21, 33.

50. Nielsen, *The Kickapoo People;* on buffering Americans, Kiowas, and Comanches, 41. On settlement in Texas, see Gary Clayton Anderson, *The Conquest of Texas: Ethnic Cleansing in the Promised Land, 1820–1875* (Norman: University of Oklahoma Press, 2005), 164–69; "Mexican Intelligence," *The Boston Daily Atlas,* June 4, 1852.

51. On land in Coahuila, see Shelley Bowen Hatfield, *Chasing Shadows: Indians along the United States-Mexico Border, 1876–1911* (Albuquerque: University of New Mexico Press, 1998). On trips to Mexico City, see *Reports of the Committee of Investigation Sent in 1873 by the Mexican Government to the Frontier of Texas,* translated from the official edition made in Mexico (New York: Baker and Godwin, 1875), 409; "Mexican Intelligence," *Boston Daily Atlas,* June 4, 1852; José Guadalupe Ovalle Castillo and Ana Bella Pérez Castro, *Kikapúes: Los Que Andan Por la Tierra: El Proceso de Proletarización y la Migración Laboral del Grupo de Coahuila* (México: Consejo Nacional para la Cultura y las Artes, 1999), 22–23. On Mier y Terán, see Anderson, *The Conquest of Texas,* 71.

52. On their 1866 acquisitions, see *Reports of the Committee of Investigation Sent in 1873 by the Mexican Government to the Frontier of Texas,* 412.

53. Na she nan et al. to Col. Cumming, Nov. 21, 1855, *Letters Received by the Office of Indian Affairs, 1824–81, Kickapoo Agency, 1855–1876,* Roll 371, National Archives. The Kickapoos were not the only Native American people to survive and cope through fragmentation and diaspora in the nineteenth century. See, for example, Sami Lakomäki, *Gathering Together: The Shawnee People through Diaspora and Nationhood, 1600–1870* (New Haven: Yale University Press, 2014).

54. On conflicts with Comanches, "Affairs in Texas," *North American and United States Gazette* (Philadelphia), Jan. 17, 1852. On conflicts with Osages, "Treaty with the Kickapoo Indians," *St. Louis Enquirer*, Dec. 8, 1819. On conflicts with Chickasaws, see David La Vere, *Contrary Neighbors: Southern Plains and Removed Indians in Indian Territory* (Norman: University of Oklahoma Press, 2000), 86. On Wichitas and Caddos, see Anderson, *The Conquest of Texas*, 6. On eastern Indians as pioneers in the trans-Mississippi West, see John P. Bowes, *Exiles and Pioneers: Eastern Indians in the Trans-Mississippi West* (New York: Cambridge University Press, 2007), 4.

55. Anderson, *The Conquest of Texas*, 8, 169, 174, 342.

56. M. M. McAllen, *Maximilian and Carlota: Europe's Last Empire in Mexico* (San Antonio: Trinity University Press, 2014), 169.

57. Quoted in Anderson, *The Conquest of Texas*, 342.

58. "Kickapoo Indians Not Satisfied," *Dallas Morning News*, Feb. 10, 1899.

59. Latorre and Latorre, *The Mexican Kickapoo Indians*, 48.

60. William Kennedy, *Texas: The Rise, Progress, and Prospects of the Republic of Texas*, vol. 1 (London: R. Hastings, 1841), 349–50.

61. Robert E. Ritzenthaler and Frederick A. Peterson, *The Mexican Kickapoo Indians* (Milwaukee: Milwaukee Public Museum, 1956), 11. Mary Christopher Nunley makes similar claims in "The Mexican Kickapoo Indians: Avoidance of Acculturation through a Migratory Adaptation" (PhD diss., Southern Methodist University, 1986), 219.

62. Alfonso Fabila, *La Tribu Kikapoo de Coahuila* (Mexico City: Instituto Nacional Indigenista, 2002), 43. On hunting, Wm. Edgar to Edward P. Smith, June 17, 1875, *Letters Received by the Office of Indian Affairs, 1824–81, Kickapoo Agency, 1855–1876*, Roll 374, 1872–1876 (Washington, DC: National Archives, 1958).

63. On pouncing and booty, see "Indian Atrocities in Texas," *Little Rock Daily Gazette*, May 28, 1866. On horse and cattle theft, see "The Kickapoos and Mexican Annexation," *Daily Evening Bulletin* (San Francisco), June 17, 1873; "Washington Letter," *Galveston Daily News*, June 23, 1874; "Ghastly Trophies," *St. Louis Globe-Democrat*, Sept. 24, 1877.

64. Richard W. Cummins to Gen. William Clark, Jan. 31, 1838, *Letters Received by the Office of Indian Affairs, 1824–81, Fort Leavenworth Agency, 1824–1851*, Roll 301, 1837–1842, microcopy no. 234 (Washington, DC: National Archives Microfilm Publications, 1959).

65. On the Kickapoos as agriculturalists, see "In General," *Boston Daily Advertiser*, April 9, 1864; "Mexicans and Indians on the Rio Grande," *Weekly Arizona Miner*, Nov. 25, 1871.

66. "Will There Be War with Mexico?" *Cleveland Morning Daily Herald*, May 27, 1873. On Anglo robbers passing as Kickapoos, see Anderson, *The Conquest of Texas*, 302, 307.

67. "Kickapoo Indians. Letter from the Secretary of the Interior, Transmitting Communication from the Commissioner of Indian Affairs relative to the Kickapoo Indians Now in Mexico," House of Representatives, 40th Congress, 2nd session, Ex. Doc. No. 340, in *Letters Received by the Office of Indian Affairs 1824–81, Kickapoo Agency, 1855–1876*, Roll 373, 1867–1871 (Washington, DC: National Archives, 1958), 2.

68. S. S. Brown, "Explanatory Letter A [1868]," in *Letters Received by the Office of the Adjutant General (Main Series) 1861–1870*, Roll 642, National Archives Microfilm Publications, Microcopy no. 619 (Washington, DC: National Archives, 1965).

69. On arranging, see S. S. Brown to Brevet Major General J. J. Reynolds, Sept. 1, 1868; on questions and camping ground, see S. S. Brown, "Explanatory Letter A [1868]," both in *Letters Received by the Office of the Adjutant General (Main Series) 1861–1870*, Roll 642, National Archives Microfilm Publications, Microcopy no. 619 (Washington, DC: National Archives, 1965).

70. Edward Hatch to General Ely S. Parker, Aug. 9, 1864, *Letters Received by the Office of Indian Affairs 1824–81, Kickapoo Agency, 1855–1876*, Roll 373, 1867–1871 (Washington, DC: National Archives, 1958).

71. Testimony of Lt. Major A. McD. McCook, Brownsville, Texas, July 30, 1872, in *United States Commission to Texas, v. 9, Proceedings July 4–Oct. 3, 1872, Depositions 1–364*, Record Group 76, International Claims Commissions. U.S. and Mexico Claims Commissions, National Archives, College Park, Maryland, 32.

72. Testimony of Lt. Major A. McD. McCook, Brownsville, Texas, July 30, 1872, in *United States Commission to Texas, vol. 9, Proceedings July 4–Oct. 3, 1872, Depositions 1–364*, Record Group 76, International Claims Commissions. U.S. and Mexico Claims Commissions, National Archives, College Park, Maryland, 32; Arrell M. Gibson, *The Kickapoos: Lords of the Middle Border* (Norman: University of Oklahoma Press, 1963), 228.

73. J. R. Bliss to the Adjutant General, Department of Texas, June 15, 1871, *Letters Received by the Office of Indian Affairs, 1824–81, Kickapoo Agency, 1855–1876*, Roll 373, 1867–1871 (Washington, DC: National Archives, 1958); John D. Miles to General J. J. Reynolds, 6th–21st [June], 1871, *Letters Received by the Office of Indian Affairs, 1824–81, Kickapoo Agency, 1855–1871*, Roll 373, 1867–1871 (Washington, DC: National Archives, 1958).

74. John D. Miles to General J. J. Reynolds, 6th–21st [June], 1871.

75. John D. Miles to General J. J. Reynolds, 6th–21st [June], 1871; Martha Buntin, "The Mexican Kickapoos," *Chronicles of Oklahoma* 11 (March 1933), 691–708. On going back to their proper reservation, see Testimony of Lt. Major A. McD. McCook, in *United States Commission to Texas, v. 9, 32*.

76. Buntin, "The Mexican Kickapoos," 698; John D. Miles to General J.J. Reynolds, 6th–21st [June], 1871; John D. Miles, report of July 7, 1871, in *Letters Received by the Office of the Adjutant General (Main Series), 1861–1870*, Roll 799 (Washington, DC: National Archives Microfilm Publications, 1965); Colonel J. J. Reynolds to Adjutant General, July 28, 1871, *Letters Received by the Office of Indian Affairs, 1824–81, Kickapoo Agency, 1855–1871*, Roll 373, 1867–1871 (Washington, DC: National Archives, 1958).

77. On the appeal to the minister, see Thomas H. Nelson to Secretary of State Hamilton Fish, Aug. 30, 1871, *Letters Received by the Office of the Adjutant General (Main Series), 1861–1870*, Roll 799 (Washington, DC: National Archives Microfilm Publications, 1965); *Report and Accompanying Documents of the Committee on Foreign Affairs on the Relations of the United States with Mexico* (Washington, DC: Government Printing Office, 1878), 206, 211.

78. "The Texas Raids," *Rocky Mountain News* (Denver), May 30, 1873.

79. H. M. Atkinson to E. P. Smith, June 14, 1873, *Letters Received by the Office of Indian Affairs, 1824–81, Kickapoo Agency, 1855–1876*, Roll 374, 1872–1876 (Washington, DC: National Archives, 1958); on strong guard and corral, see Ranald Mackenzie to the Assistant Adjutant General, May 23, 1873, Box 18, 1500–2554, 1873, U.S. Army Continental Commands, Department of Texas, Record Group 393, U.S. National Archives.

80. Gibson, *The Kickapoos*, 244–45; H. M. Atkinson to E. P. Smith, June 14, 1873, *Letters Received by the Office of Indian Affairs, 1824–81, Kickapoo Agency, 1855–1876*, Roll 374, 1872–1876 (Washington, DC: National Archives, 1958).

81. P. Sheridan to General W. W. Belknap, May 22, 1873, *Letters Received by the Office of the Adjutant General (Main Series), 1861–1870*, Roll 799 (Washington, DC: National Archives Microfilm Publications, 1965); [Mackenzie] to Col. Williams, May 22, 1873, U.S. Army Continental Commands, Department of Texas, Box 18, 1873, Record Group 393, National Archives. "Will There Be War with Mexico?" *Cleveland Morning Daily Herald*, May 27, 1873. Two accounts that lionize Mackenzie are R. G. Carter, *On the Border with Mackenzie or Winning West Texas from the Comanches*, 1935 (New York: Antiquarian Press, 1961), 422–66; Richard A. Thompson, *Crossing the Border with the 4th Cavalry: Mackenzie's Raid into Mexico–1873* (Waco: Texian Press, 1986).

82. "Kickapoo Indians. Letter from the Secretary of the Interior, Transmitting Communication from the Commissioner of Indian Affairs Relative to the Kickapoo Indians Now in Mexico," 40th Congress, 2nd Session, House of Representatives Executive Document # 340, 1868, 2.

83. Buntin, "The Mexican Kickapoos," 699.

84. "The Mexican Kickapoos," *Atchison Daily Globe*, Sept. 30, 1873.

85. Buntin, "The Mexican Kickapoos," 704–06. On the winter encampment, A. C. Williams to Enoch Hoag, Jan. 19, 1874, *Letters Received by the Office of Indian Affairs, 1824–81, Kickapoo Agency, 1855–1876*, Roll 374, 1872–1876 (Washington, DC: National Archives, 1958). On fencing, see Enoch Hoag to E. P. Smith, Jan. 20, 1874, *Letters Received by the Office of Indian Affairs, 1824–81, Kickapoo Agency, 1855–1876*, Roll 374, 1872–1876 (Washington, DC: The National Archives, 1958).

86. On the treaty, see *Mexican Border Troubles: Message of the President of the United States in Answer to the Resolution of the House of Representatives of Nov. 1, 1877* (Washington, DC: Government Printing Office, 1877), 19.

87. Carter, *On the Border with Mackenzie*, 422, 431; Wm. Schuchardt to Second Assistant Secretary of State, March 2, 1874, *Letters Received by the Office of Indian Affairs, 1824–81, Kickapoo Agency, 1855–1876*, Roll 374, 1872–1876 (Washington, DC: National Archives, 1958).

88. H. M. Atkinson to Don Victoriano Cepeda, May 17, 1873, *Letters Received by the Office of Indian Affairs, 1824–81, Kickapoo Agency, 1855–1876*, Roll 374, 1872–1876 (Washington, DC: National Archives, 1958).

89. Lieutenant-General P. Sheridan to Secretary of War W. W. Belknap, May 28, 1873, *Letters Received by the Office of the Adjutant General (Main Series), 1861–1870*, Roll 799 (Washington, DC: National Archives Microfilm Publications, 1965).

90. Hatfield, *Chasing Shadows*, 19; [Mackenzie] to Mr. Schuchardt, May 22, 1873, U.S. Army Continental Commands, Department of Texas, Box 18, 1873, Record Group 393, National Archives.

91. William Schuchardt to General, May 19, 1873, U.S. Army Continental Commands, Department of Texas, Box 18, 1873, Record Group 393, National Archives.

92. H. M. Atkinson to Hon. E. P. Smith, June 14, 1873, *Letters Received by the Office of Indian Affairs, 1824–81, Kickapoo Agency, 1855–1876*, Roll 374, 1872–1876 (Washington, DC: National Archives, 1958).

93. H. M. Atkinson to E. P. Smith, Dec. 26, 1874, *Letters Received by the Office of Indian Affairs, 1824–81, Kickapoo Agency, 1855–1876*, Roll 374, 1872–1876 (Washington, DC: National Archives, 1958); on annexation, see *El Siglo Diez y Nueve* (Mexico City), June 30, 1873.

94. On unjustified accusations, see *Reports of the Committee of Investigation Sent in 1873 by the Mexican Government to the Frontier of Texas*, 414.

95. "H. M. Atkinson . . . ," *The Galveston Daily News*, Nov. 3, 1874.

96. H. M. Atkinson to E. P. Smith, Dec. 26, 1874, *Letters Received by the Office of Indian Affairs, 1824–81, Kickapoo Agency, 1855–1876*, Roll 374, 1872–1876 (Washington, DC: National Archives, 1958); "Texas Press," *The Galveston Daily News*, March 12, 1874; "Interesting Letter from Durango," *The Galveston Daily News*, June 3, 1874.

97. H. M. Atkinson to Edward P. Smith, March 22, 1875; H. M. Atkinson to E. R. Smith, March 20, 1875, both in *Letters Received by the Office of Indian Affairs, 1824–81, Kickapoo Agency, 1855–1876*, Roll 374, 1872–1876 (Washington, DC: National Archives, 1958).

98. H. M. Atkinson to Edward P. Smith, March 22, 1875; H. M. Atkinson to E. R. Smith, March 20, 1875; H. M. Atkinson to Edward P. Smith, April 30, 1875; John H. Pickering to Respected Friend, August 14, 1875, all in *Letters Received by the Office of Indian Affairs, 1824–81, Kickapoo Agency, 1855–1876*, Roll 374, 1872–1876 (Washington, DC: National Archives, 1958).

99. John W. Foster to Hamilton Fish, June 25, 1875, *Letters Received by the Office of Indian Affairs, 1824–81, Kickapoo Agency, 1855–1876*, Roll 374, 1872–76 (Washington, DC: National Archives, 1958).

100. John W. Foster to His Excellency J. M. Lafragua, June 24, 1875, *Letters Received by the Office of Indian Affairs, 1824–81, Kickapoo Agency, 1855–1876*, Roll 374, 1872–1876 (Washington, DC: National Archives, 1958).

101. John W. Foster to His Excellency J. M. Lafragua, June 24, 1875.

102. H. M. Atkinson to E.P. Smith, November 10, 1875, *Letters Received by the Office of Indian Affairs, 1824–81, Kickapoo Agency, 1855–1876*, Roll 374, 1872–1876 (Washington, DC: National Archives, 1958).

103. On the agent and President Lerdo de Tejada's promises to remove the Kickapoos to the interior, see "Our San Antonio Letters," *Galveston Daily News*, March 8, 1876; "Texas Press," *Galveston Daily News*, March 12, 1874; "Interesting Letter from Durango," *Galveston Daily News*, June 3, 1874. On Chihuahua, see *Mexican Border Troubles*, 241.

104. Hatfield, *Chasing Shadows*, 21–28.

105. On relocation, see Castillo and Castro, *Kikapúes*, 28. Although the documentation does not specify which Guerrero, the German-speaking colony in Chihuahua makes this seem the most plausible.

106. William M. Evarts to Mr. Foster, March 31, 1877, in *Mexican Border Troubles*, 4.

107. Robert D. Gregg, *The Influence of Border Troubles on Relations between the United States and Mexico, 1876–1910* (Baltimore: Johns Hopkins Press, 1937), 51, 62.

108. The Reciprocal Consent treaty lasted until Geronimo's surrender in 1886. Daniel S. Margolies, "The 'Ill-Defined Fiction' of Extraterritoriality and Sovereign Exception in Late Nineteenth Century U.S. Foreign Relations," *Southwestern Law Review* 40 (Spring 2011): 575–603.

109. "A Hunter's Paradise," *St. Louis Globe-Democrat*, Dec. 31, 1887.

110. Hatfield, *Chasing Shadows*, 5. On the 60,000 acres in 1883, see "Texans Claim Mexican Land," *Dallas Morning News*, Feb. 25, 1909.

111. "Grazing and Farming Lands on the Mexican Frontier," *Galveston Daily News*, Feb. 27, 1883.

112. John Mason Hart, *Empire and Revolution: The Americans in Mexico since the Civil War* (Berkeley: University of California Press, 2002), 216.

113. Nunley, "The Mexican Kickapoo Indians," 45.

114. Kickapoo Indian Chieftain," *Mexican Herald*, Sept. 11, 1903.

115. Latorre and Latorre, *The Mexican Kickapoo Indians*, 90. On the contamination, see Castillo and Castro, *Kikapúes*, xii.

116. Isaac F. Marcosson, *Metal Magic: The Story of the American Smelting and Refining Company* (New York: Farrar, Straus, 1949), 215, 219, 220, 223, 280.

117. H. M. Teller, Chairman of the Committee on Indian Affairs, "Affairs of Mexican Kicking Kickapoo Indians," Senate Report no. 5, 60th Congress, 1st session, 1–12; Gibson, *The Kickapoos*, 340.

118. "Kickapoos Here," *Mexican Herald*, Jan. 25, 1901; on Thapathethea, see Gibson, *The Kickapoos*, 329.

119. On conditions in Sonora, see John Embry to S. W. Brosiuis, Agent Indian Rights Association, July 18, 1912, Folder 4; on Bentley's acquisition of land titles in 1905 and 1906, see "Abstract of Testimony, Bentley and the Seven," in Folder 3, both in Box 1, Records Concerning Affairs of the Mexican Kickapoo, 1895–1914, Record Group 75, Records of the Bureau of Indian Affairs, National Archives. On a Kickapoo residing in Sonora, see "Extradition Application," *Dallas Morning News*, Oct. 28, 1910; "Yaquis Prove They Are Worthy Foemen," *Dallas Morning News*, May 30, 1915. On the Yaquis, see Claudia B. Haake, *The State, Removal and Indigenous Peoples in the United States and Mexico, 1620–2000* (New York: Routledge, 2007), 95–96, 121–34; Eric V. Meeks, *Border Citizens: The Making of Indians, Mexicans, and Anglos in Arizona* (Austin: University of Texas Press, 2007), 2, 28–31, 72.

120. "Discuss Move to Mexico," *Dallas Morning News*, April 24, 1904. Frank A. Thackery, Plaintiff vs. R. C. Conine, L. C. Grimes, M.J. Bentley, and W. W. Ives, Defendants, Territory of Oklahoma, Pottawatomie County, Dec. 15, 1906, Folder 3, Box 1, Records Concerning the Affairs of the Mexican Kickapoo.

121. John A. Buntin to The First National Bank, Sept. 11, 1912, Folder 2, Box 1, Finance Division, Records Concerning the Affairs of the Mexican Kickapoo, 1895–1914, Record Group 75, National Archives.

122. Gibson, *The Kickapoos*, 359.
123. *Confirming the Citizenship Status of the Texas Band of Kickapoo Indians*, Hearings before the Committee on Interior and Insular Affairs, House of Representatives, 97th Congress, on H.R. 4496 (Washington, DC: U.S. Government Printing Office, 1983); on location of homes, 7, 96; garbage, 98; ceremonies, 12; citizenship status and services, 68, 74. On cane and cardboard, see Stull, *Kiikaapoa*, 83.
124. *Confirming the Citizenship Status of the Texas Band of Kickapoo Indians*, living conditions, 74; Kazen's claim, 12.
125. *Confirming the Citizenship Status of the Texas Band of Kickapoo Indians*, peace and privacy, 13.
126. Thompson, *Crossing the Border with the 4th Cavalry*, 77. The legislation created a fourth tribe of Kickapoos, the Kickapoo Traditional Tribe of Texas, which was the same as the Mexican Kickapoos but under U.S. jurisdiction; Mary Christopher Nunley, foreword to *The Texas Kickapoo: Keepers of Tradition*, by Bill Wright and E. John Gesick, Jr. (El Paso: Texas Western Press, 1996), xiii–xvi, xiv; Stull, *Kiikaapoa*, 85. On the Coahuila and Eagle Pass Kickapoos in the more recent past, see Elisabeth A. Mager Hois, *Lucha y Resistencia de la Tribu Kikapú*, 2nd. ed. (México, D.F.: Universidad Nacional Autónoma de México, 2008).
127. Latorre and Latorre, *The Mexican Kickapoo Indians*, 90–91.
128. Ritzenthaler and Peterson, 21.
129. *Confirming the Citizenship Status of the Texas Band of Kickapoo Indians*, 8.
130. Ibid.; "The Kickapoos Who Have Citizenship in two Countries," *Wassaja* 3 (September 1975): 5, in the Princeton University Rare Books Collection.
131. Latorre and Latorre, *The Mexican Kickapoo Indians*, 92–93.
132. On "Chicapoos," see Ekoneskaka, "An Oral History," 173.
133. *Confirming the Citizenship Status of the Texas Band of Kickapoo Indians*, 24.
134. Ibid.
135. *Confirming the Citizenship Status of the Texas Band of Kickapoo Indians*, 16.
136. *Confirming the Citizenship Status of the Texas Band of Kickapoo Indians*, 49. On Quintanilla, see Dennis William Stuart Selder, "Toward a Sound Methodology for Comparative Rhetoric with Aymara as a Case Study" (PhD diss., University of Arizona, 2007), 81.

Conclusion: The Nation, at Heart

1. "Thirteenth Annual Meeting Woman's Missionary Society" *Urbana Courier*, Nov. 10, 1906.
2. "Mrs. Reed Hostess to Chinese Students," *Urbana Courier*, Nov. 22, 1908.
3. "Louis Casdorf Is Home at Last," *Urbana Courier*, Dec. 18, 1909.
4. "Kinley's Speech at the Chicago Association of Commerce," May 20, 1910, Folder: Address to Chicago Association of Commerce re Pan-American Conference, Box 3, President David Kinley Papers, UIUC Archives.
5. "Mexican Heir Weds Local Girl," *Urbana Courier*, Dec. 11, 1911.
6. J. R. Stewart, *A Standard History of Champaign County Illinois*, vol. 2 (Chicago: The Lewis Publishing Co., 1918), 601–02.
7. "This Is a Small Old World After All," *Urbana Courier*, April 5, 1919.
8. John R. McNeill, "Forests, and Ecological History: Brazil, 1500–1984," *Environmental Review* 10 (Summer 1986): 122–33; Andrew Salvador Mathews,

"Suppressing Fire and Memory: Environmental Degradation and Political Restoration in the Sierra Juárez of Oaxaca, 1887–2001," *Environmental History* 8 (Jan. 2003): 77–108; Robert W. Wilcox, "The Law of the Least Effort: Cattle Ranching and the Environment in the Savanna of Mato Grosso, Brazil, 1900–1980," *Environmental History* 4 (July 1999): 338–68; on fires, see Myrna I. Santiago, *The Ecology of Oil: Environment, Labor, and the Mexican Revolution, 1900–1938* (New York: Cambridge University Press, 2006). Walker and Mulliken Company, "Odd Chiffoniers," *Urbana Courier*, Jan. 12, 1915.

9. Warren Dean, *With Broadax and Firebrand: The Destruction of the Brazilian Atlantic Forest* (Berkeley: University of California Press, 1995); Douglas McCalla, *Planting the Province: The Economic History of Upper Canada, 1784–1870* (Toronto: University of Toronto Press, 1993); Shawn William Miller, *A Environmental History of Latin America* (New York: Cambridge University Press, 2007), 18, 32, 47, 82–84; Richard P. Tucker, *Insatiable Appetite: The United States and the Ecological Degradation of the Tropical World* (Berkeley: University of California Press, 2000), 6, 16.

10. Donald B. MacMillan, *Four Years in the White North* (Boston: The Medici Society, 1925), 137; W. Elmer Ekblaw, "The Material Response of the Polar Eskimo to Their Far Arctic Environment," *Annals of the Association of American Geographers* 17 (Dec. 1927): 160, 185, 187–89; W. Elmer Ekblaw, *The Food Birds of the Smith Sound Eskimos*, New York, 1919, reprint from *The Wilson Bulletin*, 106, March 1919, 1.

11. W. Elmer Ekblaw, "The Attributes of Place," *The Journal of Geography* (Sept. 1937): 213–20.

INDEX